New World Myth
Postmodernism and Postcolonialism in Canadian Fiction

In this comparative study of six Canadian novels Marie Vautier examines reworkings of myth in the postcolonial context. While myths are frequently used in literature as transhistorical master narratives, she argues that these novels destabilize the traditional function of myth in their self-conscious reexamination of historical events from a postcolonial perspective. Through detailed readings of François Barcelo's *La Tribu*, George Bowering's *Burning Water*, Jacques Godbout's *Les Têtes à Papineau*, Joy Kogawa's *Obasan*, Jovette Marchessault's *Comme une enfant de la terre*, and Rudy Wiebe's *The Scorched-Wood People*, Vautier situates New World myth within the broader contexts of political history and of classical, biblical, and historical myths.

Vautier's emphasis on de-constructing, de-centring, de-stabilizing, and especially de-mythologizing in the study illustrates how New World myth narrators have questioned the past in the present and carried out their original investigations of myth, place, and identity. Underlining the fact that political realities are encoded in the language and narrative of the works, Vautier argues that the reworkings of literary, religious, and historical myths and political ideologies in these novels are grounded in their shared situation of being in and of the New World.

MARIE VAUTIER teaches comparative Canadian literature and Québécois literature at the University of Victoria.

New World Myth

*Postmodernism
and Postcolonialism in
Canadian Fiction*

MARIE VAUTIER

McGill-Queen's University Press
Montreal & Kingston • London • Buffalo

Legal deposit first quarter 1998
Bibliothèque nationale du Québec

Printed in Canada on acid-free paper

This book has been published with the help of a grant
from the Humanities and Social Sciences Federation of
Canada, using funds provided by the Social Sciences
and Humanities Research Council of Canada. Funding
has also been provided by the University of Victoria.

McGill-Queen's University Press acknowledges the
support received for its publishing program from the
Canada Council's Block Grants program.

Canadian Cataloguing in Publication Data

Vautier, Marie, 1954–
   New world myth : postmodernism and postcolonialism
   in Canadian fiction
   Includes bibliographical references and index.
   ISBN 0-7735-1669-7

   1. Canadian fiction – 20th century – History and
   criticism. 2. Postmodernism (Literature) – Canada.
   I. Title.
   PS8191.M97V35 1998   C813'.5409   C97-900877-8
   PR9192.6.M97V35 1998

Typeset in Palatino 10/12
by Caractéra inc., Quebec City

For Nancy, Linda, and l.p.m.

And to Joy Kogawa, whom I have met only once,
for her courage

Contents

Preface

This book is a study of various reworkings of myth in six selected historiographic novels from English-speaking Canada and Quebec, all published in the years 1975–85. It is informed in part by current theories of postmodernism and postcolonialism and in part by my observations of the particularities of the postmodern and postcolonial situations manifested in much contemporary literature from these two areas. Through comparative studies of the six novels, I attempt to illustrate the characteristics of what I call "New World Myth."

Many academic studies of myth and literature present myths as immutable, universal stories that originated in the Greco-Roman period of Western history and that are frequently recuperated in epigonic, fictional renditions of the original myths. And, indeed, myths have frequently been employed as teleological and transhistorical master narratives in literature: even studies of historical fictions from "developing nations," to use a Eurocentric term, frequently regard myths as stories that tell us who we are. New World Myth, however, works against traditional assumptions about the universality and transhistoricity of myth, and the most efficient way to illustrate these reworkings, it seems to me, is through close readings of selected texts. The six self-reflexive novels discussed in the chapters that follow destabilize the traditional functions of myth in their reexamination of historical events of the "New World." These novels' explorations of myth signal cognitive instability and ontological and epistemological uncertainty by flaunting their investigative reclaimings of the past and their self-conscious awareness of the processes involved in these reclaimings.

If, traditionally, myth is a special narrative, most frequently a classical or a biblical story that is seen as eternal, universal, and, especially, transhistorical, then what is New World Myth and what does it have to do with the histories being retold through these fictions? In the context of the fictional works to be examined here, New World Myth could be described as in a perpetual state of coming-into-being. European accounts of New World historico-political events have long informed the English Canadian and Québécois mythological universe(s), as has the traditionally dominant Christian belief system. These European-based worldviews no longer entirely suffice, however; hence the creation, in narrative, of New World Myth. In its development, though, New World Myth cannot avoid being part of the older belief system it inherited from the European viewpoint: that is to say, biblical myth and religious ritual, on the one hand, and nonindigenous historico-political accounts of New World happenings on the other. New World Myth must use these systems in order to challenge them. Similar approaches to fiction, history, and myth are found in several contemporary European novels, such as Michel Tournier's *Gilles et Jeanne*, which reworks the (hi)story of Joan of Arc, and Graham Swift's *Waterland*, which challenges the very concept of historiography. The fictional challenge to history and the postmodern play with myth is obviously not limited to post-European novels from the New World. The specificity of New World Myth, however, lies in its need to assert itself by flaunting its *opposition* to the European-inspired versions of the past(s) of the New World. As post-European entities, New World texts from English Canada and Quebec must throw off – at least to a certain extent – the assumptions contained in traditional stories about the past(s). New World Myth, then, involves a reclaiming of the past that frequently works *against* "original" – that is to say, European – versions of past events.

In my gradual migration from Eastern Quebec to Victoria, British Columbia (and from French-Québécois theory to Anglo-American-Canadian theory), where I teach Québécois and comparative Canadian literature and literary theory, I have been intrigued by interesting differences in academic and nonacademic approaches to fiction, theory, culture, and sociopolitical identity. I have also been struck by very different attitudes I observed toward stories that tell us of "our" past(s). Historical figures such as Donnacona, Louis Riel, Louis-Joseph Papineau, Marguerite Bourgeois, Lord Durham, and many others take on very different qualities and defects in alternative versions of their stories. What struck me even more, however, was the ease with which these various versions appeared to coexist and the apparent facility with which many of those who heard the stories could alter and adapt their perceptions of historical "reality" – or, as I would say in French, *patiner sur plusieurs surfaces à la fois*. As I argue in "Les Métarécits, le postmodernisme, et le mythe postcolonial au Québec," Michel Tournier's subversion of the myth of Robinson Crusoe in *Vendredi ou les limbes du Pacifique* is possible only because there *is* such a myth, known to all and forming part of the general culture, so to speak, of the West. In contrast, no such mythic certainty has ever informed the stories of the selected corpus of this study. I argue here that myth exchanges its traditional function as transhistorical master narrative (Jean-François Lyotard's *métarécits*; see *La Condition postmoderne*, 7) for a function characterized by postmodern indeterminacy, complex postcolonial attitudes, a questioning of history, and a developing self-consciousness that creates provisional and relative identities.

The analyses I undertake have a double and seemingly contradictory motivation. On the one hand, they examine the manner in which the works studied here foreground their challenges to traditional conceptualizations of myth through their metafictional rewritings of political history. Thus, they analyze the narrators' use of deconstructionist techniques common to much postmodernist fiction: irony, parody, playful self-reflexivity, intertextuality, and the undercutting of the hegemonic patriarchal ideal of the Christian liberal-humanist. There is a partial emphasis on the "de" in the methodology employed here: deconstructing, decentering, destabilizing, and, especially, demythologizing.

On the other hand, and somewhat paradoxically, this study seeks to signal the existence of a particular type of work on myth in the selected fictions. To that end, I propose a theory of New World Myth in the preliminary chapter and elucidate it in the analyses that follow. This approach is not exactly in keeping with recent discursive strategies in postmodernist and postcolonial literary practices where typologies of any kind are regarded with deep suspicion. Instead of adopting James Clifford's "collage" technique (*Predicament of Culture*, 277–346) or Michel Foucault's system of genealogies, however, I prefer to examine methodically and in detail the reworkings of literary, religious, and historical myths and political ideologies in the selected fictions. The general theory of New World Myth presented here evolved gradually from my readings in contemporary literary theory and from parallel readings of many works of fiction from English-speaking Canada and Quebec published in the years 1975–85.

As I discuss in more detail in chapter 1, theories of postmodernism from the Euro-American fields of literary criticism and theories of postcolonialism that originate in former colonies and rapidly become published (recuperated?) in mainstream journals such as *Critical Inquiry* can be productive for a discussion of the contemporary literatures from English-speaking Canada and Quebec. In the decade in which these works were published, the terms "postmodernism" and "postcolonialism" were not as well known as they are in the 1990s. I do not attempt to establish theoretical distinctions between postmodernism and postcolonialism in this work or to chart their "intersecting and diverging trajectories" (Adam and Tiffin, *Past the Last Post*, vii). Instead, I make use of discursive practices from both fields of study to elucidate the workings of New World Myth.

Most comparatists of the literatures from English-speaking Canada and Quebec – and many come to mind (Caroline Bayard, E.D. Blodgett, Jean-Charles Falardeau, Richard Giguère, Barbara Godard, Rosemarin Heidenreich, Eva-Marie Kröller, Clément Moisan, Joseph Pivato, Winfried Siemerling, Antoine Sirois, Sylvia Söderlind, Philip Stratford, Ronald Sutherland, and Christl Verduyn, to name but a selected few) – begin their essays by tackling a basic question: why compare these two literatures? E.D. Blodgett's introductory, and by now classic, essay "The Canadian Literatures as a Literary Problem" (in his *Configuration: Essays in the Canadian Literatures*) was published near the end of the decade under consideration here. The essay provides a survey of the theoretical history of the field, notes the prevalence of both thematic criticism and the binary pairing of anglophone/francophone writing, proposes a mainly structuralist approach that would stress comparisons among *all* the Canadian literatures (he opts for in-depth discussions of "minority" writers of Germanic descent – who, nonetheless, write mainly in English), and underlines the need to maintain an open-ended, exploratory attitude to comparative Canadian literature, upheld in his case by notions of "pluralism," "borderlines," and "threshold" (34–5). Blodgett touches upon two points that I wish briefly to consider. The first is his short discussion of thematic criticism; the second, his statement about the relationship between literary theory and ideology. As Barbara Godard points out in her review of *Configuration*, some of Blodgett's textual analyses recall "that metropolis/hinterland, culture/nature split which has been a characteristic of the much castigated 'thematic criticism' that has followed upon Frye's description of the 'garrison mentality'" (110). In his postscript, Blodgett suggests that the Canadian literatures may indeed require thematic interpretations: "What is more demonstrable than the theme, and what is with increasing vehemence decried? But does the thematic study appear attractive merely *faute de mieux* or is there something in these literatures that necessitates it ... Despite all the reserves I have for *Kulturgeschichte*, and especially its desire to seek national characteristics, I am prompted to say that the Canadian literatures elaborate a profoundly idealistic attitude ... Character is best seen, then, as a rhetorical configuration, the presence of idea as statement, a theme" (220–2). "Myth criticism" has frequently been perceived as synonymous with "thematic criticism" and thus has been decried by both structuralists and poststructuralists. In recent years, however, many novels have signalled a renewed interest in myth, and critical appraisals of that interest are beginning to form a new body of myth criticism.[1] The novels themselves call for a study of their various uses of "myth," and to deny them this investigation because it is de rigueur to flog myth criticism is to be unaware of the potential power of certain kinds of myth criticism to deal with postmodernist and postcolonialist tendencies in literature.

The six works of fiction I examine in this study are Jovette Marchessault's *Comme une enfant de la terre* (1975); Rudy Wiebe's *The Scorched-Wood People* (1977); George Bowering's *Burning Water* (1980); François Barcelo's *La Tribu* (1981); Jacques Godbout's *Les Têtes à Papineau* (1981); and Joy Kogawa's *Obasan* (1981). These novels, while retelling stories of the past in the light of the cultural, historical, fictional, and theoretical concerns of their "present," address and incorporate many of the present philosophical challenges of what has been designated by Lyotard and others as the postmodern age. This investigation centres on the presence of myth, especially self-conscious and ironic work on myth, in these paradoxical novels.

Blodgett's point about literary theory and ideology is succinctly made: "What we have been reluctant to assert is not only that literary theory is ideological, but that any literary theory that tries to resolve the problems of nation-states ... must be clear about its ideology" ("Canadian Literatures," 32). In the 1990s, however, most theorists are no longer reluctant to assert their ideological stance. Philosophers, anthropologists, ethnographers, and literary theorists, from Michel Foucault to James Clifford, have investigated the relationship between power and knowledge and stressed the need for an awareness of previously occulted presuppositions in any discussions of identity, history, culture, or text.[2] Indeed, essentialist notions such as "history" and "culture" are challenged by both Foucault and Clifford, with the latter arguing that any cultural commentator must be aware of the personal and cultural assumptions of the self who writes. The opening sentence of Robert Young's *White Mythologies*, a study of postwar theories of history, underlines the radical shift that has occurred: "In recent years the field of literary and cultural theory has, broadly speaking, been determined by a preoccupation with 'the political'" (vi). In fact, respected literary critics such as Laurie Ricou have signalled, tongue in cheek, the extreme pressure to be political: he titles his contribution to *A Mazing Space* "Phyllis Webb, Daphne Marlatt and Simultitude: Journal Entries from a Capitalist Bourgeois Patriarchal Anglo-Saxon Mainstream Critic" (205).

As an individual born in Quebec whose own sociopolitical outlook was strongly influenced by the nationalist movement of the 1970s, two potential areas of contention are of concern to me. This comparative work is written in English, and, as is obvious in its explanatory glosses of Québécois culture, politics, and language, it is destined primarily for an anglophone audience. Furthermore, it makes generous use of theories of postmodernism and postcolonialism – theories that are much more current in Anglo-American practice and in studies of the new literatures in "english" (Ashcroft, Griffiths, and Tiffin, *The Empire Writes Back*, 8) than in contemporary francophone studies of Québécois literature. Although there are some similarities between the concern in the 1990s in Quebec with "les théories de l'identitaire"[3] and the various manifestations of postmodern and postcolonial theoretical investigations in Anglo-American theory, I am aware that this study might well be interpreted in certain quarters as a recuperation of Québécois fiction – much as Chantal de Grandpré has accused English Canadian critics of canadianizing Québécois literature in order to meet their own needs for history and culture ("La Canadianisation de la littérature québécoise," 50–1). Such a recuperation is possible, argues de Grandpré, because English Canadian criticism occults much of the political agenda of Québécois fiction.

The present study does invoke the political contexts of all six works of fiction, situating them in the sometimes highly charged political situations of the day. That said, it is nonetheless obvious to me that many contemporary works of cultural/literary criticism written in English adopt a more personal political stance than I do in this work. No doubt my personal appreciation of the possibility of many different versions of historical reality, a necessary condition of my upbringing, along with my exposure to various schools of cultural and literary criticism, makes of me an autodidact – a "wanderer" in Edward Said's terms – one who is "essentially *between* homes," who faces "constant transposition ... 'exteriority' and 'in-betweeness'" (*Beginnings*, 8). This study of postmodern and postcolonial myth in historiographic fictions is undertaken in part because of my own strong fascination with the complex situations of politics and culture in Quebec and English-speaking Canada. None-theless, scholarship on New World Myth *is* the principal focus of this work, and, to that end, my efforts have been deployed mainly in illustrating and developing the theory of New World Myth through the reading of selected texts. For instance, while I believe that my choice of novels points to that openness and pluralism so strongly encouraged by Blodgett, I do not dwell at great length on the differ-ent racial origins or the possible political agendas of the authors of these novels. I prefer to let the texts speak largely for themselves. Thus, although I discuss Native Peoples' recent challenges to Bow-ering's portrayal of Amerindians, because it has a bearing on my discussion of New World Myth, I do not necessarily judge or con-demn Bowering for his work. My focus is more on how the text *Burning Water* exploits Eurocentric myths of Aboriginality, than, to quote Eva-Marie Kröller, on "the political responsibilities of the writer" (*George Bowering*, 84).

Nonetheless, the complex situations referred to above bring me to discuss at some length this point, the second of my concerns: the novels' problematic yet intriguing portrayal of the Amerindian figure as a device of postcolonial discourse. Both Sylvia Söderlind (in *Margin/Alias*) and Linda Hutcheon have noted the presumptuous-ness of speaking of Canada as if its political situation were equiva-lent to that of former colonies in the Third World. Hutcheon proposes that the conflation of First World colonialist experience with that of the Third World has "something in [it] that is both triv-ializing of the Third World experience and exaggerated regarding the Canadian" ("Circling the Downspout of Empire," 155). Hutcheon also raises the issue of the occulted Amerindian, arguing that "when Canadian culture is called post-colonial today, the reference is very rarely (at least explicitly) to the native culture, which might be the more accurate historical use of the term" (*Splitting Images*, 75).

Nowhere is the hesitation between varying postcolonial tech-niques and agendas more evident than in contemporary fiction's treatment of the figure of the Amerindian and the Métis. In many contemporary novels from English-speaking Canada and Quebec, a self-conscious postcolonial urge to demythologize the superiority of the European or white colonizer and to explore self/other tensions on "home ground" (Mukherjee, "Whose Post-Colonialism?" 6) coex-ists with a postmodern play with the figure of the Amerindian. Although the historical colonization of the Amerindian and Inuit peoples by the British and French is openly signalled in many con-temporary texts (which often challenge the traditions of historiogra-phy), they sometimes *use* the figure of the Amerindian or Métis to

further the postcolonial arguments of the nonnative cultural majori-
ties of their traditions. My investigation here centres on what Terry
Goldie calls the image of the Amerindian in these works – rather
than on "the people the image claims to represent" (*Fear and Temptation*, 6).

In his conclusion to *Orientalism*, Edward Said asks if "the
notion of a distinct culture ... always get[s] involved either in self-
congratulation (when one discusses one's own) or hostility and
aggression (when one discusses the 'other')" (325). Recent debates
about cultural appropriation and the politics of representation tend
to sustain this either/or stance, and it is imperative, I believe, to
address briefly here the thorny questions of the self/other paradigm
and of the appropriation of voice that has been so frequently raised
in the 1990s. In the decade since the novels discussed in this book
were published, the use and abuse of Amerindian characters in fictions by non-Natives has been strongly criticized both within and
without First Nations' communities. For instance, Gerald Vizenor
condemns W.P. Kinsella's caricature in *The Fencepost Chronicles*:
"Ermineskin is a fictional narrator, but imagination does not absolve
racialism; humor is no excuse to exploit negative preconceptions
about tribal people. The author plays Indian for a white audience"
(Review of *The Fencepost Chronicles*, 111). Frank Davey's discussion
in *Post-National Arguments* of Margaret Laurence's *Diviners* "accuses
Morag the 'white novelist' of appropriating Jules and Pique's songs
when she appends them to her novel, thereby unfairly appropriating
the 'signs of connection to the land, aboriginality, inheritance, and
'naturalness' of the indigenes" (Davey, *Post-National Arguments*, 41;
on Davey, see Kortenaar, "Postcolonial Canadian Identity," 20). I
have no quarrel with the argument made by Lenore Keeshig-Tobias
at the 1992 Vancouver conference on postcolonialism that Amerindian stories are the property of First Nations Peoples and should
therefore be told only by them ("The Identity of the Native Voice").
An awareness of and respect for Amerindian copyright systems, I
believe, is a necessary component of literary (and other) investigations. I remain intrigued, however, by the presence of the Amerindian and Métis figures in contemporary non-Amerindian literature.

Arun Mukherjee's discussion of the limitations of the binary us/
Other argument is pertinent here. While Mukherjee shares the discomfort felt by postcolonial critics such as the authors of *The Empire
Writes Back* with regard to the assimilationist and homogenizing tendencies of postmodernist theory, she objects to their "attempt to
create a post-colonial theory that can be applied to 'all' ... postcolonial writing, regardless of the differences of gender, race, class,

caste, ethnicity and sexual orientation" (2). Mukherjee raises an important point. She writes: "When post-colonial theory constructs its centre-periphery discourse, it also obliterates the fact that the postcolonial societies also have their own internal centres and peripheries, their own dominants and marginals" (6). In other words, Mukherjee proposes that when postcolonial theory maintains binary oppositions such as centre/margin, colonizer/colonized, domination/resistance, and so on, it tends to overlook "the cultural work that a post-colonial text does on its home ground" (6). Arguing against the predominant assumption that postcolonial texts are fundamentally engaged in writing back to the centre, Mukherjee warns us not to subscribe to the notion that the preeminent concern of postcolonial texts is to use parody to undercut imperial textuality. She proposes that the privileging of parodic texts limits postcolonial studies to those authors who serve up what the theory calls for, and "despite its best intentions [this restriction] ends up homogenizing and assimilating" (7). Referring at one point to national literatures of India, she writes, "Indian literatures in various languages are not in conversation with a distant outsider but with those at home." They are, like any other literature, in a "dialogic ... relation with other social discourses that circulate in the Indian society rather than with those at the 'centre'" (6).

The relationships between non-Amerindian writers from postcolonial countries in the Americas and the Amerindian characters they create or recreate cannot always be reduced to a simplified self/ other, centre/margin(alized) paradigm. Indeed, these dichotomies from postcolonial studies may perhaps hinder some serious reflection on the attempts of non-Aboriginal "mainstream" writers, such as, for instance, Rudy Wiebe or Jacques Poulin, to open up textual space in which to explore various manifestations of differing cultural representations. Thus, Rudy Wiebe's novel, *The Temptations of Big Bear*, exposes the multitiered colonial situations in Western Canada, while illustrating Eastern Canada's imperialism in Western Canada, white male Western Canadians' patronizing attitudes toward the Cree and toward women of any race, and different races' and groups' perceptions of the same event. Most of Wiebe's novels, including *A Discovery of Strangers*, indicate various degrees of willingness to explore heterogeneity. Postcolonial *studies* of *The Temptations of Big Bear*, however, tend to dwell on the non-Aboriginal status of its author, and to insist on the limitations of its characteristic postcolonial insistence on cross-cultural awareness. Thus, although Diana Brydon and Helen Tiffin acknowledge in *Decolonizing Fictions* that the novel attempts to create "an alternative view of the Other as both equal and different" (131), they conclude that "Wiebe's Christianity draws him inevitably toward assimilating the other into the established Christian framework" (134). They note, for instance, that the title of Wiebe's novel offers an "implicit evocation of a Christian context for Big Bear's heroism"(136): he is to somehow be seen simultaneously as both Christian saint and pagan warrior. The overriding pressure of the self/other paradigm in politically correct academic circles appears to be working *against* the postcolonial practices in texts by mainstream authors such as Laurence and Wiebe, in spite of the fact that they are often praised for their "sensitive responses to Native culture." One senses this in Terry Goldie's question to Daniel Moses, in their prefatory conversation to *The Oxford Anthology of Canadian Native Literature in English*. Discussing their decision not to include works by non-Natives, Goldie says: "On the one hand, Native cultures have certain values and certain powers which can to a certain extent be acquired by a sensitive and creative representation of those cultures, as in the case of *Big Bear*. But could they be acquired to the degree that they can be presented from the Native culture itself?" (xx). The question remains unanswered and almost unexplored. The preeminent postcolonial theory of the Self/Other dichotomy may perhaps be getting in the way of the attempts by Wiebe, Laurence, and other authors to explore "home-ground" issues and various manifestations of differing cultural representations.

The situation in Quebec is somewhat different. It has been suggested that the term postcolonial can hardly be applied to Quebec, given the stormy confrontation between Natives and non-Natives at Kanesatake (Oka) during the summer of 1990.[4] Racial tensions do exist in Quebec (as they do elsewhere in Canada), and I would agree with Caroline Bayard that although in Quebec "a duly elected Liberal party declared itself, by the end of June 1990, ready to commence negotiations on a different constitutional agreement with the rest of Canada, it still remained that by July 1990 the massive litigations between Native people and the Canadian as much as Québécois governments had not been attended to ... [The explosive situation at Kanasatake] signalled a profound *différend* (see Lyotard, *Le Différend*), which neither the federal government nor the Quebec Liberals nor the PQ knew how to handle" (20). However, Bayard appears here to gloss over the different hierarchial administrative levels of the federal and provincial governments, as well as the diachronical developments in Amerindian/non-Amerindian relations. Until relatively recently, the federal Department of Indian and Northern Affairs assumed responsibility for all Amerindians living within the territory of Quebec. This produced another Canadian irony at the turn of the century: English-speaking Amerindians in Quebec and francophone Amerindians in the West. Normand Delisle notes that even today in Quebec the first nonnative language of the majority of Inuit and Amerindians is still English ("Les langues autochtones," 3).

However, in spite of the politically imposed imperialist and historical split between Amerindians and francophones in Quebec, the figure of the Métis is omnipresent in its contemporary fictions. In Quebec today, two very different sorts of novels present the Amerindian and Métis figures. Some, such as Francine Ouellette's *Au nom du père et du fils*, are best-sellers, and their portrayals of Amerindians or, more frequently, Métis are not in the least subtle; they present what Penny Petrone has described as Renaissance Europe's "romanticized image of primeval innocence – the 'bon' sauvage, a Rousseauesque pure being" (*Native Literature in Canada*, 2). Other contemporary postmodern authors, however, such as Jovette Marchessault and Jacques Poulin, explore the inherent difficulties of living in nonhomogenous societies through their use of Amerindian or Métis characters. I would suggest that the societal and literary apprehensions of the Amerindian in Quebec should not be judged by the criteria that presently dominate in the English-speaking Canadian world. Worldviews can and do differ: as Stephen Richer and Lorna Wier note in the introduction to *Beyond Political Correctness*, the very term "politically correct," which has produced so much passionate debate in the English-speaking Canadian world, has "no corresponding term in French and [has received] no mass media publicity in Quebec" (18).

Indeed, Régine Robin's postface to the 1993 edition of her well-known novel, *La Québécoite*, is an excellent example of the incredulity with which some conceptions of political correctness are received in Quebec. Robin herself is a respected professor of sociology at the University of Montreal, and her fiction is usually characterized as belonging to what has come to be called *l'écriture migrante*. Her synthesis of the contemporary situation of the arts in Quebec strongly refutes those notions that have become *monnaie courante* in English-speaking Canada: "appropriation culturelle" (216) and "[un] respect *politically correct* qui équivaudrait à la mort de la littérature" (222). Instead, Robin invites a cross-cultural dialogue between what she identifies as two major streams of writing in Quebec after 1980: "La grand chance de la littérature québécoise aujourd'hui est de pouvoir faire dialoguer, même dans le conflit et la polémique (engueulons-nous, bon Dieu, engueulons-nous, mais au moins commençons à nous parler) les deux courants de la littérature québécoise, le courant légitime et l'écriture migrante, de les faire se métisser, de détisser, se ressourcer par cette grande chance d'être en Amérique" (221). Robin ends her polemical discussion by proposing that Quebecers celebrate this dynamic literature, which, in its always-already-perpetual-coming-into-being, is best defined in terms of "la fiction des bords ... pas seulement des frontières et des contacts" (224). The binary structures in postcolonial discourse from the international (anglophone) sphere of influence are not prevalent in contemporary francophone texts in Quebec. Novels such as Jacques Poulin's *Volkswagen Blues* and plays such as Jovette Marchessault's *Le Voyage magnifique d'Emily Carr* frequently present and explore a *slippage* (the idea is discussed in detail in chapter 5) among what have traditionally been perceived as separate or separable groups. As Bernadette Bucher has argued, the Métis figure is "à la fois ceci et cela, le même et l'autre" ("Sémiologie du mixte," 308), and thus offers the possibility of a less confrontational perception of difference and multiplicity. I provide a more detailed discussion of this *métissage* in chapter 3 and, especially, chapters 5 and 6.

Indeed, my argument here and in the chapters that follow is that postmodernist parodies of Amerindians might well advance the postcolonial concern of writing back to the centre, but they do not usually facilitate cross-cultural investigations of heterogeneity. However, many contemporary texts by non-Amerindian writers put parody aside in an effort to open up textual space for postcolonial discussions about home-ground issues. Unfortunately, in English-speaking Canada, the seemingly wide-scale adoption of the binary us/other theory sometimes impedes the work the novels are carrying out. The figure of the Métis, when it is not strongly marked by postmodernist parody, can facilitate a textual discussion of pluralism in political identity, although as we shall see, its use is exploratory and sometimes problematic. It is important, I believe, to be cognizant of the limitations of the self/other argument in critical appraisals of the multitiered postcolonial situations in English-speaking Canada and Quebec.

Of the six novels studied here, some are by fairly well established authors, such as Rudy Wiebe and Jacques Godbout; others, such as those by Jovette Marchessault and François Barcelo, have generated little critical commentary. All six thematize historiography and the act of narration, while foregrounding the role of the narrator in the creation of New World Myth. In chapter 1, therefore, I examine the conditions that have contributed to the formulation of New World Myth in contemporary fictions from English-speaking Canada and Quebec. A preliminary discussion signals the problematic situation of English Canadian and Québécois fictions in the current postmodern/

postcolonial debate. Chapter 1 also situates New World Myth in the broader context of classical, biblical, and historical myths, provides an overview of "myth and literature" in the French and English traditions, and concludes with a working definition of New World Myth. In Jacques Godbout's *Les Têtes à Papineau* and Rudy Wiebe's *The Scorched-Wood People*, the narrators overtly proclaim their role as myth-*makers* and emphasize the didactic nature of their mission. Their self-conscious production of New World Myth, especially through the exploitation of biblical and "primitive" myths and popular political clichés, is examined in chapter 2, as are their reflections on the changing nature of the relationships between the individual and community. The individual/community relationship is also examined in chapter 3, with a brief discussion of *métissage* and Amerindian and Buddhist mythologies informing the complex political situations portrayed in the novels discussed, Jovette Marchessault's *Comme une enfant de la terre* and Joy Kogawa's *Obasan*. In this chapter, I argue that the narrators of these two novels also challenge biblical myth through their use and abuse of the Ptolemaic and Copernican cosmogonies. In chapter 4, the investigations of historiography by these same two narrators, which follow the somewhat circuitous routes of ecofeminism, pantheism, non-rationality, speech, silence, and memory, revalorize the feminine in their apprehensions of the political past and present. Many feminist analyses involve the denunciation of patriarchy through work on language, especially in studies of *la nouvelle écriture*; I argue here that similar challenges to a patriarchal worldview are discernable in an alternative poetics of the feminine, based on a rediscovery of feminine symbolism. In chapter 5, the exploration of New World Myth focuses on magic realism and post-Europeanism in the retellings of history in François Barcelo's *La Tribu* and George Bowering's *Burning Water*. I discuss these novels' challenges to teleological evolutionism through the postcolonial technique of *slippage*. Finally, chapter 6 discusses the role of the artist and the thematization of fact, fancy, and the imagination in the same two metafictions. Their narrators ironically highlight some ethnographic practices in order to foreground the challenge of New World Myth to traditional, European-inspired ethnography through the use of irony, parody, allegory, and *métissage*.

The terminology used in this work is not always entirely to my satisfaction. "Myth," as I have noted, is a slippery term, meaning anything from Mircea Eliade's notion of "tradition sacrée, révélation primordiale, modèle exemplaire" (*Aspects du mythe*, 9) to the more contemporary acceptation of "lie, deceit, falsehood." "New World Myth" is even more problematic, as the New World is not/was not "new" to everyone. Terms such as "postmodern myth" or "post-colonial myth" however, are not operable here, for reasons that become evident in chapter 1. As comparatists such as Blodgett and Stratford have noted, it is somewhat difficult to arrive at acceptable terms for literature written in either English or French in Canada. To simplify matters, I use the terms "English-speaking Canada," "English Canadian," "French Canadian," and "Québécois" contextually, while acknowledging that such encompassing terms are not necessarily adequate to describe the complex cultural/linguistic situations that were evident in fictions from the years 1975–85 and are yet more obvious today. "Québécois" is generally applied to works written in French in Quebec after 1960. Before that date, "canadien" or "canadien-français" were used. Many commentators use the global term "Canadian" to refer to what I would characterize as works from English-speaking Canada; sometimes Québécois works are included within that global term. As far as possible, I have indicated within this study whether commentators' remarks refer to English Canadian, French Canadian (prior to 1960), or Québécois texts.

The terms "politics" and "political" also require elucidation. In the late 1980s and 1990s, "political" came to have a very wide acceptation, linked as it was to related concepts of feminism, agency, and representation. Rick Salutin defines politics as "that entire area in which we are concerned with the shape and thrust of our society, as far as these are within human control" (*Marginal Notes*, 5). In my work here, however, "political" adheres to the more limited acceptation it usually had during the years 1975–85; I use it when referring to power relationships between defined groups, as in "federal-provincial politics."

The language of quotation is equally problematic in comparative studies. I quote for the most part from the original texts, assuming that readers of this study will have sufficient knowledge of French and English. Furthermore, the close analyses I present here require the use of the original language. Occasionally, however, I use a readily available English translation of a theoretical work that was originally published in French. For the reader's convenience, my translations of the passages in Spanish are provided in the text of the study.

Acknowledgments

Many of the ideas in this study were first generated during my doctoral studies at the Centre for Comparative Literature at the University of Toronto, and I am grateful to friends and colleagues there for the stimulating environment and the intellectual support they provided. I once again thank Linda Hutcheon, J.E. Chamberlin, and Janet M. Paterson for their insightful readings of my initial research, although it must be noted that this study has evolved greatly since its first inception. Linda Hutcheon's work on postmodernism has influenced my work on myth, and I offer her my deeply affectionate thanks for the many ways in which she has supported my work.

I wish to acknowledge research grants from the University of Victoria. A warm thank you is extended to all the friends and colleagues with whom I have had useful discussions about postmodernism, postcolonialism, New World Myth, and the literatures of English-speaking Canada and Quebec. I thank my colleagues in the Departments of French Language and Literature, English, and History for their support. In particular, I express my gratitude to Dr Elizabeth Vibert for her generous help. I am grateful to the excellent research librarians at the University of Victoria's McPherson Library and particularly wish to thank Don White and Ken Cooley for their much-appreciated aid in tracking down elusive references. I also thank my three research assistants, Karyn Marczak, Andrew Gibbs, and Mary MacDonald, whose company I very much enjoyed and whose skills in library research and computer technology have contributed to this project.

Some of the ideas in this book have appeared in either French or English in *Canadian Literature*, *Studies in Canadian Literature/Etudes en littérature canadienne*, *Canadian Ethnic Studies*, and in *Les Discours féminins dans la littérature postmoderne au Québec*, edited by Raija Koski, Kathleen Kells, and Louise Forsyth. I am grateful to the editors of these pubications for their interest in my work and also to audiences in Montreal, Quebec, Vancouver, Toronto, Edmonton, Charlottetown, Victoria, Leiden (The Netherlands), Seattle, Tucson, and La Martinique for their support.

[La] liberté commence là où les certitudes s'achèvent.
　　　Pierre Hébert, "Problème de sémiotique diachronique"

1 Postmodern Myth and Post-European History: Thematics and Theory in the New World

In the 1960s and early 1970s most thematic studies of the literatures of Quebec and of English-speaking Canada, from Gilles Marcotte's *Une Littérature qui se fait* and Jean-Charles Falardeau's *Notre Société et son roman* to Margaret Atwood's *Survival* and John Moss's *Patterns of Isolation in English Canadian Fiction*, considered the problematic question of national identity to be a central issue. In the second half of the 1970s thematic criticism in both English Canada and Quebec began to give way to European-inspired structuralist interpretations. "Beyond thematics" was the place to which most critics in English Canada suddenly were expected to aspire, according to Russell Brown, although, as he himself notes, most did not get there ("Critic, Culture, Text," 175). In Quebec, applying what were commonly called *des grilles d'analyse*, largely inspired by the Tel Quel group, was de rigueur for literary academics in the 1970s. This shift from content to form, often inspired by the works themselves, was productive for many critical approaches. The thorny questions of cultural identity and nationalist politics, however, continued to hover beneath the Barthian surfaces of many contemporary English Canadian and Québécois texts. During the 1970s and 1980s, the novel, in particular, was instrumental in simultaneously constructing and challenging nationalist notions in what Benedict Anderson calls "imagined communities." In the 1980s, poststructuralism, deconstruction, and, more importantly to my argument here, the emergence of postmodernist and postcolonial theories and practices opened the door to renewed interest in the question of national identities in the literatures of

English-speaking Canada and Quebec – but an interest with a difference. As Linda Hutcheon noted, the "entire question of Canadian identity ha[d] become a kind of playground – or battlefield – for the postmodern as well as the post-colonial defining of 'difference' and value" ("'Circling the Downspout of Empire,'" 166). The complexities of these areas of investigation – identity, postmodernism, postcolonialism, and myth – form the basis of the present study.

M. Jeanne Yardley has noted the persistence of thematic criticism in comparative Canadian literary studies and the accompanying search for literary emblems. She recalls the various geometric figures that have been proposed as models for the "relationship between the two major Canadian literatures": Pierre-Joseph-Olivier Chauvreau's double spiral staircase, Jean-Charles Falardeau's horizontal and vertical axes, Philip Stratford's double helix on the DNA model, and E.D. Blodgett's idea of a lattice-work fence (Yardley, "The Maple Leaf," 252–5). Signalling Blodgett's willingness to leave models behind when appropriate, Yardley underlines the insufficiencies of searching out such emblems as a critical enterprise, noting their necessarily exclusive effect on the choice of the canon. In remarks that strike closer to home, Yardley describes the prolificacy and the limitations of myth-oriented criticism in studies of Canadian literature, noting that such criticism is frequently practised along Frygian lines and "tends to reduce all texts to a single story" (258). The present study investigates the presence of New World Myth in contemporary fictional works. Although one of the issues foregrounded in the six novels under consideration here is the double problematic of myth and national identity, this study seeks to examine various ways in which these contemporary fictions strive to destabilize the accepted workings of traditional myth.

Any university library will list hundreds, if not thousands, of works under the generic heading "myth." Where, then, does one begin? One of Said's early texts, *Beginnings*, published in the first year of the decade examined in this study, may be of some help here. Although I appreciate Jonathan Culler's criticism of *Beginnings* – a criticism taken up by several other reviewers – that it is "a manuscript in search of an editor, a sprawling work whose title claims for it a unity that it never quite achieves" (Culler, "Beginnings," 502), Said's discussion of beginnings is useful to this contemporary study of myth. Giambattista Vico's remark in *The New Science* that "doctrines must take their beginnings from that of the matters of which they treat" is the epigraph to Said's book. Vico's distinction between "the gentile or historical and the sacred or original" parallels Said's distinction between beginning and an origin (*Beginnings*, 357). Said argues that "beginning and beginning-again are historical whereas origins are divine ... [and] a beginning not only creates but is its own method because it has intention" (xiii). Origins lay claim to truth, whereas beginnings "are necessary fictions reflecting above all the desire to begin, a decision to break with a past and initiate a future" (Culler, "Beginnings," 303). Said encourages the courageous act of creating or imagining beginnings rather than seeking absolute origins. In his wide-ranging discussion Said shows how the novel has evolved from its classical form (based in autobiography, in life-story) to one wherein a beginning is motivated both by individual agency and a self-conscious awareness of the precariousness of writing as an enterprise. There is a strong tension in the novel between the *authority* proclaimed by the novelist, which is based on the power to create, to control, to intend, and what Said calls *molestation*, which he defines as "a consciousness of one's duplicity, one's confinement to a fictive, scriptive realm, whether one is a character or a novelist" (*Beginnings*, 84). Said's comments apply not only to the numerous European and American novels of the nineteenth and twentieth centuries that make up his corpus but also to the authors of fictions and of literary and cultural commentary/criticism/theory.

For Said beginnings do intend meaning: *"A beginning, then, is the first step in the intentional production of meaning"* (5), but these beginnings are provisional, marked by discontinuity, nonlinearity, disjunction. They are also marked by an intentional determination, by an intellectual "appetite" that is "always engaged purposefully in the production of meaning" (12). Writers of texts, according to Said, are increasingly aware of the burden of self-consciousness and their inability to create their work out of – and to insert it into – a long and harmonious tradition of literature and scholarship. Thus, the emphasis in the last chapter on Vico – that "first philosopher of beginnings" (*Beginnings*, 350) – as an autodidact echoes the observations in the preliminary chapter on the absence of the security of tradition for the contemporary critic, that necessary "wanderer" (8). As Welsey Morris implies, the critical, if mitigated, success of Said's *Beginnings* is perhaps due in part to its endorsing an approach that frees the American critic from the burden of European tradition: "The typical American strategy is to substitute new, 'written,' identities for the vitiating historical (generational) truth of our borrowed European ones" (Morris, "Beginnings," 743). Precisely because the modern literary critic cannot sustain himself or herself in a "dynastic tradition" (Said, *Beginnings*, 13), a different topos must be sought out. For Said this topos *is* the beginning: "Beginnings inaugurate a deliberately *other* production of meaning – a gentile (as opposed to a sacred) one ... A beginning, therefore, is a problem to be studied, as well as a position taken by any writer."

The concepts Said uses to formulate his theoretical concerns – origin/beginning(s), divine/historical, tradition/autodidact, authority/molestation – can be applied to the novels examined in this study, as well as to this study itself. Traditional myth criticism portrays myths as true stories, as sacred narratives about the actions of the gods, as explicatory models or explanations of the origins of the universe. New World Myth, however, opposes this origin/divine paradigm with one focused on beginning(s), on the historical. The narrators of New World Myth flaunt the precariousness of their beginnings while alluding to histories, to narratives, and to the act of writing. This is evident in the prologue to *Burning Water*, where the speaker reflects on his feeling that "current history and self were bound together, from the beginning" and then asks rhetorically, "How could I begin to tell such a story? I asked myself. Books do have beginnings, but how arbitrary they can be."

Said's third theoretical concern, the liberating advantage enjoyed by today's critics and novelists by virtue of being autodidacts (as opposed to being obliged to insert themselves into literary or theoretical traditions), is equally foregrounded in the texts of this corpus. Jovette Marchessault's narrator, like all New World Myth narrators, has a highly cynical attitude toward "book-learning," the written word, universities, and academics. This narrator, like Marchessault herself and like Said's contemporary critic, is both an autodidact and a "wanderer" in the geographical, intellectual, cultural, and spiritual domains. New World Myth is marked by the deliberate intention to break with mythic and historical traditions and to address the here and now, to take – to paraphrase Vico – "its beginnings from that of the matters of which it treats." While these narrators display a self-conscious awareness of the precariousness of their enterprise, they are motivated to embark upon the courageous act of creating New World Myth rather than to seek absolute origins by turning to literary or mythic traditions.

Said's remarks on authority and molestation, while interesting in their applications to the works he studies, are only partially applicable to New World Myth works. He describes a sense of authority on the part of the novelist, who is conscious of a personal power to initiate, establish, and control the "product" (*Beginnings*, 83) but who is also affected by the "consciousness of one's duplicity, one's confinement to a fictive, scriptive realm" (84). Said's discussions, however, are based mainly on works produced in the modernist Euro-American literary mainstream. In contrast, New World Myth texts are the products of more marginal cultures, and they do not reflect a similar blanket confidence in their political or literary power to control and to intend. Nonetheless, as is discussed in more detail below, these texts are marked, paradoxically, by both a strong motivation to didacticism about the historical past (which they do not perceive as confined to the fictive realm) and by an ubiquitous self-consciousness regarding the creation, through fiction, of New World Myth.

Said portrays literary critics as scholars aware of the discontinuities of their training and no longer able to insert themselves into any one strong tradition. They are thus perhaps more easily enabled to make a beginning, in spite of their consciousness of the probable frailty of the project. Thus, a critic must accept "the risks of rupture and discontinuity" (*Beginnings*, 34) because, "for the writer, the historian, or the philosopher the beginning will emerge reflectively ... already engaging him [or her] in an awareness of its difficulty" (35). I am certainly aware of the shaky uncertainty of the beginnings that are portrayed in much of Said's work: there is a definitive break in tradition in this "beginning" of mine, as my definition and illustrations of New World Myth do not insert themselves into the accepted tradition of myth criticism. This study of New World Myth was begun in an exploratory way and was formulated gradually through repeated readings of the texts themselves, so that this introductory chapter was not the first chapter of the work to be written. In this way, the theory of New World Myth, to paraphrase Vico yet once again, took its beginnings "from that of the matters of which [it] treat[s]." Where, then, to begin? First, by noting the slippery quality of the term "myth": it can – and does – mean anything from sacred story to outright lie. Second, by an overview of myth criticism and an examination of work in the field that pertains to the literatures of English-speaking Canada and Quebec. Third, by reflecting on what some contemporary authors have to say about myth. And fourth, and most importantly, by provisionally describing the perameters of what I call New World Myth.

A BRIEF HISTORY OF MYTH

In classical times, the Greeks initially equated *mythos* with true stories of the gods, but according to Mircea Eliade, from the time of Xenophanes "the Greeks steadily continued to empty *mythos* of all religious and metaphysical value" (*Myth and Reality*, 1). Slowly, a distinction came to be made between *mythos* (which has unquestioned validity) and *logos* (whose validity can be proved), and later, between *mythos* and *historia*. "Myth," says Eliade, came to signify something that cannot truly exist (2). According to Kees Bolle and Richard Buxton, few innovative theoretical perspectives on myth were developed during the Middle Ages or the Renaissance. Instead, in both periods interpretations of myth in terms of allegory or of Euhemerism (according to which certain gods were originally great people who benefited mankind) tended to predominate. This, of course, enabled Christians to incorporate myths from "the culturally authoritative" past into the Christian framework while demythologizing the gods of that past ("Myth and Mythology," 712).

Myth came to be a central focus of literature in the Western world with the rise of European Romanticism, and it grew in importance to literary studies from the end of the nineteenth century onwards, with the heyday of myth criticism occurring from the 1940s to the 1970s. Myth criticism first centred on classifying stories from the Greco-Roman tradition ("classical" myths) and on associating the gods of these stories with strong emotions: thus, Aphrodite represented desire, Athena, wisdom, and so forth. Myths were also linked to contemporary European folk tales and to anthropological studies of stories believed to be true in precontact cultures. Greco-Roman myths from antiquity and nineteenth-century folktales from popular cultures "were regarded by the Romantics as repositories of experience far more vital and powerful than those obtainable from what was felt to be the artificial art and poetry of the aristocratic civilization of contemporary Europe" (Bolle and Buxton, "Myth and Mythology," 713). At the turn of the century, one notes a proliferation of dictionaries of classical myths, as well as the publication of seminal anthropological works such as Sir James George Frazer's *The Golden Bough*, which was originally published in 1890, grew to twelve volumes by 1915, and was abridged into one volume in 1922.

Frazer's powerful impact on twentieth-century English language writers and critics was considerable, as John B. Vickery has illustrated in *The Literary Impact of the Golden Bough*. Working with information obtained from missionaries and anthropologists visiting non-European countries, Frazer proposed a diachronic development of three modes of thought: magical, religious, and scientific. Drawing on descriptions of ritual practices of precontact communities, *The Golden Bough* attempts to reconstruct elements of precontact worldviews by an examination of myths and rituals. For instance, according to Frazer, many geographically separated "primitive tribes" believed that the well-being of their communities depended upon the vitality of the king who led them, and therefore a community needed to slay its leader when his strength began to lessen, in order to replace him with a healthy successor whose vigour assured that of the "tribe." Frazer's studies of myth and ritual name, classify, and draw parallels among various ritualistic "figures" such as the divine king, the stranger, the virgin, the hanged man, the corn-mother, and the scapegoat. Northrop Frye, writing in 1957, notes that although *The Golden Bough* "purports to be a work of anthropology ... it has had more influence on literary criticism than in its own alleged field, and it may yet prove to be really a work of literary criticism" (*Anatomy of Criticism*, 109). While *The Golden Bough*'s theories of the evolutionary sequence of thought are now unsatisfactory to anthropological studies – to say nothing of Frazer's eurocentric appreciation of non-european cultures – the influence of the text can easily be traced in the writings of twentieth-century modernists: Eliot, Conrad, Faulkner, Joyce, Pound, and D.H. Lawrence, among many others.[1] Indeed, much Anglo-American myth criticism of the early to mid-twentieth century consisted of seeking out and commenting on parallels between Frazer's work and the contemporary novels and poetry of the time. *The Golden Bough* allowed critics to explore the magical and fascinating world of evil, spirits, sex, and unbridled emotions at the same time as it implied the cultural superiority of the (mainly European) world of the anthropologist.

The second major enterprise of midcentury Anglo-American work on myth was to comment on the frequently ironic allusions to myths of the Greco-Roman classical period and then to establish and elaborate on the relationships between myth and structure in the novel. This practice has come to be called the "'myth and symbol school' of American Studies, which had its heyday around the middle part of [the twentieth] century" (Hestetun, *A Prison-House of Myth?* 19).[2] The collected essays in John Vickery's *Myth and Literature* can be seen as an exemplar of this period: they present an interesting blend of Frazer-inspired myth criticism and studies of narrative structure. His later work, *Myths and Texts*, draws together many earlier essays from the myth and symbol period; its separate chapters discuss those subjects dear to New Criticism, such as structure, theme, character, narrative, and point of view. In a slightly different vein, John White's influential *Mythology in the Modern Novel* discusses how novelists used established myths as symbolic comments on modern events. The emphasis on structure in myth studies of the modernist period, along with this era's typical disregard for history, was underlined by the creative writers of the period themselves, as is seen in T.S. Eliot's famous comment in his 1923 review of Joyce's *Ulysses*: "[Myth] is simply a way of controlling, of ordering, of giving a shape and a significance of the immense panorama of futility and anarchy which is contemporary history" ("Ulysses, Order and Myth," 201).

In 1991, Bernard Accardi et al. published an annotated bibliography that provides a useful overview of material in the field. The continuing centrality of Northrop Frye's work is underlined in the introduction:

in what new directions has post-modernism, or late or decadent modernism, taken the study of literature in relation to myths? Northrop Frye, of course, both acclaimed and disavowed by such post-modern avatars as Harold Bloom and Geoffrey Hartman, stands at the centre of this stage ... By 1970 increasing uneasiness had set in with Frye's archetypal criticism, heralded by William Wimsatt's acerbic critique in *Northrop Frye and Modern Criticism* ... At the same time, the first generation of Frye's students and readers had begun developing their own ideas about his themes, often working with investigative tools and techniques unknown or unused two decades earlier. (*Recent Studies in Myths and Literature*, vii)

Frye's work on myth and literature continues to generate much discussion among theorists, and his influence on Canadian literature and theory are discussed elsewhere in this study.

Myth criticism of the myth and symbol school faded away during the heyday of structuralism (approximately, from 1965 to the end of the 1970s), and Anglo-American theories of myth began to be strongly influenced by French structuralists such as Claude Lévi-Strauss. In poststructuralist times, myth has made a singular comeback in Anglo-American cultural and literary studies, as is evidenced by the thousands of entries in Accardi's annotated bibliography, which, incidentally, deals only with myths in literature. Thus, the compilers of the bibliography omit Joseph Campbell's work on myth, although Campbell has become a quasi guru of New Age spiritualists, and his books and audiovisual presentations have contributed to the new interest in myth in recent years. Although Accardi et al. argue that "in later years he [Campbell] tended to use literary texts chiefly to support his general theories about human nature" (*Recent Studies in Myths and Literature*, vii–viii), Robert Segal's comparison of Campbell and Frazer states that Campbell's "impact on literary scholars has likewise been vast, though far more confined," with most of his followers applying his hero-myth pattern (from *The Hero with a Thousand Faces*) to novels and movies (Segal, "Frazer and Campbell on Myth," 471.)

From the late nineteenth to the mid-twentieth century, investigations of myth written in French were based loosely on the same two elements studied in the Anglo-American world of myth criticism: a strong interest in the Greco-Roman period,[3] and anthropological studies of religious and mythic practices from what were then commonly called "primitive" cultures. Mircea Eliade is the best-known practitioner of the latter approach, and the comparative, eclectic approach he adopted is representative of many twentieth-century French studies of myth.[4] Eliade's work betrays a strong belief in the superiority of the European vis-à-vis non-European cultures; as late as 1963 he could write with impunity about how "'primitive' mythologies" [had been] transformed and enriched ... under the influence of *higher cultures*" (*Myth and Reality,* 4; my emphasis). Eliade's work follows upon that of anthropologists and philosophers like Lucien Lévy-Bruhl (*La Mentalité primitive*) and Marcel Mauss (*Essai sur le don*). Their emphasis is on a combination of Eurocentric anthropology and the relationship between myth and world religions. Indeed, in the French tradition from the late nineteenth century to the era of structuralism, studies of myth were more frequently associated with studies of comparative religion than with literary criticism.[5] There is not one central figure in mid-twentieth-century French myth criticism whose influence was comparable to that of Northrop Frye in the Anglo-American world, but those scholars who focused on myth and literature generally read contemporary works of French literature in the light of classical myths.[6]

Major changes occurred in French approaches to literary criticism after May 1968, as the structuralist-inspired *nouvelle critique* led to new investigations of literature. In the 1960s and 1970s, the main promoter of *la mythocritique* was the long-time director of the Centre de recherche sur l'imaginaire, Gilbert Durand, in works such as *Les Structures anthropologiques de l'imaginaire* and *Figures mythiques et visages de l'œuvre.* A philosopher-anthropologist who has called himself a *structuraliste mitigé*, Durand argued against what has come to be called *la mythanalyse*, which is in fact the term more closely associated with linguistics and the formal studies of structuralism. Durand's work in *mythocritique* elaborates a theory of necessary dualism wherein a human being is torn by contradictory psycho-biological needs and desires that inevitably lead to conflict. For Durand, nature and culture are in opposition, and myth is seen as a way of containing, if not abolishing, the basic conflict between the biological and collective aspects of the individual in society. He studies content as opposed to form and considers myths diachronically, not synchronically. Although Durand's work is again more anthropological than literary, his early essays on "les structures de l'imaginaire" encouraged a myth criticism that studied myths and symbols as dynamic, changing entities.

Claude Lévi-Strauss is the critic most closely associated with myth during the structuralist period. In sharp contrast to previous studies of myth, his work focused not on the meaning, significance, or symbolism pertaining to a particular myth but on the underlying relationships among the basic elements of myths (predicate statements he called *mythèmes*), and then on the reticulated means by which the myths of given culture or cultures interrelate. Working with an elaborate system of binary oppositions, he strove to establish a "grammar" of mythical language, that is to say, to discover the rules and laws that govern the system of signs used in "le discours mythique": he was *à la recherche du* "sens caché derrière le sens" (*L'Homme nu*, 581). Despite the strong insistence on structural linguistics, information theory, and even cybernetics in Lévi-Strauss's work and despite its strong privileging of form over substance, its formal characteristics cannot be divorced from the Eurocentric bias in his supposedly empirical ethnographical research in works like *Tristes Tropiques*.[7] In *La Voie des masques* he offers the reader a eurocentric appreciation of the ceremonial masks of First Nations people, mainly those of the West Coast of Canada. In Paris in 1989, the Musée de l'Homme presented *Les Amériques de Claude Lévi-Strauss*, an exhibition that, in my opinion, could be critiqued along the lines of Hutcheon's discussion of the exhibition *Into the Heart of Africa* presented at the Royal Ontario Museum in Toronto in 1989–90 (Hutcheon, "The Post Always Rings Twice") or Kwame Anthony Appiah's appreciation of *Perspectives: Angles on African Art*, organized in 1987 by the Centre for African Art in New York (Appiah, "Is the Post- in Postmodernism the Post- in Postcolonial?"). Both Hutcheon and Appiah note the complexities of the politics of representation of ethnic groups in museum settings (Hutcheon, 207). However, Jean Guiart, the cocurator of the *Amériques–Lévi-Strauss* exhibition, appears to continue the us/them practices of Eurocentric ethnography in his brief introduction to the exposition: "il fallait ... montrer combien les autres, les hommes rouges, jaunes ou noirs faussement oubliés par ce que nous appelons l'Histoire, avaient accumulé de capacités rationnelles dans leurs technologies et dans leurs systèmes de représentations collectives" ("Les Amériques," 1). Levi-Strauss's studies of the "logic of myth" (*Mythologiques*, not *Mythologies*) proposes that all the variant forms of a myth have a common structural nexus and to work on myth is to discover its common structure. This push to homogenization and universality is not characteristic of New World Myth.

Perched between structuralist and poststructuralist practices, Roland Barthes's work opened the door to cultural critiques of French petit bourgeois society. His vignettes of "new" myths of French daily life, such as "The World of Wrestling" or "Striptease" in *Mythologies*, were intended to expose the parasitic, fraudulent and polluting presence of contemporary myths. Thus, myths cover the traces of their fabrication and the historicity of their production: they hypocritically pretend that they are the norm, that they represent eternal verities, when in fact they simply reflect (or – in the case of publicity slogans – exaggerate) the petit bourgeois mentality. Barthes quickly moved from an effort to reveal the duplicity of myth in language to an extended critique of how *signes* and *signification(s)* operate on social levels, developing his theories in "Eléments de sémiologie." Barthes' intent to shock the complacent (French?) reader by discovering new myths in quotidian life presupposes the notion that myths are usually understood as assuming the guise of natural or absolute truths. Again, New World Myth makes no such assumptions.

In *Beginnings*, Edward Said discusses the death of the "dynastic tradition" for the literary critic (13) and the preeminence of "paraknowledge [that] ... lies naturally alongside literature and in some way bears upon it" (7). These same comments apply to the very extended field of myth criticism in the twentieth century, for, as Eric Gould notes, "myth is now so encyclopedic a term that it means everything or nothing" (*Mythical Intentions*, 5). This supposed ubiquity of myth is due in part to the related fields of paraknowledge with which it came to be associated in the twentieth century and which, due to lack of space and to the fact that their primary focus is on matters other than literature, are not discussed here at any length.[8]

Accardi's bibliography, which annotates thousands of entries of work by mainly English-speaking authors within Britain and the United States, signals three traditional camps into which contemporary studies of myth fall: literature as an extension of mythology, literature as saving us from mythology, and structuralist studies of myth as linguistic form. It does make brief mention of new directions in myth criticism, such as a willingness to study biblical elements as myths in literature (see Frye's *Great Code*) and a growing body of feminist studies that may promote the goddess or Earth Mother myth, critique the patriarchal aspects of traditional myths of the hero, or revisit other fields of paraknowledge, such as psychology, in an attempt to create or recreate myth from a feminist point of view.[9] Accardi's survey, while useful for an examination of contemporary mainstream studies of myth, does not discuss much myth criticism outside the Euro-American sphere. One must look elsewhere for contemporary postmodern and postcolonial appreciations of myth in literature. As Sylvia Söderlind has pointed out, there is an ambiguous attitude to myth in postcolonial literature, which is "frequently busy dismantling both the myths and the literary models of the colonizer; postcolonial parodies of metropolitan canonical texts are by now numerous enough to form their own anti-canon" (Margin/Alias, 18). Let us turn now to the specifics of myth criticism in Quebec and English-speaking Canada.

In the 1960s literary criticism in Quebec was very strongly influenced by France's nouvelle critique, due in large part to the fact that many of the first generation of lay university professors had done their graduate work in Paris. La mythocritique was only one of a series of neologisms that defined the "new" hermeneutical and structuralist tools for literary analysis. In the 1970s, studies in mythocritique/mythanalyse generally followed two streams: a broadly thematic, interpretive criticism, based in large part on the writings of Eliade and on the phenomenological approach of Gaston Bachelard (L'Eau et les rêves; La Psychanalyse du feu) and Georges Poulet (Etudes sur le temps humain; Les Métamorphoses du cercle), or a more scientific, structuralist approach based on the writings of Durand and Lévi-Strauss. Myth criticism, however, was not among the popular structuralist approaches in vogue at that time, for three reasons: the frequent conflation of myth and the sacred (à la Eliade) at a time when the Québécois intelligentsia was distancing itself from Catholicism and the Church; the wish to appear scientific and structured in one's study of literature, and thus to avoid hard-to-define, "folksy," quasi-religious terms such as myth, and third, the strong insistence on le texte as écriture, whereas myth was associated with – or, according to Barthes, defined as – une parole (Mythologies, 215).

In the early 1990s, however, one finds some generalized studies of myth in contemporary literature from Quebec, such as Victor-Laurent Tremblay's Au commencement était le mythe and Antoine Sirois's Mythe et symboles dans la littérature québécoise. Occasional monographs are devoted to individual authors' use of myth, such as Paul Socken's The Myth of the Lost Paradise in the Novels of Jacques Poulin, Maurice Emond's La Femme à la fenêtre: l'univers symbolique d'Anne Hébert, and Franza Marcato-Falzoni's work on Réjean Ducharme, Du Mythe au roman: une trilogie ducharmienne, originally published in Italian). And of course, there are several articles in prestigious journals dealing with various myths – usually classical or religious – in Québécois fiction. All these studies, however, offer traditional approaches to myth. Sirois, for instance, proposes to study the influence of classical myths and biblical stories on the major writers of Quebec (11). Tremblay's work applies contemporary theories of myth and culture (Durand, René Girard, and Mikhail Bakhtin) in interesting ways to a traditional Québécois corpus (1896–1933), but he too seeks to illustrate the universality of myth in his development of a theory of *mythanalyse globale* (53). Socken's work on myth here and elsewhere is closely tied to Biblical hermeneutics; Emond follows the methods of Bachelard and Durand; and Marcato-Falzoni's study echoes Gusdorf's theory of ages of human thought, in that the order in which Ducharme's novels were written supposedly reflects an evolution from myth through religion to history. In fact, during the contemporary period (from 1960 to the 1990s), few *critics* from Quebec or from English-speaking Canada have analyzed the impending change in the treatment of myth in contemporary fictions, although creative *writers* were beginning to foreground discussions of the very concept of myth.[10]

NORTHROP FRYE, LITERATURE, AND MYTH

During the same contemporary period, few critical, in-depth studies of myth in contemporary literature in English-speaking Canada were published. Some works of criticism, such as George Woodcock's *Odysseus Ever Returning*, simply used the well-known elements of classical myth to structure their own evaluative studies of literature published during the mid-twentieth century, without specifically referring to the uses of myth in the texts. Revealingly, there is no entry under "Myth" in William Toye's *Oxford Companion to Canadian Literature*, although there are sections entitled "Folklore" and "Indian Legends and Tales." Donna Bennett's sweeping overview, "Criticism in English," in that volume underlines the importance of a group of scholars whose "criticism blends Frye's mythic or archetypal analysis with his concept of a 'thematic' criticism" (160). These "major 'thematicists,'" according to Bennett, were "more interested in developing a thesis about national identity than in participating in literary analysis" (160): D.G. Jones (*Butterfly on Rock*), Margaret Atwood (*Survival*), and John Moss (*Patterns of Isolation*). Northrop Frye's influence is noticeable here. There is almost universal agreement among critics of various backgrounds and persuasions about Frye's significance in twentieth-century studies. Since his death in Toronto in 1991, several recent publications have confirmed his status in the fields of criticism, theory, and cultural studies.[11] Frye's numerous works on myth and literature, including *Fearful Symmetry*, *Anatomy of Criticism*, *The Great Code*, and *Words with Power*, along with several volumes of collected essays, were a major contributing factor in the importance given to myth in Western literary studies of the later half of the twentieth century.

In *Anatomy* Frye examines what are for him the principles of criticism through lengthy discussions of the modes of literature: the historical, the ethical, the archetypal or mythopoeic, and the rhetorical or classificatory. It is difficult to separate out Frye's theory of myth per se from his prolific writings on criticism as a creative and investigative act, on mythology, literature as a system, and, in his later years, on the relationship between mythology and ideology. Nonetheless, his basic (and frequently repeated) arguments about myth have not changed greatly since the publication of *Anatomy*. For Frye, myth always means mythos, story, plot, narrative. Myths are immutable, transhistorical, and frequently pastoral and nostalgic. As Frye writes in the last book published in his lifetime, "To me myth is not simply an effect of the historical process, but a social vision that looks toward a transcending of history, which explains how it is able to hold two periods of history together, the author's and ours, in direct communication. It is very difficult, perhaps impossible, to suggest a social vision of this kind, even within ideology, without invoking some kind of pastoral myth, past or future" (*Words with Power*, 60–1).

Recent retrospective appraisals of Frye's very impressive body of work laud his contributions "as a theorist of culture and renovator of humanistic studies in the second half of our century" (White, "Frye's Place," 28), while frequently acknowledging that his grand project, the systemization of literary studies, is not à la mode in today's cultural studies programs. Thus, Catherine Belsey (*Critical Practice*), Fredric Jameson (*The Political Unconscious*), and Terry Eagleton (*Literary Theory*) have all respectfully taken Frye to task for his privileging of mythology over ideology and history – for what they perceive as his deep belief in the autonomy of literature and culture and therefore his supposed lack of sociopolitical engagement. Eagleton writes, "In one sense, [Frye's approach] is scornfully 'anti-humanist,' decentring the individual human subject and centring all on the collective literary system itself; in another sense it is the work of a committed Christian humanist" – one whose writings are marked by a distaste for the actual social world and for history (*Literary Theory*, 93).

While Frye's reputation as a critic of importance is evident, there is much less general agreement about the worth of his contributions to the field of specifically Canadian/Québécois criticism. On the one hand, Frye's inordinate influence on an entire generation of writers from English-speaking Canada is widely acknowledged. Woodcock, for instance, notes in 1964 that Frye's important "myth-based criticism, carried on for many years in periodicals like the *University of Toronto Quarterly* and *Canadian Forum*, [had] not merely set its mark deeply on Canadian critical writing in its early stages; it was also largely responsible for the appearance of a whole school of mythopoeic poets, led by James Reaney, Jay Macpherson, and Eli Mandel" (*Odysseus*, 2). Although Reaney and, especially, Mandel later distanced themselves from the Frygian school of myth criticism, there is no doubt that Frye influenced many writers from English-speaking Canada, as is obvious, for instance, in the very structure of Margaret Atwood's 1970 novel *Surfacing*. From a later perspective Robert Lecker writes in 1991 that "Frye himself participates in topocentrism and nineteenth-century cultural theories ... Hence Frye's criticism is both a symptom of the forces producing the dominance of romance and mythopoeia in Canadian fiction, and a contributing causal factor" (*Canadian Canons*, 201).

On the other hand, as Barbara Godard notes, "Frye himself changed hats when he came to talk about Canadian literature, leaving behind his structuralist typologies to wade into the waters of cultural history" (*"Configuration,"* 110). Blodgett, discussing Frye's conclusion to the first edition of Klinck's *Literary History of Canada* (1965), proposes that Frye felt constrained "to abandon the leading principle of the *Anatomy* and assert that Canadian literature 'is more significantly studied as a part of Canadian life than as part of the autonomous world of literature'" (Frye, "Conclusion," 1965, 822; Blodgett, "European Theory," 6). Blodgett goes on to propose that the point of departure for all Canadian critics "within the Frygian dispensation" is the colonial mentality (7), a point to which I shall return. Frye's evaluative approach to Canadian literature, particularly in that first conclusion, has been strongly challenged in recent years. Thus, Heather Murray argues that one must conclude that English Canadian literature "does not measure up to Frye's notion of literature" and that in Frye's view, Canadian literature is "unorthodox, slightly failed or fallen short" ("Reading for Contradiction," 73). Rosemary Sullivan proposes that, in effect, Frye defines the Canadian mentality as one of "defeat, denial, withdrawal," with Canadian writers "locked into a demythologized environment" ("Northrop Frye," 10). Although Frye's influence is frequently perceived as being of the

old school in today's postmodern critical circles, there is no doubt
that his double negation of the importance of Canadian writing –
admittedly in 1965 – had consequences for literature and Canadian
criticism in the past, as his opinions were transmitted widely to
Canadians through his teachings, writings, and disciples.

Frye first excludes Canadian literature from that "autonomous
world of literature" he constructs in the *Anatomy of Criticism*, relegat-
ing it to "part of Canadian life" ("Conclusion," 1965, 822). He then
insists on the absence of a specifically Canadian mythology – and the
related lack of a national identity – quoting a passage with decidedly
colonial overtones: "The art of a Canadian remains ... the art of the
country of his forebears and the old world heritage of myth and
legend remains his heritage ... though the desk on which he writes
be Canadian" (Coulter, *Deidre of the Sorrows*, vii; Frye, "Conclusion,"
1965, 840). Frye proposes that "the imaginative writer ... [find his
identity by] withdrawing from what Douglas LePan calls a country
without a mythology into the country of mythology" (839–40) – that
is, the world of literature itself. But he has already excluded Canadian literature from this world: from his perspective, Canada is a
country that, as far as literature is concerned, had not, in 1965, quite
"done it" (821).

The tensions between Frye's grand systemic structures of literary
myth and his positions regarding Canadian literature have been
qualified as postmodern in Hutcheon's discussion of his two conclusions of 1965 and 1976. She notes the seemingly contradictory pull
between "the modernist frame of reference of Frye's detached and
autonomous mythology ... [which can be seen as] a triumph of the
totalizing, organizing imagination" ("Frye Recoded," 108) and
"Frye's contradictory remarks about evaluating the quality of Canadian writing" (109). Hutcheon proposes that if one can get out of the
modern paradigm and read for discontinuity, one can appreciate the
"pesky postmodern eruptions that break through the modernist
order of [Frye's] thought" (111), especially -and significantly – in his
writings on Canadian literature. Although she does not go so far as
to argue that Frye was a "closet postmodernist" (116), Hutcheon's
interesting reading offers a way to accommodate what is often qualified as Frye's puzzling stance toward Canadian literature. It remains
probable, however, that the inherent tensions in Frye's elusive and
problematic discussions of myth and Canadian literature have contributed to the relative lack of in-depth studies of myth in contemporary literature from English- speaking Canada. To my knowledge,
there are no such surveys of myth that are comparable to recent
publications of Sirois and Tremblay.

NEW APPROACHES TO MYTH

Nonetheless, a notable call for innovations in critical methodology to match recent innovations in literature from English-speaking Canada was put forth as early as 1966 by Eli Mandel in *Criticism: The Silent-Speaking Words*. Mandel called for a type of criticism that could be loosely associated with phenomenology, a criticism that would enable the critic to participate in the work, instead of producing an evaluatory or explanatory treatise. In a sense, Angela Bowering's innovative work on Sheila Watson's *The Double Hook: Figures Cut in Sacred Ground* provides a rare example of this kind of participatory myth criticism. As Shirley Neuman notes, in *Figures Cut in Sacred Ground* Bowering follows the example of the narrator of *The Double Hook*, "speaking from *within* the text as the narrator speaks from *within* the ground of mythic knowledge and from *within* the community" (Newman, introduction to *Figures*, viii). This reading is in sharp contrast to the essays in George Bowering's *Sheila Watson and the Double Hook*, most of which follow the lead of the Frygian mythopoeic school. A second example of new approaches to that complex field of myth, identity, and literature is found in Dennis Lee's *Savage Fields*. This study of Michael Ondaatje's *The Collected Works of Billy the Kid* and Leonard Cohen's *Beautiful Losers* offers a complex and sometimes obscure reflection on the traditional liberal dualism of nature and civilization and proposes different appreciations of the world we live in. According to Lee, "earth" (energy) and "world" (consciousness), if taken as simultaneous entities, transcend the man-against-nature conflict of liberalism's worldview and exist in a dynamic tension that offers new and exciting ways of seeing the universe.

It is perhaps significant that writers such as Mandel and Lee, who straddle the fields of creative writing and literary commentary/theory, have discussed new ways of seeing the universe and the potential role of myth in that seeing. Indeed, in the contemporary period, several creative *writers* have foregrounded their fascination with the changing concept of myth, even if the subject has been largely neglected by both structuralist and poststructuralist critics. Thus, in 1973 the prolific Québécois writer Victor-Lévy Beaulieu, discussing the *bouillonnement mythologique* in the work of Gabriel García Márquez and Jose Donoso, proposed that Quebecers would get more out of this "grand courant de la littérature sud-américaine ... que des littératures européenes et américaines ensemble" ("La Grande Leçon," 15). While the critic Micheline Cambron argues in *Une Société, un récit* that the nationalist concerns of most Québécois literature of the early period of *la modernité* were relatively homogenous, Jacques Godbout, the writer and cultural commentator, signalled the need – as early as the 1960s – to rework Quebec's historical myths of identity. For instance, he has always been particularly fascinated by the myth-ification process associated with Louis-Joseph Papineau, the always ambiguous hero of the rebellions of 1837–38, and by the postmodern tensions between the Papineau myth and the assumed collectivity that created the myth. Thus, he writes: "J'ai toujours eu, pour les mythes, une admiration inquiète ... nous avons donc mythifié Papi-neau, dont tout le monde voulait la tête. Curieux mythe d'ailleurs, pour un peuple que le clergé désirait soumis, pacifique, et catholique: Papineau était en Amérique le romantique belliqueux anticlérical, rêvant d'une république indépendante et laïque (le mot eût-il existé). Papineau parlait bien, pensait juste. Le peuple se l'appropria ... On se mit à vouloir avoir *la tête à Papineau*" ("Novembre 1964," 70; God-bout's emphasis). In chapter 2, we shall see that the necessary ambi-guity of the Papineau myth problematizes the traditional historical, religious, and mythological worldview in Quebec and that it cele-brates the contemporary complexities and ambiguities of the *identi-taire* issue developed by Sherry Simon and others in *Fictions de l'identitaire au Québec*. Godbout's fascination with myth is marked by a paradoxical tension between playfulness and didacticism. It is also tied to the concepts of reinventing reality and with finding a lan-guage in which to carry out this constant reinvention.

Albertan writer Robert Kroetsch is equally fascinated with myth and its potential to reconfigure the world. Kroetsch's novels are fre-quently located in that "space between" so prized by postcolonial-ists, and his work on voice, myth, silence, language, place, and displacement indicate some similarities between his texts and those that demonstrate the use of New World Myth. Rosemary Sullivan notes a progression in Kroetsch's novels, which, while making use of various explorations of myth, move from binary structures to a place beyond – or between? – them. In this way the marked mythic pres-ence and dichotomous structure in *The Words of My Roaring* are fol-lowed by a "self-conscious self-parody in his use of myth" in *The Studhorse Man*, even if this novel retains its binary structure ("The Fascinating Place Between," 172). Then in *Badlands* Kroetsch "must not only deconstruct myth; he must go all the way and deconstruct the very binary structures that inform his thinking, in order to seek genuine meditation" (174). Sullivan's use of the imperative "must" here implies a puzzling elusiveness in Kroetsch's work on myth: he must, but does he? Indeed, although Kroetsch's fiction certainly went a long way toward introducing New World techniques such as magic realism into contemporary English Canadian writing, as Robert Wilson argues in "The Boundary of the Magic and the Real," most of his work on myth differs from New World Myth in two ways. First, he maintains a strong interest in reworking classical myths, whereas New World Myth texts, as I argue below, generally turn away from classical myth. Second, Kroetsch's explorations of myth are at once multifarious and illusive; I sense a *questioning* of the concept of myth (through his reflections on play, humour, parody, irony, and the uses of different mythological systems) more than an *exploration* of New World Myth, the perimeters of which are set out below.

With regard to myth, Kroetsch's body of work, as he himself has said numerous times, focuses on "de-mythologizing," on "de-constructing the myth," and has to do with "un-inventing the world." One sees this in the section on myth in *Labyrinths of Voice*, where the exchange of ideas between Kroetsch, Shirley Neuman, and Robert Wilson strongly illustrates the questioning and multifaceted nature of his reflections on myth. Thus, while Kroetsch proclaims his interest in the "generative possibilities of myth" (Kroetsch, "Myth," 103), he also sees myth as "very frightening because it is entrapping … [and] very powerful"; "one way out," he says, "is to retell it" (96). This perception of myth as a previously existing entity that might be controlled or manipulated through narrative recalls to mind a mod-ernist approach, and I would argue that Kroetsch's discussions of myth in both his fictional and his nonfictional writings are valuable not so much for the answers they supply as for the questions they ask. These questions, however, point to the fact that contemporary writers are aware of myth as a potential component of those ele-ments used to reimagine the world in a post-European and post-modern manner.

Margaret Laurence is another writer from English-speaking Canada who has reflected on myth, fiction, and the role and respon-sibilities of the creative writer. For instance, her discussion of the work of "two Third World novelists," Chinua Achebe and herself, addresses the tensions between fiction and history, creativity and didacticism, and the authors' "sense of particular space and particu-lar people" (Laurence, "Ivory Tower or Grassroots?" 17, 22). "Fic-tion," says Laurence, "for me at least … becomes a matter of the individual characters moving within a history which includes past, present, and future, and the emergence through these characters of beliefs which cannot be didactic but which in the most profound way are both religious and political" (17). Of course, several studies adopt traditional techniques of myth criticism to address Laurence's novels.[12]

Laurence herself, however, always tied her explorations of myth to history and to a sense of what she has called "the local." In a discussion with Irving Layton in 1970, she says: "People like my grandfather, or like the character of Harvey Lepage in *Stud-Horse Man* ... these people are our myths. This is our history. And perhaps not consciously, but after awhile consciously, this is what we are trying to set down" (Thomas, "A Conversation," 67).

It is in *The Diviners*, which was published in the year before the decade considered in this study, that one discovers several characteristics that recall aspects of New World Myth. Through her portrayal of the main character of the work, Morag Gunn, a middle-aged creative writer, Laurence instils that familiar tension between written, oral, "universal," and "local," spheres of authority, and between fiction, history, myth, and "Truth." Clara Thomas, among others, has written at length about Laurence's work on myth; she notes "three mythic sets woven into *The Diviners*: Christie's tales, which give Morag her distant past ... Jules (Skinner) Tonnerre's tales ... and the adult Morag's half-playful, half-serious myth-making of Catharine Parr Traill" ("Chariot of Ossian," 57). Thomas continues: "The passing on of the authentic heritage of their people is a central preoccupation of writers of today, particularly of writers of the post-colonial nations. Laurence of Canada, Walcott of the West Indies, Soyinka and Achebe of Nigeria – these are preeminent among writers who accept a strong social and political, as well as artistic, responsibility in writing out of their own culture and primarily for their own people" (62). While Thomas here appears to posit "culture" and "people" as nonproblematic and easily identifiable entities, Laurence, in correspondence with Thomas, signals her awareness of their complexities: "What I think I share, most of all, with [W.L.] Morton is the sense of my *place*, the prairies, and of my *people* (meaning all prairie peoples) within the context of their many and varied histories, and the desire to make all these things come alive in the reader's mind" (Thomas, "Chariot," 63). Like other New World Myth writers, Laurence foregrounds her narrator's self-conscious problematization of the past, as well as that narrator's challenge to the related notion of "Truth." Thus, when Morag provides a story about the life of her deceased parents, whom she looks at in a snapshot, she says: "All this is crazy, of course, and quite untrue. Or maybe true and maybe not. I am remembering myself composing this interpretation, in Christie and Prin's house" (*The Diviners*, 7). Morag's fascination with language, story, the power of words, and those myths that are local, known, flexible, and important to the community, points to similarities between the novels analyzed in this study and Laurence's work on myth. If there is a difference between *The Diviners* and New World Myth texts – and I am not sure that difference exists – it would be Laurence's apparent underlying belief in *a truth* of the past. As I note elsewhere in this study, New World Myth texts live with the constantly shifting grounds of certitude in the present age.

The Diviners' Morag, however, as Sherill Grace remarks, "is a successful quester in an age that disbelieves in quests, an inheritor, an ancestor, a diviner" ("Portrait of the Artist," 70). Grace applies Ronald Sutherland's tripartite thematic paradigm of the Canadian novel, as outlined in *Second Image*, to the three main stages in Morag's life. The third of these stages, or themes, Sutherland calls "the search for vital truth," and Grace suggests that, as is the case with Sutherland's typical hero, the recently separated Morag undertakes a "renewed search for meaning" (69). Grace posits that parts of the novel "portray a Morag who has completed her search for meaning. Not only does she know who she is, she knows where she is. She has arrived home and accepted the fact that the past lives within her … [Morag Gunn] comes to acknowledge the sacredness of her past and her deep loyalty to community and tradition. As long as she cuts herself off from her roots she is incomplete; her final victory is a function of her ability to embrace the totality of her experience" (70). This definitive knowledge with regard to identity and these concepts of completeness and totality are uncharacteristic of New World Myth, which always treats notions such as "the truth of the past" and "the basis of one's identity" with wariness if not with outright scepticism. I wonder, however, if Laurence's appreciation of Morag would be as definitive as the one proposed by Grace. It was Laurence, after all, who said while writing *The Diviners*: "to try and get down some of the paradoxes of any human individual with everything that has gone to influence their life – their parents, the whole bit about history, religion, the myth of the ancestors, the social environment, their relationships with other people and so on – even to *attempt* it means attempting the impossible" (Donald Cameron, *Conversations with Canadian Novelists*, 114). I strongly suspect that Laurence would at least partially share Leonard Cohen's famous formulation of a saint, the one who survives in this our postmodern world: "What is a saint? … A saint does not dissolve the chaos … It is a kind of balance that is his glory. He rides the drifts like an escaped ski … Something in him so loves the world that he gives himself to the laws of gravity and chance" (*Beautiful Losers*, 101). New World Myth writers, like Cohen's saint riding on the escaped ski, balance precariously on shifting ground as they question the past in the present and carry out their original investigations of myth, place, and identity.

POSTCOLONIALISM AND MYTH
IN ENGLISH-SPEAKING CANADA
AND QUEBEC

The presence of myth in literature has frequently been tied to the rise of nationalist sentiment. Volker Strunk points out that in the eighteenth and nineteenth centuries, Old World countries such as Germany established nationalist myths in their literatures in order to legitimize their existence, Much later, in the postwar mid-twentieth century, what used to be called "developing" – that is to say, non-European – nations sometimes adopted the same attitude, seeing a nationalist literature as an "entry ticket to the family of culturally 'established' nations" (Strunk, "Canadian Literary Criticism," 68). The hunt for myths – uniquely Canadian myths – was on, as is evidenced in Margaret Atwood's comment in 1978: "the North is to Canada as the Outback is to Australia ... It's the place where you go to find something out. It's the place of the unconscious. It's the place of the journey or the quest" (Davidson, "Interview," 204). In Quebec, the symbiotic relationships between literary myth, nationalist literature, and political ideologies have had a long history, as Sutherland points out in his introduction to *The New Hero* (1977). Writers such as Hubert Aquin and Jacques Godbout show a perhaps more sophisticated awareness of the drive behind the search for myths, but they too signal, if somewhat ironically, a place for nationalist myths that would counteract the "colonial" attitude in Québécois writing (Aquin, "L'art de la défaite,") and Québécois society (Godbout, "Novembre 1964").

Inherent in this attitude toward nationalist myth is the basic idea of progress: literatures undergo an organic process of growth toward autonomy, and the presence of nationalist myths in these literatures is taken as a marker of this growth. Implicitly, this development is seen as good. This model of literature derives from the general organic model of the Romantic period, summed up by M.H. Abrams in *The Mirror and the Lamp*, which served the purposes of Old World nationalism. Most thematic studies of the Canadian literatures operate from this basic assumption, from Northrop Frye's first "Conclusion" (1965) to Philip Stratford's more recent comparative work, *All the Polarities*. This concept of progress toward maturity is European-based, as Strunk, among many others, has pointed out ("Canadian Literary Criticism," 68), and therefore subject to reexamination in postcolonial literatures, which might well operate from somewhat different assumptions. Unfortunately, the basic liberal humanist idea of a slow evolution toward maturity in the Canadian literatures

remains largely unquestioned, even in many contemporary appraisals of them. For instance, the European Canadianist, Walter Pache,
argues that in postmodern English Canadian fiction the "ironic
destruction of realistic narrative is more than just an aesthetic exer-
cise: it is an essential step towards an independent national literature" ("Fiction Makes Us Real," 71). Many contemporary *novels* from
English Canada and Quebec, however, combine a challenge to this
notion of progress toward autonomy in literature with a self-
conscious and frequently ironic interest in the seemingly perennial
question of national identity.

While the Australian Helen Tiffin argues that postmodernism and
poststructuralism belong to the Euro-American sphere of critical
activity and are thus the very antithesis of postcolonial theories
(Tiffin, "Post-Colonialism," 170), other critics, such as Eva-Marie
Kröller, place English Canadian and Québécois texts at the conjuncture of postmodernism and postcolonialism ("Postmodernism," 53).
Stephen Slemon argues that magic realism can be seen as a marker
of postcolonial discourse in English Canadian texts ("Magic Realism," 10), while Jacques Godbout, for his part, states that Québécois
literature *is* "décolonisée": *that* battle, he writes, was fought in the
1960s ("Le Chevalier errant," 102). Nonetheless, in literary critical
circles a debate is currently raging about whether English Canadian
and Québécois literatures can be defined as postcolonial or postmodern or both.[13] As I shall illustrate in the discussions that follow, postmodernist challenges to Christian liberal humanism, including the
Whig interpretation of history, which holds that humankind is gradually progressing toward an ideal, can coexist with postcolonial
questionings of the hegemony of eurocentric world views. However,
the tensions involved in applying the terms "postmodern" and
"postcolonial" to English Canadian and Québécois literatures are
echoed in the novels themselves. There, a self-conscious postcolonial
urge *to* myth coexists with a postmodern play *with* myth, and that
"congenital art form" in Canada, the search for national identity
(New, *Among Worlds*, 101), forms an ironic backdrop to it all. On the
one hand, these novels flaunt their interest in the notion of nation
building, in that they self-consciously underline their attempts to
revise the traditional, historical definitions of their "nations." On the
other hand, these novels undermine the assumptions contained in
the liberal humanist ideal of an established national literature with
equally established literary and historical myths.

Although English-speaking Canada is frequently included in discussions of postcolonial writing, critics have noted that its postcolonial situation is not as clear-cut as that of many other former

colonies. In her contribution to the discussion of postmodernism and postcolonialism in the journal *Ariel*, Hutcheon makes a lengthy but "crucial" digression to address the basic question, Can Canada be considered a postcolonial country? ("Circling," 154–9). The punctuation mark in Albert Memmi's "Les Canadiens français sont-ils des colonisés?" signals the equally questionable situation of Quebec (*Portrait du colonisé*, 135). Although both Hutcheon and Memmi conclude that English and French Canadians have struggled with issues similar to those faced by colonized peoples everywhere, they nevertheless point to the complex situation that exists in both English Canada and Quebec today. For instance, as I noted in the foreword to this study, the historical colonization of the Amerindian and Inuit peoples by the British and French, along with the problematic relationship between the Canadian and Québécois governments and the First Nations peoples today, constitutes one component of this complex situation.

The second component of the complex postcolonial situation is that Canada does not have one cultural face to present to the world – or to itself. Whether one subscribes to the "two founding nations" theory or to the more contemporary appraisals of both English Canada and Quebec as pluriethnic mosaics, it remains that the very word "Canada" conjures up vastly different images in different contexts. In international critical practice today, Canadian literary studies are divided along linguistic lines. Studies of postcolonial literatures written in English, such as *The Empire Writes Back*, by Ashcroft, Griffiths, and Tiffin, make a token nod in the direction of Quebec, but, given their different focus, do not explore Québécois literature itself. Comparative studies of postcolonial literatures written in French, from Quebec and other former colonies, such as Maximilien Laroche's discussion of Québécois and Haitian literature in *Le Miracle et la métamorphose*, tend to ignore the literature of English Canada. Furthermore, in Quebec the postcolonial situation is debatable on two fronts: Quebec has not as yet achieved the political independence that motivated the use of the *colonisé* argument in much of its literature of the postwar years, and its first-world status as a mainly white, industrialized "nation" is not comparable to the third-world situation of most of France's former colonies. Although E.D. Blodgett argues forcibly that all Canadian literature is comparative literature ("Canadian Literature," 904), the fertile field of cultural complexity and the characteristically Canadian "perception of a mosaic has not generated corresponding theories of literary hybridity to replace the nationalist approach," much to the surprise of Ashcroft, Griffiths, and Tiffin (*The Empire Writes Back*, 36). Moreover, rapid changes in terminology in the 1990s affect discussions of post-colonialism in Canada. As Hutcheon has suggested, "postcolonial" as a generic label "may be misleading with respect to both focus and agenda. The universality implied in any such naming risks homogenizing as well as totalizing and then may mask the complexity of the colonial and postcolonial experiences of diverse individuals and societies in various times and places" ("Colonialism," 10). The multifarious uses and implications of the term "postcolonial" are raised by Stephen Slemon, who first encountered the term "as the name for a category of 'literary' activity which sprang from a new and welcome political energy going on within what used to be called 'Commonwealth' literary studies" ("The Scramble for Post-colonialism," 45). Although this statement implies that Commonwealth studies are a thing of the past, other postcolonialists – such as Vijay Mishra and Bob Hodge in their brilliant critique of *The Empire Writes Back*) argue that it is necessary to speak in terms of "many postcolonialisms," because an "undifferentiated concept of postcolonialism overlooks ... the very radical differences ... and the unbridgeable chasms that existed between White and non-White colonies" (Mishra and Hodge, "Post(-)colonialism?" 284–5).

In English-speaking Canada and Quebec, the reasons for the continued and apparently problematic presence of a nationalist thematic in their literatures lie in their particular postcolonial situations. In her study of postcolonial rewritings of Shakespeare's *Tempest*, Diana Brydon proposes that English Canadians tend to see themselves in Miranda, the "dutiful daughter of the empire" ("Re-writing *The Tempest*," 77). Prospero's values, she notes, "are internalized by Miranda but redefined through her interaction with Caliban" (86). English Canadian rewritings of *The Tempest* are clearly different from those of other former colonies. They show how "Canadians have internalized the process of their colonization: they are themselves Prospero and what he has colonized is a vital part of themselves." Brydon suggests that for this reason English Canadian texts find it harder to reject outright the imperial/colonial legacy, and she insists on the necessity to investigate "the special nature of the Canadian imagination" (87). Of course, two of the three "English Canadian" authors discussed in this study have a double linguistic and cultural heritage: Joy Kogawa foregrounds her Japanese antecedents, while Rudy Wiebe's understanding of marginalization is undoubtedly influenced by his own German Mennonite background. Their novels, nonetheless, along with George Bowering's work, strongly thematize the reshaping of that elusive Canadian imagination through their retellings of Canadian history.

Max Dorsinville's concern also lies with a postcolonial attitude to the political imagination, but in Quebec. He notes that it was more difficult for French Canadians than for postcolonial nations of the Black diaspora to decolonize their imaginations, given their closer cultural and racial ties to their imperial centre, France. For a long time, the conservative urge to nationalism in French Canada relied on an imaginative association with France, the now infamous *mère-patrie*. Only when the French Canadian writer "de-emphasizes his French origins [can he discover] … a novel sense of identity" (*Caliban*, 206) and become a Québécois. Gilles Thérien underlines the need for a postcolonial attitude as he argues for a radical realignment of Quebec's literary production: "[il faudrait] parler selon l'axe nord-sud, prendre conscience de la totalité de l'Amérique, Nouveau Monde d'un pôle à l'autre, terre de conquête et de métissage où l'Europe est venue organiser horizontalement un territoire vertical ("La Littérature québécoise," 14). This north-south axis in literature is beginning to be explored in works such as Earl Fitz's *Rediscovering the New World* and David Jordan's *New World Regionalism*. Cultural hybridity is equally discernible in the narrators of the three Québécois texts examined here, and yet they too remain concerned with imaginative retellings – and deconstructions – of Québécois history.

Teleological terms such as "nation" are frequently suspect in postcolonial practices. Since the years 1975–85, of course, the very concept of nationalism has undergone a radical rethinking, as Michael Ignatieff illustrates in *Blood and Belonging: Journeys into the New Nationalism*. Much earlier, Albert Memmi asked, "comment peut-on encore parler sans rire de nations?" (*Portrait du colonisé*, 142). The authors of *The Empire Writes Back* also adopt a critical tone, deploring the nationalist focus of much contemporary Canadian literature (Ashcroft, Griffiths, and Tiffin, 36). In fact, most international, postcolonial English-language studies point to the continuing preoccupation with socio-political identity in English Canadian literature. Beryl Langer, for example, argues that "Whereas the question 'What is an Australian?' is readily answered, however inaccurately … the 'typical Canadian' is less easily defined. Canadians are 'not American' and they're 'not British,' but the question of what they are … is [uncertain]." She goes on to argue, however, that this political ambivalence is beneficial, at least to women's writing, since the confusion about national identity in Canada leaves open possibilities for women's entry into culture that represent "a considerable advance on the Australian situation" ("Women and Literary Production," 147). Preoccupation with the flexible-identity issue opens up similar possibilities for post-European myth in contemporary English Canadian literature.

The ambivalence toward political identity in many contemporary English Canadian fictions has its origins in the ambiguous relationship that a settler colony has with the imperial centre: the battle lines are not clear-cut. A settler colony in D.E.S. Maxwell's comparative model in "Landscape and Theme" is a country, such as Australia or English Canada, where the indigenous population was overwhelmed by European colonists. Writers from settler colonies eventually came "to question the appropriateness of imported language to place" (Ashcroft, Griffiths, and Tiffin, *The Empire Writes Back*, 25). An invaded colony, such as India or Nigeria, is one where indigenous peoples were not completely overwhelmed but whose "ancient and sophisticated responses [to their environment were] marginalized by the worldview which was implicated in the acquisition of English." As with the literature of many settler colonies, it is difficult to eradicate internalized historico-political myths in English Canadian literature. Indeed, given the multitiered postcolonial situations in what is now called Canada, the notion of the imperial centre is itself a constantly shifting concept. This accounts for the underlying interest in the national identity question, even in postcolonial and postmodern texts, and points to the necessity of retaining this notion in any investigation of the contemporary literary production of English Canada. Rewriting political history is an essential component of English Canadian postmodern literature, even if, internationally, postmodernism is frequently seen as politically ambivalent (Hutcheon, "Circling," 150). The postcolonial thrust in this postmodern literature involves a rewriting of "the myths that write us"; perhaps more than other former colonies, Canadians feel the need to "decolonize the mind" (Brydon, "The Myths that Write Us," 1). English Canadian texts engage various colonial/imperial heritages in their rewriting of history and in their efforts to reshape the imagination through their work on myth. In the discussions that follow, then, the specific focus will be on the sociopolitical dimension of the novels, their self-conscious explorations and exploitations of the notion of national identity, the *active*, creative invention of the past(s), as opposed to the reactive, *passive* acceptance of the Old World systems, and lastly and most importantly, the role of myth in these fictions.

The present situation of Quebec is not one of political autonomy. Various sociologists, politicians, historians, poets, and novelists have argued that Quebec was – and remains – a political, cultural, and linguistic colony. For francophone Québécois, the political colonizers are generally seen as the British (the Conquest of 1760; the Rebellions of 1837–38) and then the English Canadians (the conscription crisis of World War II). France has come to be seen as a patronizing *mère-patrie*, especially in the cultural domain, and the more recent American influence on Québécois society is also signalled in many contemporary Québécois texts. Hubert Aquin's *Prochain Episode* is perhaps the most characteristic of the literary works published before 1975 that proposed that Quebec was *colonisé*. But major changes have taken place in the worldview of the Québécois collectivity since 1975. These ongoing changes are indicative, I would suggest, of a postcolonial reevaluation of the Québécois situation in the world. Quebec certainly sees itself as a distinct society that has been concerned with the need to establish its cultural and economic independence from dominating powers. Sociopolitical innovations during the second half of the twentieth century have created an infrastructure in Quebec that would enable it to govern itself. Thus, Quebec has its own civil service, its own police force, its own "diplomatic" offices, and, perhaps regrettably for its citizens, its own income tax. English Canada – often cryptically referred to as "Ottawa" or *le fédéral* – is perceived as "other," and is frequently peripheral to the Québécois worldview. One simple illustration of the strong sense of autonomy I am trying to describe is found in daily news broadcasts, which use *au niveau national* to mean "within the boundaries of Quebec." This sense of nation, I would suggest, was not dealt a mortal blow by the "No" votes in the referendums on sovereignty-association in 1980 and 1995, for several reasons, among them the probability, as I argue here, that the sense of nation has become – and continues to be – an integral part of *l'imaginaire québécois*.

Nevertheless, contemporary Québécois postmodern texts also struggle with dominant historico-political myths. The ambiguity in English Canadian postmodernism toward the imperialist influence over the historico-political imagination is also found in much contemporary Québécois literature, even if this ambiguity is largely ignored in comparative Canadian or English-language postcolonial studies, where it is felt that the question of national identity in Quebec has long been resolved (Langer, "Women and Literary Production," 147). The social upheaval of the Quiet Revolution did bring about welcome social, cultural, and literary reforms. It also prepared the field, however, for what Dorsinville calls novels of ambiguity, which reflect "the consciousness of the complexity of life the French Canadian never had access to when either the cult of Messianism or *le pays* meant a belief in simple creeds and answers, a reduction of life to religious or secular dogma" (*Caliban*, 181).

Dorsinville's evaluation of contemporary Québécois novels is appropriate here: these works must come to terms with the "heterogeneity of life" and somehow address the postmodern fragmentation of all aspects of traditional society. Quebec's former hesitation to modernize, its traditional linkage of *la modernité* to *Mal* (as observable in a nonreligious, free-thinking France or a materialist and capitalist America) prompts Marcel Fournier to propose, tongue in cheek, that "pour la petite collectivité francophone d'Amérique, le handicap de son accès *tardif* à la modernité, qui apparaît déjà ancienne, pourrait très bien se révéler un avantage et lui permettre de devenir postmoderne avant toutes les autres" (*L'Entrée dans la modernité*, 7). This observation, of course, is echoed in Robert Kroetsch's cryptic pronouncement that "Canadian literature evolved directly from Victorian into Postmodern" ("A Canadian Issue," 1). The postcolonial urge to get out from under worn-out, protectionist historico-political myths is the motivating force behind the postmodern work on myth in all the novels discussed in this study.

Pierre Hébert proposes that the Québécois novel has evolved through three distinct colonial periods ("Un problème de sémiotique diachronique," 218). Basing his frame of argument on Georges Gusdorf's work on myth, *Mythe et métaphysique*, Hébert proposes a loose chronology of the Québécois novel: the mythic period (1837–1940), the rational period (1940–1960), and the historical period, which he subdivides into two stages: personal history (1960–75) and collective history (since 1975). Hébert posits an evolution in the narrative voice that corresponds to these three periods; he discerns a gradual progression from *nous* through *il* to *je*. Thus, in the mythic period of the *nous*, the francophone collectivity experiences a stage of withdrawal that began after the Conquest and that is especially evident in novels published after the Rebellions of 1837–38. In the rational period, the voice of narration evolves from *il* (or *elle*) to *je*, as the colonized individual begins to distance himself/herself from his/her colonial status. In the stage of personal history, "le *je* maintenant personnalisé tente de se donner une histoire" (226). Hébert posits, but does not develop, "l'hypothèse d'un deuxième stade de l'âge historique où le projet d'écriture se déplace de la personne à la société. Cette nouvelle (?) série romanesque nous servira des chroniques, des romans historiques ... où la collectivité essaie maintenant de se donner un portrait d'elle-même, un nouveau 'nous,' mais composé, cette fois, de 'je' conscients d'eux-mêmes. Après l'indépendance de la personne peut se faire l'indépendance de la communauté" (236). This last stage is obviously of relevance here. The historiographic Québécois novels examined in this study – all published during Hébert's time frame for collective history – simultaneously reflect and help constitute a post-European worldview. A postmodern sense of fragmentation is discernible in the reworkings of myth and history in these three texts. Hébert, writing in 1982, even seems to have anticipated the 1990s preoccupation with *l'écriture migrante*, which discusses works where, indeed, the *nous* is composed of multiple *je*s conscious of themselves.[14]

Two influential studies in postcolonialism have suggested that Dorsinville's expression "post-European" may prove to be more useful than postcolonial, since its political and theoretical implications have much to offer.[15] This suggestion is especially applicable with regard to Quebec's present political situation, and I have chosen to employ the term in much of my discussion. My use of the term "postcolonial" refers implicitly to the substantial and ever-increasing body of research and scholarship in this field, while my use of "post-European" generally implies a sense of opposition – of being "anti" European models and myths. In the six novels discussed here, play with myth constitutes a self-conscious effort to decolonize the mind and to undercut the influence of inherited, European-inspired myths: post-European New World Myths are the result of these efforts.

HISTORIOGRAPHIC FICTION AND NEW WORLD MYTH

In this study, the notion of worldview is seen primarily in the socio-historical context of the New World. As Ronald Hatch has noted, in Canada, as in other New World countries, "responses to history are often formulated at least in part on the experience implicit in being a new-world country ... [By] the 1960s, it was becoming apparent to historical novelists that different narrative techniques were required to reorient the individual to history. Much of the impetus for a new sense of narrative derives from non-European novelists, in particular the so-called 'magic realists,' such as Jorge Luis Borges, Gabriel García Márquez, and Carlos Fuentes" ("Narrative Development," 79–81). One narrative technique that provides a fresh perspective on history in many postmodern English Canadian and Québécois novels is their deliberately self-conscious play with fiction, history, and myth. The overtly political character of imaginative expression found in these novels is, of course, also discernible in many nation-building novels of the late nineteenth century in European nations. While the narratorial techniques analyzed here are not entirely new, in many ways the expectations and the audience *are*. The rewriting of European-inspired history is a central concern of many postcolonial literatures; the goal is to revise, reappropriate, or reinterpret history in order to allow "those re-orderings of consciousness that 'history' has rendered silent or invisible [to] be recognized as shaping forces in a culture's tradition" (Slemon, "Post-Colonial Allegory," 159). Although the six novels discussed here do not set out to impose a new, fixed order on history, they do challenge the old European-inspired order of history by paradoxically producing works that thematize the reclaiming of the past.

Linda Hutcheon applies the term "historiographic metafiction" to novels that self-consciously thematize the historiographical process: by this she means "those well-known and popular novels which are both intensely self-reflexive and yet paradoxically also lay claim to historical events and personages ... Historiographic metafiction incorporates ... three ... domains [fiction, history, and theory]: its theoretical self-awareness of history and fiction as human constructs (historio*graphic meta*fiction) is made the grounds for its rethinking and reworking of the forms and contents of the past ... [H]istorio-graphic metafiction ... always works *within* conventions in order to subvert them. It is not just metafictional, nor is it just another version of the historical novel or the nonfictional novel" (*Poetics of Postmodernism*, 5). The six novels discussed here are historiographic metafictions; they flaunt the tensions produced by their postmodern questionings of history and traditional myths and by their contradictory urge to "establish" *new* myths of the past. However, as both theorists and novelists have illustrated, all the "foundations" upon which an emerging literature could conceivably be built have been problematized by the ontological and epistemological questionings of the postmodern age. Hence I occasionally use ironic quotation marks around terms such as "centre," "establish," and "foundation."

"Myth," of course, is often closely linked to these concepts. Indeed, myth has traditionally been regarded as one of the important determining factors of any given people's worldview. Eric Gould's attitude constitutes a traditionally accepted given of myth criticism: "What we consider essential about myth seems to me to be no more or less than its exemplary function of intending-to- interpret, whether its object is social compromise, the supernatural, questions covering the self and its place in the world, or those issues we think of as ultimate, unanswerable, and metaphysical" (*Mythical Intentions*, 34). A similar traditional definition of myth is found in the work of Mircea Eliade: "Myth narrates a sacred history; it relates an event that took place in primordial Time, the fabled time of the 'beginnings'" (*Myth and Reality*, 5). The foremost function of myth, proposes Eliade, "is to reveal the exemplary models for all human rites and all significant human activities" (8). Thus, in his schema myth serves to establish, reinforce, and legitimize the validity of human beings' existence – to answer, as Gould notes, "questions concerning the self and its place in the world" (*Mythical Intentions*, 34). Mikhail Bakhtin, for his part, claims that *the* defining factor of mythological thought is the "absolute bonding of ideological meaning to language," suggesting a worldview where experiences are expressed and categorized in language in a way that greatly restricts any challenges or changes (*Dialogic Imagination*, 369). One function of traditional myth, then, is to attempt to make unified sense of the world.

In 1979, the Conseil des universités of the Government of Quebec invited Jean-François Lyotard to write a report on knowledge and learning in the contemporary era. In that report, translated as *The Postmodern Condition*, Lyotard states, "Simplifying to the extreme, I define *postmodern* as incredulity toward metanarratives" (xxiv). Lyotard gives as an example of a metanarrative the "Enlightenment narrative, in which the hero of knowledge works toward a good ethico-political end – universal peace" (xxiii–xxiv) and in which the "possible unanimity between rational minds" (xxiii) is accepted as what I would call a given. Myth, as characterized above by Gould, would obviously constitute one of these metanarratives. This does not mean, however, that all forms of myth are metanarratives. The present study constitutes an admittedly tentative effort to examine a form of myth found in post-European fictions. Its particular focus is on how the selected fictional works manipulate myth, a traditionally accepted metanarrative of the Old World, in their formulations of what I have chosen to call, following Margery Fee, "New World Myth" ("Making New World Myth," 8).

When a developing form defines itself against the form from which it derives, it can easily generate tension. This is, in fact, the predominant effect created by the narrators of the New World Myth novels analyzed here. Tension is first generated by the obvious conflict between historical reality and novelistic fiction, which draws readers into the debate: "did it really happen this way?" Second, the narrators' drive to affirm their version of the past ("it happened *this* way") conflicts with their and our awareness of a fundamental epistemological uncertainty about ever really knowing the past. Third, a refusal of certain givens – such as history as taught by the colonizing powers, or God, or religion – conflicts with the need to use the givens in order to illustrate and then problematize their power over the imagination. Fourth, the narrators' overt awareness of the narrative process ("listen, I am telling you this story") conflicts with their self-consciousness about its limitations and the readers' awareness of the techniques being used in the text. Fifth, the very term "New World Myth" could be said to generate tension. Articulating itself against that out of which it originates, New World Myth introduces not only a notion of flexibility but also a social, political, historical, and temporal component into the traditional concept of myth as something immutable, eternal, and, especially, transhistorical. The term itself is oxymoronic; it deliberately introduces a historical dimension into traditional notions of mythic universality. New World Myth in these novels is an imaginative attempt to explore world views more suited to the world in which we live. This New World Myth is anchored in historiography; it is highly political; it is concerned with both epistemological uncertainty and the need to know, and is intent on imaginatively reclaiming the past while flaunting its awareness of the processes involved in this act.

The six novels studied in detail here problematize issues tradition-ally accepted as givens – issues such as knowledge, history, certitude, truth, or God. Although it could be argued that debate on such issues has always constituted the subject matter of novels every-where, the positivistic, relatively unquestioning *acceptance* of their unproblematic nature in French and English Canadian writing is fre-quently remarked upon in literary overviews and studies in cultural history, and has only begun to be challenged in contemporary stud-ies such as Robert Lecker's *Canadian Canons* or Pierre Nepveu's *Ecologie du réel*. New World Myth novels are in the process of self-consciously (and, usually, ironically) "developing" their respective mythologies. They have progressed beyond the survival attitude that has been so heavily promoted and so closely studied by cultural historians. In contemporary Canadian literature, Frye's frequently cited provisional concept of the garrison mentality is replaced by a self-conscious embracing of ideas that are not marked predominantly by fear, defensiveness, and the need for survival. The six novels examined here are exploratory works: in turning to the study of the past, they seek to present themselves as inevitably partial testimoni-als to a vibrant historico-political identity that recognizes, affirms, and celebrates the very fragility of its nature. Myth, in these post-modern works, serves as a cognitive, imaginative tool in the novel-istic exploration of a new post-European worldview.

HISTORY AND NEW WORLD MYTH

In the mid-twentieth century, there seems to have been a general acceptance of what I have called "givens" in the work of English and

French Canadian writers – at least insofar as few radical challenges to these givens can be found in the texts of the time. In Europe, however, at least one of these issues was often problematized. History was perceived as a threatening element in many European novels of the early and mid-twentieth century. The frequently cited utterance of James Joyce's Stephen Dedalus about history being a nightmare from which he is trying to awaken (*Ulysses*, 34) is an apt illustration of the general feeling of malaise about history in the modernist period, especially after the devastation of the First World War. Hayden White has discussed the hostility of twentieth-century mainstream literature toward the historical consciousness. Stating that the "modern writer's hostility towards history is evidenced most clearly in the practice of using the historian to represent the extreme example of repressed sensibility in the novel and theatre," he illustrates this point with examples taken from the works of authors such as André Gide, Aldous Huxley, André Malraux, Thomas Mann, Wyndham Lewis, Jean-Paul Sartre, Albert Camus, Kingsley Amis and Edward Albee (*Tropics of Discourse*, 31). After exploring the notion that there is "a revolt against history in modern [fictional] writing" (39), White proposes that both science and art have "discovered the essentially *provisional* character of the meta-phorical constructions which they use to comprehend a dynamic universe" (50). Therefore, coherent notions of continuous history might well also be seen as provisional. White ends this chapter by suggesting the need for a "history that will educate us to discontinuity more than ever before; for discontinuity, disruption, and chaos is our lot" (50). Arthur Kroker and David Cook suggest in *The Postmodern Scene* that the present period constitutes a good example of this chaos: "Ours is a *fin-de-millenium* consciousness which, existing at the end of history in the twilight time of ultramodernism (of technology) and hyper-primitivism (of public moods), uncovers a great arc of disintegration and decay" (8). Although I do not share Kroker and Cook's pessimistic appraisal of the postmodern age, White's description of our lot as one of discontinuity and disruption nevertheless forms the background to this study. While turning toward historiography by reexamining and retelling events of the English Canadian and Québécois historico-political past(s), the novels examined here are in fact exploring worldviews that correspond to postmodern changes in the contemporary cultures of English Canada and Quebec.

Although the term "modernism" is sometimes associated with English Canadian poetry, as in Brian Trehearne's *Aestheticism and the Canadian Modernists*, its applicability to Canadian prose fiction is highly debatable. Dennis Duffy, for instance, argues that there is only one "full-blown instance of literary modernism" to be found in the Canadian corpus – O'Hagan's *Tay John* – and that this work is a presager of postmodernism ("Losing the Line," 175–6), while Stephen Scobie argues that Leonard Cohen's *Beautiful Losers* may be read as a highly organized book: "Cohen is trying to become a post-modernist, one might say, but he is going about it in a very modernist manner" ("End(s) of Modernism," 66). Fiction writers of what is loosely and infrequently termed the "modernist period" in English Canada are generally characterized as realist writers; they do not appear to have adopted the wary attitude to history displayed by their European counterparts. Referring to the work of Grove, Callaghan, MacLennan, Richler, and Laurence, Larry McDonald notes that "Canadian modernism was shaped in the '30s; the majority of our writers affiliated themselves with some form of socialism and the result was a modernism whose aesthetic placed the work of art squarely in the world of social and historical determinants" ("Post modernism," 30).

The same argument might be made for French Canadian writers of the same period – writers such as Roy, Lemelin, Yves Thériault, and the early Anne Hébert. However, there are formal and ideological differences between the retellings of history in the English and French Canadian fictions of the mid-twentieth century and the postmodern works analyzed in this study. Compared to the works of the authors cited by McDonald, the texts analyzed here make more blatant use, in their challenges to history and to historiography, of the techniques that have come to be considered the markers of postmodernism in fiction: autoreferentiality, intertextuality, playful self-reflexivity, parody, irony, and multiple, often contradictory, retellings of the same event. They also thematize many concerns of postcolonial literatures: the centre/margin debate; place and displacement; language, speech, and silence; written versus oral history; and multiple challenges to the hegemony of the Christian liberal-humanist worldview.

A further distinction is the attitude toward myth in these contemporary works. While the European modernists escaped from history into myth, the narrators of the works discussed here turn *toward* history in their exploration of a different sort of myth. Like Gérard Bessette's apprentice-historian Guito in *Les Anthropoïdes*, the New World narrator strives to "imager en paroles" (17) in an effort to discover the perimeters of a post-European, post-colonial, and post-modern (in the sense of literary period) worldview. Such a discovery, however, as Paul Simon's song says, keeps "slip-slidin' away." This is due to the collision, in a manner of speaking, between the narrators' didactic interest in retelling the past and their awareness of the constantly shifting grounds of certitude in the present age. Rudy Wiebe, for instance, is the speaker in the two passages that follow. The first underlines his strong sense of didactic/historical mission: "For in forcing me to discover the past of my place on my own as an adult, my public school inadvertently roused an anger in me ... *All* people have history. The stories we tell of our past are by no means merely words: they are meaning and life to us as *people*, as a *particular* people; the stories are there, and if we do not know of them, we are simply, like animals, memory ignorant, and the less are we people" ("Big Bear," 134). The second passage reveals his suspicion of any certitude, even in a retelling of historical facts: "Well, you need the facts so you can make something out of them. To discover facts or to discover details of geography are things that are done ... But, then, when it's done, it's finished with. The act is in the past. The fact is always in the past, but a fiction is what you make of it. And you have to have a certain amount of facts to make a fiction out of them. Something that will last" (Mandel and Wiebe, "Where the Voice Comes From," 152).

Eli Mandel has noted the lack of a strong sense of history in Canada: "Of the French in Canada, we know Lord Durham said, 'They have no history.' Of the English in Canada, English parliamentarians might be tempted to say, 'They know no history.' And of both, the perennial question remains (as Northrop Frye puts it) not: who are they? but: where are they? The etymology of the name 'Canada' is, in one version, Portuguese, 'Ca nada' – translating crudely as 'There is no one here' or 'Nothing here at all'" (*Family Romance*, 29–30). One could easily argue that the explosion, in the last decade or so, of historical novels, documentary fictions, and fictional biographies and autobiographies manifests a desire on the part of many creative writers to respond to – and to self-consciously problematize – both the question of 'who' and the question of 'where' in the passage just quoted.

The six historiographic texts studied here have been selected precisely because they allow for discussions of specific aspects of the role of myth in the creative rewriting of the history of that "who" and that "where." I chose them because I liked them, but also because I felt they would provide an opportunity to illustrate various workings of New World Myth. Many other novels would have served the purpose, but I wanted to look closely at the work on myth in a selected – and therefore necessarily limited – number of novels of that period. These novels form part of a much larger corpus whose thematic focus is to recreate fictionally events of the English Canadian and Québécois historico-political pasts. Some works of that larger corpus are straightforward historical novels; they present an unproblematic fictional situation in which the "novelist researches his [or her] chosen period thoroughly and strives for verisimilitude" (Cuddon, "Historical Novel," 309). However, other contemporary texts actively engage history in order to problematize the past. Instead of turning *away* from historical events, by creating, for example, purely imaginary events and characters in what is commonly called a "fictional situation," these works rewrite history in a fictional mode that has much to do with challenging any monolithic sense of how we acquire knowledge of the past in the postmodern age.[16]

The issue of the American influence on – many would say "colonization of" – English Canadian and Québécois cultures is not a central concern of this study. This is because the six texts studied here, while aware of this American influence, mainly thematize the retelling of the conflicts of more remote history, or else their concern lies with the internal political situation of Québec or Canada or both. As Hutcheon points out in a discussion of English Canadian art and literature, *historical* colonization concerns the British – or, more broadly, the European – factor, whereas present day "colonization" is carried out largely through the American media (*Politics of Representation*, 12). In the case of Quebec, of course, there is at least a double historical colonization, with the French preceding the British factor.

The six novels discussed here were published in the years 1975–85. On the political level, this period was one of extreme turmoil. The election of the Parti Québécois in 1976 was followed by the referendum on sovereignty-association in 1980, and the subsequent defeat of the referendum proposal demanded a political adjustment of major proportions in Quebec. English Canada was also politically perturbed, as events in Quebec and Ottawa, culminating in the repatriation of the Constitution in 1982, provoked intense debate about the historical reasons underlying the political uncertainties of the period. The six novels are united by the fact that the reflections on the past found in their nontraditional narratives contain an awareness of the political present. In some of the novels, such as Godbout's *Les Têtes à Papineau*, that political present is frequently signalled; in others, such as Kogawa's *Obasan*, its muted presence is found in occasional references to contemporary issues that were not necessarily perceived as problematic in the past.

These metafictional novels flaunt their focus on politics and their explorations of elements such as fantasy, myth, and play as cognitive tools in the retelling of past events. Patricia Waugh has noted how

self-reflexive fictions, while making readers aware of their expectations, propose a partial answer to the "need to know" through an
investigation of what she, somewhat vaguely, calls "the mythic": "As
novel readers, we look to fiction to offer us cognitive functions, to
locate us within everyday as well as within philosophical paradigms,
to explain the historical world as well as offer some formal comfort
and certainty. [Robert] Scholes argues that the empirical has lost all
validity and that a collusion between the philosophic and the mythic
in the form of 'ethically controlled fantasy' is the only authentic
mode for fiction [*Fabulators*, 11]. However, metafiction offers the recognition, not that the everyday has ceased to matter, but that its
formulation through social and cultural codes brings it closer to the
philosophical and mythic than was once assumed" (*Metafiction*, 16).

Play with traditional mythic elements is evident in postmodern
English Canadian and Québécois texts. Laurent Mailhot, discussing
the work of Québécois writers such as Louis Caron, Victor-Lévy
Beaulieu, Jacques Poulin, Gérard Bessette, and Michel Tremblay, in
an article significantly entitled "Romans de la parole (et du mythe),"
discerns two major categories in contemporary Québécois writing. In
contrast to the experimental, theoretical texts of *l'écriture* by novelists
such as Nicole Brossard and François Hébert, there exists a sophisticated, but undefined, mythic fiction "qu'il faut situer quelque part
entre l'oral et l'écrit, entre la tradition et la modernité, entre l'épopée
et la critique (l'autocritique)" (84). While the novels of *l'écriture* flaunt
their European intertextuality, Mailhot notes that novels of the
second category are definitely grounded in the North American context. He seems to find it easier to define novels of *l'écriture* than novels
"de la parole (et du mythe)." He foregrounds the exploratory nature
of the latter: their fictions are situated "somewhere between" various
poles, and although they give the appearance of being popular or
folkloric, they also contain a sophisticated rhetoric that can constitute
an opposition – or even a reaction – to the formal, intellectual novels
of *l'écriture*. Mailhot notes a common trend in these contemporary
texts: their exploration of the past and of their own nature incorporates a study of myth. While he does not offer a precise definition of
myth, he does propose that these North American fictions look to
various sources for their inspiration, sources which include self-
conscious usage of biblical writings and techniques from what has
been called the archaic or precontact "primitive" period: "Parole,
parabole, parolade, parade: le roman/récit québécois cherche son
commencement, son histoire, son sens … Hubert Aquin se mesurait
à Joyce, Jacques Ferron se mesure à Molière, à Lewis Carroll, à

l'éloquence indienne ... [L]a démesure de la parole, du mythe, passe les bornes et déplace les frontières. Où situer telles nouvelles fantastiques? ... La guerre se fait à l'intérieur même de l'univers fictionnel [des textes étudiés dans cet essai]" (86).

Mailhot is not alone in positing that the play with myth in many contemporary Québécois fictions is somehow related to a distinction between the Old World (Europe) and the New World. Eva-Marie Kröller, discussing the attractiveness of Herman Melville's work for George Bowering and Victor-Lévy Beaulieu, states that Melville's work "interjects itself between the Canadian authors and their reaction to European predominance ... Melville [may be perceived] as part of a utopian concept of America, the promise of a mythic new space in which European notions of man-made order are no longer applicable" (Kröller, "Postmodernism," 54). In the contemporary texts examined here, there is a sophisticated awareness of a "mythic setting" – the New World – and a wish to distinguish the English Canadian/Québécois territories of the imagination from those of the "old" colonizing nations, England and France. These novels obviously do not uphold the European-inspired myth of the New World as a natural, uncontaminated paradise, where humankind can begin anew. As the Caribbean writer Derek Walcott points out, "the apples of [the] second Eden have the tartness of experience" ("Muse of History," 115). These novels investigate, through their reworkings of myth, the possibilities of a new, but not naïve, historico-political vision of the New World.

CLASSICAL AND BIBLICAL MYTH

The obvious question is, what is to be called myth in the context of English Canadian and Québécois historiographic metafiction? In its most general formulation, a myth is a story of special significance. This criterion would obviously include such common notions as classical myth, defined as "of, having to do with, or designating ancient Greek and Rome, especially with respect to their art and literature" (*Gage Canadian Dictionary*, s.v. "classical"). James Joyce, for instance, makes use, via the text of the *Odyssey*, of the story of Ulysses in *Ulysses*, his modern novel about Ireland. The novels studied here do *not* make extended and coherent use of classical myths. In many New World Myth novels, there is a deliberate attempt to turn away from the European worldview, so strongly influenced by the idea of a classical education, and to use what is known and at hand in the New World as a source for New World Myth. Thus, the narrator of Madeleine Ouellette-Michalska's *La Maison Trestler* deliberately refuses an Old World Myth to concentrate on the historico-political happenings of the New World. Asked by a "real" historian if she possesses letters written by Iphigénie, a significantly named member of the Trestler family (whose existence she is fictionally recreating), the narrator thematizes in the following passage her awareness of the narrative and of historiography, her preoccupation with "les gens d'ici," and her refusal of Antiquity and its myths: "Je panique en entendant parler [des lettres d'Iphigénie] ... Mon stylo se déplace de fantasme en fantasme, aidé de quelques documents et d'une imagination démente ... Je renonce à Iphigénie ... [qui] me conduirait chez les Grecs, chez Agamemnon ... Or, je suis déjà débordée par l'Amérique, le Canada *a mare usque ad mare* [sic], la guerre de Sept ans ... Je ne saurais me mettre l'Antiquité sur les bras sans périr. Mon cheval de Troie ne peut galoper aussi loin" (191–2). This is not to say that all English Canadian and Québécois novels of this period put classical myths aside. Louky Bersianik's *Le Pique-nique sur l'Acropole*, as Patricia Smart has noted, is "a denunciation and reversal of the Greek myths inherent in Western psychology" ("Culture," 10); and Robert Kroetsch also parodies classical myths in his retelling of stories of the Canadian prairies. Nonetheless, many contemporary historiographic novelists in English-Canada and Quebec follow Ouellette-Michalska's lead and overtly foreground their rejection of classical myth as a paradigm for myth.

Rather than turning to the classical tradition, New World Myth turns in part to the biblical tradition, that is, to the well-known religious stories implanted in the New World that have gradually taken on a mythic life of their own. Viewed from a mythic perspective, the four books of the New Testament tell stories of special significance about a god – Jesus Christ. Among biblical scholars there exists an ongoing argument about the applicability of the term "myth" to the Bible, given its special status in the Western Christian worldview, and there is frequently a resistance to the reduction of the sacred Scriptures to the mere level of myth. Thus, Lee W. Gibbs believes in the teleological power of Jewish and Christian myths, which "possess the inherent power to convert the time process from meaningless repetition and absurdity into a cosmic drama in which men may find meaning, purpose, and value through their own existential involvement and participation" ("Myth and the Mystery," 19). His colleague, W. Taylor Stevenson, notes that the mythological stories of Greece and Rome "[became] trivialized and [were] made a matter of literature in the Hellenistic period" ("Myth and the Crisis," 5). Speaking as a Christian, Stevenson argues against a similar fate for biblical myth. He too believes in the totalizing power of myth, particularly biblical myth: "The fundamental function of myth ... is one of cosmicization; of giving meaning and shape to the world; of stating what is really real, self-founded, true, and good ... Because the myth speaks authoritatively of the real and the true, it perforce speaks of the sacred" (5).

In Catholic Quebec, and perhaps to a lesser extent in English-speaking Canada, it has been considered sacrilegious to term anything in the Bible a myth; the Bible was to be taken literally as the word of God. This resistance is clearly due in part to one connotation of the term myth as "untruth" (Frye, *Anatomy*, 75). More to the point, myth criticism of the Bible has frequently been viewed as a method of lessening its power to shape and maintain the Christian worldview. Myths, however, sometimes "take on a new lease of literary life once their connection with belief and cult disappears, as Classical mythology did in Christian Europe" (Frye, "Literature and Myth," 33). Although Frye implies that a myth stays the same while the external events surrounding it change, I would propose that postmodern novels assume control over the myth-making process and that a New World Myth is not as immutable as Frye suggests myths should be. Through their manipulations of biblical myth, the historiographic fictions examined here create a certain distancing from the traditional unquestioning acceptance of Christian doctrines. Some narrators tend to denounce vehemently and to attempt to destroy the traditional hold of the Christian belief system over the imagination; others use biblical myths to confer importance on the characters and events they recreate. All the narrators, however, maintain a critical distance; they operate within the Christian belief system to further their own myth-making, but they are aware of it and posit it as a *constructed* system. They all use and abuse biblical myths – in particular, the Christ story – in coming to grips with the strong biblical influence on our literatures.

Both J.J. White (*Mythology*, 73–4) and Northrop Frye (*Anatomy*, 101) have noted a decline in scholarly knowledge about classical myth; Frye posits the same decline with regard to biblical stories (*Anatomy*, 14). Although there may well have been a decline in serious scholarly knowledge, I would suggest that a popular *awareness* of biblical stories still constitutes an integral part of those contemporary English Canadian and Québécois worldviews that have been formed by the Christian religious system. Religious practice, of course, may have declined greatly, but the *stories*, perhaps subconsciously, can still affect world views. The extremely deep vein of what could be called religious writing, in both Québécois and English Canadian fiction, has been noted by cultural commentators from Northrop Frye ("Conclusion," 1976, 328) to George Bowering ("Modernism," 5). Although the novels discussed here *challenge* what they consider to be an untoward predominance of the biblical element in the traditional Western worldview by subverting the sacred in biblical writings, they all *use* biblical myth in their narrative exploration and development of New World Myth.

One distinction made above is worth stressing: the extremely strong monopoly held by the Catholic belief system over imaginative thought in the traditional Québécois worldview, especially prior to the Quiet Revolution of the 1960s. This monopoly was due to several factors, almost all of which no longer form a large part of everyday life in Quebec, but which at one time strongly shaped the imaginative capacities of the Québécois collectivity, especially those members of it who, like the authors studied here, were born before 1960. In an article published in 1985, Benoît Lacroix notes the surprising absence of any serious research on the traditional religious mythology of French Canadians ("La mythologie," 63). Lacroix argues that the Catholic religion was transplanted from Old to New France and that its transporters, the French religious communities, were directly inspired by the philosophy of the Middle Ages. This catholicity survived in North America until about 1960, without being affected by the major upsets – the three Rs – that touched European catholicity: the Renaissance, the Reformation and the French Revolution. Pre-Vatican French Canadian catholicity, then, was traditional in the extreme. Lacroix further notes, in a patronizing tone, that the power held by the priests in the centuries after the fall of New France affected the worldview of the traditional French Canadian: "Il ne se préoccupe pas trop des 'grandes vérités' de la foi: croire n'est-il pas assez? 'Les prêtres pensent pour nous.' Son sens historique n'est pas des plus précis: Adam, Abraham, Moïse lui font penser aux ancêtres de sa famille. La légende le passionne autant que l'événement. Il adapte, il transpose, il imagine à même sa croyance; l'affectivité du moment joue constamment dans sa manière d'être religieux. Dans un tel contexte, il est normal que la mythologie intervienne" (63). The religious monopoly over education and most aspects of social life in Quebec ensured that this traditional mythological worldview was known to most francophones. Although change occurred rapidly with the secularization of education during the Quiet Revolution, the novels examined here ironically illustrate the sway the traditional Catholic belief system exercised over a (still) relatively homogeneous Québécois society. Despite his somewhat pedantic attitude, Lacroix is one of the few critics who has set forth the blurring between matters religious and mythological in the worldview I am trying to describe. This blurring of religion, mythology, and narrative does not produce the "historyless" New World writing proposed by postcolonial writers such as Derek Walcott. These Québécois novels engage history, but in so doing, they assume and then challenge a common mythico-religious past that must be underlined in any comparative study.

NEW WORLD MYTH

In all six novels under consideration here, there is a foregrounded awareness – and wariness – of biblical myths as having been an extremely strong force in shaping the traditional, inherited thought-system that previously dominated the respective literary canons. The deliberate narratorial weakening of the status of both classical and biblical myths paves the way for the presence of a third form, New World Myth, which is, of course, the major focus of this study. Margery Fee notes that a frequent criticism levelled against the New World is "its lack of an indigenous mythology." Fee refutes this criticism, arguing that Howard O'Hagan's *Tay John*, a New World novel, is "filled with mythic power" ("Making New World Myth," 8).[17] "*Myth*," Fee writes, "is used here loosely, as O'Hagan appears to use it ... [it includes] a wide variety of conventional patterns: native myth and local legend; literary genres, modes, and archetypes; popular stereotypes; and even intellectual categories. All are or have been accepted widely and uncritically as true, and used as valid ways of viewing the world" (9–10). Fee shows how O'Hagan, in *Tay John*,

rigs up a new myth out of the pieces of the old ones, revealing in the process how it's done. His "enemy" in this novel, then, is not myth, but the belief in one complete immutable myth: the Truth. It is impossible to think or talk without believing in something, starting from somewhere, standing on some taken-for-granted ground. But in *Tay John* those who refuse to shift ground, or to feel the ground shifting under their feet, are defeated, while those who wonder and doubt survive ... The world [O'Hagan] moves [the reader] into is filled with the elements of myth, but, unlike the Old World myth, immutable, authoritarian, timeless, and universal, his New World myth is rather a paradigm of myth, revealing how myth is created to suit a particular need in a particular time and place ... O'Hagan undermines various Western ideologies ... [and] shows how a borrowed indigenous myth can be adapted to immigrant needs in a way that will distinguish Canadian novels from others. (10)

Elsewhere in the article, Fee states that these "dominant and inter-connected ideologies [are] idealism, Christianity, patriarchy, class, and capitalism" ("Making New World Myth," 9). She attributes the liberating quality of New World Myth to its self-regulated distancing from the dominant Judaeo-Christian worldview – a distancing that gives individuals the freedom to think and imagine for themselves. In her analysis, Fee notes that the process of rewriting myth begins with the importing of "a version of Judaeo-Christianity [the Christ story] and a version of Platonic idealism [the allegory of the cave] into the traditional beliefs of the Shusway tribe into which Tay John is born" (11). The rewriting process continues with O'Hagan's use and abuse of Amerindian and white settlers' stories to build his New World Myth of *Tay John* (13). O'Hagan, argues Fee, is attempting "to re-make not only Old World mythology, but also Old World literary genres, to suit the New World" (17). The coming-into-being of New World Myth is tied to the commonplace, and O'Hagan's tale "has a popular origin, being formed in the main by indigenous oral genres: myth, legend, tall tales, gossip, rumour, and hearsay" (11). In *Tay John*, therefore, myth "is not immemorial, immutable, and universal, but flexible, time-bound, and appropriate to its setting" (23). O'Hagan is engaged, proposes Fee, in a "process that Robert Kroetsch has argued is characteristic of recent Canadian fiction" (17). Kroetsch has written: "In recent Canadian fiction the major writers resolve the paradox – the painful tension of appearance and authenticity – by the radical process of demythologizing the systems that threaten to define them. Or, more comprehensively, they uninvent the world" ("Unhiding the Hidden," 239). Fee portrays Jackie Denham, the narrator of the middle section of O'Hagan's novel, as having what Kenneth Bruffee qualifies as a "European mind" (*Elegiac Romance*, 239). Denham, notes Fee, "spends the novel overcoming a kind of culture shock ... [He] must learn to change the European attitude that sees nature (and the associated women, native people and indeed, reality itself) as objects to be mastered" ("Making New World Myth," 18). Fee implies that for O'Hagan possessing a Euro-pean mind is not advantageous and points to his attempt to remake Old World mythology and Old World literary genres. She further argues that the shift in narrators in *Tay John* makes "the reader aware that all narration is incomplete, and that stories exist independently of their authors." Fee's basic argument is that the novel moves "from certainty to doubt": "This is not to say that O'Hagan turns to radical irony. He wants us to believe in doubt, to make myths while under-standing that they are of necessity inadequate, and will be replaced by versions of others ... Thus, this is a New World myth, egalitarian, popular, practical, peaceful, agnostic. In that it rejects both Dobble's American and materialistic realism, and Denham's Anglo-Irish and aristocratic romance, it is also specifically Canadian" (20).

Fee further develops the politico-cultural aspect of this last point, noting that the hero/ine of the new myth, the child of Ardith Aeriola and Tay John, will be "a mixture of her obscure Central European past, and his Irish-Indian heritage: a new Canadian" (23). Throughout the article, Fee argues that New World Myth, produced by the dismantling of the old myths, takes possession of a new literary and intellectual territory "formerly excluded from literature, the 'colonial'" (11). Discussing New World Myth in terms of the colonial situation and the need to use what is at hand in the overt *construction* of New World Myth, Fee notes that O'Hagan flouts "the dogmas of 'Imperial' criticism in creating a colonial myth. Denham trails behind him into virgin territory the whole European literary heritage, the dreadful burden of the colonial writer. Yet it proves fruitful. He supplies from local materials those things identified as lacking by critics like Rupert Brooke" (24). Brooke's infamous comment about the lack of mythology in the New World is frequently cited in postcolonial studies: "Look as long as you like upon a cataract of the New World, you shall not see a white arm in the foam. A godless place. And the dead do not return" (*Letters from America*, 155). Fee concludes that despite "'victories' over old ideologies, the survival of the myth is problematic ... [However, for] O'Hagan, the future is not simply determined by the past. In the precarious present, the moment of action, of 'promise,' clarity of vision can create a new and perhaps less oppressive myth" (24–5).

It was in the context of Fee's analysis that I first defined New World Myth in my own work. Since this study concentrates on novels published much later than *Tay John* and as since these novels foreground their interest in historico-political situations in a way that the narrators of *Tay John* do not, many characteristics of New World Myth in my analyses are extensions rather than illustrations of those developed by Fee. For instance, New World Myth encourages a renewed interest in reclaiming the past, and yet flaunts its re-*creation*, through story, of that past in the here and now. Its emphasis on what Dennis Duffy terms the "malleability of material" (*Sounding the Iceberg*, 66), as well as the emphasis on the narrator as the creative teller of "untold tales that wait for their telling" (Kogawa, *Obasan*, 226), underlines the flexibility of New World Myth. The texts studied here explode the concept of a "commonly experienced, objectively existing world of history" (Waugh, *Metafiction*, 6) by their narrators' recreation of – and challenge to – the very notion of past reality and how we know it. These novels contribute to what Patricia Waugh describes as a "sense that reality or history are provisional: no longer a world of eternal verities but a series of constructions, artifices, impermanent structures" (7). The presence of classical myth that Fee notes in *Tay John* is not an important factor in these historiographic works; indeed, there is a deliberate putting-aside of classical myth in many New World Myth novels. The political aspect of both the past and the "precarious present" receives more attention in these texts than it does in *Tay John*. In addition, the metafictional aspect is more strongly stressed in the later fictions, lending more weight to the discussion of the creative *making* of New World Myth.

TERMINOLOGY AND NEW WORLD MYTH

As is the case with New World Myth, there is a potentially problematic tension in any usage of several terms that recur frequently in this study: fiction, history, reality, myth, mythology, and mythologization. Warner Berthoff's "Fiction, History, Myth" provides a basis from which to begin to define three of these terms and to explore the relationships among them. Berthoff assumes that it is possible to define precisely fiction, history, and myth and offers definitions that, in the context of this study, could be qualified as conservative or traditional. He posits that all three are modes of narrative, and he underlines their *cognitive* basis. A fiction, writes Berthoff, describes "something made up" by an individual maker, the author (269). A fiction is particular to this individual maker, and, if not made by him or her, it would remain "unknowable" (271). A fiction in this schema is an imagined narrative, a particular writer's invention.

A history, according to Berthoff, is "that species of narrative in which we try to describe something that happened according to the discoverable testimony about it and by means of certifiable techniques for gathering and identifying such testimony" (270). Contrasted to a fiction, which is, Berthoff notes, "constitutive or inventive," this second type of narrative is descriptive. Whereas the critics' concern with a fiction revolves around its "veracity," their concern with a history centres on the problem of "verification" (272). Although Berthoff realizes that ambiguities develop with the concept of history, he thinks that "on the whole they are manageable ones ... History, in brief, is the story of happenings that are, or might be, otherwise knowable" (270-1). Thus, for Berthoff, a history is a narrative that is "meant to reveal a pre-existent order of actuality" (272).

A myth, writes Berthoff, is a narrative that is "*told*," as opposed to "*composed*" (as is the case with a fiction) or "reassembled" (as is the case with a history). We do not know the origins of myths; we do not know them as a making, only as a telling. There is "an element of unchangeability in the structure of the telling" of a myth that endows it with "the authority of the ritually stabilized" (276). Another characteristic of myth, claims Berthoff, is that it constitutes a "collective activity of uttering and re-uttering (with all manner of local, idiomatic variation) certain relatively unchanging formulas of statement" (277). A myth is stabilizing, "inseparable from ritual" (278), and has both an intimate association with religious life and, as Frye notes elsewhere, a "special category of seriousness" (Frye, "Literature and Myth," 28). Myths exist, states Berthoff, to bring "things that are known about ... into an order in which they will continue to exist and be serviceable" (281). According to Berthoff, then, the "basic function or purpose of myth is thus not *explanation* (in the sense of interpretation) but *recovery, preservation, organization, continuance*" (281).

A New World Myth is something quite different. The frame of argument of Berthoff's article suggests that one can separate out – and keep separate – fiction, history, and myth. In fact, Berthoff somewhat disapprovingly mentions "a certain over-confident waywardness and libertinism of imagination among post-modern writers of fiction," referring in passing to the work of Günter Grass and Peter Weiss (272). Berthoff's approach clearly does not allow for any blurring of the boundaries among these three modes of narrative. Such a cut-and-dried system, however, proves to be inapplicable to the historiographic works discussed here, because in these novels there is a deliberate narratorial blurring of the boundaries of the fictional, the historical, and the mythical. Although these novels may claim to be fictional works, some of them are what Allen Thiher calls "not always fictional fiction[s]" (*Words in Reflection*, 190) whose concern is the creative retelling of actual past events. Thus, contrary to Berthoff's definition, the "event(s)" of the narrative would not remain unknown without the novel. The critics' concern with history, says Berthoff, is verification. However, the fictional retelling of historical events (with the only sometimes acknowledged filling-in of the gaps) brings fiction into the problematic realm of history and puts history into the equally problematic realm of fiction. In these works of fiction, verification can also be a concern. The incorporation by these novels of real historical documents is but one example of the numerous narrative techniques that add to this blurring of the boundaries and render fiction inseparable from history and "reality." These novels also "take on" history: they problematize the past, and they put forth their retellings as equal to, or superior to, those recorded by the supposedly certifiable techniques of historical research. The very acknowledgment within these texts that their version is *one* version of the past (and that there are therefore other possible and perhaps equally acceptable versions) contributes to the generic blurring of the boundaries between fiction and history. The textual use of documents (trial records, letters, memoirs, descriptions of photographs) illustrates that these traditional aids to historical objectivity are only what the imagination makes of them. Berthoff's article offers a traditional concept of myth: an eternal, traditional, teleological, transhistorical narrative that lends shape, unity, and what Shirley Neuman calls "integrated wholeness" to the story (Kroetsch et al., *Labyrinths of Voice*, 129). However, as we shall see in greater detail in the following chapters, the ongoing crises in theories of historiography, of knowledge, and of fiction also have their equivalent in discussions of myth. To the postmodern list that includes "fiction" that is not always fictional, "history" that is not always an objective record of past events, and "knowledge" of the past that is relative, personal, and perhaps, "the ultimate fiction" (Waugh, *Metafiction*, 107), we may now add the concept of "myth" as comforting *and* disquieting, structuring *and* decentring, old and traditional, *and* new and generative.

The other three terms that recur frequently in this study are "reality," "mythology," and "mythologization." With regard to the novels discussed here, "reality" refers to that which is traditionally outside fiction: simple, empirically verifiable facts that should be objective because they apparently leave no room for diverse interpretations or for necessarily biased assembly. Thus, a statement such as "Jovette Marchessault is the author of *Comme une enfant de la terre*" belongs to the realm of "reality." However, the unnamed narrator of this novel has a father whose name changes from John-marchait-eau to John Marchessault. Thus, this narrator brings reality into the realm of fiction and fiction into the realm of reality. Again, as W.J. Keith has noted, when the narrator of Rudy Wiebe's *Scorched-Wood People* tells of the shout "Vive le Nord-ouest libre!" during the celebration dance of the Métis (31), the phraseology is not politically innocent or, in all likelihood, historically accurate (*Epic Fiction*, 90); it incorporates de Gaulle's similarly phrased exclamation at another politically charged celebration and illustrates how narrative techniques can deliberately occasion a blurring between fiction and reality.

Northrop Frye defines a mythology as a "definite canon of stories," a "body of traditional and religious data" ("Literature and Myth," 28, 31). He describes the process of mythologization as a movement *downward*: myths degenerate from stories about gods to stories about legendary heroes, to stories about human beings (*Anatomy*, 51). But

the narrators in the texts studied here are struggling *against* the domination of definitive mythologies, such as the biblical and the colo-
nial-historical ones. Frye's tone, created in part by his frequent use
of first-person plural pronouns, implies that these mythologies are
"our" inherited traditions, our primary data for understanding our
situation in the world ("Literature and Myth," 27). The narrators of
the texts being considered in the pages that follow, however, challenge these "given" mythologies and address their self-imposed task:
to mythologize at least their, if not our, past(s) in a manner appropriate to New World nations.

By "mythologization" (and its verbal form, "to mythologize") I
mean a deliberate according of the quality Hans Blumenberg calls
"significance" to the characters and events in the texts: "[Myth] has
something to offer that – even with reduced claims to reliability,
certainty, faith, realism, and intersubjectivity – still constitutes satisfaction of intelligent expectations. The quality on which this depends
can be designated by the term *significance* [*Bedeutsamkeit*], taken from
Dilthey" (*Work on Myth*, 67). Although Blumenberg argues that "significance" cannot be defined, but only explained and that "Equip-
ping something with significance is not something that we can
choose to do" (68), I would argue that in New World Myth, where
the emphasis is placed on myth-*making*, the narrators do set out to
confer significance on the events and personages of the stories they
retell. "Significance," in the context of this study, refers to a characteristic quality of certain stories, a quality that makes them important, notable, valuable, and of consequence. In these self-conscious
fictions, of course, the according of significance is often ironically
undercut by those who use it to mythologize individuals or historical
events.

In outlining the traditional definitions of the six terms just discussed, I have been working toward a fuller definition of New
World Myth by suggesting that in the novels under scrutiny here
there is a perpetual tension between the traditional definition of
each term and the narrators' treatment of the concept. Similarly, the
narrators instil a tension between Old World myths and their particular versions of New World Myth. They do this by actively working
at breaking down the barriers between myth and history or fiction
and by deliberately blurring the boundaries between what constitutes a myth and what does not.

INDIGENOUS MYTH

The post-European fictional works discussed here use that which is
at hand – that which is *local* – to create, underline, and ironically

problematize the significance of what which is being recounted. One difference between New World Myth and the perhaps more conventional use of myth in the modernist period is seen in Eric Gould's suggestion that James Joyce's re-use of motifs from *The Odyssey* is part of his work of "mythological plotting" (*Mythical Intentions*, 12). "In other words," writes Gould, "we undoubtedly have *The Odyssey* in mind as a working analogy for *Ulysses*, which is what Joyce intended, and Stuart Gilbert, T.S. Eliot, and everyone else confirms. We are not disappointed to find that Joyce's novel reflects, residually at least, the 'archetypal order' of the geography of Ulysses' quest" (140). Joyce's work, Gould implies, comes out of a strong tradition: his *Ulysses* assumes a general knowledge of *The Odyssey* and gives ample work, as Gould points out, to those critics who "see the business of reading as that of fitting together motifs and archetypes into a solution to a giant puzzle" (140). The general strength of such a literary tradition has been underlined also by Frye, who proposes that in "a fully mature literary tradition the writer enters into a structure of traditional stories and images. He often has the feeling, and says so, that he is not actively shaping his material at all, but is rather a place where a verbal structure is taking its own shape" ("Conclusion," 1965, 836).

In order to see the difference between this concept of tradition and the challenge to it by New World Myth, one could imagine a vertical pole with various types of myth placed on it in a hierarchical order. In the traditional literary scheme, classical stories would be at the top (important) end of the pole, while gossip, hearsay, and local-interest stories would occupy the bottom (frivolous) end. In New World Myth, however, this hierarchical order is challenged. Instead of having traditional myths come down from the heights to enhance an ordinary story and keep the paradigmatic original story alive in a contemporary form, the narrators of New World Myth novels make use of the elements situated at the base of the imagined vertical pole. That is to say, they emphasize what has frequently been dismissed as local colour or *des histoires de village*. Margery Fee insists upon the liberating quality of New World Myth and the important role of what she calls indigenous popular genres in its formulation. Examples of the latter are legend, the tall tale, gossip, rumour and hearsay – all of which inform the text of *Tay John*. This novel, Fee notes, "buries its references to 'high' culture in allusions and echoes that are not essential for its comprehension"; its author, in his creation of New World Myth, "turns from 'high' to 'low' cultural forms" ("Making New World Myth," 24). Laurent Mailhot makes approximately the same point in his overview, "Romans de la parole (et du mythe)," where narrative fluidity is linked to orality and popular, local discourse (88). In *Le Romancier fictif*, André Belleau makes a different distinction between "romans du code et romans de la parole" in Québécois literature (57–89). He too notes, however, that "romans de la parole" are usually first-person narratives by potential fictional authors whose interests concern real-life issues. As Romanticism rediscovered fairy tales in reaction to the Enlightenment, so, perhaps, New World Myth turns to indigenous popular genres, such as local stories, folk songs, and political slogans, in reaction to the influence of more traditional givens, such as classical myth and European worldviews, on the literatures of English Canada and Quebec.

New World Myth also investigates what used to be generally called, in the context of myth criticism, "primitive" myth. This word has recently, and deservedly, fallen on bad ideological times, as have the anthropologists who contributed to its general usage in many fields.[18] Prior to approximately 1960, however, primitive was the term generally employed to describe archaic or prehistoric examples of myth. Characteristics of this "primitive" myth are anonymity of authorship, freedom from the limitations of chronological time and physical space, a strong sense of tribalism and collective activities that reinforce bonding among members of the tribal collectivity, and belief in the magical and the occult. Georges Gusdorf's introductory chapters in *Mythe et métaphysique* give as good a description as any of this category. Gusdorf posits that in a primitive worldview, no distinction is made between the objective world of reality and the world of myth and that there is only "une lecture unique du paysage" (57). For the "primitive," writes Gusdorf, "la conscience mythique imprime directement son sens au réel vécu, sans que soit possible la moindre ambiguïté" (68). Gusdorf further proposes that in the prehistoric period the individual is not distinguished – and does not distinguish himself or herself – from the group: "L'époque préhistorique est le règne de l'impersonnalité. Les individus n'émergent pas de la masse. Le *je* est prisonnier de l'*on* qui l'englobe" (162). Good examples of the postmodern play with this primitive category of myth in contemporary Québécois and English Canadian literature are to be found in large sections of Gérard Bessette's *Anthropoïdes* and Geoffrey Ursell's *Perdue: Or How the West Was Lost*. In the novels discussed in detail here, the notion of primitive myth is sometimes used to uncover and then to abuse inherited misconceptions. This is particularly the case in the novels by Barcelo and Bowering. Amerindian myths, however, are present without irony in Marchessault's work, reflecting her use of what is local, *known* (Marchessault is part Amerindian), in her production of New World Myth.

Story-telling is also a concern of this investigation of myth, especially as it relates to knowledge of the past in a New World context. The major part of Lyotard's *Postmodern Condition* is devoted to the present status of *scientific* knowledge in postindustrial societies, but his remarks concerning *narrative* knowledge are of relevance here. His salient points are the breakdown of the metanarrative, the decline of narrative per se, and the effect of this change on contemporary society. Summing up this part of his argument, Lyotard writes, "Lamenting the 'loss of meaning' in postmodernity boils down to mourning the fact that knowledge is no longer principally narrative" (26). Using as an example a tale of a primitive Cashinahua storyteller, Lyotard suggests that it is "the preeminence of the narrative form in the formulation of traditional knowledge" that separates the "customary state of knowledge from its state in the scientific age" (19). Narrative, then, in the postmodern period – according to Lyotard – is no longer an important conveyor of knowledge. I would argue, however, that in the contemporary fictions studied here narrative – that is to say, story-telling – *is* linked to the problematic of the acquisition of knowledge in the postmodern age. There is indeed a refusal of "the great historical systems of the past" (Thiher, *Words in Reflection*, 200) in much recent fiction written in Quebec and English Canada. Accompanying this refusal, however, is an acceptance or, more appropriately, an *exploration* of precisely those narrative components that Lyotard dismisses along with his primitive storyteller. This study, by examining the creative retellings of stories of past happenings in the context of the present, examines the role of story-telling in New World Myth, particularly in the context of its relationship to history and knowledge. In the novels under study here, the narrators explore a combination of the traditional markers of myth (such as cyclical structure, naming as a creative and magical act, and the poet as the voice of the gods) and postmodern play with various "indigenous popular genres" (Fee, "Making New World Myth," 24). This dual concentration works to produce the tension that is inherent in and generative of New World Myth. As we shall see, the narrators of these texts flaunt the paradoxes that arise from thematizing "primitivism" in a highly technological age, orality in a printed text, or storytelling as a means to knowledge in what has long been considered a rational, scientific society.

Textual blurring of fiction, history, and myth frequently provokes a certain malaise. Historiographer Louis O. Mink, for instance, warns that "myth serves as both fiction and history [only] for those who have not learned to discriminate" and suggests that we not "forget what we have learned" ("Narrative Form," 149). It is possible, however, that, in going beyond the need to set up boundaries between fiction, history, and myth, the novels discussed here are in fact offering their readers a new cognitive tool: an alternative way of viewing the past as an imaginative, *narrated* construct.

Kroker and Cook state polemically that "Jean-François Lyotard is ... wrong when he argues ... that we are living now in the age of the death of the 'grand récits,' [in] a post-historical period ... In fact, it's just the opposite. We're living through a great story – an historical moment of implosion ... [that] traces a great arc of reversal, connecting again to an almost mythic sense" (*Postmodern Scene*, 14–15). I would challenge part of this argument: the novels studied here do involve an eventual rejection of dominant historical systems – the metanarratives of Lyotard's work. Narrative as *story*, however, is alive and well in these texts: the "tales that wait for their telling" (Kogawa, *Obasan*, 226) are being told through the textual construction of New World Myth. Precisely because of their metafictional awareness and their particular construction of New World Myth, these texts offer their readers a fictional mythologization of history as a way of acquiring a necessarily provisional knowledge of the past(s).

Although Paul Veyne and historians of the Annales school propose a historiography that would be different from the dominant *histoire-traité-et-batailles* mode (*Comment on écrit l'histoire*, 31), many English Canadian and Québécois historiographic metafictions of the years 1975–85 turn to precisely those periods of history that were periods of conflict: the Conquest, the Rebellions of 1837–38, the two world wars, the October Crisis, the referendum of 1980. This leads to a slightly different version of the question posed above: apart from the putting-aside of classical myth, the use and abuse of biblical myth, and the foregrounding of what Fee calls "indigenous" myth, is there anything *new* about New World Myth?

In typical postmodern fashion, there is both an "installing" and a "subverting" process (Hutcheon, *Poetics*, 3) in novels of New World Myth. The installation process self-consciously enhances the significance of the historical characters and events being retold. It is in the second stage – the subverting process – that a clearer answer to the question posed in the last paragraph may be found. The subverting of the mythologization process keeps New World Myth from becoming fixed and rigid. This subverting process is linked to the metafictional aspect of these novels. It is also connected to the ongoing discussion, within the novels themselves, about the self-conscious power of the imaginative, creative act to influence our cognitive capacities and our basic attitudes regarding knowledge of the past.

The "tellers" of the stories in these texts, by foregrounding the tensions between the historical past and the political present and by emphasizing and then deconstructing their own privileged position as narrators, contribute to the creation of a necessarily fluid New World Myth. They metafictively lay bare their acts of mythologization in the full knowledge that in this, our postmodern climate, the resulting mythology is and will be temporary, adjustable, and continually shifting.

Denied, then, a traditional function of myth, which is to offer intellectual security in the form of an established, definitive worldview, the presence of New World Myth in these texts serves other functions. By overtly exploring – and challenging – the notion of what Eric Gould calls "mythicity" (*Intentions*, 3), the narrators of these historiographic metafictions encourage the liberation of the concept of myth from its traditional function and allow for its rejuvenating presence in the literature of the postmodern age. Margery Fee concludes her study by noting the creation of "new and perhaps less oppressive myth" in "the precarious present" ("Making New World Myth," 25). Although not all contemporary fictions include the two factors necessary for the tensions that generate New World Myth – the installing and the subverting processes – I would suggest that both are contained in the six novels analyzed here. New World Myth fills a need to reimagine the world in a post-European and postmodern manner.

2 Making Myths, Playing God: The Narrator in Jacques Godbout's *Les Têtes à Papineau* and Rudy Wiebe's *The Scorched-Wood People*

In Jacques Godbout's *Têtes à Papineau* (1981) and Rudy Wiebe's *Scorched-Wood People* (1977) the first-person narrators explode the concept of a "commonly experienced, objectively existing world of history" (Waugh, *Metafiction*, 6) by their comments on – and challenge to – the very notion of a single past reality. Through the narrators' treatment of important historical events, these texts explore the concepts of narratorial control, historical instability, and the fictional mythologizing of the past. Two central concerns here are the textual blurring of history and fiction and the ostentatious use of the narrators as myth-*makers*.

Political history is a concern of many postcolonial texts. In rewriting eurocentric interpretations of past events that took place in the New World, postcolonial writers can partially repossess the past while remaining aware of the flexible nature of history. Not all New World writers, however, enthusiastically set about rewriting their pasts. For instance, Derek Walcott, the Caribbean poet and essayist, sees the postcolonial rewriting of history as an endless spinning of wheels and has what might be called a mythic reaction against history: "The truly tough aesthetic of the New World neither explains nor forgives history. It refuses to recognize it as a creative or culpable force" ("Muse of History," 112). Walcott advocates "historylessness" – the clean-slate syndrome: "No history, but flux, and the only sustenance, myth" (118). Instead of adopting Walcott's approach, however, Godbout's and Wiebe's novels take on history, thereby illustrating a continuing concern with the nationalist stance discussed in the previous chapter. By "nationalist," I do not necessarily mean pan-Canadian, which is the meaning intimated by Alan Twigg's brief description of Wiebe's novel: "*The Scorched-Wood People* (1977) is an account of Louis Riel's Métis people struggling to retain a sense of communal integrity and political autonomy in the face of encroaching nationalism" (Twigg, *For Openers*, 207). Nor do I at all wish to suggest the negative meaning associated with the term and its homologue, "nationalism," in the 1990s, after the ethnic conflicts in Africa, the former Yugoslavia, and Eastern Europe. As Peter Alter remarks, "the plethora of phenomena which may be subsumed under the term 'nationalism' suggests that it is one of the most ambiguous concepts in the present-day vocabulary of political and analytical thought" (*Nationalism*, 4). In Quebec and in English-speaking Canada during the period studied here, the concept of nationalism was generally taken as a positive quality, although in keeping with the intriguing nature of these areas and the peoples who inhabit them, it usually meant different things. For instance, during Centennial year (1987), while many *Canadians* invested great energy in Centennial projects (such as, for instance, creating community parks), Montrealers took great pride in Expo '67, seeing it as a celebration of *Québécois* autonomy and a manifestation of Quebec as a nation of the world. Reflections on nationalism in the novels of this study are tied to a sense of belonging or not belonging, or both: they demonstrate strong interest in all aspects of a particular community, which is not necessarily the same thing as an ethnic group, a race, or the people(s) of a nation. The question of community is discussed below, but for the moment, suffice it to say that the narrators of Godbout's and Wiebe's texts deliberately refer to specific historico-political events in their investigations of New World Myth; they problematize the concept of history in order to permit the elaboration of alternative and imaginative perspectives on the past.

New World Myth novels tend to foreground the use of a narrator (or narrators) in their stories and to flaunt the situational complexity of these narrators. For this reason, this study focuses on the narrators and narratorial intentions, as opposed to the authors, of these texts. The insistence on a first-person narratorial voice, as opposed to an epistolary form of address or an omniscient third-person narration – to mention but two alternative narratorial possibilities – permits two elements to operate within the texts. First, the use of a narrator facilitates the illustration of self-reflexivity in a text: self-conscious narrators, by laying bare their story-telling techniques and by insisting on their own problematic and sometimes fractured natures, emphasize the arbitrariness of any story. Second, the presence of a narrator in

New World Myth texts allows a reflection on the question of community, as narrators who (re)tell history are frequently taken as representatives, cultural custodians, or spokespersons of a given collectivity. The notion of community itself, as Zygmunt Bauman notes, has become a concern of postmodernists: "It is precisely because of its vulnerability that community provides the focus of postmodern concerns, that it attracts so much intellectual and practical attention, that it figures so prominently in the philosophical models and popular ideologies of postmodernity" (*Intimations of Postmodernity*, xix). The post-European focus of New World Myth narrators problematizes and investigates this notion of community, in various ways. Where do people find their identity? In the *collectivité*? In their ethnic group? In their gender? their geographical location? their individuality? Is there such a thing as a definite identity? How do different communities interact? Are there enemies to community? If so, are these enemies within or without – or perhaps both? One demonstration of the ironic dimension of the treatment of community in the two novels examined in this chapter is that Wiebe's narrator openly, and futilely, strives to construct a collectivity, while Godbout's narrators, products of what has become a stifling *collectivité*, strive to break out of the deeply engrained nationalist stance of the Québécois *chez nous* (77), which has been defined by Micheline Cambron as "une idéologie où la collectivité ... est conçue comme un 'nous' englobant" (*Une Société*, 176).

The omnipresent first-person narrator of *The Scorched-Wood People*, the Métis poet and song writer, Pierre Falcon, recounts the lives of Louis Riel and Gabriel Dumont and the rise and fall of their New Nation, an appellation that is capitalized throughout the text. In this retelling of the rebellions at Red River in 1869–70 and on the Saskatchewan in 1885, the narrator's sympathies lie with the Métis. Directly addressing the reader/listener, Falcon underlines his attempt, through his story-telling, to accord "significance" to the leader of the Métis: "Let me tell you immediately, Louis Riel was a giant. If God had willed it, he could have ruled the world. No, no, hear me out, and you will believe it too" (36). The conclusion of Falcon's narrative exemplifies the one-on-one tone of the entire story, as well as its nationalist and religious overtones: "That is all the story I can tell you. Our New Nation blossomed and faded for a few short months in Manitoba in 1869–70, it blazed up in 1885 and in less than two months died on the Saskatchewan. Our prairie vision was too strong ... O God I pray again, let our people not be confounded. Give them that faith again" (348–51). In Coral Ann Howells' words, this narrative "gives us the world of the Northwest Rebellion in stories, making us relive the process and see the problematics of history in the multiple claims being made on/in the West in the 1870s and '80s. Wiebe does not deny History ... but what he does do is offer the chance for its creative revision" ("Wiebe's Art," 20). Of course, Wiebe also uses these stories of the past to convey the strong political tensions of the 1970s between the marginalized "West" and what it perceived as the powerful centre, even while calling it the "East."

Godbout's novel *Les Têtes à Papineau* is a political allegory that comments on the state of affairs in Quebec at the moment of the 1980 referendum on sovereignty-association. As Stephen Slemon has argued, allegory can be an effective method of subversion for post-colonial challenges to any monolithic presentation of history ("Post-Colonial Allegory," 158). Godbout's use of allegory not only offers such a challenge to history, but it also illustrates the New World Myth challenge to dominant myths that shaped traditional cultural worldviews in Quebec. Bicephalic Charles and François Papineau are the main characters and the first-person plural narrators of the text. Unlike Riel and Falcon, they are *not* historically authentic personages. Indeed, they are rather improbable creatures: Charles and François are the names of two heads joined at the neck and sharing a single body. Like Siamese twins with independent minds, emotions and discourses, they live an increasingly frustrating life, bound together physically and yet partial to different aspirations. Charles and François agree to have an operation that will unite their two brains, thereby giving them *one* head. The narrators decide to write a journal about their "évolution, jusqu'au scalpel" (28). Divided into eight relatively short chapters, their journal tells of their first twenty-five years in Montreal and the surrounding area. Their infancy deliberately recalls that of the Dionne quintuplets from Ontario, who in the 1930s were kept from their parents by the medical community and exhibited to the general public as a curiosity. The Papineau family ties are maintained, however, when the heads' parents, Alain-Auguste and Marie Lalonde, kidnap them from the hospital, thereby saving them from a similar fate.

Charles and François continually flaunt the particularity of their bicephalic condition and, at the same time, stress their monstrosity. The allegorical import of their two-headed existence has been noted in practically every review of the novel: "Charles-François Papineau symbolise le Québec" (Alain Piette, "Les Langues à Papineau," 120). Although Piette and also Patricia Smart note that this double name might well be associated with the English-French conflict within

Canada, both critics conclude that the heads are, in Smart's words, "plutôt les côtés 'canadien' et 'français' de la psyché québécoise" (Smart, "L'Espace de nos fictions," 27). Charles and François Papineau are indeed representative of the Québécois collectivity. The tension they feel as they contemplate the operation recalls the situation in Quebec prior to the referendum of 1980. Their internal conflicts have obvious political undertones: "Aujourd'hui … nous n'envisageons plus l'avenir, ou ce qui en reste, de même manière. Nous sommes, pour ainsi dire, idéologiquement séparés … Il n'est plus question de tenir des discours chacun de notre côté. Ce n'est plus le temps des élections. Nous n'en avons plus le courage. Il nous faut faire face à la situation" (29). In the hospital room, their sister's question again underlines the political import of the operation, as well as their contradictory responses to it:

"Et si nous tenions un référendum?" lance Bébée qui nous embrasse par-derrière. "Pour trancher la question?" …

"Pourquoi voudrais-tu un référendum?" demande Charles.

"Parce que vous ne vous appartenez pas tout à fait," répond Bébée. "Vous vous devez à votre public. Vous êtes l'orgueil de la Nation …"

"Dites, vous avez déjà choisi? Dites-le-moi?"

"Oui," répond Charles.

"Non," répond François. (145–8)

The final chapter of the novel consists of a letter written by Charles F. Papineau to the prospective publishers of the heads' journal. Written in English, the letter explains that the operation produced a unilingual one-headed Papineau, thereby fulfilling the heads' prophecy that "les têtes à Papineau … sont condamnés à disparaître" (150). The political implications of the heads' complicated existence, then, are foregrounded throughout the text.

Godbout and Wiebe have both emphasized the power of creative writing to influence our understanding of the past. Godbout has said: "Toute entreprise d'écriture est une entreprise pour masquer, transformer, transmuer les choses, et non pas pour les dire comme elles sont … [Ecrire, c'est] Briser la chronologie, briser la représentation" (quoted in Donald Smith, "Jacques Godbout," 54). For Godbout, then, writing is an act of transformation that is different from a direct chronological representation. The exterior presentation of his text as artifact thematizes its mythical and historiographic concerns. On the back cover of the original Seuil edition of the novel, Charles-François Papineau is presented as a "real live person," complete with definite birthdate (1955), birthplace (Montreal) and age (25). The "reality effect" to which this passage aspires is greatly strengthened by the fact that it first mentions the celebrated Dionne quintuplets and then leads on, without the slightest change in tone, to the existence of Charles-François, "le seul enfant à deux têtes qui ait survécu si longtemps."[1] This phraseology implies that there have been other two-headed children, as there have been other sets of quintuplets. Instead of touting the *novel* as being worth its price, the entire publicity blurb emphasizes verisimilitude, the *life* of "les têtes": "Leur vie est un roman plein de contradictions et de surprises."[2] The title of Joan Miró's painting reproduced on the front cover, "Le disque rouge à la poursuite de l'alouette" (which was incorrectly attributed to Paul Klee on some copies), is doubly indicative of the political slant of this allegorical novel – the *alouette* being a traditional symbol of things French Canadian. "Papineau" recalls Louis-Joseph Papineau, the leader of the *Patriotes* during the 1837–38 rebellions. The adjective *rouge* traditionally described the rebels: Papineau is the "name of one of Québec's most famous *Rouges*" (Kröller, "Two Heads," 112). As Piette argues ("Les Langues à Papineau"), the historical Papineau has undergone a process of mythification that makes of him a crystallized heroic figure of the past. The exterior presentation of the work, then, strongly suggests that its main characters, bizarre and fabulous as they may be, have a historical reality and occupy a particular time and place. This presentation also indicates that the text will discuss the historical and mythological discourses of Quebec. Indeed, the title of the painting on the cover indicates the action of the novel: the fictional Charles and François Papineau, while playing on the significance of their name, challenge the historical traditions of the Québécois. They are, indeed, "à la poursuite de l'alouette."

Rudy Wiebe shares Godbout's view of writing as an act of transformation. The research he did for *The Temptations of Big Bear* enabled him to write *The Scorched-Wood People* at a faster pace, as he had already acquired a knowledge of the historical background of the period (Bergman, "Rudy Wiebe," 166). This common research is significant because of the prefatory address in *Big Bear*: "No name of any person, place or thing, insofar as names are still discoverable, in this novel has been invented. Despite that, and despite the historicity of dates and events, all characters in this meditation upon the past are the product of a particular imagination; their resemblance and relation, therefore, to living or once living persons is to be resisted." This passage is indicative of Wiebe's attitude to storytelling or, more appropriately, to story-making. As we saw in chapter

1, Wiebe considers facts to be the raw material from which he shapes his story. This concern is reflected in the epigraph printed under the title of the hardcover edition of *The Scorched-Wood People*. Although no source is given, the epigraph is in fact modelled on the last stanza of a song composed by the historical figure Pierre Falcon.[3] Ironically, Falcon's version comes to us as a translation of a written version of the oral story that Falcon is purported to have sung. Wiebe's epigraph, reprinted here, most closely resembles the version of "The Battle of Seven Oaks" (La Bataille des Sept Chênes) printed in Davis's *Poetry of the Canadian People*.

And who has made this song?
Who else but good Pierre Falcon.
He made the song and it was sung
To mark the victory we had won;
He made this song that very day,
So sing the glory of the Bois-brûlés.

As in the original (?) French text, the hearer/reader is being urged to participate. This work, then, may have the power to shape our perception of the way things were. Although – perhaps because – it is the product of a particular imagination, it can mediate between the reader and the past.

In an effort to destabilize the traditional versions of past events, the narrators of *The Scorched-Wood People* and *Les Têtes à Papineau* present *themselves*, as well as their stories, as a mixture of fictional elements and historical personages. In this way, they challenge the reality of their own existence, as well as the traditional version of the (hi)stories they retell. At the same time, and paradoxically, they stress the importance of their narratorial role and the seriousness of their textual productions. The historical and fictional worlds of the novels are inextricably bound together here. While shifting the focus in their retellings of the events of the past, the narrators of both novels self-consciously blur fiction and history in their creation of New World Myth.

The historical Pierre Falcon died in 1876, but Wiebe's Pierre Falcon is not bound by time or space as we know them. He is both in his fictional world and not in it. At one point, as participant, he is singing his "silly, ironic, ribald songs" (322); at another, as distanced observer, he is commenting upon the life of the twentieth-century Métis. Falcon breaks openly with the objective or neutral narrator convention. The articulation of his society and its leader is his poetic

– and political – function and the raison d'être of this text: "During my lifetime I was given many songs, and I have often prayed to the Good Father ... I have prayed, give me to make this song of Riel. You gave me so many songs ... Give me this song too ... I prayed for that for some years, and that song of Riel was not given me until I lay on my deathbed" (140). The repetition of the pronoun "this" suggests that the text we are reading *is* Falcon's song of Riel: with these written words, he is expressing the histories of his Métis people – even if it is done from his dwelling-place after death. The following passage, with its Romantic overtones of European feudal halls, illustrates the privileged position of the maker of this "song" as the articulating "voice" of the people:

"Grandfather, how long must one live before he can speak for the dead?"

"I am nearly old enough to sing for them," I said, and his glance leaped to mine.

"You have made a new song for us."

And I laughed aloud. To be known again, our Métis glory! All of a day's driving from White Horse Plains, and my head bulging once more with words and music and rhythm, I chuckled and laughed until they all thought I was at last truly crazy, feeling again after years all those wild sounds of frogs plains and words clashing and liberators and lords drinking their death in enormous halls that had spun in my head for half a century.

"Yes, yes. You Métis boys have given me another song." (36)

This passage has been erroneously interpreted as an indication that Riel is Falcon's grandson (Dueck, "Rudy Wiebe's Approach," 195). The term "grandfather," however, is commonly used in Canadian French to signal respect for the figure of the older person, the oral transmitter of knowledge about the past. In "Romans de la parole (et du mythe)," Laurent Mailhot remarks on the narratorial utility of the "grandfathers" that one finds in contemporary Québécois literature: "[Ils] sont moins des personnages (émouvants) que des moyens (efficaces). Plutôt que de parler d'eux, et même de les faire parler, la narration passe par eux. Ils font le pont entre l'ici-maintenant du conteur-scripteur et l'ailleurs-autrefois du mythe" (86). Wiebe's use of the bard figure as the elderly, wise, representative *voice* of a *chosen* people reflects the liberal humanist attitude toward the artist's role in "nation building." It also makes use of the notion in traditional myth criticism of the inspired artist as the holder and guardian of the tribal history and mythology. In this, it illustrates the postmodern tension in New World Myth novels: even while Falcon is striving in every way to establish the collective myth of the Métis New Nation, the metacommentary of the novel is rewriting Canadian history and commenting upon the past and present-day fragmentation of the country.

Falcon's supernatural qualities, such as his retrospective powers of clairvoyance, induce incredulity in the twentieth-century reader. Thus, the fact that the historical Falcon died nine years before the events described at the end of *The Scorched-Wood People* has been interpreted as an "unnecessary implausibility" by George Woodcock ("Prairie Writers," 14). However, Wiebe's portrayal of Falcon as an improbable grandfather-figure permits this Métis songwriter to introduce New World Myth tension through his histories of the past. It is through his particular brand of narration – a chatty, informal address – that Falcon conveys his own special qualities to the listener/reader. After the battle at Fish Creek, Riel tries to comfort his people. Witness Falcon's subtle intimation of his own powers to inspire the Métis leader: "he [Riel] needed Will Jaxon, broken and crying in a small room; he needed Louis Schmidt ... he needed Father Ritchot; he needed the songs of – dearest God how? – but the words came to him then; he could continue, for the light of his vision shone like a single fire blazing in a night storm" (273). Elsewhere in the text, Falcon tells us how in later years, Gabriel Dumont, reflecting on the Métis' final defeat, reproaches himself for his lack of understanding when the horses bringing Riel back from Montana balked at crossing the railroad. And in the following passage, Falcon promotes his own "understanding" as being somehow beyond this world: "Why had he [Gabriel] not then understood that moment as premonition? I might have told him, but the sometime clairvoyance of the aged usually comes when it is of no earthly use to anyone, especially those still able to do things beyond understanding. In my lifetime I thought about 'understanding' a great deal, about 'moments' that are telling you the essence of things: I had a little longer than Gabriel to do so" (194).

Falcon is conscious of the fact that his articulation of the way things were is a strain on credibility. "Quoting" Riel directly, he says: "I must leave [Riel's] words to stand in all their unmemorable bareness: their unearthly power will have to be seen in the effect they had ... And most of all, I suppose, in their impossibility" (141). Despite his awareness of the effect his version of past events may have upon his audience, Falcon is primarily concerned with explicating the Métis' worldview to those outside the Métis' universe. If the world of the Métis is a closed circle, then Falcon's role as narrator may be illustrated diagrammatically by placing him on the circumference. As Métis, he can move within the circle; as narrator-with-a-mission, he can reach outside the circle by means of this written text and explain the Métis to the non-Métis. His repeated efforts to explain the religious cosmological concepts of the Métis underline the fact that he is addressing himself to the uninitiated, as Métis do not need to explain their commonly held worldview to each other. Near the end of the novel, while discussing the political and religious crises of his people, Falcon sends a message to the reader about this text: "The word and understanding is very near you: you need no revelation from beyond the grave; as our Jesus said when he was on earth, if you will not believe what is already discernible on earth, then neither will you believe that which comes extraordinarily from beyond" (284). Falcon, the narrator of this text and the singing poet of the Métis, is "from beyond the grave" but his words are, indeed, "near" us. This narrator solicits our recreation of the historical past.

Many critical studies of *The Scorched-Wood People* assume that Wiebe uses Falcon mainly as a mouthpiece for his own spiritual convictions. Thus, Woodcock insists that "Wiebe was writing a religious and not a political novel," and that the Métis in this work are "used to illustrate a religious theme" ("Prairie Writers," 15); while W.J. Keith suggests that in this novel there is a "coalescing of the viewpoints of author, narrator and protagonist" (*Epic Fiction*, 102). Wiebe's deliberate problematization of the narrative, however, also allows for a problematization of the narrator. The style of Falcon's "song" is complex and polyphonic and consists of many layers of embedded narrative. As Penny van Toorn writes, "*The Scorched-Wood People* consists of Wiebe's authorial utterance, which allegedly consists of Falcon's narration, which in turn contains the utterances of all the other characters including Riel, whose voice dominates the text and contains the utterances of numerous other characters. By using Pierre Falcon as narrator ... Wiebe turns the dialogue between the author and the characters into a multi-tiered structure" (*Rudy Wiebe*, 143). Van Toorn makes use of Bakhtinian theories of monologic, dialogic, and polyphonic narrative forms to illustrate the complexity of Wiebe's narrative technique: "Analysis of the text reveals a degree of internal dialogization unparalleled in any of Wiebe's other works, a shifting, labyrinthine pattern of refraction of the authorial voice" (158). Falcon, as narrator, frames the stories, but the text's polyphonic sentences, which frequently conflate several characters' contradictory words and differing attitudes, create a counterforce that dialogues with Falcon's narratorial voice. As van Toorn notes, Wiebe sometimes "allows voices which play a minor compositional role in the text to rise above their official station and address readers more directly ... In short, the text re-enacts the political struggle it depicts: rebellion erupts in the text as in the historical North West" (150).

The situation in *Les Têtes à Papineau* is somewhat different, although Charles and François pose a similar narratorial problem: *who* is doing the narrating? The first word of the text, *nous*, suggests that this diary will be a harmonious coproduction, as does the heads' stated intention to produce a "récit bi-graphique" (28). However, as early as the fifth paragraph of the novel, the *nous* breaks down and a third-person narration is added. Although the *nous* remains the main narratorial voice, this breakdown occurs frequently; as a result, the heads are perceived as being different persons. The narrators' statements and attitude imply that their coexistence is rooted in reality, but even their father, Alain-Auguste, who is partly responsible for their creation, underlines the particularity of this coexistence in an article he writes for *La Presse*, the newspaper that employs him. The title of his article, "Faits divers ou fait divin?" (46), at first ironically undercuts the importance of Charles-François' birth: a *fait divers* is an unimportant piece of news. If the birth is a *fait divin*, however, it will give a quasi-religious status to the self-important Alain-Auguste, putting him "dans la foulée d'Abraham et de Jacob, serviteurs du Très-Haut" (47). This passage is an example of the frequent use made of religious discourse by the narrators of this novel. Their parodic references to the practices of the Catholic Church would be immediately recognized by most Québécois born before 1960, whose education at home, at school, and in church was dominated by religious themes. Charles and François take this common background of their readers for granted. Colloquial Québécois language has a strong religious vocabulary, and the ironic undertones of the heads' discourse permits their text to parody the traditional religious belief system of the perhaps more traditional Québécois. The father's uncertainty about his offspring is also reflected at a purely grammatical level: should he write *nouveau-né* or *nouveau-nés*? (47). The relationship between Charles and François is problematic and, as we shall see, their story is affected by the stresses inherent in being a "Bicéphale ambigu" (130). The political implications of this cohabitation are highlighted in the narrator's hyphenated name: "Charles-François" strongly evokes *canadien-français*. The *nous* designates not only the "personnages-narrateurs," but also "toute la collectivité québécoise" (Piette, 122). François appears to represent the traditional group that looks nostalgically toward the past; Charles is oriented toward the future. Throughout the novel, Godbout demonstrates his awareness of the changing socioeconomic scene in 1980: Charles is the embodiment of the typical Québécois businessman – the *p.d.g.* (CEO) of a *P.M.E.* (small and medium-sized businesses) – whose existence was beginning to be recognized outside Quebec in the 1980s.[4] Charles and François have different reactions to history: François "se sent comme un bien national, un morceau du patrimoine" (113), but Charles "ne croi[t] pas aux traces" (22). He feels that "nous avons payé assez cher ... notre filiation aux Papineau" (22). By exploring and questioning the premise of an existing world of history and by illustrating two different reactions to the past and its effect on the present, this novel underlines the incompleteness of knowledge of the past, while preparing the way for its narrators to function as myth-*makers*.

The heads discuss their relationship as coauthors in the fourth chapter. Charles proposes that each write his separate version of the adventure; otherwise, the reader will never know who they truly are. It is eventually decided that the primary function of the text is to communicate their evolution to each other. If the world of the text is again a closed circle, then the narrative role of the heads may be illustrated by placing them within the circumference. Readers may observe the inside communication from outside the circle by reading this text, but the purpose of this "récit bi-graphique" (28) is basically an explanation of themselves to themselves. As François says, "L'essentiel, crois-moi, c'est d'être confrontés dans la même phrase jusqu'à la phase finale" (64). This text is an internal discourse. Charles and François, while aware of the reader outside the closed circle of their text, do not facilitate this reader's comprehension of their discourse. They introduce themselves only after five pages of text. They can, and do, keep parts of their communication from the reader: "Nous avons convenu de ne pas transcrire ici le jeu de mots qui vient de traverser l'esprit de François" (37). By adopting a seemingly superficial attitude to life, to politics, and to the upcoming operation, and by refusing to reveal to their readers their individual identities, Charles and François, as narrators, are as improbable as Pierre Falcon, who speaks to the reader from beyond the grave.

Near the end of Godbout's novel, however, is a passage that echoes Falcon's message to the reader about understanding the text: "Mais les gens croyaient que [Charles] blaguait. Les gens s'imaginent *toujours* que nous blaguons. Parce que nous avons deux têtes, parce que nous utilisons deux discours; ils croient que nous jouons avec les mots pour des effets de langue. Comment pourraient-ils prendre un monstre au sérieux? Quand sauront-ils que nous disons *toujours* la vérité? Quand il sera trop tard?" (138). This is an invitation – almost a plea – to take the narrators seriously. The constant fluctuation between playfulness and seriousness in *Les Têtes* is comparable to Pierre Falcon's passage through different time frames, coupled with his personal style of recounting past events. The narrators of both novels deliberately focus on the process of storytelling *and* on the fact that they are subverting the reality of their own narratorial existence. Falcon installs narratorial tension by underlining his fictional *and* historical nature. Charles and François install a similar tension through their play with their existence as "real live persons" and as allegorical, if ironic, representations of the Québécois collectivity. The reader is openly reminded that both the narrators and their texts have a provisional existence. In these works, historical and narratorial instability reigns.

Pierre Falcon, the narrator of *The Scorched-Wood People*, establishes himself and his stories as being partly rooted in what Linda Hutcheon calls "'real' historical and political realities" ("Challenging the Conventions of Realism," 36) and partly rooted in the order of the "non-real." He also destabilizes the notion of historiography as he addresses a recurrent theme of New World Myth: a strong dissatisfaction with the supposedly authentic *written* documents of history as a means of communicating knowledge of the past. Dissatisfaction with written language is, of course, not specific to New World Myth. In his discussion of "the postmodern order of not always fictional fiction," Allen Thiher has suggested that this type of fiction "aims at probing how one can refer beyond language and appropriate an order of the real that may or may not be linguistic" (*Words in Reflection*, 190). Thiher goes further, however, and posits a European, postmodern "ahistorical vision of history" (197). The New World Myth texts discussed here, however, do not reflect an *ahistorical* approach.

Summing up what might be considered a traditional attitude to written records, Thiher writes, "For history, for a record of the real, the basic form of articulation should be writing, the trace that, if it could perdure, would be the foundation of the lasting memory" (208). However, in his discussion of Latin American – that is to say, New World – writers, Thiher does note that they suffer "perhaps more acutely than others from the feeling that history cannot be written" (205). Thiher's "others" refers to European writers such as Günter Grass. He remarks that, in Gabriel García Márquez's *One Hundred Years of Solitude*, "books come apart, lose their pages, and disintegrate" (208). It is Pilar Tenera, the only character to survive from the beginning until the end of the novel, who retains memory – tribal memory, mythic memory, that moves backward and forward in time. In *The Scorched-Wood People*, Pierre Falcon, the grandfather, assumes a similar role as the self-appointed memory-bank of the

Métis. However, the particular postcolonial situation of English (and French) Canada is evident here. Unlike Tenera, who must read "the past in cards as she had read the future before" (Márquez, *One Hundred Years of Solitude*, 53), this settler colony has "authentically certifiable" historical documents – such as the historical Riel's memoirs – at its disposal. As W.J. Keith points out, Wiebe uses these documents to form part of the structure of his story (*Epic Fiction*, 85–91). Paradoxically, Falcon, that Métis storyteller, displays an aversion to reading and writing as means of acquiring and preserving knowledge. His bias against written words is evident at the beginning of the novel, which describes a confrontation between representatives of the Métis and representatives of the Canadian government. Neither group can establish control of the Northwest by means of the written word: "[Governor] McDougall ... clutching that paper which would prove everything and [the Métis secretary] Schmidt, not seeing him, of course, clutching his paper and already reading into the wind the words he had carried seventy winter miles from Fort Garry ... But McDougall, like any paper man, hadn't heard a word; he was too busy thinking about his own words pondered so long, written so carefully" (16). In Falcon's worldview, spoken words and direct actions carry far more authority than any words that are written, and in this initial conflict Gabriel's *actions* eventually triumph over the paper men's useless written words when he throws the governor's driver into the snow and has his men scoop McDougall up between their horses and take him for a ride (13–19).

Wiebe's novel sets up a tension between the written and the spoken word by dwelling on the differences between Riel and Falcon with regard to writing, speaking, singing, and permanence. The text itself self-consciously points to its own existence as a fictional construct by the intermingling of "song" and "[written] word." The Métis poet's *songs* articulated the power of his people, but in this novel, his singing voice has become a written text. With this textual product Falcon does what Riel had hoped to do with his writings, that is to say, give a voice to the Métis people. Falcon, however, is wary of written words. For Riel, "the words [wrote] themselves" (171), and he used them "to give his unwritten people a place on paper before the frozen earth closed them away one by one and no one would hear them" (245). But for Falcon, these words of Riel are "words to be used against him [Riel], for every written word called to judgement" (245). Falcon had wanted to shape the Métis' vision into song while still on earth, because a written text, for him, is frustratingly insufficient when compared to song. Song moves people, as is evidenced by Gabriel's emotional and physical reactions to

Falcon's "Sad Ballad of King Muck": "And with one surge of his immense body he hurled the chair high above the fire. Down it crashed ... and the sound torn from all of us then was the joyous scream of a woman, rapture and agony, delivered at last" (41-2). Falcon, then, would rather that we heard his song, as he is not at all sure of his control over potentially dangerous written words: "The letter was lying there, and letters are dangerous ... The words crouch black on pale paper, unchangeable and deadly" (170). Falcon here expresses a frustration common to many metafictional writers: written words are fixed, rigid, and limited in their ability to fully communicate anything to the reader. Falcon underlines his knowledge of the limitations of the written textual product by contrasting voice and song with written word and paper and by using imagery that recalls the act of writing. By means of the written word – and in spite of it – he transmits his dissatisfaction with writing while admitting to his need of it in order to communicate the story of his people.

As Fredric Jameson points out in his foreword to Lyotard's *The Postmodern Condition*, "it is obvious that one of the features that characterizes more 'scientific' periods of history ... is the relative retreat of the claims of narrative or storytelling knowledge in the face of those of the abstract, denotative, or logical and cognitive procedures generally associated with science or positivism" (xi). If, however, there is now a marked return to an emphasis on storytelling in postcolonial literatures, as is evidenced by the narrator of Wiebe's historiographic novel, then it perhaps follows that the scientific method of apprehending the past might be insufficient to his needs. And indeed, there is an implied disrespect for and wariness of institutions of learning and formal knowledge in Pierre Falcon's worldview: he prefers direct action and storytelling to "paper men." Falcon accords little value to book-learning; at the end of a story he has just *told*, he says sarcastically, "when Charles Boulton was nearly a Manitoba senator he told this story in a book where it can be read for all time" (78). Hutcheon has pointed out a similar tension between oral and written modes of communication in Wiebe's *Temptations of Big Bear*: "while Wiebe is obviously and seriously exploring the oral/written dialectic, he cannot escape one final, anti-McLuhanesque irony, and he knows it ... Big Bear's dynamic oral presence can only be conveyed to us in static print; the oratorical power that goes beyond words can only be recounted in words; and perhaps, the truth of historical fact can only be presented in novelistic fiction" ("The 'Postmodernist' Scribe," 292).

In contrast to Falcon, the Riel of *The Scorched-Wood People* feels the need of factual knowledge and learning: he yearns for the qualities inherent in a liberal-humanist worldview. In the Parliamentary Library, Riel's "perception flipped as if a fever had galloped through him; he was surrounded by books, the thoughts of all the wisest men who had ever lived, the poets and popes and philosophers and giants of men, if he could only stay here ... he would cram this beautiful room full to its top with the white living beauty of magnificent thoughts and create a country men would sing forever of its freedom and love, and knowledge" (134). Significantly, in the paragraphs following this passage, Falcon ironically recounts Riel's expulsion in absentia from the House of Commons and his necessary exile to the "small safety of a room" across the river in Hull. The knowledge contained in the sacrosanct library, where the "greatest men of history stood around him like sentinels" (135) is thus forever denied to him. In the same passage, Falcon denigrates the "great figures" imposed upon our history by European standards. Thus, Riel, left alone in the Parliamentary Library in Ottawa, is overwhelmed by the world of beautiful architecture and of books. His soul is torn, however, because this perfect place is the domain of that stone woman, Victoria. Adrift, Riel loses his sense of direction: "He stared up; the world turned like roaring in his head and he might have been staring down into some perfection, into a stone-polished symmetry that horrified him as nothing he had ever felt before. He reached down – up – he could barely touch the irrevocable ordered marble of her name: cold like rot in his nostrils" (134). In his thirst for knowledge, Riel is caught between his revulsion for the colonial powers of the "centre" – here symbolized by that statue of Victoria – and his liberal-humanist respect for booklearning. It is easier for Falcon, however, who is impressed by Riel's supernatural access to knowledge of "a new world under the subterranean breath of God" (20) but not by his knowledge of the legalese of Ottawa. In the following passage, Falcon's choice of vocabulary accords significance to the supernatural Riel. In a trance-like state, Riel "sees" the unknowable: "the knowledge of looking into water, once learned, cannot be removed by silvered glass. It is like the knowledge of looking behind your own eyelids, at the aura which flames at the surface of your own perfect purple sun. If you have one" (20). Knowledge, then, for this New World Myth narrator, is other than that contained in written texts. Necessarily partial knowledge of the historico-political past may be obtained, suggests the *narrator* of this admittedly written text, by listening to the singing of the song.

Pierre Falcon flaunts his text as an historical construct. He occasionally interrupts his own narrative to refer to the historiographic act: "I know of no historian who has commented on this to say the least strange legal distinction that the men who shot and killed Canadian soldiers only *intended* to wage war, while Riel ... had actually waged war" (316–17). Comments of this sort point out Falcon's knowledge of other historical interpretations of the Riel rebellions. They also stress that his Métis worldview differs from the traditional view of history. In fact, this text, like Godbout's work, is overtly political. For Elizabeth Waterston, the confrontation described in *The Scorched-Wood People* is a prism that catches "recent intensely troubling conflicts: French-English, white-Indian, centrist-hinterland, pragmatic-idealist, aesthetic-technological. Wiebe ... provides in *The Scorched-Wood People* release, sublimation, and perspective on more recent disharmony – his own, and Canada's" ("Disunity Remembered," 103). Waterston notes the importance of the choice of Falcon as narrator, a choice that allows Wiebe "to transmit in native terms the story of the insurgence against white repression." Unlike Falcon, Waterston here conflates "native" and "Indian" with "Métis." She sees Wiebe's choice of narrator as representative of a deep disunity – "in the political history of the country, in the events of the 1970s, and in the psychological development of the author" (104).

Eli Mandel, discussing the use of history, myth, and voice in *Big Bear*, states that no "other writer of white culture has come as close as Wiebe to the culture he writes of" and that Maria Campbell, herself a Métis writer, had told Wiebe that when he wrote that novel, the spirit of Big Bear was speaking for him (Mandel, "Imagining Natives," 45). In a subsequent interview with scholars in Baroda and Delhi, India, Wiebe was asked if he had not been part of the culture that did injustice to the Indians. His response drew on his experience as a Mennonite immigrant who spoke no English until he went to school, and he claimed that people of "English culture" treated Low German-speaking Mennonites and nonwhites in similar ways: "that imperial world, which is part of the expression of Canadian suppression of Native Indians and taking over their land, to me is just as strange and just as repulsive now as it is to a Native Indian. So I'm equipped, I think, to perceive the problems in that imperial world and how it considers someone from a different culture" (Juneja et al., "Looking at Our Particular World," 9).

Wiebe, like many New World Myth writers, draws on the heterogeneous elements of his own cultural experience to open up textual space in which to explore various manifestations of differing cultural representations. Significantly, in the interview the discussion turned to Third World writers and to the interviewers' thesis that Wiebe's work bears striking similarities to the Third World novel, which has "community" as its central character. One interviewer proposed that in the Third World novel "there is a shift in form itself from the individual consciousness to the consciousness of the community. This has been happening primarily in the Third World, but definitely there are writers like you [Wiebe] within the white situation also" (10). Wiebe replied: "A clash of communities, of worldviews, more than character. Well, I find that very interesting because I don't think that that kind of criticism is being written in North America" (10). Although New World Myth does not set out to totally replace the individual with "community," there is no doubt that its investigation of the interaction of different worldviews and its problematization of the notion itself is indicative of its postcolonial slant.

Postcolonial societies also have "their own internal centres and peripheries, their own dominants and marginals," as Arun Mukherjee has noted ("Whose Post-Colonialism?" 6). Sam Solecki characterizes the tensions that consequently arise in Wiebe's work in Sartrian terms as "contestational"; when Wiebe "writes about western life and history from a western point of view his fiction stands in opposition to the homogeneous view of Canadian experience whose geographical centre is Ontario and whose ideological origins are in the Laurentian thesis and 'national' history; as a Mennonite who happens to be a western writer his novels stand in opposition to a secular and capitalist worldview whose centre is everywhere – Edmonton as well as Toronto" ("Giant Fictions and Large Meanings," 5). Pierre Falcon presents a decided bias against central Canada in his anachronistic retelling of Western history: "Out of the total bankruptcy, again, which President George Stephen wrote Macdonald about on March 26, 1885, the Canadian Pacific Railway exploded from the so-called Second Riel Rebellion to rival the Hudson's Bay Company itself as the most powerful business empire in Canada; one of the most perfect monopolies on earth. I have often felt the CPR might at least have named a hotel after Riel" (*The Scorched-Wood People*, 247). Falcon implies that different "true stories" are made by different narrators. Furthermore, the presentation of the "end" of the story – the hanging of Riel – in the first paragraph of the novel subverts regular historiographic and novelistic processes, both of which tend to explain events in chronological order and lead up to a climactic ending. The frequent use of flash-forwards has the same effect. By not giving the sources for the documents he uses, by treating them as just another aid in the storytelling process, the narrator subverts the concept of linear historiography and story, and makes the reader aware that *his* version of the past is being constructed.

Along with his deliberate blurring of history and fiction, Falcon further prepares his position as myth-*maker* by challenging the traditional respect for historical figures of the past. Thus, in *The Scorched-Wood People*, Prime Minister John A. MacDonald is a scheming hypocrite and the Mounties hardly ever get their man. And though Falcon says he cannot sing of the "machinations of eastern politicians" (328), the following passage certainly retells events in a nontraditional light: "no Opposition would now dare vote against the last gigantic loan which could complete the financing of the Canadian Pacific Railway for the massive benefit of Canada from Sea to Sea and, quite incidentally, for the benefit of CPR shareholders. Riel had created the catastrophe, an outbreak worthy for Conservative purposes of elevation to rebellion, as the Prime Minister would explain carefully to the Governor-General as soon as the fighting was over" (247). While ridiculing the "great figures" of Canadian history, Falcon also indicates that he is self-consciously constructing an alternative historical world. His demolition of the reputations of MacDonald, Cartier, and the Mounties creates a vacuum that permits him to propose a new historical and mythological perspective on the story he is retelling. As we shall soon see, Falcon's exploration of New World Myth centres on the person of Louis Riel.

In *The Scorched-Wood People*, the theme of the difficulty of translation also insists upon the existence of this text as a construct. The Métis, as we know, spoke French: this text makes us read, in English, about their inability to speak English. This point is driven home by Michel Dumas' incomprehension when he and other Métis eavesdrop upon Colonel Wolseley's plans to attack them: "'What's that English,' Michel whispered, 'what?'" (119). The problem of translation is related to one of the major themes of the novel: the conflict produced when different linguistic and religious groups with different worldviews come into contact with one another. In this novel, Falcon's sometimes awkward use of the English language underlines, on a linguistic level, the frustrations he experiences in his efforts to explicate the Métis' worldview to outsiders. For instance, his account of the hunters' court that judges Thomas Scott points out that Scott is killed, not for political reasons, but because of the effect his blasphemy has on the Métis. Linguistic and cultural incomprehension is evident in the following passage, where Falcon, long afterwards, tries to explain the event to an English Canadian:

"It is the cursing" [Goulet] said ... "The few French words aren't so bad, but to understand English, it's so ... at home I soak my head in cold water, in snow, but the blasphemy ... "

"Shoot a man for telling you to go to hell!" MacLeod burst out.

"If you really know ... " but how do you explain the eternal annihilation of your soul to someone who doesn't want to know he has one? (80)

Cross-cultural confusion, such as we see here, is frequently portrayed in New World Myth novels. By insisting on the problems of translation, the text thematizes Falcon's struggles to "translate" the history of his people. Contrary to traditional historiographic practice, this text does not seek to deny or to efface the narratorial voice: the reader is made aware that this song is *Falcon's* particular meditation upon the past.

New World Myth, having discredited the traditional respect accorded to some important political personages of the past, does not set out to install a fixed, rigid mythology in its place. The narrator of *The Scorched-Wood People* is aware of the (mainly) English Canadian historical process that initially condemned Riel as a moccasin-clad madman who deserved to hang for treason. Falcon is also aware of the (mainly) French Canadian glorification of Riel as a martyr for the French in Canada. As was noted above, this narrator's sympathies lie with a third group, the Métis. The Louis Riel (hi)story has been retold frequently in English Canadian and French Canadian/ Québécois literature, theatre, and song. Margaret Osachoff's comprehensive review of the literary manifestations of the Riel story indicates that this political figure has become part of the historico-literary landscapes of both English-speaking Canadians and Québécois. She notes the initial linguistic and religious polarization that saw Riel as hero/martyr or traitor/murderer and observes that, subsequently, writers of fiction, history, drama, or poetry "often used Riel as a vehicle for their own ideas about Canadian politics and culture" ("Louis Riel," 61). Wiebe's novel uses these contradictory attitudes to the Louis Riel (hi)story to its advantage, using them to underline the postmodern fragmentation of history.

Another narratorial concern in this novel is the postcolonial desire to change the site of the "centre." Here, the happenings of the New World are no longer seen to be on the periphery of the Old (Euro-centred) World, but become, through the narrators' version of events, the central subject of concern. An example of this shift of focus is found in the following passage, where, in his somewhat peculiar storytelling mode, Pierre Falcon underlines the New World focus of Riel's protestations to Bishop Taché: "Asking, when he [Riel] came to see him at last, 'What does the Holy Father say to us?' and, 'What is the point of being "Holy Father" if he does not know us? He sounds like "The Great Mother" in England. Who needs all this greatness, this holiness far away and ignorant across oceans? We are ourselves, people living here'" (105). This one passage expresses a general desire of the narrators of all the New World Myth texts examined in this study. Through their stories, the narrators reexamine historico-political events of the past(s) of the "people living here" from a New World point of view. Of course, that shifting centre is also the centrifugal federal government of the late 1970s – nationalist tensions are a component of English Canadian and Québécois post-colonial texts.

In *The Scorched-Wood People*, the narrator's creation of New World Myth makes extended use of the Bible, and in particular of the Christ-figure, in its mythologization of the historical personage of Louis Riel. Biblical mythology is frequently used in the production of New World Myth. By parodying the known biblical stories, New World Myth narrators can often lay bare an unquestioning and unacknowledged attitude toward biblical "truths" adopted by those English-speaking Canadians and Québécois raised within the framework of Christian belief systems. Such an attitude underlies much of Northrop Frye's work: he argues that the "mythology that has been decisive for the cultural tradition which we ourselves inherited is the Biblical one" ("Myth as the Matrix," 474). Although I have no quarrel with Frye's argument about the influence of biblical mythology on English Canadian and Québécois literatures, I suspect that the first-person pronouns in the preceding quotation – "we ourselves" – most probably were not meant to represent the First Nations peoples or the Métis.

The narrator of *The Scorched-Wood People*, by contrast, makes his reader/listener aware of the need for a flexible approach to various "cultural traditions." For instance, differences of race and religion divide human beings into several groups in this novel: the Cree Indians, the English half-breeds, the French Métis, the Catholic priests and nuns, the Protestant whites from Ontario, the law-enforcing RCMP, the politicians from Ottawa, and those from Quebec. Each group has a different worldview, and Falcon's disjointed narrative style portrays the confusing culture clashes among them. For instance, the Métis sometimes mix the religious practices of their various heritages. A striking example is Falcon's story of the buffalo hunt of 1852, where the Métis have been surrounded by the Sioux and are dying of thirst on the blazing plain. Catholic and Amerindian worldviews are both represented here. The Métis pray to God for rain; their Catholic priest marches around their circle holding a cross and chanting in Latin; the Sioux then flee before the Black Spirit-maker, just as a dark cloud of the Thunderbird comes over, blessing them with Saint Joseph's rain. Falcon's portrayal of cross-cultural confusion in this passage is characteristic of New World Myth texts, whose narrators struggle against the Eurocentric, liberal-humanist bias evident in many English Canadian and Québécois essays on "our" cultural traditions.

The tensions inherent in New World Myth novels are manifest in the fact that the narrator of *The Scorched-Wood People* is a self-proclaimed practising Catholic. Pierre Falcon's use of the biblical stories in his development of the myths of Riel and the Métis is not overtly parodic, as is the case in many other New World Myth narratives. In this story, Falcon makes the reader/listener aware of the "supernatural" qualities of Riel by having recourse to biblical stories that he knows and respects. This is not to say that the *author* of the novel, Rudy Wiebe, is unaware of the possibilities for parody and irony in the retelling of various religious rites. Here again, one finds the tensions inherent in the struggle to get out from under the dominant myths of the liberal-humanist Christian worldview. Wiebe, who has frequently reflected on his upbringing in the Mennonite tradition, *uses* biblical myths to construct the story of the Métis. However, given the political nature of the metacommentary on the past and on the present in the novel, the use of biblical mythology here can be problematic. Whereas, traditionally, the Christian worldview strives for hegemony in a hierarchical situation, the revision of history and contemporary politics in this novel searches out the opposite effect. The tension between Falcon's straightforward use of the Catholic tradition in his myth-making and Wiebe's ironic revision of traditional interpretations of Canadian history through Falcon's story remains unresolved.

Falcon constantly draws parallels between the Métis and the Israelites and between Riel and Jesus Christ. Riel, in his youth, was to have become a priest, but he has an uneasy relationship with the organized Church. As a submissive student in a grey Montreal seminary, he never knows the correct behaviour and must "hold tight an uncommitted face while juggling off-balance in a world that would never be his" (*The Scorched-Wood People*, 80). His submission to the priests disappears when he becomes the leader of his people, faced with the task of giving them a world that would be theirs. For he believes that he has a "great mission to fulfil" (223): he is the appointed leader of God's Chosen People and must lead them to the "outstretched arms of God ready to raise them into a new paradise of belief untouchable by earth's mud and horrors" (274). While denying a role to the organized Church in the religious education of the Métis, Riel draws on its sources for inspiration. Biblical imagery dominates the parts of the novel that concentrate on the formation of the New Nation. For instance, the Métis are innocents: the death of the innocent Young Bertie at the beginning of the novel parallels the immolation of the sacrificial lamb: "Riel watched him go [to his death], the halo of his call circling him like snow" (37).

Falcon's most striking use of biblical imagery in the novel is found in his identification of Riel with biblical figures. When Riel goes from Montana to Saskatchewan, he must cross the railroad. His son and the burden of his mission weigh him down, as the Christ-child was a weight for St Christopher: "Tired soon, the boy rode his father's shoulders ... the immensity of carving out and tying down this long double steel rested like rocks on Riel's shoulders ... he felt so gaspingly small; it was impossible to walk ... Especially carrying a child" (*The Scorched-Wood People*, 193). Sara Riel names her brother "David" after the singer-king. Like David, Riel is a leader and a poet; in his visions, God tells him: "You are the David of Christian times" (161–2). Like the dancing David, he sings the psalms and feels "the glory of God over his naked body" (163); he knows himself to be a "white naked flame" (162) in the gloom. Riel believes that the time has come for a new religion in the West: "The lights of civilization move through the ages from the east to the west: man born on the banks of the Euphrates, Christ in Palestine, the Papacy established for a time in Rome. A new order is coming" (165). Falcon also identifies Riel with Moses (140). Riel, as leader of his people, must receive the Word as Moses received the tablets, and lead his people out of bondage into the chosen land of God. Even the Montana countryside is used to portray Riel as the founder of a new seven-hilled Rome: "The knobby hills, like seven sentinels marching to the mountains, were dappled with the May snow, but the evening sunlight came in ... washed the room all over as with gold" (170).

Falcon confers special significance on Riel by associating him with Christ. The narrator insists upon Riel's "beginningless and endless immortality" (96). He can move out of time and out of body into his vision-world. The pastor/flock imagery is strong throughout the novel; little children come unto him, following him while he wanders the hillsides or goes to prayer. Like Christ, he has a Mary and a Martha: Marguerite, who "always accept[s] perfectly, without question, everything he [tells] her" (171), and Madeleine, who questions him in fear and anger but who eventually feels that "she [is] part of him, this hard, solid rock" (268). Two passages in particular strongly convey the Riel/Christ metaphor: the baptism of Will Jackson and the scene of the sacramental meal. Minutes after Riel proclaims the Provisional Government of the Northwest, he baptises Will Jackson as Henri Joseph Jaxon, new Son of the New Nation. Falcon puts himself in Jaxon's place, "seeing that hand, that ecstatic face, reach for me in welcome. One revelation. I must count Henri Joseph Jaxon happy" (225). During the sacramental meal, Riel asks God's blessing on the bannock (which, like the Catholic host, is unleavened bread) and milk that he and his men eat after they have proclaimed the Provisional Government and declared Riel to be a prophet; the men feel that this is "beyond comprehension, revelation!" (251).

This recreation of the scene of the Last Supper confers significance on Riel, giving him a larger-than-life stature in Falcon's story. The narrator's desire to confer mythical status on Riel is also apparent in his use of supposedly timeless biblical stories: by blurring the boundaries between the biblical and the historical stories, Falcon strives to annihilate the difference between Christ's time and Riel's time. In the same way, Falcon's "song" of Riel's passage through time gives a mythic dimension to *his* story, striving to annihilate the distinction between the historical past and the present of this text. The text itself, however, underlines the ongoing political and historical tensions in present-day Western Canada. Dennis Duffy's reading of *The Scorched-Wood People* argues that Wiebe seeks to replicate the scriptural project: "Wiebe is stating in effect that a new Bible can be written about things here, in Canada, in a time past when the fate of the world centred upon the doings of our own peoples. Readers may not wish to walk all the way with an author on a journey of that scope, but no reader can deny that he is in the presence of extraordinary narrative indeed. Some primal act recalling the foundations of narrative in our culture is occurring here" (Duffy, "Wiebe's Real Riel?" 205). Narrative, myth, history, and place are all conflated in Wiebe's text.

In many mythologies, the image of the circle is representative of unity, eternity, repetition: the *éternel retour* of Mircea Eliade. Although the narrative of *The Scorched-Wood People* is mainly linear, the novel does have a cyclical structure. Echoing the first sentence of García Márquez' *One Hundred Years of Solitude* ("Many years later, as he faced the firing squad, Colonel Aureliano Buendia was to remember that distant afternoon when his father took him to discover ice" [11]), the first paragraph of Wiebe's novel deals with the final moments of Riel's life on earth: "Sixteen years later Louis Riel would be dressing himself again, just as carefully" (*The Scorched-Wood People*, 10). This same episode is described in practically the same terms near the end of the novel. That Riel's life on earth was part of a mythical, cyclical pattern of events is summed up in Gabriel's statement at the end of the novel, in his conversation with a former Mounted Police officer: "You think like a white ... You can't help it, that's okay, but you think Riel is finished? He said a hundred years is just a spoke in the wheel of eternity. We'll remember. A hundred years and whites still won't know what to do with him" (351). Past and present are narratively linked in the preceding passage, as they are in many New World Myth works. The song of the Métis poet, that is to say, the text of the present novel, is being "sung" to give voice to the myth of Louis Riel.

The leader of the Métis is always at the centre of the circle of his people. The god-like subject of the centripetal gaze of his people, Riel controls all action from the centre of his "court," Fort Garry. The image of the circle underlines two aspects of this novel: the centrality of Riel in the saga of the Métis nation and the symbolic linking of this saga to eternity. The irony, of course, is that the Métis "nation" was not eternal. In Riel's vision, he hears himself say the following words, although he does not understand them: "My nation holds my life ... my nation has no other life than mine. A hundred years is but a spoke in the wheel of eternity, a hundred years, a hundred" (*The Scorched-Wood People*, 301). After the death sentence has been passed on him, Riel begins to comprehend; his mission, he says, is to bring about practical results, "and even if it takes two hundred years to achieve it, what does that matter? God's time is not ours" (326). His own and Gabriel's previously quoted remarks link Riel to the wheel of eternity. Riel must hang to be a saint; in dying he gives life to the story of his people. Riel's last sight before his death is "the immense circle of prairie" (345); he is one with this world. The cyclical structure of the novel ties this Christ-like sacrifice to eternity. Falcon produces a revolutionary view of history by drawing parallels between Louis Riel and Jesus Christ and other biblical figures. And yet, as Osachoff points out, in this novel "Wiebe has changed Riel from French-Catholic traitor/martyr into Western Canadian hero; he becomes a symbol of all the injustices that all Western Canadians, and not only the Métis, have suffered at the hands of Central Canada and of a federal government which always favours what we in the West call 'the East'" ("Louis Riel," 69). The tension in New World Myth between past and present, then, is foregrounded in this novel's use of biblical imagery in its retelling of the historical past.

Even though the narrator of *The Scorched-Wood People* draws most heavily on the biblical frame of reference, Falcon also uses other mythical elements to confer significance on Riel and his New Nation. He does this by exploiting various elements of pagan imagery – such as that of the dying god, whose death and rebirth are associated with the cycle of nature. As Northrop Frye points out with reference to Frazer's *Golden Bough*, the dying god is often associated with the colour purple, with the sun, with cannibalism, and with the notion of the scapegoat (*Anatomy*, 141–62). In Wiebe's novel, the royal colour purple is frequently associated with Riel. Falcon's narration deliberately draws attention to this imagery when, upon Riel's triumphant return to the Northwest, a young Métis woman presents him with "an immense saskatoon bough clustered thick with purple – royal indeed he was laughing! – berries" (*The Scorched-Wood People*, 191). Riel is also associated with the sun, and sometimes the two images blend, as in the previously quoted sentence about his visions: "It is like ... looking behind your own eyelids, at the aura which flames at the surface of your own perfect purple sun" (20). Images of nature and of cannibalism are present at Riel's death. He sees the kingdoms of the world at his feet, and yet, at the end of the rope, he is one with this world: his feet brush the dead prairie grass. By the time Sheriff Chapleau gets Riel's body, bits of its clothing, beard, hair, and even eyebrows have been cut off. The "god" has died, and his people take parts of his body away with them.

Sara refers overtly to Riel as a scapegoat who carries the sins of his people. It has been suggested that Riel is not a true scapegoat, because "by a tragic irony Riel's death coincides with that of his nation instead of being a surrogate for it" (Keith, *Epic Fiction*, 95). Gabriel, however, does not feel this way. He knows, as Riel knew, that Riel had to die; it was necessary for his body to be at the end of that rope so to "prove forever how Canada destroyed [the Métis]" (*The Scorched-Wood People*, 351). Falcon, of course, by retelling the story from the Métis point of view, can underline other political groups' lack of comprehension about the Métis while promoting *his* version of events. Thus, he reports Gabriel's conversation with a non-Métis:

"There's no white country can hold a man with a vision like Riel, with people like us who would understand it and believe it, and follow. Canada couldn't handle that, not Ontario, and not Quebec, they're just using him against the English. They all think he was cracked, mad."

"He wasn't...mad?" ...

"By the grace of God," Gabriel said, "he received the vision" ... [Gabriel] saw that poor white who had never, would never find such a man to know stare at him in consternation, and he roared with laughter as only our Gabriel could when he was completely, overwhelmingly happy. The huge bar rang. (351)

Gabriel's happiness here underlines the differences between the "white" and the Métis worldviews, and underlines the tension inherent in the various versions of the Riel (hi)story.

Although Falcon's narration concentrates on presenting the *perfection* of Riel in his god-like state, it remains true to New World Myth, and does not permit this presentation to crystallize. In other words, this narrative installs and then subverts the "godliness" of Riel. Thus, Falcon deliberately judges Riel's *lack* of political judgment: "Riel seemed to have lost his decision, another one of those strange cycles in his life which would repeat itself on the Saskatchewan fifteen years later" (*The Scorched-Wood People*, 112); "he had naïvely assumed Macdonald would pay him a salary for administering Red River" (124). Elsewhere in the text, Falcon intimates that Riel's relationship with his sister Sara borders on the incestuous; as a boy, he is "running in terror at what he was being made to think and at her [Sara's] white body ground down, at what his own thudded into him as he ran achingly" (176). After he makes love with his wife, Riel's thoughts turn to Sara: "I could never touch her as a man does a woman" (178). Just before his death, Riel realizes that soon, he "would look into the face of God Himself and ask him why, why, and he would touch Sara" (345).

In another destabilization of the idea of Riel's "perfection," Falcon characterizes him as a "god" of the underworld; this demonic imagery is particularly obvious in the passage describing Riel's incarceration in the Montreal insane asylum. Iron bars and steel-laced doors haunt Riel's dreams; sunshine frequently comes to him through the bars of a window. Cannibalistic imagery is rampant in this underworld. Riel, fighting physically, bites a restraining arm. Wrestled back to his room, his body convulses, tears and is torn. Elsewhere in his story, Falcon exposes the aimlessness that besets Riel. The god figure is not perfect: "'Brass,' Riel said; 'heaven is sealed over, frozen brass ... I am cut off!'" (214–15). A final aspect of this demonic imagery is that of the stake with the hooded heretic attached to it. First, Riel can see his own skull "set out of a collar at its own peculiar, dreadful angle" (21). At one point he witnesses Wolseley and his men burning his effigy after breaking its neck. And at the end of the novel he is a white-hooded figure and, figuratively, he burns: his vision blazes up before him, consuming him in "searing eternal fire" (346) as he is freed of the earth.

Falcon points out Riel's use of the Bible in the formulation of his vision. He then intimates that he himself can only "offer" Riel's words to us – that he has no other means with which to communicate his knowledge. As we have seen, however, Falcon does make extensive use of biblical imagery to partially mythologize Louis Riel and his New Nation. In this story, his use of other mythical elements such as the cyclical structure and the dying god imagery also accord significance to Riel. The use of both demystifying faults and demonic imagery, however, prevents the myth of Louis Riel from crystallizing into a fixed element in the reader's historico-mythical imagination.

In accordance with New World Myth, Falcon insists that his narration is *his* particular version of the events he is retelling. His story, like any other story of past events, is and will remain flexible, adaptable, open-ended.

The narrators of *Les Têtes à Papineau* employ some of the same narratorial techniques as those used by Pierre Falcon to explode that concept of an "objectively existing world of history" (Waugh, *Metafiction*, 6). Charles and François flaunt their disregard for formal knowledge and academic institutions; they underline the existence of themselves, their text, and their (hi)stories as constructs; and they blur the boundaries between fiction and history in their exploration of New World Myth.

The two heads share Pierre Falcon's disregard for formal and official attempts to transmit knowledge of the past. Knowledge acquired at higher institutions of learning, they imply, is outmoded, dry, distanced, and tainted by the official version of events. Thus, Charles-François: "Seul l'âge nous a empêchés d'entrer à l'université en couches. Il nous a fallu attendre notre quinzième année. Les autorités croyaient qu'un enfant dévaloriserait leur science. Charles s'est inscrit en lettres. François aux HEC. Le plus difficile fut d'harmoniser les horaires; pour le reste, ce fut comme sur une pinotte. Nous avions terminé nos thèses avant même la scolarité. Enfin. L'université est une vaste salle d'attente" (*Les Têtes à Papineau*, 105). The heads' scorn for universities as centres of learning is again evident in the following passage. Also very clear is the ubiquitous subtext of this novel – the political Referendum of 1980: "Invités en Belgique, en France, en Angleterre, dans les universités américaines et japonaises, pour y donner des conférences, nous avions développé une technique à toute épreuve: le discours dialectique ... l'un faisait les citations, l'autre le texte ... Le sujet préféré des organisateurs de colloque? L'autonomie" (109–10). By linking their own history to that of the collectivity throughout the text, the heads stress that history itself is a "personal reconstruction" and, perhaps, "the ultimate fiction we are all living" (Waugh, *Metafiction*, 107). As we shall soon see, the formerly sacrosanct notion of the Québécois collectivity is also ironically parodied in this text.

The heads' narration of their own evolution underlines the fact that history is a construct. Theirs is not presented as a chronological sequence but as a continual alternation between past and present. Personal significance is frequently given to historical dates. Thus, in this overtly political text, 1960 is important, not because it marks the beginning of the Quiet Revolution, but because it is the year in which the heads celebrated their "première et dernière communion" (*Les Têtes à Papineau*, 98). Paradoxically for the heads, writing this text is no different from constructing their history: this text *is* their history, and they are a grammatical construction within it. When Charles stops the narration to read over what has been recorded so far, the construction of this history – and by extension, any history – is laid bare. Like us, the heads exist in the present and reconstruct the past from fragments. They eventually seem to lose control over their own existence: they are told they belong to the public, to the nation, and to science. The impossibility of separating Charles' and François' private lives from their role as representatives of the evolving Canadien-français/Québécois people reflects the many-faceted approach to history and reality in this text.

Destabilizing the traditional assumption that there is one true version of events is a trait of New World Myth texts. In *Les Têtes à Papineau*, the conflicting tensions of the prereferendum period are evident in the "perpétuel tête-à-tête" of Charles-François: "De plus en plus nous nous regardons comme chiens de garde, les babines retroussées sur nos dents pointues" (15). "Jusqu'à l'année dernière nous nous accommodions assez bien de nos différences de caractère. Aujourd'hui ce n'est plus guère possible" (29). If these narrators are, as they say, ideologically separated, some conflicting aspects of their coexistence might cause the reader to be ideologically confused. For instance, the pragmatic and future-oriented Charles "s'inscrit en lettres," the former traditional ghetto for the French Canadian élite, whereas François, who *is* traditional and oriented toward the past, studies at the Hautes Etudes commerciales, a business school for the ambitious Québécois entrepreneur of today. Charles' position is on the (conservative) right of the heads' body, even though he is the progressive partner "[qui] voudrait ... n'avoir aucun passé ... [qui] désire devenir un homme neuf" (22). Neither Charles nor François, then, is a perfect stereotype of the progressive or traditional Québécois. Each character has his own internal contradictions, and the tensions in this doubly divided being reflect the prereferendum tensions of Quebec.

Puzzles are a frequent textual image in the novel, since they are the preferred pastime of Charles-François. Discussing their successful completion of a jigsaw puzzle in biblical terms – "un morceau double ... permettait enfin de réconcilier le ciel et la terre" (*Les Têtes à Papineau*, 86) – the heads philosophize on the fragility of everything: "N'était-ce pas la preuve que nous avions refait le monde? Mais aussi qu'il pouvait se défaire, à tout instant, en deux mille cinq cents morceaux?" (86). In this novel, where "[d]u coup, il n'y [a] plus d'autorité qui tienne!" (99), contradictory aspects of the heads' coexistence emphasize the contradictory attitudes of the Québécois toward the past and the future in the prereferendum year. In fact, at least one passage in the novel underlines a negative apprehension of nationalism. The heads have gone to their parents' home for dinner with the purpose of discussing Dr Northridge's proposal to amalgamate them. The parents' home, located in the "*square mile* des intellectuels" (68) in Outremont, is full of guests. When Alain Auguste understands Northridge's proposal, he proclaims with a "faux véritable accent allemand[:] Ein Kultur, ein nation, ein head, Ein Fürher! Ya?!" (69). This obvious reference to the Nazi régime and its implied criticism of nationalist fervour is immediately followed by a description of the guests' behaviour – behaviour that I remember observing frequently in the prereferendum months, when one did not always know where the political sympathies of one's fellow guests lay: "Les invités ne savaient plus s'ils devaient rire, se retirer ou participer au débat. Ils so contentèrent de faire circuler, de main à main, le plateau de fromage" (69).

The heads underline the internal contradictions of the Québécois "nation" through exposing their love-hate relationship with each other: "J'ai de plus en plus la tribu en horreur, répondit Charles. Puis il cracha au loin, de dépit, sans s'expliquer plus avant. Bicéphale ambigu" (130). "La tribu" here represents the traditional and supposedly united "peuple canadien-français" – a collectivity that has usually been perceived as agrarian, God-fearing, and submissive to secular and religious authority. Through his narrators' mockery of this outdated self-portrait, Godbout is here exploding this "traditional" self-image. And yet, elements of this portrait, as we have seen, form part of François' – and even, at times, Charles' – character.

The heads have an ambivalent relationship with the Québécois collectivity. The general public's morbid curiosity about their condition is evidenced by the line-ups at the hospital shortly after their birth. The heads detest this aspect of the Québécois: "Des milliers de *morons* unicéphales" (45). Paradoxically, the heads' very existence is inextricably tied to their "québécitude"; this same gaping public finds in them a source of pride. At the top of a photograph of Charles-François in the arms of Alain-Auguste, supposedly published in the almanac of 1956, the legend proclaims: "Impossible n'est pas canadien-français" (97). This pride, however, emanates from a distance; the average Québécois is uncomfortable in close proximity to the heads. Mothers pull their children away from the sandbox when Charles and François come out to play; people turn away, embarrassed, when they walk down the street. Even though their television talk show makes them the hosts of the year, they remain "définitivement célèbres et profondément solitaires. Solitaires" (112–13). The insecurities in the relationship between Charles and François, and in the relationship between the heads and their "public," reflect on an allegorical level the ambivalent attitude of the Québécois people toward the internal changes taking place in their society in the aftermath of the Quiet Revolution.

Charles and François deliberately present themselves as monstrous creatures: "une Erreur, au départ" (21). The capitalization of "Erreur," however, indicates their self-valorization. The frequent narratorial practice of capitalizing words that refer to the heads promotes their singularity. Thus, in the text the day of their birth is the "Jour de la Grande Distraction Divine" (18); their first sexual experience is a "Coïncidence miraculeuse" (127); every so often, when they have surpassed themselves, they capitalize the "t" of "les Têtes à Papineau" (30, 79, 101). There is a continuous subtext of monsters, freaks, dwarfs; the heads, who resemble no one, feel at home only in the presence of *other* freaks, such as the Fontaine family of dwarfs or the physically abnormal members of a travelling circus. Are we to understand, then, that Québécois are freaks? No. In this novel, which turns traditional values upside down, being monstrous is a positive quality; it confers significance on Charles-François. Thus, their official biographer notes that "L'enfance des monstres n'est jamais une sinécure ... non seulement doivent-ils s'ajuster à un environnement où ils ne se retrouvent pas du tout ... [mais ils] savent qu'ils ne sont pas de ce monde" (79–80).

The biblical echoes in the preceding quotation are taken up in the following passage, where the heads "go public" to the whole world: "La vie cachée de Jésus, a-t-on dit, s'est terminée quand il atteignit l'âge de douze ans et vint au temple. La vie obscure et humble de Charles-François Papineau se termina peu après notre arrivée à l'université ... Non seulement nous étions bicéphales mais aussi étions-nous intelligents. 'Un jeune monstre sur la montagne,' titrait un quotidien du soir parlant de notre arrivée à l'Université *Montis Regii*. Enfin. La nouvelle fut reprise de Singapour à Yaoundé" (106–7). Charles and François flaunt their physical abnormality to foreground their significance. It is in this light that they describe their surgeon, Dr Northridge, as a Frankenstein. His surgical skills, while normalizing them, will put an end to their monstrosity and thus lessen their significance: "Le couteau de Northridge va nous trancher dans l'*être*. Après ce sera le néant! Enfin" (28). By using intertextual references such as this one to Jean-Paul Sartre's *L'Etre et le néant* (1943), the narrators further the blurring of the boundaries between the world of fiction and, paradoxically, the "reality" of the text. Furthermore, this reference to the operation blurs the boundaries between the fictional world of the novel and the reality of the political operation, which is itself foregrounded in the publicity blurb on the back cover. Godbout's text here ironically links the referendum to Shakespeare, to Sartre, and to the Québécois: "A la veille de prendre une grave décision existentielle – être ou ne pas être deux, c'est en effet la question – 'les têtes à Papineau' nous font partager leurs souvenirs intimes."

An ironic undertone in the text plays with traditional myths about the birth of a divinity, even while maintaining a sardonic, political metacommentary about the supposed singularity of the Québécois as a distinctive francophone collectivity in North America. A sect in Korea has chosen the heads as "divinité," and "quelque part en Afrique une tribu [les] a incorporés dans sa lignée" (21). At the moment of their conception, according to their parents, unnatural happenings occurred: "A cet instant suprême ... ils furent soudain tous deux plongés dans un silence profond et une noirceur totale" (34). Although the parents' explanation for the darkness is the famous New York City blackout, the heads' biographer intimates that they have been conceived, as are many gods, by an extraterrestrial force: "Se peut-il par contre que Marie Lalonde et Alain-Auguste Papineau aient eu une rencontre inexpliquée avec un extra-terrestre? Qu'un Vénusien égaré à New York se soit glissé dans leur lit, sous les draps, invisible à leur yeux, mais présent comme Dieu en toute chose? Que cet enfant qui leur est né soit mi-terrestre, mi-lunaire? Le fils inattendu des galaxies?" (35). Godbout's terminology and syntax here parody the infamous "Petit Catéchisme de la Province de Québec," mentioned elsewhere in the text (100), which formed a part of the rote learning imposed upon all Catholic schoolchildren prior to ecumenical reforms in the 1960s. They also echo a popular Christmas hymn in Quebec, "O Divin Messie," which contains the line "Un enfant nous est né." The heads have verified the dates in their parents' story of their conception and have concluded that, once again, their father is producing new realities. They refute their parents' version of events and make clear to the reader that there is little factual basis for the tale. They do not, however, refute their own powers to inspire the creation of new myths, as is evident in their ironic description of their first trip to the ocean, which parodies the annual descent of thousands of Québécois to the beaches of the New England states: "En caleçons de bain nous jouions au monstre sorti de l'océan! Avec de l'écume et du varech sur les épaules! On en parle encore sur les plages de la Nouvelle-Angleterre jusqu'à la fine pointe de Cape Cod. Ainsi naissent les mythes. Ceux qui ne nous avaient pas contemplés dans les vagues à marée basse nous ont imaginés" (30–1). The heads' play with the recreation of myth centres on the myth of Papineau.

Whereas Pierre Falcon challenges the "truth" of historical documents – and written texts in general – by promoting his *oral* retelling of history, Charles and François provoke uncertainty regarding the fixity of written texts by their metafictional play with language. In other words, they go to the other extreme of Falcon's orality in their attempts to discredit the concept of *one* written version of events. Thus, *Les Têtes à Papineau* illustrates its existence as a fictional product by insisting on its linguistic nature. For instance, the frequent repetition of the last word of a sentence provokes a break in the rhythm and forces the reader to become aware of the act of writing and doubling: "Dès qu'on met le doigt dans les rouages politico-juridiques on en a pour l'éternité. L'éternité" (96). The same result is produced when the narrators interrupt their discourse to underline the effect of a sound: "embryonnaire, an-bri-yo-nère" (84). The exchange of consonants in the following sentence not only plays with the doubling technique but also pokes fun at nationalistic values, given that *chrysostome* is a typical – and unique – *juron québécois*: "'C'est tout de même ainsi,' répondit François, 'que nous avons conservé nos traditions, notre langue, notre foi, nos chansons et nos chromosomes. Chrysostome!'" (80). And Charles-François, the "parfait bicéphale *bilingue*" (96), ironically sums up the financial benefits of this particular condition through a linguistic pun: "Freak show. Fric chaud" (106).

As the date of the operation approaches, the heads are placed in quarantine and hooked up to a computer. Their internal communication can continue, since they each have access to a keyboard. But since the surgeon Northridge has programmed the computer to distinguish between single and plural pronouns (*je* and *nous*), not all their sentences show up on the two screens. This episode, of course, underlines Charles-François' existence as a linguistic construct. According to François, the operation is already in progress, since their written discourse has been divided. This text becomes progressively more difficult to write, as the number of "interférences" (119) increases. Each head has to approve of the text; their failure to agree on the written word can bring their narration to a halt: "Les discours se croisent, se bousculent, s'entrechoquent" (119). Their knowledge that neither will write the final chapter of the journal helps to slow down their production. There is no solution to the impasse that was described at the beginning of the diary: "Nous sommes, pour ainsi dire, idéologiquement séparés. C'est pourquoi ce livre ne peut être un effort de raccordement" (29). The written document is insufficient to their needs; if we stay within the limits of the narrators' text, it will not be published. This work, then, overtly flaunts its conditions of textuality.

Les Têtes à Papineau also places much emphasis on the distortion of reality. The reader is made aware of the narrators' predilection for the construction of alternative worlds. Speaking of Charles, François says: "il aime lui aussi inventer des univers inconnus" (22). The heads acknowledge that they can – and do – change their own perception of things: "Nous adaptions notre discours à la sauce littéraire ou politique suivant le lieu" (110). Many characters are creative transformers of reality: performers, actors, writers, journalists, and computer programmers. Even the computer is a manipulator of characters, and this makes it a producer of an alternative reality. This narration thus makes us aware of the fictional construction of the text and of the textual creation of alternative worlds.

In their efforts to destabilize the traditional, "objective" retelling of the past, the narrators of the novel deliberately flaunt their use of rural folk traditions of Quebec as a major intertextual tool. Thus, François, discussing the biological danger inherent in their two hereditary, defective *luettes* (a part of the throat, the uvula), jokes: "Ah luette! Je t'y plumerai" (17). His "other half" interjects a fragment of another well-known folk song in his comments on the preponderance of hereditary diseases in Quebec: "'C'est trop drôle'," dit Charles, 'un plein bateau d'êtres humains ratés, visa le noir, tua le blanc, des centaines de Canadiens français qu'il faudrait recommencer!'" (81–2).[5] Just as the heads subvert the political impact of what were nationalist folk songs in the 1960s, so does this novel subvert the traditional image of the Messianic French Canadians and the more recent one of the politicized Québécois of the Quiet Revolution. In both worldviews, the notion of a united collectivity was of paramount importance, and, in that they assumed a *nous-autres* versus *les autres* stance, these worldviews resembled Frye's theory of the garrison mentality. This postmodern novel, however, dares to challenge that dominant myth of the collectivity and presents other possibilities for political myth in a New World context.

The heads also perform linguistic operations on well-known historical quotations, thereby reinforcing the idea of history as a construct. For instance, Henri Bourassa, the famous journalist and politician, was the founder of the very influential newspaper *Le Devoir* (known for its political commentary) and the grandson of Louis-Joseph Papineau. His well-known axiom, "la langue est gardienne de la foi," is altered by the narrators' verbal play. Dr Northridge's mother, a French-Canadian postulant from Saint-Boniface, became pregnant to protest the disappearance of her race. Her baby was adopted by an Anglo-Catholic family in Winnipeg, and the heads' ironic political comment is: "Déjà, au Manitoba, la foi n'était plus gardienne de la langue!" (19). The fact that the Supreme Court of Canada was reexamining Manitoba's language laws in 1979, a year close to the period of the writing of the novel, is perhaps peripheral here, but it does underline the constant slippage between past history and the present of the text. By inserting fragments and deformations of well-known Quebec folk songs into their discourse, and by altering equally well-known historical and political slogans, the heads create a tension between the fabulous world of two-headed beings and the "real" world, the one with an historical setting. This technique brings alternative worlds into contact and creates the tension typical of New World Myth.

In *Les Têtes à Papineau*, Charles and François also self-consciously display their awareness of the *making* of history. This novel is an allegorical comment upon a political event of the recent past, the referendum of 1980, and upon the historico-political evolution of Quebec that had led it to this important moment. Its narrators, by constantly playing off the "historical" world against alternative worlds, confuse our perception of all worlds. They suggest "that history itself is a multiplicity of 'alternative worlds,' as fictional as, but other than, the [world of the novel]" (Waugh, *Metafiction*, 104). For instance, the heads insert "real" historical events and personages into a fictional context. In this novel, reference is made to the Shah of Iran, Maurice Duplessis, and the Dionne quintuplets, and to events such as the Battle of the Plains of Abraham and the New York City blackout. At times, the distance between the worlds of history and fiction is reduced to a minimum: the centrefold of the 1956 *Almanach du Peuple* is said to portray, on the left-hand side, the Dionne quintuplets in the arms of their father, and on the right, Charles-François in the arms of Alain-Auguste. Elsewhere, the heads describe this Almanac, which is still widely used as a reference book in rural Quebec, as their "véritable livre d'histoire! L'histoire" (98). The ironic repetition of the word "histoire" here signals the heads' play with historiography. The blurring of history and fiction in this text permits the heads to rework the myth surrounding a mythico-historical figure of Quebec, the leader of the Patriotes, Louis-Joseph Papineau.

Patricia Smart, discussing Godbout's film on Hubert Aquin, writes:

A writer or public figure becomes a *myth* when his or her life corresponds to or crystallizes something central in the collective consciousness. An evolving, changing society needs to shake off the influence of those mythical figures that tend to paralyze rather than liberate. The most obvious examples of changing myths are Dollard des Ormeaux and Madeleine de Verchères, symbols of the Golden Age of New France during that period of conservative nationalism in Quebec. Both disappeared without a struggle with the advent of the Quiet Revolution. A whole line of tragic figures central to the literature of French Canada has been harder to get rid of ... It was Hubert Aquin who analyzed this tragic archetype most lucidly in an article titled "L'Art de la défaite," relating it to the paralysis of a nation unable to shake off the inner split and lack of confidence of a colonized people. Aquin included the Patriotes of 1837 ... in his list of tragic ancestors, and argued for the need to transcend the national neurosis by political growth. ("Filming the Myth," 20)

The "têtes à Papineau," by means of their deliberate play on their symbolic name, set about destabilizing the myth of Papineau. Gilles Pellerin has noted the continuing importance of the *historical* politician to the Québécois: "Car Louis-Joseph Papineau est plus qu'un politicien ambigu du siècle dernier: il est au foyer d'un miroir concave où chaque exégète, historien, politicien, poète, romancier ou dramaturge qui prétend en parler, projette en fait sa propre idéologie, le critique littéraire y compris" ("*Papineau*," 46). Pellerin makes an interesting comment, given the subject matter of this chapter, about the evolving mythic dimension of another historical figure from Canadian history: "Dollard des Ormeaux et Montcalm ne faisant plus recette, il n'y a que Louis Riel à avoir un potentiel mythique comparable à celui du seigneur de Montebello" (47).

Alain Piette has proposed that in *Les Têtes à Papineau* the nationalist problematic is inscribed in its very title: "il s'agit d'une mythification du passé cristallisée dans le personnage de Papineau" ("Les Langues à Papineau," 123). Piette suggests that Godbout's title plays with the standard expressions – "C'est pas la tête à Papineau" and "Faut pas se prendre pour la tête à Papineau" – both of which imply a negative judgment on the intelligence and knowledge of the person being discussed. To have a "tête à Papineau" means to be capable of brilliant intellectual activity: "Référence à Louis-Joseph Papineau, brillant tribun et homme politique de chez nous dont le nom est passé dans l'usage populaire."[6] As Jacques Pelletier notes, "Une tête à Papineau, on le sait, c'est dans la mythologie québécoise une grosse tête, une intelligence généralement imbue d'elle-même qui tout à la fois fascine et agace: 'Prends-toi pas pour la tête à Papineau,' entend-on dire souvent au sens de 'Prends-toi pas pour plus fin que tu ne l'es'" ("*Les Têtes à Papineau*," 52).

Godbout's title, however, totally subverts the raw material he started out with: the clichés concerning Papineau. The use of the plural form centres the reader's attention on the collectivity rather than on the individual Papineau. As Piette has noted, "la négation a disparu: il ne subsiste qu'un groupe nominal ouvert à toutes les possibilités au niveau des qualifications ou des actions" ("Les Langues à Papineau," 123). Godbout's novel reflects the need of the Québécois nation to shake off "those mythical figures that tend to paralyse" (Smart, "Filming the Myth," 20). The narrators' play with the myth of Papineau is a reflection of the struggle of New World Myth to open up myth, to make it as liberating and flexible as possible. Their overt exploration of the notion of myth itself is coupled with their ceaseless self-identification with the nation and, paradoxically, with their efforts to explode the traditional self-characterizations of Québécois as the "chosen people" of the nineteenth and early twentieth centuries, or as the *gens du pays* of the 1960s and '70s. Charles and François doubly and onomastically underline their "filiation" to Quebec and its historical past. As we have seen, they frequently and ironically associate themselves with the Québécois as a group. In the palace of mirrors of a Montreal amusement park, they exclaim: "Ah! Ces corridors infinis de miroirs convexes! Concaves! Tordus! ... Il fallait voir ces monstres que nous renvoyaient les glaces, nous multipliant à l'infini. Nous avions envahi la planète. Nous n'étions plus uniques! Des milliers de têtes de c.-f. se contemplaient médusées" (137). The tension inherent in New World Myth is evident here in the deliberate ambiguity of the abbreviation: is "c.-f." Charles-François or *Canadien-français*? Such blurring of boundaries between the various worlds in this novel allows the narrators to purposely confuse our perceptions of myth, mythology, history, fiction and reality, and to call for a new way of looking at the world.

As in Wiebe's work, Christian mythology is frequently used as an intertext in Godbout's novel. The respect that Falcon demonstrates for the traditional biblical stories, however, is absent from the heads' narrative. Charles and François set up ironic parallels between their life and the life of Jesus Christ. Their birth, for instance, is presented as a mystery and a miracle, and the final meeting of the family before the operation is described as the Last Supper (*Les Têtes à Papineau*,

146). The internal division of the bicephalic creature is again fore-grounded in this scene; as Yvon Bellemare has pointed out, "François, qui se voit comme le Sacrifié, estime son vis-à-vis comme un 'Judas,' un traître" (Bellemare, "Les Têtes à Papineau," 161). In this text, the narrators' play with biblical mythology serves two pur-poses. First, the heads' ironic use of religious words and images, which formed an important part of the traditional Québécois' vocab-ulary, here parodies the outdated image of the steeped-in-religion *Canadien-français* and suggests that a new self-image is needed. Sec-ond, biblical mythology is presented in this novel as one possible myth-system among others. In these narrators' textual production, deliberate confusion of various mythological worlds underlines the many-faceted, constantly shifting surface of New World Myth. The narrators' explorations of alternative mythological systems and their confrontation of their own precarious historico-political mythology with that of these other systems reinforces the idea that New World Myth self-consciously creates itself to suit particular and changing needs.

A clear example of the narratorial play with myth-making and mythology is the use the heads make of the derogatory term "frog." Charles and François repeatedly use the frog image as a political metaphor that permits them to comment on the uniqueness of their situation and on their internal tensions. By incorporating a pejorative term normally used by anglophones into their discourse, the heads are readjusting their own mythology, resituating themselves as myth-makers and assuming the controlling power over their own mythological system. It is significant that in their "image publique la plus répandue" (*Les Têtes à Papineau*, 17), a plaster statuette sold in supermarkets everywhere, the heads are cast on the *back* of the frog, that is to say, in a position of control. Alain Piette has suggested that "la charge négative [du 'frog'] est beaucoup moindre ici que dans la réalité québécoise. Cela tient en bonne partie à la présentation que les narrateurs-monstres font d'eux-mêmes: ils rendent sympathique 'ce monstre sorti de l'océan' (p. 30), cet 'animal préhistorique,' ce 'serpent de mer' (p. 124)" ("Les Langues à Papineau," 120). How-ever, in accordance with the slippery quality of New World Myth, this positive image of the frog does not completely dominate the text. The heads do foreground their desire to reinvent "Le cri des gre-nouilles" (*Les Têtes à Papineau*, 123). They wish to alter the fact that "dans l'océan anglophone tout ce qui ne saxonne est un batracien" – a fact that they first dismiss as "[q]uerelles de vieux pays qui ont fait long chemin." But the photograph that the starlet takes of them in the swimming pool reveals them to be a "vilaine grenouille ... Cette photographie comme un rayon x révélait notre structure intime. Intime." And the heads then wish to "couler a pic. Nous noyer. Avaler du chlore tiède ... Nous avions assez d'être une grenouille" (124–5). It is only after making love with the starlet, who, significantly, is of French origin, that the heads can try to come to terms· with their bicephalic existence: "Nous avons convenu que si les starlettes rêvent de monstres nous allions, en tant que Grenouille, chercher des lèvres de princesse et devenir un homme. Des hommes" (129). It is not clear, however, whether the princess's kiss is going to turn them into "*un* homme" or "*des* hommes" (one man or two). In any case, as their psychoanalyst later tells them, this love-making means they were suffering from a temporary desire to regress. By returning to the safety of the (French) womb, they would undoubtedly be protected from the surgical (political) intervention of Dr Northridge, a man whose name resembles (in reverse) that of Pierre Eliott Trudeau. Fairy tales, culturally pejorative expressions, high-tech surgery, political allusions – all these elements are adopted and then adapted here by the narrators in their efforts to rework a clichéd image of the people they represent. The shifting quality of the narrators' use of the frog image reflects a general move in this novel toward the destabilization of any fixed elements in history or myth.

The entire novel reworks the traditional portraits of the evolving French Canadian/Québécois people by subverting the notion of a definitive version of its historical past. It also presents a puzzling commentary on the postcolonial situation of Quebec. I refer of course to the last chapter of the work, entitled "Enfin," where a unilingual Charles F. Papineau has embraced the technological world: he writes to a Québécois publishing firm from a computer science centre in English Bay, Vancouver, on Canada Day. This chapter, which significantly does *not* form part of Charles' and François' internal discourse, constitutes a metacommentary on the political ambivalence alluded to elsewhere in the novel. While the two *narrators* of the journal assume their uniqueness, which is anchored in their monstrosity, and confidently engage all the political and religious mythologies that have shaped the worldview of the evolving French Canadian/Québécois people over the centuries, this passage implies a surprising resolution to Quebec's political dilemma: assimilation into the North American anglophone world. This conclusion is all the more surprising because it was invented by Jacques Godbout himself, when, in a famous essay entitled "Ecrire," first published in 1971, he somewhat sardonically proclaimed the necessity of what has become known as the *texte national*: "Ce que tout jeune écrivain québécois devrait savoir, c'est qu'il n'échappera pas au

chantage du Pays, car justement il découvrira ayant perdu sa virgi-
nité que ce n'est pas lui qui écrit ses livres (qu'il signe), et *qu'il n'y
a au Québec qu'Un seul Ecrivain: NOUS TOUS* ... Un écrivain québécois
ne peut chercher à exister en dehors du texte québécois, il lui faut
participer à l'entreprise collective, autrement c'est le néant" (150). In
Les Têtes à Papineau, Godbout explodes this *nous tous* notion of a
political collectivity, a notion that, as Jacques Michon critically notes,
Godbout himself helped to perpetuate: "Après avoir travaillé avec
des écrivains de sa génération pour exorciser la disjonction cana-
dienne-française en affirmant la réalité unique du Québec, Godbout
semble maintenant revenir sur des positions bien reconnues"
("Romans," 340).

When pressed in the interview with Donald Smith ("Jacques Godbout") to explain this radical rethinking of the *texte national* and the
political collectivity, Godbout's answers were contradictory: he
asserted at one point that this novel is really a political text, but
elsewhere in the interview he denied that the final chapter is political
in nature, claiming novelistic immunity for it: "C'est ce qui se passe
dans le livre, point à la ligne" (56). But Yvon Bellemare, among others, sees the ending of Godbout's novel as a betrayal of the *indépendantiste* movement and a return to a colonial worldview: "la fin
tragique de Charles-François Papineau doublement colonisé" is an
illustration of Godbout's "désillusion" ("Les Têtes à Papineau," 157).
Godbout himself, however, pointed to a different interpretation of
the novel – one that calls for an end to protectionist colonial attitudes
and a postmodern acceptance of instability, change, and flux. Playing
with the *monstre/Québécois* metaphor, he proposed "si nous sommes
des monstres, d'une certaine manière, c'est parce que nous avons
toujours refusé l'étranger. Il s'agit de savoir si nous allons continuer
longtemps encore à performer dans le cirque québécois, ou sortir de
sous la tente et affronter le monde. La tentation du cirque est
grande" (Smith, "Jacques Godbout," 61). Godbout reiterated this call
for openness, occasioned by postcolonial confidence, in another
interview that underlined the need to situate Québécois literature in
an international context: "Dans le fond, 20 ans que l'on se croit au
centre du monde ... on sait qu'on existe, l'identité est là. Il est peut-
être temps que l'on se place dans l'univers par rapport aux autres
nations, aux autres langues, qu'on se préoccupe de l'Occident et que
l'on cesse de demander aux gens de ne penser qu'à nous" (Guillot,
"Godbout le réducteur," 27).

Charles' and François's persistent destabilizing of dominant ideological myths reflects Godbout's exasperation with those protectionist worldviews in Quebec that have, apparently, more than run their

course. A typical postmodern indeterminacy permeates the meta-commentary of the last chapter, however, leaving the reader with many questions regarding Godbout's overtly political allusions. Is the anglicized Papineau a warning about the essential outcome of the rejection of traditional myths? Is Godbout proposing that the process of change, clearly already begun, will inevitably lead to the disappearance not only of the outmoded notion of the collectivity but of francophones in North America? The political tensions of New World Myth are strongly evident in the conflict between the narrators' text, which pushes for change, and this last chapter, which offers a disappointing prognosis, from a Québécois nationalist point of view. Indeed, the contemporary predilection for a nationalist stance, discussed in the preceding chapter, springs to the fore here. Godbout's narrators, as we have seen, embody conflicting attitudes to everything, including the allegorical operation and the formulation of their journal. This last chapter reflects, perhaps, the similarly contradictory outlook of its author, torn as he appears to be between his earlier urges toward *l'écriture* as *texte national* and his intuition, as expressed in *Les Têtes*, that contemporary historiographic literature is driven by different concerns.

While Godbout's position as "one of Quebec's most prominent novelists, film-makers and intellectuals" holds firm in English-speaking Canada, as is evident in Richard Hodgson's review of Godbout's diaries ("Critical Juncture," 84),[7] his standing in these areas has come under attack in recent years in Quebec. One senses this in some reviews of his latest work, such as André Vachon's discussion of Godbout's 1993 novel, *Le Temps des Galarneau*. The "Galarneau" of the title is of course an intertextual reference to *Salut Galarneau!* (1967), a literary allusion not lost on Vachon, who notes that Godbout's earlier novel portrayed a culture "québécoise-de-souche et on ne peut plus traditionnelle" ("Qui serons-nous?" 118) and implies that Godbout's more recent work, like its author, has not changed to accommodate the changing cultural scene in contemporary Quebec, which is qualified as "une société *à inventer* ... une identité *à faire*" (126). *Liberté*, the journal in which this review appears, has had long and close associations with Jacques Godbout; in its recent issues one finds a strong polemical discussion of Godbout's role in contemporary Quebec.

This discussion turns, in part, on the allegorical and problematic presentation of cultural identity and politics in *Les Têtes à Papineau*. The polemic began with a statement by Godbout himself in issue 203 of *Liberté*, titled "Le Québec des écrivains." Godbout wrote: "Pour ce qui est de l'ensemble des Québécois, nous sommes partagés par le milieu, comme les Têtes à Papineau. Ca n'a pas changé, en douze ans, et pourquoi est-ce que cela changerait?" ("Les Ecrivains," 42). In a subsequent issue, *Liberté* 206, Serge Cantin responds to Godbout's short text with a long article entitled, significantly, "La fatigue culturelle de Jacques Godbout." He discusses, among other things, the role of the intellectual in Québécois society and the paradoxical praxis *and* stasis of this society's political engagement. Cantin sees Godbout's work as encouraging political stasis and condemns his "profond et délétère attachement à une vision statique et minoritaire du Québec qui contredit le dynamisme de sa durée" (27). Again, *Les Têtes à Papineau* is invoked as illustrative of Godbout's fence-sitting: "Rien ne témoigne davantage de la persistance de cette antinomie dans la conscience historique actuelle que "les têtes à Papineau" de Jacques Godbout, qui, sous le mode de l'allégorie euphémisante, nous invitent à foncer têtes baissées dans un faux et fatal dilemme qui trahit une 'tentation du vide idéologique' ... exaspérée jusqu'au délire et confinant à la schizophrénie. Deux têtes dans les nuages, ou plutôt dans le sable, jouant à l'autruche" (20–1).[8] In yet a third article, in *Liberté 212*, Alain Roy offers a rebuttal of Cantin's argument and notes that "Godbout, contrairement à Cantin, se donne volontiers le rôle de l'avocat du diable, ce qui peut l'amener à critiquer une option pour laquelle il semble globalement favorable et à louer telle qualité dont ferait preuve la partie adverse" ("La Sagesse de Mireille," 98).

Devil's advocates, of course, may ironically imply something contrary to what they mean; they frequently make use of irony as a rhetorical tool. However, Vachon's review of Godbout's work, along with most of the discussion in *Liberté*, seems to occult Godbout's use of irony in *Les Têtes* and elsewhere in his impressive corpus. It is interesting that irony has come under close critical scrutiny in English-speaking Canada (in part because of the overt irony of much postmodern literature) but that it is rarely addressed in studies of contemporary literature in Quebec. In fact, I sense that critics did not know what to *do* with *Les Têtes* and that their bafflement was reflected in the relatively small number of serious critical articles devoted to this novel. As Josias Semujanga succinctly remarks, several critics, "tout en reconnaissant l'importance de la dimension ironique du roman de Godbout, lui accordent une signification très limitée" ("Onomastique littéraire," 81). Semujanga explores the play with proper names in *Les Têtes* and argues that although the text apparently sets up a binary opposition that "s'appuie en outre sur un discours monologique de l'identité/altérité ... l'installation d'une énonciation ironique déstabilise les discours ainsi convoqués et cette symétrie en apparence oppositionnelle des noms propres" (81). In *Les Têtes* irony is used at the level of onomastics to destabilize the binary us/other opposition; as I have been arguing in this chapter, irony is also used as a tool to destabilize traditional historical and mythological world views. Godbout's proclivity for the use of irony and his pleasure in playing devil's advocate in texts that comment on the contemporary political scene set him apart from many other writers of his generation; this "serious playfulness," perhaps, is the cause of the unease with which his recent novels and films have been received in Quebec.

The Scorched-Wood People and *Les Têtes à Papineau* provide a good introduction to New World Myth, in that their narrators rework the historico-political myths surrounding two problematic figures from the past. These reworkings include an illustration of the tensions between fiction and history and between the historical past and the political present. The narrators' use and abuse of various mythological systems points to their urge to *make* New World Myth, to retell the past from the viewpoint of the here and now. Paradoxically, however, the narrators' metafictional flaunting of themselves, their "texts," and their (hi)stories as constructs underlines the instability of all versions of past events and indicates the postmodern impossibility of imposing one definitive mythological system upon past or present worlds.

3 Reshaping Religions, Challenging Cosmogonies: Jovette Marchessault's *Comme une enfant de la terre* and Joy Kogawa's *Obasan*

Daphne Patai, in *Myth and Ideology in Contemporary Brazilian Fiction*, remarks on the declining influence of classical mythology and the persistence of biblical mythology in contemporary Brazilian fiction that is equally discernible in much English Canadian and Québécois fiction: "In an age of mass media and mass education ... even an acquaintance with occidental [classical] mythology may be beyond the range of the average reader ... By contrast, biblical mythology (whose continued currency makes many people unwilling to refer to it as 'mythology') is still very familiar to most Westerners ... In a Catholic country such as Brazil, a writer may reasonably expect the reader to have some specific knowledge of Christian mythology since this still forms an important part of the general cultural frame of reference" (148). Such a remark could aptly be applied to the awareness the "average" Québécois or English Canadian reader has of biblical mythology. The two texts examined in this chapter, Jovette Marchessault's *Comme une enfant de la terre* (1975) and Joy Kogawa's *Obasan* (1981), make use of this general awareness of biblical mythology in their different yet complementary investigations of New World Myth.

Both novels were first novels for their authors, although in 1975 Marchessault was a recognized sculptor/painter and Kogawa, in 1981, a recognized poet. Marchessault's novel is the first of a trilogy; the subsequent novels in the series are *La Mère des herbes* (1980) and *Des Cailloux blancs pour les forêts obscures* (1987). Even before the publication of this third novel, however, Marchessault had turned her considerable energies to writing plays.[1] Linda Gaboriau, who has translated some of Marchessault's work into English, explains Marchessault's shift from fiction to drama: she "was immediately seduced by the power of a public forum where women's voices could be heard, literally and figuratively, by a larger and more varied audience than that usually reached by the smaller literary presses that tend to publish new work by women. She also found the flesh and blood embodiment of her work particularly fulfilling" ("Jovette Marchessault," 93).

Marchessault can be called an "ex-centric" (Hutcheon, *Poetics of Postmodernism*, 67); part Amerindian, she is a self-proclaimed lesbian and feminist, although she did not come out as a lesbian until 1979.[2] Furthermore, having quit school in grade eight to work at various menial jobs in the East End of Montreal, she is largely self-taught. Her grandmother would bring her books from the library, and Marchessault would work her way through the classics – not only those well-known occidental works to which one would be introduced within the context of a typical classical Québécois education but also those of other cultures and religions. This undoubtedly eclectic education must have contributed to the strange intensity and the evident cultural and mythical conflation in Marchessault's writing. In her presentation of the special issue of *Voix et Images* on Marchessault's work, Claudine Potvin speculates that although academic and cultural institutions tend to eventually recuperate significant marginal works, Marchessault's writing does not stand much of a chance of ever being recuperated, or as she puts it, "faire son chemin jusqu'au centre" (214). Potvin proposes that Marchessault's linguistic excesses, strong sense of drama, and especially, her creation of an "espace autre" – a different, women-centred space – have puzzled the cultural community, which has not given Marchessault's œuvre the serious attention it deserves. The advantages of being marginal, however, are indirectly signalled by Potvin. Marchessault's work, she proposes, has been generally ignored by the academic community because it upsets far too many structures: "mentales, sociales, culturelles, sexuelles, raciales, spirituelles, structures patriarcales avant tout" (214). As an ex-centric – a *marginale* – Marchessault is on the periphery of any cultural circle, and thus, perhaps, in a better position than mainstream writers to explore the development of New World Myth and, as I argue here and in the next chapter, its relationship to biblical mythology, feminism, and historico-political knowledge.

When Marchessault was thirty-one years old, her beloved grandmother died. Marchessault subsequently went through a period of grief and an intense personal crisis that led her to decide to explore her own creative energies. After sitting for six months before a blank page, incapable of writing, she began to paint and to sculpt, producing the telluric sculptures that were once her trademark. In a riveting section of Dorothy Todd Hénaut's National Film Board film *Les Terribles vivantes*, Marchessault describes how as a cleaning lady she once opened the door of a company boardroom in Montreal, only to stand there, mop in hand, looking at one of her own paintings hanging in the place of honour on the wall. Plagued by financial difficulties, Marchessault tried once again to write, and the result of her efforts was the definitely different *Comme une enfant de la terre*. While Marchessault's style remains polemical and even, according to several critics, "excessive," there has been a major shift in her expression of strong emotions: she has moved from definitive expressions of anger and a condemnation of repression in her early novels to themes of spirituality and of reconciliation in her later work. Elaine Naves argues that the portrayal of men in Marchessault's recent plays, from the male guardian angel in *Le Voyage magnifique d'Emily Carr* to the "positive and beautiful" man in *Le Lion de Bangor*, are unique: "there is nothing like this in Québécois theatre and in fact in contemporary theatre altogether" ("Magnificent Voyage," 31). To get *to* reconciliation, however, Marchessault had to get the anger out. In 1988 Marguerite Andersen's discussion of several important women writers of Quebec noted that "Marchessault can be angry" and described the three monologues that make up *Triptyque lesbien* as "frankly explosive" ("Subversive Texts," 137). Naves makes similar observations about Marchessault's "first two autobiographical novels [which] pulsate with a manic energy and bubbling rage, an apparent overflow of feelings suppressed during the long years of stultifying poverty and dronelike work" ("Magnificent Voyage," 29). Anger and a strong didactic tone dominate *Comme une enfant de la terre*, although the novel also explores spirituality and mysticism. The theme of reconciliation is definitely more central to Marchessault's later plays.

It is interesting to note the inverse progression of similar emotions in Joy Kogawa's work. Contrary to the initial reception given to Marchessault's text, Kogawa's *Obasan* was immediately acclaimed as "the most discussed and celebrated first novel of the year" (Bilan, "Fiction," 316).[3] Reviewers and critics almost unanimously acclaimed its literary worth, and the novel continues to be the subject of several serious critical commentaries more than a decade after its publication. Unfortunately, several solid critical appraisals of Kogawa's *Obasan* suggest an unsuitable appropriation of the text, claiming it as exemplary of "Asian American fiction." This has lead to convoluted and ridiculous constructions, such as this one from Shirley Geok-lin Lim: "Her mystification, Naomi learns later, derives from her *Japanese American* community's silent submission to *Canadian* racism" ("Life Stories," 291; my emphasis). Indeed, this attempted cultural takeover has interesting ramifications, not the least of which is the practice, in several articles and books with a strong American focus, to occult all references to Canadian political issues in the novel. Thus, Kogawa's references to highly charged Canadian political "texts," such as the national anthem, usually disappear from these commentaries, having been replaced by ellipses. At a 1995 conference in Seattle, Washington, I chaired a panel on Vancouver writer Sky Lee's *Disappearing Moon Café* and Kogawa's *Obasan*. Some participants saw the practice of identifying these texts as Asian American as a transnational approach to "ethnic" literature, such as that embodied in Lim's publication: "*Obasan* is quickly becoming recognized as an Asian American novel" ("Life Stories," 310). Other participants, led perhaps by panellist Karlyn Koh's presentation, "Thinking Through Canadian 'Post-Nationalism' and a 'Pan-Asian Sensibility,'" argued that this practice constituted an attempted cultural takeover.[4] As panellist Donna Bennett noted, the loosening of "national" boundaries in the current discussion of fiction by "ethnic minorities" points to a pressing need to determine the new parameters of discussions of these kinds of fictions. In the present study I refer when appropriate to the work of those critics who characterize *Obasan* as an Asian American text, although I would suggest that many of these critics misread the text by occulting its evident discussion of Canadian issues. My main focus, of course, is on the work as representative of New World Myth novels.

Although there is some division of opinion regarding the tone of Kogawa's *Obasan*, it is generally described as subtle, reflective, poetic, meditative, or ambivalent. Thus, for Teruyo Ueki, Kogawa utilizes the "subtle art of 'expression through subtraction.' The book conceals an enormous depth beneath the surface of a calm, modest, natural narrative" ("*Obasan*," 5). Although Kogawa published *Naomi's Road*, a children's version of *Obasan*, in 1986, it was not until 1992 that *Itsuka*, an adult sequel to *Obasan*, appeared. *Itsuka*, which means "some day" in Japanese, continues the story of Naomi Nakane while focusing on the eventually successful struggle for redress carried on by Japanese Canadians during the 1980s. In this second novel, Naomi has moved to Toronto, but she does not feel at home there. *Itsuka* also traces the changing and sometimes problematic relationships Naomi has with her Aunt Emily, as well as the slow development of her love relationship with Cedric, a college chaplain of mixed heritage. Anger against injustice is a strong theme of the novel, as is coming to a wary acceptance of love and reconciliation. However, as more than one reviewer has noted, the thrust of the novel is strongly didactic: it presents "a fierce desire to teach us as much as possible about both the Japanese Canadian past history of repression and its recent history of redress" (Hutcheon, "Someday," 181). The subtlety of *Obasan* is not frequently evident in *Itsuka*, and, revealingly, this long-awaited sequel has generated scarcely any critical commentary at all. While Marchessault has gone from anger to reconciliation, Kogawa appears to have moved from a hesitant (yet powerful) subtlety to an overt expression of anger. *Itsuka* is direct, didactic, and crammed with facts – yet its overall effect is much less powerful than the carefully restrained prose of *Obasan*.

Kogawa's third novel, *The Rain Ascends* (1995), has as its central subject a woman coming to terms with her father's sexual abuse of children. He is a kind and well-loved Christian minister. Here again, Kogawa deals with a central issue of her work: finding the courage to first face, and then tell, a truth about the past. This third novel discusses, through the metaphors of fog and light, the thorny questions of anger, mercy, guilt, and reconciliation. The direct expressions of anger and the didactic tone of *Itsuka* have given way in *The Rain Ascends* to something reminiscent of Kogawa's style in *Obasan* – a subtle, mythic expression of the complexities of life: "In the beginning is the fog, the thick impenetrable fog. In the beginning there is also an unquenchable light ... From within the density, this much alone is known: the way out of the lie is through mercy, the name of the path is mercy, the one who stoops to help is Mercy" (*The Rain Ascends*, 2).

As is the case with Marchessault and her book, there are similarities between Kogawa herself and the narrator of *Obasan*. In an interview, Kogawa explains that much of her own family's experience during the war is found in *Obasan*: "We journeyed from comfort in Marpole, Vancouver, to a shack in Slocan and to an even smaller shack in Coaldale. That's one of the sugar beet centres in southern Alberta. Dad, as an Anglican clergyman, was rarely home since he had to be 'on the road' visiting the dispersed community" (Redekop,"Literary Politics," 15). Kogawa is the daughter of a Christian minister who has the same family name as the minister in *Obasan*: the Reverend Nakayama.

Patricia Merivale asserts that Kogawa has a "complexly ambivalent relationship ... to traditional Christianity" ("Framed Voices," 81).

Nowhere is this ambivalence more evident than in an early interview: responding to questions about the influence of the Bible and
of Christianity on her work, Kogawa underlines her respect for the
mythology put forth by the Bible, describing it as "a pretty strong
grid on my mind." She accepts biblical mythology "for its peculiarity
and its uniqueness, but not in any sense for its superiority" (Meyer
and O'Riordan, "Joy Kogawa," 29). Criticizing the "arrogant superiority [that] is still within some churches today," Kogawa describes
herself as a "closet Christian" who is "embarrassed about it, especially when [she is] among some of [her] feminist friends who find
this aspect of [her] a great aberration" (30). Both Marchessault and
Kogawa, then, underline the feminist resistance to the patriarchal
mythology espoused by Christianity. Reflecting elsewhere on her
personal stance toward politics and religion, Kogawa states, "The
private and the public, the personal and the political, the internal
and the external are all co-extensive" ("Is There a Just Cause?" 20).
She describes her own retreat "into silence and withdrawal" (24) as
a Nisei "who suffered the drawn-out trauma of racial prejudice
during [her] formative and young adult years" and affirms that
"what draws us together is not sermon, but story" (21). Like her
narrator, then, *Obasan*'s author has had to struggle to come to story.

The tensions inherent in Kogawa's struggle are also present in the
"urge to tell" manifested by the narrators of both novels discussed
here. These narrators possess a particular knowledge of the past and,
eventually, a desire to transmit that knowledge. Paradoxically, they
underline the indeterminacy of any one definitive portrayal of the
past and their self-conscious awareness of their *making* of their ver-
sion(s), which they offer up against other worldviews. The present
chapter examines New World Myth approaches to biblical mythology in its discussion of the novels' use and abuse of various religious
practices and rituals and in its illustration of these authors' postmodern challenges to previously dominant belief systems. In chapter 4
these same two novels serve to illustrate aspects of New World Myth
reworkings of history and historiography, as well as to illuminate
some feminist apprehensions of the past and of the present. Thus,
while this chapter examines the narrators' challenges to Christian
belief systems, the following chapter looks at womens' empowerment in fiction.

Before addressing the reworkings of biblical mythology in Marchessault's work, I wish to touch briefly on the questions of Amerindian
writing in Quebec and of Marchessault's mixed heritage and its place
in a discussion of *Comme une enfant de la terre*. In Quebec in 1975 there

was no such thing as a strong community of Amerindian writers who used French as a language of communication. Indeed, there is no strong francophone Amerindian/Inuit community of writers in Quebec today. Although some Amerindian/Inuit novelists and playwrights are beginning to publish their work in French,[5] the numerous publications of First Nations people writing in English, as well as the considerable body of work from English-speaking Canada that presents and analyses Amerindian writing and issues, such as the *Oxford Anthology of Canadian Native Literature in English* (Goldie and Moses 1992), do not have their equivalent in Quebec.[6] This situation is gradually changing, and some Amerindian writers in Quebec are choosing to publish in French instead of English, as Pierre Turgeon, the editor of "Liberté aux Indiens," remarked in his introduction to a special 1991 issue of *Liberté* devoted to Amerindian writers of Quebec. However, with the exception of the Hurons (who have lost their own language and speak French) and some Algonquins and Montagnais, in the years 1975–85 there were few communities of First Nations people in Quebec who functioned comfortably in French as the language of communication, whereas many First Nations people in English-speaking Canada have been communicating and publishing in English for some time.

Gilles Thérien's and Diane Boudreau's work on the Indian/Métis has begun to address the small body of Amerindian writing in French in Quebec,[7] while a Montreal journal, *Recherches amérindiennes au Québec*, is addressing the presence of the Amerindian in Québécois society. And in 1993 a research group published *Répertoire bibliographique*, a bilingual (English/French) bibliography of writings by Amerindians. Nonetheless, there is still no established *littérature amérindienne*, as Boudreau notes at the end of her overview of those Amerindian writers who do publish in French in Quebec ("L'écriture appropriée"). Pierre L'Hérault's recent work on Québécois theatre supports this theory; as he noted at a presentation of his research at a 1995 conference, while playwrights from the *écriture migrante* group, such as Marco Micone, have produced a significant body of plays, "l'Indien demeure toujours une figure dans l'imaginaire québécois" ("Figures et langage(s) de l'ethnicité"). The very small proportion of Amerindian communities that communicate with others in French is the result of several factors, among them the historical reasons I touched on in the preface to this book, such as the hierarchical and linguistic tensions between the federal and provincial governments with regard to the administration of First Nations people, as well as the diachronic developments in Amerindian/non-Amerindian relations. Thus, even in the early 1990s in Quebec the first non-native language of the majority of Inuit and Amerindi-ans is still English (Delisle, "Les langues autochtones," 3), and this linguistic difference has produced some linguistic and racial tension in recent years. However, those who would see only racial tensions between francophones *de vieille souche* and First Nations people in Quebec must forcibly ignore the historical French-Amerindian rap-port and the intermingling of races in New France. In "Ne sommes-nous pas tous des Amérindiens?" Pierre-André Julien has proposed that closer attention be paid to the practice of *métissage* in historical French Canadian/Amerindian relations, a practice that has been receiving much critical attention in the writings on hybridity and *mestizaje* in Latin American discourse (Chanady, *Latin American Iden-tity*, xvi). This complex relationship between francophones and Amerindians is addressed in more detail in chapter 5 of this book, in my discussion of François Barcelo's *La Tribu*. What I wish to suggest here is that Marchessault's double heritage is an example of that *métissage*.

This is not to say that there are no racial tensions in Quebec, because of course such tensions do exist. I propose, however, that someone like Marchessault, writing out of an Amerindian and fran-cophone culture in 1975 in Quebec, might have a different mytholog-ical worldview from the one underlying the self/other argument frequently put forth by the politically correct criteria presently obtaining in English-speaking Canada. Worldviews can and do dif-fer. For instance, Sylvia Söderlind has noted the ambivalence, or hes-itation, that characterizes the literatures of English-speaking Canada and Quebec. She writes: "Canada's past is, as the ambivalence of its literatures often indicates, a double one: it has been colonized by the French and British, but it is also a colonizer of its indigenous peo-ples" (*Margin/Alias*, 3). This frequently cited comment assumes an identical situation of English-speaking Canada and Quebec as colo-nizers of Amerindians and does not discuss the different attitudes toward – and portrayals of – Native Peoples in works of fiction and nonfiction from these two areas. I would argue, however, that there are basic differences in how the two literatures incorporate the fig-ures of the Amerindian and Métis into their textual discussion of postcolonial issues. These differences are rooted in part in the histor-ically divergent relationship to Amerindians in the two linguistic groups and in part in the two groups' very different perceptions of what has come to be called political correctness.

Ever since the publication of Edward Said's *Orientalism* in 1978, the question of the Other as an element in the identification of Self has gained currency in contemporary cultural discourse. Simplifying greatly, one could summarize Said's argument thus: the West identifies itself as different and superior from what it perceives to be "of the Orient." Said assumes a set binary opposition: the (Euro-American) West, which constitutes itself against its set construction of the Orient. If one tries to apply this binary opposition of self/other to the treatment of the Amerindian in the postcolonial literatures of the Americas, however, things begin, to parody Chinua Achebe, to fall apart.

It is my theory that the surprising absence of serious critical reception of Marchessault's work has a great deal to do with the absence of a self/other (Québécois/Amerindian) dichotomy and the creation of what I call a "double insidedness" in the text. Marchessault, unlike other writers, writes from deeply *within* a feminist perspective *and* a complex Québécois/Amerindian identity. Some of the passages of *Comme une enfant de la terre* touch on European techniques of colonization and others reflect aspects of Amerindian mythology. However, Marchessault's ironic and frequently angry challenges to the dominant Catholic belief system in *Comme une enfant de la terre* do not so much criticize French Quebec's exploitation of the Amerindian culture as propose an intriguing blend of Québécois nationalism and Amerindian worldviews. In this novel, the power struggle is therefore *not* white French Quebec *versus* Amerindian, as some contemporary cultural commentators would perhaps wish to frame it (see Di Brandt's "Tenderness and Rage"), but French Quebec *plus* Amerindian *versus* Catholic Church. In this first novel by Marchessault, New World Myth is worked out as a means of "getting out from under" the dominance of the patriarchal Catholic church, which is portrayed as a very powerful and controlling social and mythological *system*.

Marchessault's work is strongly marked by Québécois nationalism and by the conflation – not the opposition – of Amerindian and Québécois cultures and identities. Articles by Jeanne Morazain, Pierre-André Julien, Gilles Lesage, and Normand Delisle in *Le Devoir* during the summer of 1992, as well as several studies in *Recherches amérindiennes*, indicate that the historical evolution of the relationship between native peoples and Québécois has not followed the same path as the relationship between Amerindians and English-speaking Canadians. While it is highly probable that aspects of the Amerindian/Québécois relationship have changed since the New France period, and even, perhaps, since 1975, Marchessault's creation of New World Myth is similar to that found in other texts in this corpus. That is to say, New World Myth may proclaim oppositional conflict (such as this novel's denunciation of the Catholic church), but it also highlights cultural conflation and "cross-cultural confusion," a term which some might equate with apparent contradiction, but which I most certainly do not. In the cultural discourse in Quebec in the 1990s, the related concepts of *l'identitaire* and *convergence culturelle* can be applied to Marchessault's ground-breaking novel of 1975. Out of Marchessault's anger comes the creation of a society in which the conflation of previously differentiated identities, *as well as* the insistence on the multifaceted aspects of any identity, plays an important part. As we saw, this partial conflation of cultural groups was also evident in Wiebe's work, and it is foregrounded in various ways in New World Myth novels. Compared to Wiebe, however, Marchessault shows little evidence of an explanatory focus. She creates, without so much as subtly acknowledging that she is doing so, another reality – one in which she exists so completely that it presents difficulties for Patai's "average reader" from the mainstream.

According to Marchessault's note on the back cover of her novel, the book is entitled *Crachat solaire* and is the first volume in a series entitled *Comme une enfant de la terre*. The novel is generally referred to, however, as *Comme une enfant de la terre*. At first it received a generally negative reception in Quebec: Jean Basile's strongly negative review in *Le Devoir* accused Marchessault of being full of rage and of undiscriminatingly piling words upon words (*"Le Crachat scolaire,"* 14). Nevertheless, the novel was granted the prestigious 1976 Prix France-Québec, winning out over thirty-three other submissions. Marie-Andrée Beaudet notes that even the subsequent publicity failed to generate much serious critical commentary. She blames the esoteric quality of the undertaking and Marchessault's uncharacteristic use of language for the poor reception of the novel (*"Comme une enfant de la terre,"* 170). Gradually, however, critics and other creative writers began to review the novel much more favourably, and both in French and in its English translation it continues to surprise and to shock. Thus, Di Brandt: "Yvonne Klein's fine translation makes available to English readers the dizzying, delirious prose of Jovette Marchessault ... It's hard to talk about this book, hard to name what's happening artistically in it, because it opens up so much wild, uncharted territory, unheard of in English-Canadian writing" ("Tenderness and Rage," 23). Brandt, however, incorrectly identifies Marchessault as "a Native Canadian woman," and completely occults the strong pro-Québécois nationalism in the text. Brandt's longer study of Marchessault's trilogy in *Wild Mother Dancing* explores the shamanic quality of *Comme une enfant de la terre*, noting Marchessault's interest in "origins" and in "envisioning a holistic and woman-affirming cosmology" (83). However, she does not address Marchessault's obvious pro-Québécois nationalist discourse, which in my view is central to the New World Myth offered by the text. It is possible that these inaccuracies are due to the fact that the translator, an American, uses American terms in her translation ("Native Americans" as opposed to "First Nations") and, more probably, to the omission, in the translation, of entire sentences from the French text that refer to the political history of New France and Quebec. I believe that there is also critical silence from the mainstream because *Comme une enfant de la terre* is one of the first fictional works in Quebec to externalize, in large part through its reworkings of biblical mythology, the internal reshaping of the Québécois mythological world.

The well-known twentieth-century historian, Lionel Groulx, reflecting on the traditional relationship between the Catholic faith and the Québécois collectivity, wrote, "French Canada is ... a child of the Church ... [A] whole epoch of her history grew out of faith and mysticism" ("Why We Are Divided," 239). This relationship had not greatly changed in Quebec society prior to 1945, where the ideological focus was on survival: *la survivance*. Although in the people's thinking there was "the realization that the church alone could no longer be the bulwark of the French-Canadian nation ... The central element in this ruling ideology was still the nationalism of survival that kept its vigil over the church, the language, and the established rights of the French Canadians ... The recurrent themes of this ideology were that Heaven was the essential thing, that the people were poor, Catholic, and French ... It was an essentially negative nationalism ... Its sole ambition was to preserve the established order, which meant the preferred position of the clerical and bourgeois élite of Quebec" (Monière, *Ideologies in Quebec*, 226–7). This negative nationalism was dominant during the Duplessis years (1936–39; 1944–59), but there was a major ideological readjustment in the 1960s as the Quiet Revolution provided for a general strengthening of Québécois nationalist identity. One of the indications of this affirmation, proposes Monière, was the decline of the temporal power of the Catholic church: "As far as the church and all its works were concerned, the sky was falling in Quebec ... The old Catholic Quebec took up religious toleration and slid quietly towards a mass exit from the churches." Monière notes that although "[t]hese changes all went deep into Quebec society, and they would have decisive effects on its future ... [i]t should not be imagined ... that they occurred in an atmosphere of perfect progressive unanimity" (257). Indeed, it can be argued that the traditional worldview of Catholic Québec, as described in chapter 1 of this book, was deeply entrenched in the cultural and mythological identity of many Québécois, and that in spite of the rapid changes in Québécois society after 1960, it has taken slightly longer to alter this mythological worldview, anchored as it is in biblical mythology and in linguistic and historical references. I refer here to the traditional worldview of French Canadians in Quebec, which was largely constituted by the formerly omnipresent Catholic education system.

The separation of the church and the state in education in Quebec began as late as 1964, the year of the founding of the provincial ministry of education. This is not to suggest that the Church's authority was sacrosanct from the settling of New France until the Quiet Revolution. A current of opposition to ecclesiastical power is discernible among the francophone inhabitants of the New World, from the *coureurs de bois*, who defied the Church's recommendations to stay home and start families, to the anticlericalism of the Patriotes of the 1830s. Following the failure of the 1837–38 rebellions, however, the Church, with the full blessing of the then British state, consolidated its powers, and the ensuing *réaction catholique* insured that a numerically important and increasingly influential clergy would install and promote a unified worldview in predominantly rural Catholic Quebec.[8] Thus, liberal-minded groups such as the Institut Canadien (a cultural organization founded in the 1840s, whose members called for the separation of church and state and reached out to the general public by founding libraries and organizing conferences) were strongly opposed by the organized church. The latter won out. The resulting, and perhaps abnormal, *idéologie unitaire*, to use Jacques Grand'Maison's term ("L'Eglise et les idéologies au Québec," 294), had a strong impact on the traditional mythology of Quebec, as we saw in chapter 1. Grand'Maison defines this ideology as one that strongly linked and even conflated the Catholic, French and agricultural "vocations" of French Canadians in North America (294). Richard Arès elaborates on the unquestioning *acceptance* of this religiously inspired worldview, which he calls "une chrétienté":

à partir du milieu du XIXe siècle, surtout après l'échec de la tentative d'insurrection de 1837–1838, le peuple canadien-français, sous l'influence et la direction de l'Eglise catholique, a accepté de se constituer en chrétienté; c'est-a-dire ... de devenir socialement chrétien, de faire que ses usages, ses institutions, ses lois aident ses membres à atteindre leur fin surnaturelle, de se laisser animer par l'esprit chrétien, de réintroduire le religieux dans le social, autant que possible sans nuire au respect des nécessaires libertés individuelles. Désormais et durant plus d'un siècle, il y aura au pays du Québec trois signes distinctifs de l'existence d'une chrétienté, savoir: (1) une union – de fait sinon de droit – de l'Eglise et de l'Etat; (2) un entremêlement des institutions religieuses et des institutions civiles, accompagné d'un rôle prédominant des clercs; (3) un rayonnement de la foi des individus sur le plan social et dans la vie publique. Situation qui a duré au Québec jusqu'aux environs du milieu du XXe siècle, époque où la chrétienté québécoise a commencé à ne plus rencontrer l'approbation générale, et même à être durement contestée, et peu à peu s'effriter et s'effondrer. ("L'Evolution de l'Eglise," 270–1)

Because the ideological assumptions which underlie this traditional, religiously inspired mythology formed part of *l'héritage collectif* over many generations, any challenge to them had to penetrate to what I identify as a "deeper level of knowing." The social upheaval brought about by the Quiet Revolution challenged the dominance of the Church-as-institution and the religious framework upon which much of Québécois society had been built. Nonetheless, at a deeper, mythological level, this profoundly entrenched world view has been slower to evolve. Political and social changes in Quebec in recent decades, however, have more than begun to alter the worldview of the collectivity, and a reworking of Catholic Quebec's traditional mythology is discernible in postmodern fictional works such as *Comme une enfant de la terre*.

English-speaking Canada has not had as homogeneous a worldview as the one that dominated traditional Québécois society up until the Quiet Revolution. Indeed, some cultural commentators argue that it is through its very diversity that English Canada defines itself, that its cultural richness is due to the coexistence of several worldviews. Robert Kroetsch suggests in the title of an article that I alter slightly here that "disunity as unity might be a Canadian strategy." This diversity of worldviews, however, does not diminish the influence biblical mythology has exerted on much English Canadian literature, as both Frye and D.G. Jones have argued.[9] English-speaking Canada cannot be qualified as a Catholic nation, but it can be argued that its *traditional* cultural and religious worldview has been predominantly Judeo-Christian, although such a generalization is most probably no longer applicable in the late twentieth century. In this study, "Judeo-Christian" or "Christian" are used to distinguish the English Canadian religious worldview from the Catholic worldview of the Québécois.

Although a theological discussion is inappropriate here, I would agree with Lucinda Vardey's premise that there are some differences between how these two groups see the world (*Belonging*, 200–14). She lays stress on the enduring ritual and public performance of the Catholic Mass, as opposed to the more functional manifestations of spirituality in Protestant communities. Ronald Sutherland's discussion of the "Calvinist-Jansenist Pantomine" presents a different argument. He compares American Puritanism, which was so extreme that it was not practicable and "fell apart" (*Second Image*, 65) to the more moderate and therefore more workable Calvinism in English-speaking Canada. Sutherland argues that there are very strong similarities between the Calvinist attitudes of English-speaking Canada and the *Janséniste* philosophy that reigned in Quebec Catholicism. Both operated from the principle that it was important to show *la résignation chrétienne* (63), to do one's duty on earth, to not enjoy earthly pleasures, especially pleasures of the flesh, but to suffer one's purgatory here on earth. What is most important here is Sutherland's accurate observation of Canadians' "security of reliance upon a church establishment" (65) and upon the power of that church as controlling social system: "The stress, in fact, was evidently placed upon the human-insignificance-and-impotence part of the Puritan ideology, making man more than ever dependent upon the church institution as custodian of God's grace" (68). Christian belief systems are behind that deeper level of knowing discussed above, as Sutherland seems to indicate here: "Whatever the case, this country's Calvinist-Jansenist tradition, whether in English Protestant, Irish Catholic or French Catholic context, whether officially recognized or officially denied, whether conscious or unconscious, has certainly been stamped by the power to hold onto its own" (79).

Obviously, this statement might lead us to reflect not only on the strength of the Calvinist-Jansenist tradition but also on the absence of discussion of non-Christian religions, both in Sutherland's essay and in much of my work here. Without ignoring the multifaceted practice of many religious and spiritual manifestations in contemporary English-speaking Canada and Quebec, however, I would argue that it is Christian belief systems that are (perhaps unconsciously) mythologically highlighted in the work of the writers discussed here, even if they are actively working *against* the power of these systems. This makes sense, of course, if one sees biblical mythology as a meta-narrative that was and is being challenged, even if it is still, in Patai's formulation, "an important part of the general cultural frame of reference" (*Myth and Mythology*, 148) in the New World – be it in Brazil, Quebec, or English-speaking Canada. In the years 1975–85, the power of the biblical mythology of the majority cultures had to be laid bare precisely so that it could then be subverted. It is indeed significant that the authors of all three English Canadian texts examined in this study have publicly focused on the sometimes troubling influence that Christian religions have had on their own formation. Rudy Wiebe was raised in a Mennonite family; Joy Kogawa's father was a Bhuddist before he became an Anglican minister; and George Bowering comes from a Baptist background with an admixture of Mennonite. In contrast, all three Québécois writers studied here were educated in the pre-Vatican II Catholic school system of Quebec.

Biblical imagery has been used in English Canadian literature as a structural and shaping device. It has also served as a means of exerting subtle social and moral controls on an inherited Eurocentric worldview. "Canada's long history as a colony," writes T.D. Maclulich, "meant that there was no attempt to define the Canadian as a new man [such as the New Adam figure in American literature], free from the guilts and anxieties engendered by European society. Canadian authors feel that the restrictions imposed by religious and social conventions are necessary to control the Old Adam" ("Our Place on the Map," 203). "Religion," claims Northrop Frye, "has been a major – perhaps the major – cultural force in Canada, at least down to the last generation or two" ("Conclusion," 1966, 832). The comfortable acceptance – the tacit approval – of the social and moral control exerted by religious elements in this literature, as noted by Maclulich, has been questioned in recent years by both literary works and critical theorists. This challenge is part of the larger postmodern movement discussed in chapter 1: the questioning of traditional, authoritative "givens" that Jean-François Lyotard has termed "metanarratives" (*The Postmodern Condition*, xxiv). Although the first-person narrator of *Obasan*, Megumi Naomi Nakane, does not denounce all things biblical with the unrelenting vehemence that drives Marchessault's unnamed narrator, she does question the ability of the Christian belief system to help her come to terms with the injustices of the past, and she concludes that this system is inadequate to her needs. Her Christian religion, Anglicanism, does not help her establish, as she says in another context, a "safe enough" worldview (*Obasan*, 227). Indeed, both New World Myth texts examined here, through their references to biblical mythology and their questioning of Christian religion(s), foreground the insufficiencies of the traditional interpretation of the Christian belief system for the postmodern era. Three traditional "givens" are particularly challenged in *Obasan* and *Comme une enfant de la terre*: biblical mythology, patriarchal catholicity, and the official version(s) of our historico-political past(s).

Comme une enfant de la terre is composed of twelve *chants* of relatively equal length. *Chant* may be translated as "canto," "song," or "hymn."

As is the case with Wiebe's narrator, Pierre Falcon, the use of a song as a rhetorical device indicates the tension between written and spoken (or sung) language. The narrator's story is difficult to follow. This is due in part to the mystical language she employs, in part to her predilection for "quantitative elaboration," piling words upon words (Herz, "A Québécois and an Acadian Novel," 179), and in part to the fragmentation of the *je*. The narrator's full identity is never totally revealed; the text insists on the undecidability of her species and her essence, though not her gender: she is always female. At different times, she is a kiwi bird (*Comme une enfant*, 18), a being with a barely human face (29), and of celestial origin (11). The constant use and abuse of *various* mythological systems render the narrator's origins confusing: she is part mythical, part animal, and part human. Furthermore, the typical New World Myth blurring of various political issues is evident here: the narrator's Amerindian heritage is stressed throughout the text, as are her "québécitude" and her gender. The emphasis is on storytelling; the narrator follows her own inclinations and frequently changes stories in midstream. She is aware of the unusual, nonlinear quality of her story and celebrates all aspects of its indeterminacy.

La Parole – the Word, or speech – is thematized throughout the work, with the narrator making unequal progress in her efforts to express the ineffable (*Comme une enfant*, 105). When she feels threatened, she flirts with various belief systems in her search for protection. Thus, she seeks comfort from carrying out rituals from both biblical and Amerindian mythologies. Frightened, she makes the (Catholic) sign of the cross but also seeks reassurance from "les mamelles de la Grande-Oursonne" (11), the Great Goddess in the sky, which was the narrator's own home before she "fell" to earth. In this passage, the narrator is playing ironically with the biblical notions of the Fall and of the birth of Christ, but she is also making reference to a myth that originates in Amerindian matriarchal mythology. I refer here to the myth of "Sky Woman," a curious sky dweller who, fascinated by the blue space below her home, was happy to fall to earth through a hole she had made in the clouds. This myth is retold in Beth Brant's significantly entitled short story "This is History," which presents a creation story that strongly emphasizes the matriarchal quality of Amerindian myth.[10] Marchessault places a matriarchal mythology comparable to the myth of Sky Woman up against the patriarchal mythology of the Bible here and elsewhere in her novel. Di Brandt notes the radical elements in the birth scene: "It is difficult, I think, for readers steeped in Western thought to appreciate the implications of this vision, and the radical challenge it offers to non-Native, dualistic thinking: there isn't a fall into conception, there isn't a fall away from Idea, or Word, or Spirit, into the body, there isn't a fall away from father sky to mother earth. There is rather a passage, a birth-giving, from one state of physical/ spiritual being into another, through the celestial body of the She Wolf, her ear canal, her mouth, helped along with a swat from the paws of the presiding Great She-Bear of the sky" (*Wild Mother Dancing*, 79). Although Brandt sees this birth as radically and completely different from the birth scene in Christian mythology, Marchessault does play with the "givens" of Christian mythology, so strongly internalized in Quebec before the Quiet Revolution, in her presentation of an alternative worldview.

Of course, Marchessault is not the only woman to link the oppression of women to organized patriarchal religions in the West. In 1978 Mary Daly's vehement denunciation of patriarchy spoke as strongly as Marchessault does through her narrator: "*Patriarchy is itself the prevailing religion of the entire planet* ... All of the so-called religions legitimating patriarchy are mere sects subsumed under its vast umbrella/canopy ... And the symbolic message of all the sects of the religion which is patriarchy is this: Women are the dreaded anomie. Consequently, women are the objects of male terror, the projected personification of 'The Enemy,' the real objects of attack in all the wars of patriarchy" (*Gyn/Ecology*, 39). Marchessault's novel, however, strongly expresses anger at the oppression of women by the Catholic church, in particular. One method of expressing that anger is by undermining the traditional structure of Québécois mythology at that "deeper level of knowing" previously discussed, in order to destabilize her readers' dependency on *any* belief system.

In the first *chant*, the narrator's world is falling apart: she has been pushed back into "l'orbite du temps" by the "grande soufflerie du ciel" (*Comme une enfant*, 14). Couching her lamentation in biblical terms, she proclaims the total lack of structure in which she must struggle to survive: "En vérité, en vérité, quelqu'un a enlevé les bornes, les balises et effacé les points de repère" (12). In the Bible, especially in the Gospel according to John, Jesus' frequent use of the expression "en vérité, en vérité" usually precedes a divine pronouncement about the Way to the Kingdom of Heaven. Thus, "En vérité, en vérité, je te le dis, / à moins de naître d'eau et d'Esprit / nul ne peut entrer dans le Royaume de Dieu" (3.5). While Jesus was concerned with the criteria for entering the Kingdom of Heaven, Marchessault's narrator is initially focused on survival on earth. The notion of biblical truth is ridiculed in Marchessault's novel, where the recognizable biblical expression *en vérité* frequently precedes insignificant details: "J'imagine ... un mille-pattes (en vérité, en vérité ils n'en n'ont jamais plus de 170 et jamais moins de seize)" (*Comme une enfant*, 31). Alluding to another biblical term, the narrator states that she wishes to "déchirer le rideau de brume de la lamentation." Jesus' death, of course, was marked by the tearing of the curtain of the Holy of Holies in the Temple. For the goddess-like narrator to rend her curtain, to regain "l'immensité du royaume oublié," certain needs must be met – needs that are rooted in nationalist politics, Amerindian traditions, and mythical allusions: "Rendez-moi mon canot! Rendez-moi mon pays! Rendez-moi mes avirons, mes forces … et la substance de la vie avec ses fleuves souverains, ses animaux fabuleux qui apportent des messages en voguant dans l'eau, dans l'air" (20). This passage, along with many other similar passages in this politically engaged New World Myth novel, contains highly charged intertextual allusions. Marchessault frequently conflates biblical references, mystical language, and references to Québécois nationalist slogans. For instance, the passage just quoted contains references to several well-known folk songs and folk tales handed down orally from the time of the voyageurs – songs that became a means of expressing nationalist tendencies during the *indépendantiste* period in Quebec during the 1970s.[11] *Comme une enfant de la terre* is marked by the nationalist *collectivité* argument of the 1960s and '70s. This is not surprising, given that it was published in 1975, whereas the other texts discussed here were published during the 1980s. Although Marchessault's novel adheres to the *collectivité* argument in a way that Godbout's and Barcelo's texts do not, it is not content with the status quo and argues for an expansion of the notion of the *collectivité* by its dual foregrounding of female and Amerindian mythologies.

The narrator's desire for change is expressed first by her rejection of her self – "Je veux me quitter" – and then by her hunger to revisit her homeland, which is obviously a Quebec linked to her mythological and political concerns. Her enumeration of beloved place-names is followed by mythical concepts and vocabulary: "Je veux pousser une pointe jusqu'à Tadoussac, jusqu'à ce cap en sentinelle à l'entrée du Saguenay … Je veux aller jusqu'à Dolbeau, jusqu'à Mille-Vaches, jusqu'à Sault-au-Côchon … Je veux aller jusqu'à mes embouchures, là où je commence, où je finis" (*Comme une enfant*, 21). At the end of the first *chant*, she joyfully welcomes her entry into time and into the present, couching this acceptance in the biblical terms of Genesis, while working in a reference to the frozen lakes of Quebec: "Une épée de feu vient de frapper nos fleuves, nos rivières, nos lacs gelés … Voici venu le jour du baume universel … Voici enfin le temps du principe, le temps de l'eau et de la terre … Le monstre-lamentation se métamorphose en beauté et toutes griffes dehors il s'agrippe à l'univers" (23–4). Bizarre and fabulous as its lyrical, mythical language may be, this first section of the text nonetheless introduces many of the major areas of concern of New World Myth: the rejection of established authoritarian order, be it temporal or spiritual; politics and nationalism; the thematization of *la parole* and the tensions inherent in its relationship with *l'écriture*; and a reworking of mythological systems, with particular attention given to inserting aspects of Amerindian matriarchal mythology and Quebec social mythology into the narrative while subverting the traditionally inherent power of biblical mythology.

The next four *chants* (2–5) are couched in the same mythical language with occasional didactic passages. The narrator has been in Mexico with her friend Francine. Driven by a desire to "revoir [ses] terres, prendre racine à [ses] rives; parler tous les jours [sa] langue naturelle" (*Comme une enfant*, 102), she heads north, accompanied by Francine as far as Phoenix, Arizona. There, in an underground café, while discussing male-female relationships, she has a spiritual experience that is related to her control over self-expression (100–9). Her previous blockage as "un animal muet [qui ne sait] rien prononcer" (60) is suddenly replaced by a feeling of liberty: "Les mots m'apparaissent comme des escaliers en spirales qui aboutissent à une porte. Qui s'ouvre!" (105). This image indirectly introduces another important theme of this novel to which I shall return: by regaining their power over speech, women permit themselves to retell their histories – personal and political – and thus to alter the status quo of the patriarchal world. The spiral, referred to in the passage just quoted, has become a symbol of women's power for many Québécoises, as Nicole Brossard explains in Hénaut's film, *Les Terribles vivantes*.

Chants 2–5 include several digressive and highly original passages that seem to have little bearing on the already confusing story, such as asides on the voyages of Christopher Columbus and on the origins and growth of banana trees. These digressions in the story mainly parody the European-inspired stories of the "discovery" of the New World and are typical of New World Myth narration. A highly personal tone dominates here. The narrator's retellings are in fact long chats with her friend: "Je t'écoute, ma chère Francine; je bois tes paroles et je m'empoigne, je m'énumère jusqu'à la nausée" (69). In this text, Marchessault's narrator deliberately engages patriarchal society's stereotypical appreciation of nonlinear exchanges between women (otherwise known as chit-chat) as essentially female and therefore of little significance. She does this by actively promoting chatting as a positive aspect of female communication, one that permits and encourages female reappropriations of "*his*-story."

In the sixth *chant*, the narrator, now travelling alone toward her homeland, reflects at length on *l'écriture* and *la parole* and on her gradual liberation from the limitations of what traditionally has been described as a man's way of thinking – that is to say, linear, conceptual, logical reasoning. More confident now, she proclaims: "je suis le Scribe! J'acquiers une main glorieuse et je relate. J'invente ... J'interprète et je parle ... J'écris avec cette main radieuse afin que la nuit où me seront comptées mes années, je sois en mesure de prononcer les paroles de la lumière. Avant que je commence ce récit, plusieurs soleil [sic] sont déjà morts en moi. J'ai appris peu à peu à faire sauter les amarres du raisonnable, à faire table rase des théories" (135–7). This desire to get *beyond* the "raisonnable" by eliminating "les théories" is an important factor in the female mythology explored in this text, as well as in its postmodern challenge to the rational, logical acquisition of knowledge.

The seventh *chant* is addressed to the voices of her friends – voices that "retentissent sur les tambours de nos mémoires" (144) – and leads into a detailed loving description of the physical geography and political history of Quebec. Memory, as we shall see, is another important concern of Marchessault's narrator in her attempt to retell history from a feminine perspective. This seventh *chant* also contains the fantasy-story of the "sickness of silence" that befell Quebec at an unspecified time; it bears a definite resemblance to the "sickness of forgetfulness" that beset the inhabitants of Gabriel García Márquez's Macondo (*One Hundred Years of Solitude*, 52–5) – with similar political allegory intended.

The eighth *chant* consists of a description of the narrator's city, Montreal; it recounts a nontraditional history of its foundation. In the next three *chants*, the narrator returns to personal, instead of public, history: she describes the lives of her Amerindian grandfather and her part-French, part-Amerindian grandmother and their epic journeys across America. Again, this tale is interspersed with anecdotes that seem to bear little relation to each other or to the narrator's personal and public history. They do, however, signal yet once again the conflation – not the conflictual opposition – of Francophone and Amerindian interests.

The last *chant*, by its incantatory language and its mythical and biblical allusions, recalls the tone of first one: "Et voici que quelque chose resurgit ... Cette chose se fait air, feu, eau, terre matérielle, image corporelle dans l'Image unique, dans l'Idée unique" (327–8).

Here is the narration, in mythical terms, of the narrator's wild flight across the skies before she is born – daughter to her earthly mother and a female celestial force, and a goddess in her own right. The last sentence emphasizes the cyclical structure of the text, relating, as did the first sentence of the text, the birth of the narrator: "et je plonge, je plonge, je descends en flèche comme un crachat solaire" (348).

As is the case in other New World Myth novels, Marchessault's narrator deliberately problematizes her identity. Thus, the novel draws correspondences between the unnamed narrator and the author of the text. The front cover of the novel depicts one of Jovette Marchessault's frescoes, which, as we learn on the copyright page, forms part of Louise and Jacques L'Archevêque's art collection. Within the text, the narrator discusses this fresco, thereby drawing attention to the tension between the reality of the text and the reality outside it. Elsewhere in the novel, one of her many "tales" recounts the mock-epic journey of her maternal grandfather, and in the process, illustrates how he came by his name: "John marchait. John marchait-eau, John Marchessault et toutes les villes de l'Amérique sont marquées au fer rouge sur sa peau" (279). The narrator also shares several autobiographical details with the author: both are self-taught, both have worked at menial jobs, both have travelled extensively in North America, and both have a part-Amerindian heritage.

In *Comme une enfant de la terre*, the narrator's role is to affirm and to protect her "Terre promise" (65) – Québec – from afflictions that beset it, such as sexual inequality and self-denigrating colonial attitudes. She presents herself ironically as both sacrificial lamb and as oracle. Through her travels, her use of memory, and, eventually, through her "witnessing" – her retelling of history – she will attempt to redeem her *pays*. Aware of her lack of training and her marginality, the narrator is at first reluctant to undertake an altruistic mission in a patriarchal world dominated by the Christian belief system: "Je suis comme une lutteuse qui s'est mal préparée au combat; qui ... [est] sur le point d'être disqualifiée parce qu'il n'y a plus de maître" (103). After her liberating experience in the underground cave, however, she is ready to assume her role, which is to speak up, to defend her world, and to challenge Québécois catholicity and patriarchy. The narrator now is able to orally express the inexpressible: her untold history. Having consciously decided to act, she gladly accepts the chaotic New World situation within which she must operate and, in a parody of Christ, announces the (Good) Word to the multitudes: "Je m'arrête là, au centre du chaos, je bois et je danse, je tire des plans pour une vie nouvelle ... J'annonce ma résolution à la foule des multitudes, aux enfants du déluge avec des mots, des sons qui vont de la joie profonde à la détresse, de la colère à la menace ... Le temps presse ... je dois partir avant que le papillon ... pénètre dans ma bouche pour y piller les mots qui dorment sur ma langue" (106–7). A blurring of boundaries among the natural (animal, mineral) world, the familial world, the Amerindian world, the nationalist world (Québec), and the human and the heavenly worlds is common in Marchessault's text. Nationalism, as would be expected, is particularly foregrounded in those parts of the text that focus on the narrator's *pays*. As was the case with the works studied in chapter 2, the text thematizes the uncertainty of historical knowledge in the postmodern age, through its insistence on narratorial insecurity. Thus, this novel emphasizes the metamorphosis of the narrator, her identification with the physical geography of her *pays*, her retelling of history, her preoccupation with her double Amerindian/Québécois heritage, her concern with animism and theomorphism, and her exploration of what has been called "newly rediscovered female mythology" (Lewis, "Introduction," 8).

Kogawa's *Obasan* also foregrounds the uncertainty of historical knowledge, the problematization of the notion of community, and the questioning of traditional markers of myth. Two major stories are told in the novel: the government's mistreatment of Japanese Canadians on the West Coast of Canada during World War Two and the narrator's particular reactions to that mistreatment and to other personal concerns. While Jovette Marchessault's text deals with European-inspired oppressions in the New World, Kogawa's text addresses the recent historico-political past of English-speaking Canada itself. As R.P. Bilan points out, *Obasan* sheds light on what has been "one of the least known – and most frightening – aspects of Canadian history" ("Fiction," 317). Several nonfictional works now offer retrospectives on this historical period.[12] *Obasan*, however, struck deep and effected change. The novel, in the words of Douglas Hill, is a "quietly savage indictment of Wasp-Canadian racism" ("Ethnic Fiction," 31). The Canadian government, in particular, comes under attack: "Aunt Emily sends letters to the Government. The Government makes paper airplanes out of our lives and files us out the windows" (*Obasan*, 242). *Obasan* contrasts with the many historiographic fictions published in English Canada and Quebec during 1975–85 that deal mainly with colonial, as opposed to indigenous, injustices. Interestingly, an overtly political review of *Obasan* in *L'Actualité* ties the indigenous to the colonial, drawing strong parallels between the dispersal of the Japanese Canadians and the *Grand Dérangement* of the Acadians: "Kogawa et *Obasan* racontent en témoins oculaires les misères des familles, réplique de la répression de Murray et de Winslow contre les Acadiens en 1755" (Keith Spicer, "Les Acadiens aux yeux bridés," 28). To my knowledge, no other critic or reviewer has drawn this historical and cultural parallel.

As is common in novels dealing with myth, *Obasan* has a cyclical structure: the passage in chapter 1 describing Uncle and Naomi's annual visit to the coulee is reflected in the narrator's return visit there in the last chapter to honour the deaths of her mother and uncle. The epigraph, a biblical passage taken from the Book of Revelation, is the first indication of the novel's religious frame of reference, while the prefatory address signals the blurring of the boundaries between the real and the fictional so common in New World Myth texts. Kogawa writes, "Although this novel is based on historical events, and many of the persons named are real, most of the characters are fictional." The proem refers to many of the central concerns of this strongly political text: the difficulty of speech and the opposition of speech to silence; the different mythical worlds of the Copernican and Ptolemaic universes; imprisonment, birth, and freedom, and a strong desire to "tell": "Unless the stone bursts with telling, unless the seed flowers with speech, there is in my life no living word."

Chapters, or parts of chapters, consist of flashbacks, and it is only at the end of the novel that the mystery of what happened to the narrator's mother is finally solved, as the story of the mistreatment of the Japanese Canadians is finally told. The constantly shifting narration describes the adult Naomi's relationships with her very different aunts, Obasan and Emily, and the child's life before, during, and after the war. The ubiquitous question of national identity and its relation to race is underlined by the textual inclusion of governmental documents, newspaper clippings, and "toneless form letter[s]" (37):

I held the pages [of the pamphlet] ... There it was in black and white – our short harsh history. Beside each date were the ugly facts of the treatment given to Japanese Canadians. "Seizure and government sale of fishing boats. Suspension of fishing licences. Relocation camps. Liquidation of property. Letter to General MacArthur. Bill 15. Deportation. Revocation of nationality."

Wherever the words "Japanese race" appeared, Aunt Emily had crossed them out and written "Canadian citizen."

"What this country did to us, it did to itself," she said. (*Obasan*, 33)

The narrator's initial reluctance to address the question of political injustice, to "tell the story," is foregrounded in the opening scenes of the novel. The painful personal past, she says, "does not bear remembering" (49). At the beginning of the novel she is also unwilling to be a voice of remembering for her people, but Aunt Emily, during her infrequent visits, provokes Naomi to delve into the past and to relive her memories. *Obasan* is composed of three interconnecting narratives: the child narrator's story, the adult narrator's story, and Aunt Emily's diary. All three sections are first-person accounts of personal and political events.

Puzzled by the questions that still haunt the adult narrator, the child takes refuge in silence. Naomi feels guilt about her mother's disappearance, because it happens soon after her first sexual awakenings. A neighbour, Old Man Gower, sexually molests her, and soon she goes willingly to his lap: "His hands are frightening and pleasurable. In the centre of my body is a rift ... My mother is on one side of the rift. I am on the other. We cannot reach each other" (*Obasan*, 65). The confusion in the child narrator's worldview about this episode and other equally complicated ones is translated through her frequent references to riddles and to fairy tales. When her brother calls her a "Jap," and her father corrects this – "No ... We're Canadian" – her solution is to see things as a riddle: "We are both the enemy and not the enemy" (70). As an adult, the confusion remains for her, and it is again transmitted through the use of childlike imagery: "I've never understood how these things happen. There's something called an order-in-council that sails like a giant hawk across a chicken yard, and after the first shock there's a flapping squawking lunge for safety. One swoop and the first thousand are on ships sailing for disaster" (188–9). This image of chickens and danger is taken up in various ways in the novel, and, as Cheng Lok Chua points out, it frequently refers to the problem of identity in community. For instance, as a child, Naomi innocently places some live Easter chicks into a mother hen's compound. Chua explains: "Contrary to Naomi's naive expectations, however, the mother hen pecks at the chicks and kills them; Kogawa's ironic comment upon the treatment of Japanese by Caucasian Canadians in their own homeland is clear when one notices that the chicks are yellow and the mother hen is white" ("Witnessing the Japanese Canadian Experience," 103; see *Obasan*, 58). (The complexities of being both "the enemy and not the enemy" (*Obasan*, 70) are discussed in chapter 4, below.)

After the war, Naomi becomes a worker on a beet farm in Alberta. The word for life there, the narrator notes cryptically, is "hardship." One of the basic themes of the novel, the tension between official history and "reality," is conveyed by the narratorial gloss of a newspaper photograph entitled "Grinning and Happy," which shows a

Japanese Canadian family standing around a pile of beets. "I cannot, I cannot bear the memory," says the narrator (*Obasan*, 194). "'Grinning and Happy' ...? That is one telling. It's not how it was" (197).

As the narration proceeds, Naomi gradually recollects the sufferings of herself and her people. At the end of the story, the secret of her mother's disappearance is revealed to her when the Anglican minister, Nakayama-sensei, reads aloud a letter written in Japanese that Naomi herself cannot read. A victim of the atomic bomb dropped on Nagasaki in 1945, her mother remained alive for an indeterminate period of time in Japan. It was her wish to spare her children any knowledge of her agony. Aunt Emily, Uncle, and Obasan have known of the tragedy since Grandmother Kato's letter arrived in 1954, but there has been "no telling" (232) to Naomi and Stephen. Once Naomi realizes that her mother's silence was a message of her love, the rift she has always felt in her body is somewhat healed. Reflecting that "Somewhere between speech and hearing is a transmutation of sound" (245), she determines that "wordlessness" has been her destruction and implies that she will not remain lost in her silences (243).

Obasan is structured around strong tensions between different worldviews. First, there is continual tension between things Japanese and things Canadian. Their coexistence is underlined on the linguistic level. As Erika Gottlieb points out, Kogawa's style "is the result of extensive linguistic experimentation, presenting us with the special flavour of Japanese Canadian speech patterns and their underlying sensibilities" ("Concentric Worlds," 39). The narrator conveys the linguistic confusion so typical of New World Myth novels by occasionally blending English and Japanese phrases: "'Nothing changes ne,' I say" (*Obasan*, 1). By explaining instead of translating Japanese expressions, she underlines the basic differences behind the separate linguistic systems: "If Grandma shifts uncomfortably, I bring her a cushion. 'Yoku ki ga tsuku ne,' Grandma responds. It is a statement in appreciation of sensitivity and appropriate gestures" (56). The political implications of cultural tension are clearly signalled. Thus, in Obasan's living room, a "bright purple maple-leaf-fringed cushion" clashes with the clutter of "Japanese-language newspapers" (222–3). Kogawa does not hyphenate "Japanese Canadians," although it is hyphenated in some reviews of her novel. Could this orthography be part of the narrator's effort to point out how Japanese Canadians are rendered marginal even at the purely linguistic level? Thus, there are Canadians and then there are those "others": Japanese-Canadians. This technique, if it is one, recalls the change from "Canadien-français" to "Québécois" in Quebec during the Quiet Revolution: in rejecting a hyphenated naming, this change indicated a refusal to assume a subjugated identity.

In addition to the first tension between things Japanese and things Canadian, there is a second tension to which I shall return, that subtle one between Christian and Buddhist mythologies. There is a third tension between the Christian worldview of love and forgiveness and the narrator's reactions to historical injustices, which do not always correspond. Fourth, there is tension between the governmental view of the "Japanese situation" and the Japanese Canadians' view of their own role in wartime Canada. Fifth, there are internal tensions in the narrator's evolving worldview. Should she retell her stories or forget the past? Did her mother love or abandon her? Is she Canadian or Japanese? Which aunt's reaction should she emulate – Obasan's silences or Emily's vehement claims for justice?

The impetus to tell the story comes from the narrator's desire for change, her desire for life, and her overriding need of the "living word" (proem). The telling, however, does not alter her knowledge of the immanent quality of life and of story. Describing a family photograph, with its message that "for ever and ever all is well," the narrator, a teacher, asserts the uncertainty of everything: "Even my eleven-year-olds know that you can't 'capture life's precious moments,' as they say in the camera ads" (*Obasan*, 20). Nonetheless, by retelling the private story of her childhood anguish and the public story of the dispersal, the narrator seeks to gain partial control over her own worldview, all the while foregrounding the impossibility of ever coming to total knowledge and understanding of the past. Like many other New World Myth texts, then, this novel emphasizes its deliberate blurring of the personal, the political, and the religious; the thematization of speech and the struggle to overcome silence; the speech/writing debate; the fiction/history debate; and the prevalent tensions inherent in New World Myth. These tensions lead to a fundamental question posed by both *Comme une enfant de la terre* and *Obasan*: what, in this postmodern age, is the function of an historiographic work of art?

A partial answer to this question may be found in the reworkings of the traditional concept of myth in the novels studied here. As Ernst Cassirer declares in *The Myth of the State*, "we must know what myth *is* before we can explain how it *works*" (4). This assumes that myth can be clearly defined. However, as Michael Palencia-Roth points out in *Myth and the Modern Novel*, "myth 'is' different things for different people, and thus it 'works' differently" (13). He further notes that writers on myth may examine wildly different aspects in their discussions: "The more psychological stress, naturally enough, the unconscious and dreams. The more literary emphasize stories or, like Aristotle, the plots and structure of these stories. The more religious accentuate myth's sacred, transcendental, and cosmogonic qualities. The more anthropological point up myth's ritualistic aspects. The more philosophical of course focus on myth as a kind of thinking" (13–14). As we saw in the introductory chapter, most studies of myth in literature, including those devoted to English Canadian and Québécois literature, assume or overtly posit myths as master narratives. For instance, Northrop Frye's theory of the Ptolemaic and Copernican universes proposes a diachronic development of two all-encompassing mythic worldviews. This theory of Frye's is referred to in many of his publications; a clear presentation of its basic concepts is to be found in "New Directions from Old." Although Frye's structured system building is not helpful in theorizing about New World Myth, his succinct explanations of the Ptolemaic and Copernican systems are useful here as a point of departure. They describe diachronically evolved mythological systems, with the Ptolemaic topocosm preceding the Copernican one.

In the West, according to Frye, the Ptolemaic cosmology was the dominant structure of the mythological universe until the Renaissance, when it was slowly replaced by that structured on the Copernican model (Frye, "New Directions," 63–4). The Ptolemaic cosmology consisted of a four-level topocosm, which Frye defines as the "background of roughly four levels of existence" such as are found in the work of Dante, Spenser, and Milton (63). The "old structure of authority was an ordered hierarchy with God on top, the perfect world he had made (and to which it is our primary duty to return) directly underneath, the 'fallen' world into which we are born below that, and the demonic world at the bottom" ("Myth as the Matrix," 475). Although "[s]cience blew up the Ptolemaic universe ... Christianity, after feeling itself cautiously all over, discovered that it had survived the explosion" ("New Directions," 52). With Romanticism, according to Frye, the Copernican model appears: "another 'topocosm,' almost the reverse of the traditional one, begins to take shape. On top is the bleak and frightening world of outer space. Next comes the level of ordinary human experience, with all its anomalies and injustices. Below ... is the buried original form of society ... On the fourth level, corresponding to the traditional hell or world of death, is the mysterious reservoir of power and life out of which both nature and humanity proceed" (64).

Frye, that "Canadian mythographer" par excellence (Sullivan, "Northrop Frye," 1), not only presents his theory of these supposedly mutually exclusive systems, but he explains the usually occluded assumptions under which proponents of each system operate. Frye's theory, however, cannot be applied successfully to Kogawa's and Marchessault's texts, because these two novels subvert the teleological nature of traditional myth (and myth studies) by underlining the coexistence of *each* of these two systems, the Ptolemaic and Copernican topocosms, within the texts themselves. Thus, Frye's theory is useful in that it describes the parameters of the two dominant cosmologic systems that have been at the root of worldviews and attitudes to "God" in what is commonly called the West. However, the theory is inapplicable to these novels, in that they present a conflation or a convergence of topocosms that, in Frye's view, are in a necessarily diachronic relationship. Indeed, in these works by Marchessault and Kogawa, the hegemony of *any* fixed mythological system is challenged. New World Myth, with its drive to reject metanarratives in life *and* literature, foregrounds its postmodern awareness of the indeterminacy of history and of the decentring of all systems – mythical ones included.

Frye argues that the Ptolemaic universe continued to influence poetic thought for centuries, but that its dominance of even that territory has worn out as the "inherited structure of authority in the Western world is undergoing a process of revolutionary change" ("Myth as the Matrix," 475). I would argue, however, that the pre-Renaissance worldview (see chapter 1, above) has prevailed in the Catholic Québécois worldview – and not only in its cultural expressions of poetic thought – for far longer than it has in most occidental worldviews. Quebec's isolation in matters pertaining to theology prior to the Quiet Revolution contributed to its formation of a surprisingly hegemonic worldview. As Robert Viau has argued, "La Réforme et ses conséquences – laïcisation, étatisation, montée de la bourgeoisie – ont eu peu de répercussions dans la colonie agricole isolée et dominée par le clergé" (*Les Fous de Papier*, 34). The narrator of *Comme une enfant de la terre* deliberately foregrounds her challenge to the Ptolemaic/Christian universe and, to a lesser extent, to the Copernican universe, thus calling into question the traditional authority structure inherent in either mythological system. In Frye's scheme, the Christian worldview is modelled on the Ptolemaic universe. This novel decries Catholic patriarchal worldviews and strongly challenges the Ptolemaic mythological structure, which underlies much traditional Québécois mythology.

In traditional Catholicism, heaven is the home of God, and the sky is thus the natural element to which a Catholic symbolically aspires to attain. The widely accepted mythological framework of a vertically ascending movement toward God, however, is shattered by the narrator of Jovette Marchessault's work, who sets up two coexisting systems that provoke topocosmic confusion. In her article on the use of myth in this novel, Micheline Herz rightly associates this "cosmogony gone wild" with the conflict between imagination, on the one hand, and reason and logic, on the other ("A Québécois," 177). This conflict, however, is also rooted in a mythological culture clash. Herz notes that the "vertical schemes are those of the fall ... [and also] of an ascent towards celestial life," but she summarily dismisses this narratorial play with direction by stating that "she who goes down knows that she can go up again" (176). Such a simplification, I would suggest, does not give sufficient weight to the narratorial blurring of the Ptolemaic and Copernican universes in this complex text. Neither does it take into account the presence of Amerindian mythology in the novel.

Frye points out that "[a]s long as poets accepted the Ptolemaic universe, the natural place for the point of epiphany was a mountaintop just under the moon, the lowest heavenly body" (*Anatomy*, 204). In the Ptolemaic scheme, the "upper world is often symbolized by the heavenly bodies" ("New Directions," 58–9). Its opposite point is the "lower world, reached by descent through a cave or under water [which] is more oracular and sinister, and as a rule is or includes a place of torment and punishment." There are "points of particular significance in poetic symbolism ... the top of a mountain ... [and] a mysterious labyrinthine cave" (59). This order, as we have seen, is inverted in the Copernican worldview, with the sky becoming a cold and forbidding element and the depths of the earth a life-giving force. In Marchessault's work, this ascending and descending vertical imagery is presented differently in different parts of the text, bringing the two worldviews into conflict. One clear example of this topocosmic confusion is provided by two separate images of the underground cave. The first is clearly within the Ptolemaic/Christian pattern. A substantial part of the eighth *chant* consists of a description of Jos Beef's demonic tavern, hidden away in the small streets of the Port of Montreal. There, a nightly *sabbat* provides entertainment for sailors. Jos Beef, whose historical existence has been signalled in other literary works, such as David Fennario's 1991 play, *Jos Beef*, is portrayed as a demonic high priest presiding over the communal torture and sacrifice of wild animals he has imprisoned beneath a trapdoor in his establishment. All the expected accoutrements decorate the scene: the fire, the demonic circle traced in blood, the excitement of the participants in the ritual, and the invocations to the gods of the underworld. In typical New World Myth fashion, this last demonic element includes a salutation to today's type of "god": "Salut à vous tous les présidents-directeurs-généraux-subalternes-en-uniforme-de-piastre-agenouillés" (*Comme une enfant*, 227). The New World Myth narrator ties this underworld to twentieth-century social history, working condemnations of Sigmund Freud and Adolph Hitler into the text. Freud is particularly condemned for his pretensions to universal, rational knowledge of all human beings – and his derogatory comments about women – as the narrator here articulates her preference for mythical schemes in her exploration of the "secrets" of the essence of humanity. As might be expected, the narration of this horrifying demonic spectacle takes its semantic framework from the Bible. Thus, Jos Beef "savait faire cuire le pain magique sur lequel il traçait des signes" (217); the smells from the subterranean holding-pen are a "[p]arfum du troisième jour de la création" (224), and the action ironically takes place under a plaque that is "décorée d'une scène biblique: celle des Noces de Cana" (219). The narrator notes that demonic imagery has its necessary place in the scheme of things: "Et pourtant, la pestilence et la fièvre, par leur infernale ronde, portent témoignage aussi bien que les étoiles, des lois immuables et de l'harmonie de l'univers" (225–6).

The second image of an underground cave, that of the subterranean café in the significantly named Phoenix, Arizona, falls within the Copernican topocosm. Here, beneath the city that onomastically recalls the mythical bird's ascension from ashes into new life, the narrator has a liberating, transcendental experience. Frye, we have seen, describes the primary (lowest) level of the Copernican topocosm as a "mysterious reservoir of power and light out of which both nature and humanity proceed. This world is morally ambivalent, being too archaic for distinctions of good and evil, and so retains some of the sinister qualities of its predecessor" ("New Directions," 64–5). In *Comme une enfant de la terre*, the narrator first accords mythical significance to this city: "Je peux même penser que l'Ancienne-des-Temps et les étoiles dont les révolutions s'accomplissent en de grandes années, décrivent au-dessus de cette ville, un cercle immense sous l'action des courants opposés qui ont lutté ici" (96–7). She and her travelling companion, Francine, penetrate into a dark, labyrinthine canteen: "Nous allions vers de basses demeures, des temps inférieurs ou intérieurs, je ne sais plus" (97). There, they encounter "[d]es âmes sœurs ... [qui] se rassemblent à heure fixe pour réparer l'éclat du monde" (98). This subterranean cavern, the perfect point of epiphany of the Copernican universe in this section of the text, is thus a source of rejuvenation, of hope, and of liberty for the narrator.

It gradually becomes evident that the narrator, while using here the imagery of a Copernican framework, does not consistently maintain it. Instead, she flits back and forth between the topocosms of ascent and of descent, presenting several distinct paradoxes in the text. For instance, in the midst of generally positive Ptolemaic/Christian ascent and birth images, she refutes traditional symbols of ascension: the narrator "[n]e sai[t] pas voir plus loin que [sa] défaite et nie l'arbre, l'échelle, le mât où circulent des escalades sans fin" (18). Elsewhere in the text, Ptolemaic images that usually suggest self-improvement and personal growth (such as the metamorphosis of the chrysalis/butterfly) or means of attaining to the "au-delà" (such as bridges and rainbows) are subverted by the narrator. Playing with the accepted symbolism of these images, she deliberately lays bare the underlying assumptions of both topocosms, and distances herself from each: "L'ordre de l'univers ... en serait il perturbé? Peut être que oui ... Peut-être que non" (32). The narrator's refusal to choose one topocosmic system over another permits her to challenge the authority structure inherent in either mythological system. By deliberately contrasting two cosmological systems in one story, the narrator foregrounds them both as systems and effectively diminishes their power to shape any worldview. In particular, the narrator illustrates the insufficiencies of the pre-Renaissance worldview – the Ptolemaic/Christian one – which, as I argue, has prevailed until recently in the Québécois worldview. She thus prepares for a New World Myth point of view.

Kogawa's *Obasan* presents both differences from and similarities to Marchessault's treatment of the Ptolemaic and Copernican universes in *Comme une enfant de la terre*. The Ptolemaic topocosm, closely associated to the Catholic worldview, is more vehemently attacked in Marchessault's work. In Kogawa's text, Christian beliefs, images, and patterns, as well as Biblical citations and allusions, are everywhere. As Merivale points out, a problematic "Christianity 'binds' together on levels other than the political or social: it binds together *the book*" ("Framed Voices," 73). I argue here, however, that in spite of its underlying Christian framework, Kogawa's novel is a quiet testimonial to the insufficiencies of the Christian belief system today.

The predominant topocosmic structure of *Obasan* is the Copernican model. Kogawa's own comments in an interview gloss this choice of topocosm: "The feminist theologian Rosemary Ruether argues that humanity went through a crisis after the Second World War when it had to face the power of its destructive capacities at Auschwitz and Hiroshima. I think what Ruether is saying is that the experience was felt as one of our abandonment by God. We were forsaken and lost … It may be that we are swinging on the 'transcendence-imminence' pendulum in the direction of imminence, the argument being that our cries to the Help 'out there' were met by silence and that we did not seek out the Help that is available here in our human condition" (Garrod, "Joy Kogawa," 141). Kogawa's use of the phrase "out there" is revealing. In the Copernican system, the sky is no longer the welcoming home of the Christian god but a bleak and frightening empty space. In the proem to *Obasan* the sky repulses the narrator: "I hate the staring into the night. The questions thinning into space." The sky, she notes, maintains its "silence" and "swallow[s] the echoes … There is no reply." This poetic version of the Copernican universe in the proem is echoed in the narrator's everyday language. Thus, sitting with her Uncle on the slope above the coulee, Naomi admits to feeling dominated by the sky: "Above and around us, unimaginably vast and unbroken by silhouette of tree or house or any hint of human handiwork, is the prairie sky. In all my years in Southern Alberta, I have not been able to look for long at this" (*Obasan*, 3). Frye notes that after "the rise of Copernican astronomy and Newtonian physics … [t]he stars look increasingly less like vehicles of angelic intelligences, and come to suggest rather a mechanical and mindless revolution" ("New Directions," 64). This view of the universe as a cold, impersonal machine that shapes her life first comes to Naomi when her mother is called away from her side. Years later, on the Barker farm, the sky is again seen as a malevolent controlling force: "The clouds are the shape of our new prison walls – untouchable, impersonal, random" (196).

Naomi's dreams are full of imagery suggestive of "something mechanical and malignant in human nature" (Frye, "New Directions," 64): robotic animals and trained, unfeeling white soldiers "eager for murder, their weapons ready" (*Obasan*, 227). As Gottlieb suggests, the various figures in the dream of the British martinet are presented as mechanical beings who "manifest the destructiveness of evil as part of our unfeeling, indifferent, machine-like civilization" ("Riddle," 44). The Copernican topocosm is reflected in the lack of goodness (and godliness) in the political injustices suffered by Naomi's family and by the Japanese Canadian community. Referring to the impersonal tone of the custodian's form letter to Aunt Emily, the narrator rhetorically asks: "Did he experience a tiny twinge of pleasure at the power his signature must represent? Did B. Good sometimes imagine himself to be God? Or was it all just a day's mindless job?" (37).

Frye notes that "in the twentieth century … images of descent are, so to speak, in the ascendant … [In the Copernican system] the reward of descent is usually oracular or esoteric knowledge, concealed or forbidden to most people, often the knowledge of the future" ("New Directions," 62). In Naomi's case, however, the knowledge in question is not knowledge of the future, but, ironically, knowledge of the past. *Obasan*'s proem emphasizes the descent to underground knowledge, with speech being privileged in the narrator's particular worldview: "Beneath the grass the speaking dreams and beneath the dreams is a sensate sea. The speech that frees comes forth from that amniotic deep … If I could follow the stream down and down to the hidden voice, would I come at last to the freeing word?" A movement of descent (rather than ascent) may be productive of knowledge. Thus, the narrator welcomes her descent into "white windless dream" with "prayers descending" and "[f]ingers tunnelling" (*Obasan*, 28), and the remote possibility of knowing the secrets of the past. Recovering from her near drowning, Naomi again associates descent with her loved ones and with safety, wanting to go "down to the moss-covered door on the forest floor that opens to the tunnel leading to the place where my mother and father are hiding" (151). On the Alberta beet farm, the only peaceful places are *in* the earth: the main irrigation ditch and the root cellar. Naomi perceives God as being far away and human beings as cogs in an uncaring and impersonal machine. The sense of powerlessness typical of the Copernican universe is reflected in the following imagery: "Sometimes when I stand in a prairie night the emptiness draws me irresistibly, like a dust speck into a vacuum cleaner, and I can imagine myself disappearing off into space like a rocket with my questions trailing behind me" (186). In this politically engaged novel, the machine imagery is equally applicable to the Canadian government, whose faceless employees issue unfeeling orders to Japanese Canadians.

The dominance of the Copernican universe in *Obasan*, however, is contrasted at different places in the novel with images from the Ptolemaic/Christian topocosm. As is the case with Marchessault's narrator, the confusion in Naomi's worldview is reflected by the confusion between the two cosmogonies in the text. The Ptolemaic imagery is most evident in the passages describing life in Slocan, the ghost town that has "sudden fresh air … open space … a lake … [and] mountains covered in trees, climbing skyward" (*Obasan*, 119). For a relatively short period of time Naomi glories in the paradisiacal beauty of the ghost town. In the Ptolemaic universe, as we have seen, up is good and down is bad. Vertical ascension imagery is particularly evident during Naomi's hike to the highest lookout point above the town. Here, "up" is good because it gives a view, an understanding, and thus at least the illusion of a certain control over events that shape the world: "here we are, suddenly looking down on Lilliput from the top of the world. A dizzying kingdom … The world is as immense as sky and tiny as the pin-dot flowers in the moss" (141). This Ptolemaic world of ascension is also evident in the narrator's use of negative connotations of descent imagery in her description of her family's forced journey into the British Columbia interior in 1942: "We are going down to the middle of the earth with pick-axe eyes, tunnelling by train to the Interior, carried along by the momentum of the expulsion into the waiting wilderness" (111). Naomi, however, has happy memories of community life in Slocan. As she remembers years later, in 1945, "the gardens in Slocan were spectacular. In the spring there had been new loads of manure and fertilizer and the plants were ripening for harvest when the orders came" (183) – inhuman, mechanical, governmental orders to disperse, destroying the microcosmic earthly paradise the Japanese Canadians had managed to carve out of the wilderness.

The occasional testimonies to the Ptolemaic/Christian universe in this text serve to subtly underline the narrator's topocosmic confusion. So too does the imagery of things turned upside down, a common trait of New World Myth novels: "I am overcome with dizziness. I cannot tell which direction the beach is, where the raft is, where the nearest point of safety is. Sky and lake swirl as I gasp and swallow … Again and again I am plunged and twirled in the frantic dizziness" (*Obasan*, 149). This same topocosmic confusion is evident in the narrator's reflections on her Uncle's death. Instead of drawing consolation from the Christian teachings on eternal life, whereby the soul of the deceased ascends into heaven, Naomi wonders: "What, I wonder, was Uncle thinking … Had the world turned upside down? Perhaps everything was reversing rapidly and he was tunnelling backwards top to bottom, his feet in an upstairs attic of humus and memory, his hands groping … down to the underground sea" (14). In "Broken Generations in *Obasan*," Mason Harris notes the problematic relationship between the nature imagery of ascent and descent and Naomi's inner conflicts regarding her past, without discussing the mythic structures I examine here. On the one hand, notes Harris, the sky in the novel represents a "cold threatening outer world" and the earth, on the other, "an inner world of silent warmth" (48). This obvious Copernican framework contrasts with Harris's proposal (which corresponds to the Ptolemaic schema) that "the only cure for the dichotomy of earth and sky would be upward growth from Naomi's earthbound world" (49). Although Harris, like many commentators on *Obasan*, seeks to illustrate a final unity – a "sense of resolution" (41) – in Naomi's struggles, Naomi's topocosmic confusion is not completely resolved, as I argue here, in her coming-to-story.

The confusion of the two topocosms in Naomi's worldview is indicative of her bewilderment about personal and political injustices. When she asks questions as a child, the "answers are not answers at all" (*Obasan*, 135). As an adult, she realizes that neither topocosm can provide the answers: "Like the grass, I search the earth and the sky with a thin but persistent thirst" (3). Even when Naomi has the "answer" to her mother's disappearance, the Ptolemaic/Christian system is insufficient to her needs. Although the Anglican minister recites the Lord's Prayer after reading the letter from Nagasaki, Naomi is elsewhere in her mind: "it is as if I am back with Uncle again, listening and listening to the silent earth and the silent sky as I have done all my life" (240). Indeed, Magdalene Redekop has noted the irony, at the end of *Obasan*, of the narrator's prayer to the "gentle Mother, gentle Mother" being interwoven with the "Our Father Who Art In Heaven" ("Literary Politics," 14). As Cheng Lok Chua remarks, Kogawa's technique of using "subtly recurrent leitmotifs drawn from Christian rituals and symbols ... puts an ironic question to the Christian ethic professed by Canada's majority culture" ("Witnessing," 99). In the final scene, Naomi's actions reveal that she has not resolved the topocosmic confusion. From the *bottom* of the coulee, which constitutes a point of epiphany in the Copernican universe, the narrator looks *up* at the moon in the night sky, the point of epiphany of the Ptolemaic system.

Topocosmic confusion in *Obasan* and *Comme une enfant de la terre*, then, indicates the insufficiencies of both the Ptolemaic/Christian and the Copernican systems to the worldviews of these two narrators. These novels suggest that the traditional ways of making sense of the world through inherited cosmogonies need rethinking. So too, perhaps, do the past histories of these worlds.

In *Comme une enfant de la terre*, two related religious elements are parodied: some are rituals of the Catholic religion and some biblical myths of the Western tradition, with particular emphasis placed on the Christ-myth. The text's challenge to these two elements enables a reconsideration of biblical mythology and of the church- and male-dominated version of Quebec's historico-political situation. Several factors in Quebec's social and political history were responsible for the predominance – until relatively recently – of biblical mythology and the Ptolemaic worldview: the inordinate political power of the

Catholic church when most French administrators and many seigneurs returned to France after 1760; the church's quasi monopoly over education until the 1960s; and the isolation of Quebec catholicity, which, for reasons already explained, did not have to confront the challenges to its monolithic belief system occasioned in Europe by the "three Rs" – the Renaissance, the Reformation, and the French Revolution. Although the practice of the Catholic religion in Quebec today may have changed because of the reforms initiated by Vatican II (1962–65), the Québécois novels discussed here engage the former domination by Quebec catholicity of religious, social, and mythological worldviews.

Marchessault's narrator begins her parody of Catholic ritual by laying bare the linguistic imprisonment of Québécois French in a dominant, if perhaps dying, religious system. Ironic humour is a successful rhetorical tool in this process: the narrator juxtaposes fixed expressions from Catholic religious practices with equally fixed political expressions – or political sore points. Witness the following confrontation between religion and reality *à la québécoise*: "C'est le mois de Marie, c'est le mois le plus beau, c'est le mois de mai à Montréal et les rues défoncent." Not only does this parody of a well-known religious hymn recall to mind the petty arguments that occur every spring over Montreal's deep potholes, which are a constant source of embarrassment to the city's politicians and a major annoyance to its citizens, but it juxtaposes the daily grind of the street with the saint who has always been portrayed in the church's teachings as being above all that: the extraterrestrial Virgin Mary, the saint to whom young church-educated Québécois sang every May. Religion and federalism are given a similar ironic treatment in Marchessault's text: "[le fleuve passe devant] collèges et couvents de la race fière qui sait porter le chapelet, qui sait porter la croix" (*Comme une enfant*, 180). The narratorial adaptation of well-known songs – here, a popular religious hymn and the Canadian national anthem – is, as we have seen, a frequent device in New World Myth novels. This sabotaging of given linguistic clichés, as it were, foregrounds the narrator's ability to subvert the layer of complacency and the unthinking state one generally assumes when mouthing the traditional words. By juxtaposing the sacred with the commonplace, the narrator illustrates her disdain for the former and makes place for the latter in her story. In the second example, the complement of the anthem ("les Canadiens savent porter la croix" as conquering missionaries) is here turned into a criticism: the people were bent under the double yoke of the cross and the rosary, kept in a submissive state by the Catholic

Church. This linguistic subversion is also an illustration of the fact that the narrator's animosity toward the oppressive church is inseparable from her political and historical concerns.

The lyrical passages of *Comme une enfant de la terre* frequently parody biblical mythology and the rites of the Roman Catholic Church. The strong influence that the Catholic mass and biblical texts have traditionally exerted on the Québécois language is evident everywhere in Quebec – especially, and ironically, in Québécois swearwords. Based on the life of Jesus and the rites of the Mass, this profane vocabulary is quite different from French, English Canadian, or American curses. Marchessault's text, which strongly rejects the Catholic Church and the Catholic patriarchal god, nevertheless contains excerpts from the Bible, parts of traditional religious hymns, direct addresses to Christ, and parodies of the sacraments. In other words, it uses the "system" extensively – in order to abuse it. Prior to the 1960s, Catholic Quebec's mythological universe was very much influenced by the ceremonial rituals of the church and by traditional biblical expressions, both of which have permeated the linguistic systems – sacred and profane – of this still fairly homogeneous society. Like many other Québécois novels published since the 1960s (works by Marie-Claire Blais, Gérard Bessette, Anne Hébert, and others), Marchessault's novel strongly attacks institutionalized religion. The narrator of this text deliberately sets out to shake up and then transform the firmly entrenched, biblically and historically inspired mythology of Quebec by self-consciously playing with the collectivity's deeply anchored and linguistically encoded knowledge of biblical mythology and religious rites.

The second way in which the narrator calls into question the Catholic Church is through her exaggeration of some of its defining aspects, such as prayer, ritual, and ceremony: "Oh Christ! Nous sommes christianisés. Oh Christ! Nous sommes tombés dans le puit [sic] de vérité avec ses soleils pâles ... Oh Christ! Nous serons asservis définitivement par toutes nos institutions, nos lois, nos églises. Oh Christ! Nous perpétuerons cette duperie millénaire" (*Comme une enfant*, 289). This prayer-like imploration is not a prayer at all, but a condemnation of the subservient state in which, according to the narrator, the Catholic Church sought to maintain its members. Elsewhere in the text, the narrator's desire to replace patriarchal Catholicism with a female spiritual lineage is discernible in her ironic adaptations of Catholic rote expressions. For instance, the traditional Sign of the Cross, a universal symbol of Catholicism, was accompanied by the standard prayer: "Au nom du Père, et du Fils et du Saint-Esprit, ainsi-soit-il." The narrator's ironic rendition

of this incantatory prayer underlines the patriarchal slant of Catholicism by including a reference to a female addressee: "Oh Christ!
Donnez-nous la force de continuer, au nom du père, de la mère,
ainsi-soit-il" (290). For those used to mouthing the ritual words, this
insertion of the female noun shocks and abruptly calls attention to
the absence of women in traditional prayers to the deity. In another
equally ironic adaptation of Catholic prayer, the narrator emphasizes
her point that the church encourages passivity by comparing the
waiting stage of the chrysalis to the political inactivity of the people,
a stage that will persist as long as they continue to be church-
dominated (312–13).

The third element of the narrator's denunciation of the Catholic
system is her ridiculing of the numerous sacrifices formerly expected
of young Catholics. For instance, during her travels she orders a
cheese sandwich that is so dry she has difficulty swallowing it. Calling out to Christ to save her from suffocation, the narrator enumer-
ates the many sacrifices she has made throughout her life, such as
kissing the cross while on her knees and offering up her nickels to
save "de petits Chinois, de petits nègres du Bengale" (*Comme une
enfant*, 135). Calling out for a miraculous intervention, she mocks the
popular interpretation of the Jansenist tradition in Quebec Catholicity, whereby the amount of suffering undergone on earth was
directly proportionate to the reward received in heaven.

In the paragraphs that follow this passage, it becomes evident that
the sandwich is associated with the Sacramental Host and that the
narrator is parodying the Catholic communion service and mocking
the doctrine of transubstantiation. The dry cheese sandwich, like the
Host of Communion, sticks in her mouth. She is repulsed by the
presence of this dead matter in her body and plays on the familiar
body/temple image of the New Testament. Here, her body is profaned and she cries out ironically, "Je suis une poubelle ... Seigneur,
sauvez-moi de ce destin; donnez-moi des pains sanctifiés" (*Comme
une enfant*, 134–5). This phrase is a good example of the narrator's
frequent use and abuse of biblical language. Allusions to two fragments of the Lord's Prayer are discernible here: "Que Votre Nom soit
sanctifié" and "Donnez-nous aujourd'hui notre pain quotidien."
Such parodic allusions to fragments from the Bible, the Mass,
prayers, hymns, and other fixed expressions occur frequently
throughout this work.

Instead of swallowing the Host without chewing it, as a faithful
Catholic was supposed to do, the narrator, through her own extreme
efforts, rids her mouth of the undesirable presence. Once the narrator
has expelled the "dead bread" and freed up her mouth, she reveals

herself as the replacement of the Christ-priest; she is "en mesure de prononcer les paroles de la lumière" (*Comme une enfant*, 137). She sets herself up as an alternative saviour – a female goddess. The traditional separation of the spiritual and material worlds, which was passed on to Catholic Quebec through the work of the missionaries and the subsequent development of Catholicism in Quebec, does not apply here. Marchessault's narrator does not subscribe to the traditional Eurocentric construction of paganism, which sets up a bipolar and hierarchical structure, with the spiritual world having a higher value than the material one. Indeed, Marchessault here recalls to mind Amerindian traditions, which see all matter as inherently sacred and spirit as intrinsic rather than "wholly other." Her narrator tends to conflate the spiritual and material worlds, and her "saving of the world" has much to do with the historical, political, and social inequalities of Quebec's past and present. The tension between the traditional religious cosmogony and the narrator's rejection of it is evident in the narrator's parasitical use of religious vocabulary. In her new-found state of liberation, although she throws off the restraints of her Catholic upbringing, refuting "ces temps préhistoriques des chapelles au cœur des écoles ... des ciboires, des calices ... des psaumes pas ordinaires" (104), it is again through biblical language that this narrator conveys her desire to throw off her human vanities and to bear witness for her "terre amérindienne ... terre subarctique ... Québec" (117): "'Que les pouvoirs de ma bouche me soient restitués, que je puisse prononcer les paroles de la Puissance'" (116). She makes ironic use of easily recognized biblical language and rhythm in order to defamiliarize, depower, and demystify them.

The narrator's challenge to the former dominance of Québécois society by the Catholic Church leads to a second challenge, this one directed at its god, Jesus Christ. Biblical myth is patriarchal, male-centred, and exclusive, as Frye notes: "it consistently opposed the mother-goddess cults that were so prominent in the east Mediterranean world at the time [of Christ]" ("Myth as the Matrix," 474). Frye suggests that the Bible's god is male because of a need to break out of the cycle of Nature: "In the older, or Jahwist, account of the Creation ... Adam emerges from the dust of the ground, the *adamah*, or mother earth ... The maleness of God seems to be connected with the Bible's resistance to the notion of a containing cycle of fate or inevitability as the highest category that our minds can conceive. All such cycles are suggested by nature, and are contained within nature – which is why it is so easy to think of nature as Mother Nature"

(*The Great Code*, 107). It is highly ironic that in Marchessault's text a similar need lies at the origin of the narrator's urge to break out of the equally imprisoning cycle, or, more aptly, system of Christianity. In *Comme une enfant de la terre*, the narrator challenges the portrayal of a masculine god in biblical mythology by setting up ironic parallels between herself and Christ. Like God, she chooses her earthly parents. While she does have a token earthly father, she has in fact chosen to be the child of a female goddess and a human mother. Once again, the parodic references to the biblical stories about Jesus Christ are interwoven with Amerindian myth: in a solely matriarchal lineage, Sky Woman gives birth to First Woman with the help of Turtle, the "Mother of all things" (Brant, "This Is History," 24). Thus, both Amerindian and biblical mythologies contribute elements to the "new" – and decidedly political – mythology created in this text.

Furthermore, the relationship between the narrator and her friends parallels that between Christ and his Apostles. These friends have undertaken a specifically political mission. Travelling to every corner of Quebec, they challenge the dominance of the traditional colonial and church-dominated systems, by orally retelling Quebec's political history to its inhabitants. They are to "recréer ... le récit de notre résistance dans les filets du gouvernement colonial, dans la mâchoire du vampire clérical" (144–5). Like the Apostles, they courageously face hardships so that they may "[d]escendre aux plages les plus basses porter la bonne nouvelle, comme des prophètes, des gesteux, des rois mages boulangeant le pain des anges" (175). Through her mythically inspired vocabulary, the narrator gives significance to the travels of these friends: "nous sommes de la même famille, nous, les vivants et les morts et vos voix cheminent en nous, jusqu'au nord du nord, jusqu'à Ivujivik car elles sont greffées sur l'antique racine du Verbe et de l'émotion cosmologique" (144). The friends' oral transmitting of history and culture is very similar to the narrator's self-imposed mission. She too wants to use *words* in a new way: to communicate the history of her *pays* – and to underline its mythological dimensions. As the narrator metafictively notes, she creates these "nouvelles constellations de mots" (136) so that the mythological and historical points of view will be changed. Her words will not participate in her people's "déchéance" – a word that has both biblical and historical connotations as "fall from grace" or "decline of a race." Instead her words will create a new mythology that uses the structure of biblical mythology even as it parodies it. Recalling to mind Christ's ridding the temple of the merchants who profaned it, the narrator desires to free this new mythology from the clerical domination under which it has been suppressed: "Rangez ...

vos prêtres ... Laissez-moi passer! Je suis en route pour l'éternité" (140).

There are loose parallels between the structure of Marchessault's text and the Bible. The first *chant* contains ironic references to episodes found in Genesis, such as that of the Tree of Knowledge. The later *chants* describe the personal life of the narrator, as the books of the New Testament describe the life of Jesus Christ, and the last *chant*, in its biblical and mythical vocabulary of superlatives, is similar in tone to the Book of Revelation. At one point in the first *chant* the narrator claims she been on earth for more than thirty years, and, like Christ at approximately the same age, she is aware that her private life has almost come to an end. Traditional Catholic theology in Quebec teaches that Christ was sent to earth by God the Father to atone for Adam's original sin: the eating of the forbidden fruit of the Tree of Knowledge. In this same first *chant*, the narrator is also on her way down to earth. She sees a Tree of Knowledge, but the traditional biblical story is subverted in this passage. The fruit is not forbidden, but feeds gifted humans, such as visionaries, prophets, shamans, and artists (15). It gives them access to previously censored knowledge. The implication is that the narrator's mythology, when compared to the biblical one, is liberating. Esoteric knowledge will become exoteric here.

In the biblical story of Genesis, the serpent tempts with forbidden knowledge. In this novel, the biblical symbol of evil, the snake, is an object of beauty. Jean Bolen points out in *Goddesses in Everywoman* that "Snakes had been symbols of the pre-Greek Great Goddess ... and serve as symbolic reminders (or remnants) of the power once held by the female deity ... [W]omen who gain a sense of their own power and authority [are] 'reclaiming the power of the snake,' which was lost by feminine deities and human women when the patriarchal religions stripped the goddesses of their power and influence, cast the snake as the evil element in the Garden of Eden and made women the lesser sex" (283–4). In Marchessault's text, the narrator uses the snake, a rejuvenated symbol of womankind, to introduce a political commentary into passages such as the following, which resonate with both biblical and political allusions: "[Ce] beau serpent aux yeux de saphir est occupé dans l'instant, depuis l'éternité, à faire des nœuds lunaires qui effraieront les gnomes hystériques qui gouvernent l'Amérique" (16). Women, this passage implies, are about to reclaim their right to knowledge of past and contemporary events and to form their own historico-political worldviews. The narrator's Christ-like mission is to retell her personal history and the political history of Quebec, and to promote the importance of *woman* – human being, legendary figure, and mythological goddess.

The narrator of *Comme une enfant de la terre* articulates her own divinity through her association with the cult of the Great Goddess. Also referred to as the Earth Mother, this goddess is known by many names: Ashtoreth, Au Set, Anat, Brigit, Coatlicue, Chicomecoatl, Danu, Devi, Hecate, Hera, Innana, Ishtar, Jezanna, Kunapipi, Kybele, Mawu, Mboze, Nu Kwa, Rhea, and Yemanja (Tuttle, *Encyclopedia of Feminism*, 127–8). Marchessault's narrator does refer occasionally to a few of these goddesses, along with others of Middle America (such as Ixmucane), but she is more interested in la Grande-Oursonne and other goddesses. La Mère-des-herbes, la vénérable Grande-Mère, l'Ancienne-des-temps, and, especially, La Grande-Oursonne are the celestial forces to whom the narrator gives homage. The power of these goddesses outshines that of other deities and legendary figures: their light is "incomparable, une lumière qui a depuis longtemps dépassé la terre, le vieil Oedipe, la sagesse de Salomon, la passion du Christ ... les plumes du dieu Pan" (*Comme une enfant*, 93). The Grande-Oursonne here reclaims her rightful place from Father Sky, the traditional male procreative force in some precontact mythologies. As God the Mother, she dominates the heavens; "vaste comme le ciel" (337), she controls all movement in the universe.

Barbara Godard points out that "the ancient telluric myth of origins, of the marriage of the sky father with the earth mother [is] ... important in Quebec social mythology ... [Marchessault] undertakes a critique of the masculine domination of this tradition, centered, as it has been, by the sermon of a priest, representative of the Christian sky father, so that the full erotic and creative potential of the earth mother has been denied. In western culture, this female principle has been relegated to the lower, earthly realm. Marchessault reclaims for the Great Mother her earlier status as Queen of Heaven as well as of Earth" ("Flying," 10). Through her parodic use of well-known biblical scenes, Marchessault's narrator ridicules and then rejects traditional Catholicism's attitude toward this Queen of Heaven – and toward women in general – through such techniques as the adaptation, mentioned above, of a hymn addressed to the Catholic Virgin Mary. Such a technique is typical of Québécoises' feminist writing. Denise Boucher's 1978 play, *Les Fées ont soif*, which set off major controversies and demonstrations in the Quebec cities in which it was first performed, rejects this outdated stereotype by foregrounding the limitations of the traditional Catholic concept of the Virgin Mary in a similar way. In Marchessault's novel, the female narrator has replaced the masculine Christ as the perfect Saviour. Marchessault, then, presents another type of female divinity for women: not the pure, apolitical, and, especially, asexual Virgin venerated in biblical mythology and Catholic teachings, but a goddess who assumes both her sensuality and her sexuality, as well as her political awareness and involvement.

In this narrator's scheme, women should also replace the masculine heroes of mythology and history. Thus, when her friend Francine names her heroes, "Moïse, Jésus-Christ, le Roi Arthur, ... Mandrin, Boudha, Don Juan," the narrator counters with her own – all women: "Judith, la Vierge Marie, Isis, Iseult" (67–8). Her list is long, and it reflects the novel, in that it moves from these biblical women and mythological goddesses to finish with an odd collection of two well-known figures from Quebec social mythology, one visionary, and one fairy-tale character: "Madeleine de Verchères, Rose Latulippe, Thérèse de Lisieux, le petit Chaperon rouge" (68). This purely female lineage also reflects one of the narrator's goals: to disempower the male lineage of patriarchal Catholicism and to promote the importance of women, particularly Québécoises, in her reworking of traditional mythologies. Many practitioners of l'écriture au féminin in Quebec, such as Nicole Brossard, France Théoret, and Madeleine Gagnon, wish to promote the importance of women on all fronts. Marchessault's strong insistence on accomplishing this promotion through reworkings of mythology, however, has perhaps closer affinities with the work of the novelist and journalist Madeleine Ouellette-Michalska, and in particular, with her essay on knowledge and myth, L'Echapée des discours de l'œil. The very title of this work indicates its argument: a female being escaping from the dominant male discourse, represented here and in many mythologies by the symbol of the Eye. Ouellette-Michalska argues forcibly that women, previously empowered in matriarchal societies, have been subjugated by the dominant, "scientific," male discourses. In her "collage" writing, which is punctuated with scientific "facts" and with personal comments in italics, Ouellette-Michalska takes apart the scientific arguments of a Lévi-Strauss, of a Freud, of a Lacan. In the final chapter of the book, attention is given to the effective changes brought about in the twentieth century. Offering an overview of the work of diverse women writers, such as Hélène Cixous, Jeanne Hyvrard, Marguerite Duras, Anne Hébert, Madeleine Gagnon, Annie Leclerc, and Marchessault herself, Ouellette-Michalska notes that the sheer quantity and quality of l'écriture au féminin has "détruit l'Œil à jamais" (295). Interestingly, her conclusions resemble mine, in that she sees this new writing as one that must first unsettle myths-as-master-narratives: "Après avoir franchi plusieurs étapes, la contre-ritualité finira par abolir la mère paternelle et les anti-Mères servant de repère à l'histoire des hommes. L'opération de dé-genèse s'effectue dans la dérision – 'En ce temps-là,' 'en vérité je vous le dis,' 'bonheur à toi, ô terre,' etc. Elle déconstruit les mythes et discours théogoniques. Luce Irigaray s'en prend à Nietsche et Platon. Freud, Lacan, Lévi-Strauss sont analysés et ridiculisés. Le métalangage est passé au crible. Les sciences 'humaines' sont révisées" (304). For Ouellette-Michalska, playing with linguistic clichés taken from a deeply rooted mythology is one way of laying bare their power. For Marchessault, this operation is indeed one of *dé-genèse* and of *dérision*, as far as biblical language is concerned. However, she also proposes the possibility of a fluid construction of a new mythology with nationalist, Amerindian, and feminist concerns.

The narrator of *Comme une enfant de la terre* accords significance to *herself* as female goddess through her use of biblical language, images, and stories. Her retellings of the Christ stories parody these "sacred Truths," revealing them as elements in a belief system that has more than run its course – at least for women. The gender subversion of the novel, whereby the god has (re)become goddess and is aggressively female, is the most obvious biblical parody in the text. Another is that of the Tower of Babel. This biblical story recounts how humans try to reach heaven through their own means: they build a tower. God reacts angrily to this effort, causing the workers to speak many languages, and the ensuing linguistic confusion brings the construction to a halt (Genesis 11.1–9). In *Comme une enfant de la terre*, however, the divine linguistic curse is reversed, and in the inverted tower – the underground cavern – the narrator glories in the fact that her sister soul mates "[utilisent des] mots parlant français, anglais, italien, espagnol, portugais, allemand, araméen" (98) – according to the narrator, a splendid linguistic potpourri. This subversion of the biblical myth is echoed by Robert Kroetsch, who reads the Tower of Babel myth as a positive one, because, as one of his interviewers says, it "broke up our primordial collectivity" ("Myth," 116). He proposes elsewhere that (English) Canadian literature "comes compulsively to a genealogy that refuses origin, to a genealogy that speaks instead, and anxiously, and with a generous reticence, the nightmare and the welcome dream of Babel" ("Beyond Nationalism," xi). Contrary to the sentiment contained in the title of this latter article by Kroetsch, Marchessault's work, I would suggest, does not aim at getting beyond nationalism (in the sense of overcoming a handicap) but at opening it up through a reworking – not a refusal – of the notions of primordial collectivity, origin, and genealogy. The nationalist thrust in this novel is in keeping with the strong political drive in Québécois fiction in the mid-1970s, but the widely accepted and male-dominated Québécois mythology of the *collectivité* at that time is challenged here by the narrator's demands: this mythology must make room for feminist reworkings of biblical and historical myths. For instance, in the Bible, Christ *descends* to earth, dies, and then *ascends* to heaven. In Marchessault's text, this order is challenged; in the last *chant*, as in the first one, the goddess comes *down* to earth. There is no need for resurrection here: this *enfant*, although a goddess, is also *une enfant de la terre*. Heaven has been replaced by the nation – Quebec.

Although the narrator underlines the negative effects of the traditional masculinity of Catholicism, she does not simply replace masculinity with femininity. Instead, she liberates herself and her new mythology from the set patterns of the system by frequently altering the well-known scenarios of the biblical stories. For instance, although the gender-shift is central to this text, the narrator's "apostolic" friends are not all female, even though in the church's teachings Christ's apostles are all male. This creation story also deviates here from the myth of Sky Woman, which, as we have seen, describes a strongly matriarchal lineage. The narrator's flexible mythology is fluid and free of rigidity: it does not necessarily have to meet the expectations aroused by its resemblance to biblical or Amerindian stories, though it can – and does – play with them.

The narrator of *Comme une enfant de la terre* also subverts the importance of biblical myth by according it the same – and not a greater – significance as that conferred upon other mythological systems. For instance, she quotes freely from among many books held to be sacred in other societies: the *Popol Vuh* of the Quiché-Maya or the *Livre des morts des Egyptiens* (125). This exploration of other mythological systems originates in an effort to downplay the importance of biblical mythology. Thus, the narrator emphasizes her relationship with the sun, the central heavenly being, particularly through her identification with the colour yellow. Sun-worship is one of the earliest forms of religion, with the sun being perceived as a *male* life-giving force. In this text, the sun-goddess – the narrator – is, of course, female. Born out of the mouth of the "louve solaire," she herself is a "crachat solaire," and thus the central subject of her personal solar system: "je suis unique … ma vie est unique … je suis un microthéos!" (206).

This solar cosmology is frequently associated with the narrator's exploration of – and self-insertion into – native North American mythological systems. Although parts of the novel dwell briefly on indigenous Central American mythology, through excerpts from the *Popol Vuh* and references to the goddesses of the Aztecs, the Maya, and the Toltecs, the narrator turns her back upon these cosmogonies: "Je comprends mal le Mexique; je le jette à pleine main dans le ciel du soleil et des aigles. Il me semble vital de retrouver mes demeures aquatiques en terre du Nord" (77). North American Amerindian mythology, particularly that of the Eastern Woodlands peoples, who lived in the area of North America first explored and colonized by Europeans, permeates the narrator's tale.[13] Thus, storms are presided over by l'Oiseau-Tonnerre (Thunderbird), who is assisted by minor deities, such as the corn and tobacco gods. As in several historiographic novels of English Canada and Quebec during this period, the buffalo is the mythical animal par excellence (30, 61, 93, 256, 265, 270). Reference is made to other mythical Amerindian animals, with the typical ironic New World Myth inclusion of a new, rather more political, one: "Je flaire ma piste … je croise en passant celle du lièvre téméraire, du tamias rayé, du coyote nerveux, du loup affamé, du renard gris qui court sur les murs, les clôtures, du castor en train de construire le Haut-Canada" (109). Biblical stories therefore form but one of many mythological systems with which the narrator associates herself, but it is, nevertheless, biblical mythology that is most strongly parodied in this text. The narrator, then, challenges the power of this predominant mythology by her use and abuse of its stories, especially those about its central deity. She implies that she considers Amerindian myths and stories about different cosmogonies as having a status equivalent to biblical mythology, and she gives herself the same status as any other god – Christian or otherwise. Out of the story she creates emerges a desire, as we have seen, to retell the post-European history of Quebec, to promote the cause of women, and to remake a mythological universe in their image.

The critique of the Bible and of Christian practices in *Obasan* may best be introduced by Joy Kogawa's reaction to a question put to her in the interview with Andrew Garrod. Asked about the relationship of her faith to her female identity, Kogawa responded, "my feminist identity seems to leap to the front of the stage when there is an unloving challenge to it – which of course is experienced often in the realm of patriarchal religion" (143). This obvious criticism of the shortcomings of patriarchal religion is taken up elsewhere by Kogawa, who has condemned the "tradition of arrogance within Christianity" (Meyer and O'Riordan, 29). In *Obasan*, criticisms of the male-dominated Christian belief system are best examined in parallel with the novel's positive portrayal of woman, and its less than positive portrayal of men, who are seen as inoffensive but ineffectual human beings. As we shall soon see, the subtle but persistent presence of an alternative belief system, that of Buddhism, also affects the novel's apparent submission to the tenets of Christianity and what Kogawa calls "Biblioatry."

In Slocan, the old grandfather must be helped to take a bath, and Stephen must be helped to move when his leg is in a cast. Even Naomi's father is ineffectual: "Father is as if he is not here. If my mother were back, she would move aside all the darkness with her hands and we would be safe and at home in our home" (*Obasan*, 69). The narrator's father and brother escape into music when "real life" becomes unbearable. In contrast, women are constantly portrayed as the strong human beings, those who "are burdened with all the responsibility of keeping what's left of the family together" (101). Donald Goellnicht uses Lacan's theories of language and psychological development to propose that Naomi, like any "girl from an immigrant racial minority," lives a "situation of potential double powerlessness – of being woman and minority" ("Father Land and/or Mother Tongue," 123). My reading of *Obasan*, however, differs from his: in Naomi's world, women are more powerful than men. As Frank Davey points out, the men in this novel falter in confusion and withdraw from life, in spite of "their inherited Japanese culture [as one] of male privilege" (*Post-National Arguments*, 104).

Biblical language is often used to lend significance to the women of the Nakane and Kato families. Thus, encouraged by her grandmother's example, Naomi dares to immerse herself in the extremely hot water of the familial bath: "I go into the midst of the flames, obedient as Abednego, for lo, Grandma is an angel of the Lord and stands before me in the midst of the fire and has no hurt" (*Obasan*, 48). Biblical expressions are also used to poke gentle fun at the respected matriarchs: Obasan, who never throws anything away, is baptised "Our Lady of the Left-Overs" (45). The thematization of female empowerment through narratorial play with biblical mythology, however, is not as evidently foregrounded in Kogawa's text as it is in Marchessault's novel. There are other important ramifications to the very frequent use of biblical allusions in *Obasan*; its narrator examines the incapacity of the Christian belief system to respond adequately to the injustices of the recent historical past.

In *Obasan* the narrator portrays various characters and settings in biblical terms. Once again the communion service is parodied: the narrator wonders, for instance, if Uncle's "last act" was the making of his infamous "stone bread" (12). However, unlike Christ's last eucharistic act, which will be repeated by his followers, "there will be no more black bread" now that Uncle is gone (13). Biblical allusions frequently do not inspire hope. Naomi, as child narrator, uses biblical language and syntax to describe her surroundings, particularly – and ironically – when she is feeling insecure. The following typical passage describes the family's arrival in Lethbridge: "Ah. We have come to a city of wind with stores and streets and people angled against the gusts and behold we are sitting safely out of the blowing debris in a restaurant at a round table" (190). The use of biblical language, however, does not help the narrator: from this restaurant, she is taken to the beet fields, which are described in apocalyptic terms as a "place of angry air" on "the edge of the world" (191). Apocalyptic imagery is appropriate to this text, as Gottlieb points out, because "direct quotations and numerous allusions to the Bible have prepared us to see the conflagration of Nagasaki as the doomsday vision of the Apocalypse, the destruction of the world by the powers of evil" ("Riddle," 49).

The personal, the political, and the religious are deliberately blurred in this novel. The following passage, for instance, conflates the disdain the narrator feels for the empty rituals of her Anglican religion with her indictment of the government's unfeeling bureaucracy and her frustration at Aunt Emily's useless "paper battles" (*Obasan*, 189): "In Aunt Emily's package, the papers are piled as neatly as the thin white wafers in Sensei's silver box – symbols of communion, the materials of communication, white paper bread for the mind's meal. We were the unwilling communicants receiving and consuming a less than holy nourishment, our eyes, cups filling with the bitter wine of a loveless communion" (182).

This conflation of the political and the religious is also evident in the narrator's frequent sardonic adaptations of the Canadian national anthem. Thus, crying out against past injustices, Naomi adapts the New Testament parable of the sower (Mark 4.1–20) in this ironic, political comment: "Oh Canada, whether it is admitted or not, we come from you we come from you … We come from the country that plucks its people out like weeds and flings them into the roadside … We grow where we are not seen, we flourish where we are not heard" (*Obasan*, 226). Parables and other recognizable biblical passages are used by the narrator to portray her despair at understanding the troublesome events of her past and at her lack of trust in God. Significantly, it is through her use of biblical language that she criticizes the unfeeling God of the Copernican system. She too uses – paradoxically – the language of the system to criticize, albeit indirectly, the God of that system. Whereas Aunt Emily ends one of her diary entries with "I asked too much of God" (106), Naomi's animosity toward God is expressed indirectly through her sardonic use of biblical terms. The child narrator in Alberta notes that Aunt Emily's words "are not made flesh. Trains do not carry us home. Ships do not return again. All my prayers disappear into space" (189). The adult narrator has not resolved this lack of faith. She notes that her Uncle, unlike Lazarus, "does not rise up and return to his boats. Dead bones do not take on flesh" (198).

In *Obasan*, the church-as-institution is also weak. For instance, the efforts of the missionaries in Slocan to influence the government's policy of relocation are ineffectual. The missionaries themselves, in spite of their good deeds, have little beneficial effect on the narrator. Naomi notes the racism of the church: Uncle is turned away from the communion rail, and a United Church parson "says to 'Kick all the Japs out'" (102). Even the Japanese Canadian representative of God on earth, the Anglican minister Nakayama-sensei, is portrayed as a well-meaning but incapable man. Over and over again Naomi notes that the prayers he offers are "not understandable" (129), and that his words seem to "stop before coming out of his mouth, so that the sound is swallowed up" (129). Elsewhere in the text, Aunt Emily mixes political and religious metaphors, describing this minister as a "deeply wounded shepherd trying to tend the flock ... [but] all the sheep were shorn and stampeded in the stockyards and slaughter-houses of prejudice" (186). When Uncle dies, the minister, a tired old man, has "no words of comfort to offer" (182).

The first biblical reference in *Obasan* is in the epigraph: "To him that overcometh / will I give to eat / of the hidden manna / and will give him / a white stone / and in the stone / a new name written" (Revelation 2.17). The proem links this stone imagery to the absence of speech – to silence: "I fail the task. The word is stone. / I admit it. / I hate the stillness. I hate the stone." Gradually, the narrator builds on this imagery to convey the idea that in order to "over-come" she must break the stone and turn silence into the "freeing word" (proem). The thematization of *la parole* in Marchessault's text is equally evident in Kogawa's novel, where the narrator is endlessly fascinated with "the word." This is of course a biblical allusion to the Gospel of John: "In the beginning was the Word, and the Word was with God, and the Word was God ... And the Word was made flesh, and dwelt among us ... full of grace and truth" (John 1.1, 14). In "Speaking the Silence: Joy Kogawa's *Obasan*," Gary Willis associates "the word" with God. He suggests that for Naomi the "way to safety is speech, and the 'speech that frees' is the word of the 'wordless word' that is God" (248). I argue, however, for a different reading of

Kogawa's text. Willis implies that Naomi has come to a Christian acceptance of the painful past. He writes: "Remembering both the small sins committed by herself and her mother and the terrible sins perpetrated by nations, she [Naomi] invokes a prayer spoken by the priest Nakayama-sensei years ago at their Grandmother Nakane's funeral ... 'We are abandoned yet we are not abandoned ... Teach us to forgive'" (248). At that funeral, however, Naomi says that the meaning of the minister's words is unknown; his words themselves are "not understandable" (*Obasan*, 129). After listening to Nakayama-sensei's reading of the letter that tells of her mother's fate, Naomi dismisses both the minister and his prayer: "I am not thinking of forgiveness. The sound of Sensei's voice grows as indistinct as the hum of distant traffic" (240). The Christian belief system has been tried and found wanting by the narrator of *Obasan*. In spite of the biblical epigraph to the novel, in which God promises to reward "him that overcometh," I would argue, along with Erika Gottlieb, that "In spite of the rich and consistent texture of the Biblical imagery, the plot does not fulfil our expectation of the vision of a 'New Heaven and New Earth'" ("Riddle," 50).

Jovette Marchessault's integration of other mythological systems – in particular, Amerindian mythology – is echoed by Joy Kogawa, who makes use of Buddhist imagery in *Obasan*. In keeping with the calmer tone of Kogawa's work, however, the presence of Bhuddism as an alternative religious system is presented as a secondary option, which flows naturally out of her narrator's dual heritage. Thus, before describing her grandmother's funeral pyre, the child narrator notes matter-of-factly that her grandfather is Buddhist, and it is accepted as perfectly normal in the ghost towns that Nakayama-sensei, an Anglican clergyman, should preside over the Buddhist rites of that ceremony. In another example of the conflation of religious practices, Obasan, a devout Christian, respects Buddhist rites by gathering the grandmother's bones from the remains of the fire and sending them to the grandfather.

In their detailed and sensitive readings of *Obasan*, Gottlieb and Teruyo Ueki discuss at length the effects of the inclusion of Japanese/Bhuddist elements within the text. Both speak in terms of cultural, linguistic, and religious bilingualism, of superimposition or double exposure, hinting at what I have been calling "cultural conflation." Gottlieb first signals her appreciation of Kogawa's exemplary use of language, while noting the effects of the inclusion in the text of Japanese expressions: "To say that Joy Kogawa has a language of her own is not sufficient. Many good poets or writers do achieve

that. But in Naomi's narration one often has the feeling that the
writer is virtually reinventing language. Unmistakably, the style is
the result of extensive linguistic experimentation, presenting us with
the special flavour of Japanese Canadian speech patterns and their
underlying sensibilities. The writer translates Japanese expressions,
often including the Japanese turn of thought" ("Riddle," 39). Ueki,
for her part, elaborates on the passage in *Obasan* where Naomi, discussing one of her nightmares, mentions the "two ideographs for the
word 'love'" (228) that contrast "heart," "hands," and "action" to
"heart," "to tell," and "a long thread." Ueki shows how these Chinese ideographs are linked to the love, silent or otherwise, that
Uncle, Obasan, Emily, and especially Naomi's mother have for
Naomi, and how, thanks in large part to her dreams, Naomi recon-
ciles "the languge of silence and the language of speech" ("Revelations," 18). Like Marchessault, then, Kogawa is praised for the
radically different quality of her word-power, and its capacity to
affect the reader's appreciation of what Gottlieb calls the novel's
"cosmic dimension" ("Riddle," 48).

In spite of its unobtrusive presence, the very existence of Buddhist
imagery in this novel weakens the authority of the Christian belief
system. One example of the reworking of what might be an expected
scenario is the double import of the image of the "Tree of Life,"
which, as Gottlieb explains, means different things in the different
traditions:

Coincidence of Buddhist and Christian symbols ... present the effect of
superimposition or double exposure. Although the "new name" on the
tablet and the vitality of the living waters that feed the Tree of Life have their
particular consistency significant in the Biblical drama of Apocalypse and
resurrection, the same images also have their consistency in the Buddhist
tradition. Here the Tree of Life becomes the family tree, and the concept of
resurrection evokes Naomi's affirmation of renewal through the nature cycle,
that is, through the continuity between ancestor and mourner in the family
line ... As the wake for her dead becomes enriched by allusions to the
Buddhist and the Biblical tradition, the images of tablets, water, stone, flower
and fruit assume their multi-dimensional significance. ("Riddle," 50)

Gottlieb also notes that in spite of the undoubtedly Christian context
of the novel, "several aspects of the sequence and a great deal of the
spirit of Naomi's ritual of mourning are reminiscent of ancient Japanese tradition." She mentions, for instance, the practice of offering a
single flower with a long stem before the coffin (a single branch of
Shikimi); the inscription of family names on a wooden tablet (an

ihai), and the giving of a new name to the deceased, who will pass on his or her spirit to a newborn member of the family; the tradition of commemorating all the dead of the family at the same time; the importance of maintaining a respectful silence during the time between death and the funeral (in the novel, the temporal framework for most of Naomi's recollections is the time between Uncle's death and his funeral); and the Buddhists' pantheistic, nature-centred tradition. All these elements are contained within the novel, although they are frequently presented within a Christian framework. Thus, the "white stone" with the "new name" is from the Biblical epigraph, but it "may also allude to ancient Buddhist or Japanese folk tradition" (Gottlieb, "Riddle," 53).

Teruyo Ueki's work on *Obasan* continues this discussion of the subtle but definitive presence of Buddhist practices within the text. Building on Gottlieb's description of the structure of the novel as "a concentric pattern" (Gottlieb, "Riddle," 34), Ueki proposes that the "structure of the grey cardboard folder and the structure of the novel correspond to each other in their design" ("Revelation," 9). This folder contains the letters that finally reveal the secret of Naomi's mother's disappearance (*Obasan*, 45, 221) and, according to Ueki, this "folder structure evokes the structure of a Buddhist shrine, with its two flapping doors, inside of which Kannon, goddess of Mercy, in enshrined." Through detailed readings of selected passages, Ueki then examines the divine role assigned to Naomi's mother in the novel. She proposes that Mother "appears in the novel as a symbolic presence carrying out dual as well as paradoxical roles – a silent sufferer evoking the image of the Christian God and a tender comforter associated with the Buddhist Goddess [of Mercy]" (13).

The Buddha taught that "life is permeated by suffering or dissatisfaction," but that suffering can cease if one can learn to no longer crave or grasp that which one desires (Smart, "Buddhism," 41). Furthermore, the Buddha "did not believe in a Creator, and seems to have found the existence of evil and suffering to be an insuperable obstacle to such a belief." He believed instead that by successfully proceeding along the stages of the Noble Eightfold Path, an individual could attain nirvana. This appreciation of suffering and desire is discernable in *Obasan*: both Gottlieb and Ueki dwell on the fact that Naomi had to cease desiring an explanation for her Mother's silence before she could learn of her Mother's love. For Gottlieb, Naomi "cannot receive the message she so eagerly has searched for until she learns to give up the search" ("Riddle," 47); for Ueki, the "abandonment of mankind by God as told in Genesis and his abandonment of Jesus in the New Testament for the sake of a great purpose, which is to say, a greater love of his creation, is paralleled by the mother-daughter relationship in the novel" ("Revelations," 16). Di Brandt also signals the complexities of the mother in this novel, noting that the absent mother is associated with an absent God: "It is our human responsibility, Kogawa would argue, to honour the 'impotence' of God, the silence of the earth, the mother, matter, to recognize and embrace its helplessness in the face of the human will to destruction" (*Wild Mother Dancing*, 122).

Ueki's detailed discussion of love and Mother is linked, I would argue, to Kogawa's interpretation of the Christian God and love. In an interview with Ueki, Kogawa expounded upon a point she had made several years previously in the interview with Meyer and O'Riordan. In both interviews, she cited the American feminist theologian Rosemary Ruether who wrote, "Each of us must discover for ourselves the secret key to divine abandonment – that *God has abandoned divine power into the human condition utterly and completely, so that we may not abandon each other*" ("The *Faith and Fratricide* Discussion," 256). This statement forms the epigraph to Kogawa's novel *The Rain Ascends* (1995), and, as I mentioned at the beginning of this chapter, the goddess of Mercy plays an important role in that text. In the Meyer-O'Riordan interview, Kogawa explains: "What I get from that [Ruether's statement] is that there is no God who is going to come down and rescue us, but that the power we once invested in that belief is now within us to rescue those who are abandoned. That power is real. It is within the human condition ... I do believe this" (Meyer and O'Riordan, "Joy Kogawa," 31). This belief echoes my argument that for Kogawa, there is no answer to be found "out there" in the mechanical sky of the Copernican topocosm. Ueki summarizes her discussion with Kogawa about Ruether's writings: "Our age, which has undergone the traumatic experience of holocaust, is the age of disbelief, chanting the theme of 'God's death.' Kogawa's *Obasan* ... is to be viewed as a statement of 'continuing faith in a terrifying love' in the age of God's absence" ("Revelations," 18). In this way, the silence from "out there" obliges us to rethink where our help lies. Kogawa suggests that it is "in our midst" (18). The distant male God of the Copernican universe is not the answer.

In another interview, Kogawa agreed with the idea of a "switch from the notion of a patriarchal god situated outside of oneself to the feminist way of bringing choice and responsibility into the context of daily affairs" (Garrod and Kogawa, "Joy Kogawa," 142). This statement suggests that there are similarities in Aboriginal and Oriental belief systems, at least insofar as they are reflected in

Marchessault's and Kogawa's novels. Both narrators struggle out from *under* the traditional eurocentric constructions of Catholicism/Christianity, which separated the spiritual world from the material one hierarchically, and where, as Sutherland notes, one accepted one's purgatory here on earth (*Second Image,* 62–5). Instead, both these narrators argue the importance of speaking up as women and of acknowledging the historical, political, and social inequalities of the past and the present. They also insist on the necessity of challenging the usually unquestioned authority of the Catholic/Christian belief systems by incorporating elements of alternative mythologies into their texts. As we have seen, a plurality of belief systems is typical of New World Myth texts, which challenge any form of exclusivity. This plurality, of course, also questions the hegemony of any *one* belief system, be it religious, mythical, historical, or political.

Although the word-imagery in *Obasan* is undoubtedly biblically inspired, the solution to Naomi's predicament is not found in the Christian belief system, but in her retelling of her personal and political pasts. Indeed, in keeping with the indeterminacy and flexibility of New Word Myth, the novel proposes no complete resolution to the issues it raises. As the narrator says, "no doubt it will all happen again, over and over with different faces and names, variations on the same theme" (199). This justifiably pessimistic attitude overrides even the one passage in the novel (the departure from the British Columbia coast) that has been read as an optimistic portrayal of the Christian sacrifice (Gottlieb, "Riddle," 42). In that passage, the narrator ironically describes the dispersal in terms, once again, of the Gospel of John: "We are the man in the Gospel of John, born into the world for the sake of the light ... We are sent to the sending, that we may bring sight" (*Obasan,* 111). As was illustrated in the discussion of topocosmic confusion, however, all the rest of the imagery of this passage is negative in tone and politically accusatory. "Reality" does not bear out the biblical message; those who are supposed to "see" remain blind.

Naomi does find a partial solution, however, in "the word." This "word" has little to do with the presence of God or the sacrifice of a chosen people, but it has everything to do with one individual's courage to articulate "story." Only by overcoming the silence of which she was both a willing and an unwilling prisoner will Naomi break the stone and find the "freeing word" (proem). Naomi begins to articulate those episodes in the painful past that need to be acknowledged, and, eventually, comes to realize that wordlessness had been her destruction (*Obasan,* 243). She eventually comes to understand the necessity of examining and then discarding those aspects of the worn-out, biblically inspired system that do not contribute to her well-being-in-the-world. As we shall see in the next chapter, the narrators of *Obasan* and *Comme une enfant de la terre* explore New World Myth through their personal evolutions as women and as storytellers.

4 Political History in the Feminine: Jovette Marchessault's *Comme une enfant de la terre* and Joy Kogawa's *Obasan*

Jovette Marchessault's *Comme une enfant de la terre* and Joy Kogawa's *Obasan* examine (and contribute to) present-day uncertainty in the face of collapsing traditional worldviews. In Quebec and in English-speaking Canada, these worldviews were based in part on biblical mythology and on official versions of history. Dennis Duffy suggests that one of the reasons for the present flourishing of the genre of historical novels in Canada is the decline of the Christian belief system: "What the Bible does for the Judeo-Christian tradition, historical fiction and history provide for the yearnings of secular man" (*Sounding the Iceberg*, 75). Man, yes, and woman too. As was suggested in the last chapter, the questionings of the Christian patriarchal systems in *Comme une enfant de la terre* and *Obasan* are linked to their narrators' desire to retell history, making room in these retellings for a feminist apprehension of the past and present. The yearnings mentioned by Duffy, however, will not be assuaged completely in these narrators' texts. Uncertainty is the order of the day.

Internationally, the relationship between feminism and postmodernism is an uneasy one, as Alice Jardine, among many others, has pointed out (*Gynesis*, 65). What Jardine calls "gynesis" is "a crisis in the master narrative of western culture ... a crisis characterized by the decentering of the subject ... and the writing of the feminine into discourse" (Smart, "Postmodern Male Narratives," 146). However, as Patricia Waugh argues, the postmodern urge to deconstruct the subject, to do away with the self-centered "I" of liberal humanism is sometimes problematic for feminists. Women have traditionally been constituted through a male gaze as Other: "Subjectivity, historically constructed and expressed through the phenomenological equation self/other, necessarily rests masculine 'selfhood' upon feminine 'otherness'" (*Feminine Fictions*, 8). If women have not yet experienced a "'whole' or 'unitary' or 'essential' subjectivity," it follows that the desire "to become subjects (which dominates the first phase of post-1960s feminism) is likely to be stronger than the desire to deconstruct, decentre, or fragment subjectivity (which dominates post-1960s postmodernist practice)" (12). The narrators of Kogawa's and Marchessault's texts face not only this double pull to construct identities while deconstructing master narratives but also that third problematic issue discussed in chapter 1: an ongoing preoccupation with – and problematization of – "collective identity" in a blatantly postmodern world.

On the international front, feminist writings and theories increasingly appear to parallel rather than intersect postmodernists' concerns. For instance, Craig Owens deplores the lack of feminist contributions to the debate on postmodernism in the United States ("The Discourse of Others," 62). However, in English-speaking Canada and Quebec, where women writers are very visible participants in the production of contemporary theory, the situation is different. In Quebec, especially, literary theory often appears to be driven by *l'écriture au féminin*. In both Quebec and English-speaking Canada, postmodernists' and feminists' projects can and do intersect, especially in their efforts to deconstruct imposed hegemonic worldviews, such as that proposed by authoritative historical discourse.

As I have argued elsewhere, the term "postmodernism" is a recent import in Quebec; more usual terms were *la modernité* or *la nouvelle écriture* ("Les Métarécits," 43–4). That the term as such has not been unilaterally accepted by feminist writers and critics is evident in theoretical/ fictional works such as *La théorie, un dimanche*, which presents collective reflections by Louky Bersianik, Nicole Brossard, France Théoret, and others. Nonetheless, *l'écriture au féminin* in Quebec often uses subversive strategies employed by postmodernists – such as deconstruction – to advance a different worldview. I agree with Barbara Godard's appraisal of the situation: in Quebec, "the feminist project has been at the heart of postmodernism" ("Re: Post," 141). In the (English) Canadian context, as Godard argues, "poststructuralism has been preeminently a theory of postmodernism. Poststructuralist criticism in a variety of modes – deconstruction in particular – has been used as a theory of reading postmodern texts ... Feminist criticism especially has privileged the texts of contemporary women writers such as Atwood, Munro, Laurence, and Thomas.

Poststructural theory in Quebec, even more than that of English-speaking Canada, has emphasized the political over the aesthetic tendencies" ("Re: Post," 139). It appears that in both English Canadian and Québécois feminist discourse one finds that blurring of postmodernist techniques and problematic nationalism discussed in chapter 1.

In their explorations of New World Myth, the narrators of *Comme une enfant de la terre* and *Obasan* partially resolve the dichotomy between their urge to personal and collective identity and their acknowledgment of necessary fragmentation. As Waugh argues, much contemporary feminist fictional writing has produced "an alternative conception of the subject as constructed through relationship, rather than postmodern/post-structuralism's anti-humanist rejection of the subject" (*Feminine Fictions*, 13). The study of relationship in Marchessault's and Kogawa's texts revolves around three activities: celebrating the feminine, deconstructing historiography, and living as women with the political, cultural, and community-based contradictions of the past and of the present.

Diana Fuss has noted that while "historians like Hayden White have busily been trying to get out of history, feminist literary critics have been just as energetically trying to get into it" ("Getting Into History," 95). Writers such as Kogawa and Marchessault are also carving a place for women in "history" – or, rather, telling the story of women and making evident their place in it. Writing women into "history," as Judith Newton points out, "might well mean that traditional definitions of 'history' would have to change" ("History as Usual?" 100). My investigation of the rewriting of history in Kogawa's and Marchessault's texts is indeed outside the usual studies of history as it appears in fictional works: the double focus of this chapter is the narratorial promotion of women's worldviews and the retellings of political history in the feminine.

These two elements are examined here through the narrators' thematization of the presence (or absence) of sensuality, non-rationality, speech, and memory in their stories. Related versions of these concepts are central to feminists' concerns, as some feminist historians, known as the Clio Collective, point out: "Activities and debate within the movement were focused on four major themes: the body, work, speaking out, and power" (*Quebec Women*, 368). In this chapter, I want to expand the notion of the body to the more encompassing one of sensuality, and relate *la parole* – "the word" – to the narrators' need to speak out. The Clio Collective's discussion of the third element, work (the second element in their list), centres on women's unremunerated housework. This is not a major issue in Marchessault's and Kogawa's texts, although, as Gayatri Spivak points out, it was and remains a feminist concern: "it is the long history of women's work which is a sustained example of zero-work: work not only outside of wage-work, but, in one way or another, 'outside' of the definitive modes of production" (*In Other Worlds*, 84). In Marchessault's and Kogawa's texts, the female narrators' approaches to history are also outside the definitive modes of production; they actively promote the non-rational as an alternative to the traditionally male-dominated rational and linear study of the past. By remembering, retelling, and liberating their versions of the past through their stories, these two narrators undertake a different kind of work.

Undoubtedly, certain aspects of a feminine worldview have usually been either ignored or treated disparagingly in the West. Thus, Catherine Belsey names "irrational intuition" as one of the determining characteristics of "specifically feminine discourse offered by society" (*Critical Practice*, 65), implying that it is generally perceived as a negative attribute. In a reversal of this attitude, the narrators of *Comme une enfant de la terre* and *Obasan* promote the feminine by celebrating the non-rational in their retellings of the historical past. The Clio Collective cites power as the fourth major concern of feminism. The notion of empowerment is central to both texts examined here: to remember and to retell is to claim power over the past. These four aspects of what I see as constitutive of Marchessault's and Kogawa's particular feminine worldviews – sensuality, non-rationality, speech, and memory – are all important factors in the narrators' concern to retell sociopolitical history. Their exploration of a personal sense of feminine identity – of what it is to be women living in history – is inseparable from their personal concerns regarding political nationalism. The narrators adopt similar – though not identical – approaches to retelling political history in the feminine.

An emphasis on the feminine puts Marchessault's text into the stream of feminist poetics in Quebec – more precisely, into one of two streams described in detail in "Flying Away With Language," Barbara Godard's introductory essay to another of Marchessault's works, *Lesbian Triptych*. Of course, the term "feminine" is fraught with difficulties of definition, as are "female," "feminist," and other related terms. I use the term here as Godard uses it: to distinguish between two poetics of feminist writing. According to Godard, the first of these two streams, the poetic of feminist deconstruction, challenges the oppression of women mainly through its work on language. Wendy Waring has suggested that the "patriarchal stronghold on language works on a number of levels, and feminist writers subvert everything from syntax to semantics, from linear discursive patterns ('logical' argument) to the unconscious assumptions about the speaking situation (that 'I' is a man) in the battle against a garrisoned language" ("Strategies for Subversion," 17). She proposes that in Québécoises' prose, the language issue has focused chiefly on grammatical markers of gender in syntax and morphology.

Although Marchessault's text includes many of the grammatically subversive strategies examined by Waring, its main focus is on the other stream: the poetic of the feminine. In its attempt to promote a community of women, this second stream, according to Godard, concentrates on the rediscovery of feminine symbolism, which has been excluded from the dominant patriarchal worldview. While Marchessault's novel does employ the "techniques of doubling – satire, inversion, parody and other self-reflexive modes" common to the deconstructionist feminists – its main emphasis is on the practices of "feminine writing" ("Flying Away with Language," 18). This type of writing, in spite of the fact that it *is* writing, seeks to transcend the printed page by its insistence on corporeality and speech. In feminine writing, "the Word is made flesh of woman's body and the emphasis is on the surfaces of the body, on the cry, on a wealth of experience that has remained always on the other side of language, in the realm of bodily experience" (20). Sensuality is a marker of this writing: emphasis is placed on women's need to regain contact with their physical and emotional selves, a contact that in Quebec had been curtailed by the "Catholic dualism which separates saintly motherhood from sinful sexual pleasure" (18–19). Indeed, in Marchessault's novels and plays, attention to female bodily functions such as menstrual bleeding, love-making, giving birth, and lactating promotes the female body and seeks to "produce the fluid, associative, irrational writing that ... is opposed to the rational linearity of masculine discourse" (21). This emphasis, however, can be problematic. It can signal that writers who emphasize female bodily functions "are still caught within the definition of the 'eternal feminine' as it has been used to exclude them ... close to body and nature ... Privatized, this experience cannot enter the public domain as herstory" (21–2). *Comme une enfant de la terre* promotes the sensual and sexual aspects of the feminine and yet doubly inscribes this "be-ing" in the public domain through two related discourses: ecofeminism, to use Françoise d'Eaubonne's term (*Le Féminisme ou la mort*, 216), and feminist political nationalism.

Ecofeminism, that marriage of feminist and ecological concerns, is linked to a resurgence of earth-based spiritualism (sometimes called "paganism" within the dominant Christian system), which includes Amerindian religions and Goddess worship.[1] The term and the concept of ecofeminism are not universally accepted by feminists, partly because there is a fine line between ecofeminism and "the 'maternal feminist' movement of the late 19th century" (Prentice, "Taking Sides," 9), and partly because the term is sometimes criticized as a watered-down form of militant feminism (Cameron, "Why I'm Not an Ecofeminist," 12). Ecofeminism, however, can provide useful insights into Jovette Marchessault's novel because it explores pre-Christian, Goddess-centred myths. Ecofeminism addresses not only man's destructive domination of the earth, but "domination itself, in all its forms – whites over people of color, men over women, adults over children, rich nations over the Third World, humans over animals and nature" (Lindsy Van Gelder, "Mother Nature," 61). One of the tenets of ecofeminism is that "Rationalism is the key to the connected oppressions of women and nature in the West" (Plumwood, "Nature, Self, and Gender," 3).

In *Comme une enfant de la terre*, Marchessault mounts an all-out attack on rational thought, tying it to the hegemonic discourse of traditional historiography and to the sociocultural undervaluing of women by men. Ecofeminism, according to Joyce Nelson, undertakes a critique of the "patriarchal Western worldview paradigm" because it makes explicit "the connections between a misogynist society and a society which has exploited 'mother earth' to the point of environmental crisis" ("Speaking the Unspeakable," 15). The traditional masculine point of view assumes a hierarchical, oppositional stance: rationality, logic, and a mechanist cosmogony are male and separate from nature; relating, nurturing, and sexuality are consigned to the feminine/earthy realm. Nelson names three notions that are central to ecofeminist's concerns: interconnection (all parts of the living cosmos are linked), immanence (sacredness is inherent in all Creation), and compassion (valuing other lives – including animal and plant life – as we value our own). Traditional mythography has of course categorized this approach as "primitive" animism, while Jungian scholars and mythographers have reduced the Great Goddess to the notion of the eternal feminine, as Andrée Collard has argued in *Rape of the Wild*. In *Comme une enfant de la terre* the narrator's blurring of the boundaries among the plant, animal, human, and goddess worlds is indicative of the interconnections between all living things. "Animals are mere machines" in the rational Cartesian framework (Hallen, "Making Peace with the Environment," 14), but the narrator of *Comme une enfant de la terre* animates machinery and discerns souls and personalities in animals and plants. For instance, she dialogues with the Greyhound bus in which she travels north to Quebec from Mexico, giving it a mythical dimension and identifying with it on a personal level (43–4). The narrator's pursuit of those feminine qualities denigrated by traditional masculine rationality empowers her to complete her mission. Thus, she actively seeks physical and emotional nurturing from the Great Goddess and from other goddesses, from her grandmother's warmth, from her friend Francine – from a complex network of female support: "la grande femelle de l'humanité" (335). For the narrator, all the universe is mythical, and she herself is sensually centred in all things: "Par l'univers j'entends aussi bien l'herbe des champs, les vers de terre, les poissons des rivières, les nébuleuses qui tirent des chariots d'étoiles et de bisons célestes, que mon père, ma mère, les ancêtres et vous tous" (106). Marchessault thoroughly conflates all scientific categories of species and race, reinvests both the earth and the sky with feminine power, and actively promotes Earth/Goddess worship. Her writings, as Gloria Orenstein points out, cumulatively create "un univers de Déesse-mère (matristique), éco-féministe … où toutes les espèces vivent ensemble en harmonie dans un monde où tout se définit à partir d'images féminines" ("Les voyages visionnaires," 257).

Nevertheless, there is a difference between the international ecofeminism of the 1990s and that found in Marchessault's 1975 novel: ecofeminist concerns in *Comme une enfant de la terre* are bound up with the Québécois nationalism of the 1970s. The narrator's interest is in the earth – Mother Earth, yes, but specifically, her "terre amérindienne/terre de Québec," which she sees as a mythical life-giving force. Thus, in her "grand Lévrier," the greyhound bus that brings her back to Quebec from Mexico, the narrator underlines the mythical dimensions of Quebec, rejecting the cosmogonies of Latin America and the United States. Techniques common to many nationalist texts of the '60s and '70s are found in this text: for instance, a lengthy, elegiac list of Québécois place-names is in the seventh *chant* (169–80). The narrator's variation on this traditional theme of Québécois *indépendantiste* writings consists of a curious mixture of Earth worship, Amerindian legends, and Québécois nationalist sentiments. This passage celebrates the beauty of Quebec's countryside. It also proclaims the creation of a new race, descendants of Quebec's Amerindian tribes and francophone Quebecers, who have united to celebrate Quebec and who are to protect it from colonizing forces. The narrator's friends in this *chant* – themselves apparently a mixture of Amerindians and Québécois – condemn the human exploitation of Quebec's environment, criticizing in particular the owners of the pulp mills, whose English names provide a hard contrast to the poetry found in the numerous French and Aboriginal place-names.

The narrator's love of Mother Earth, then, is expressed in part through her political accusations of the colonial exploitation of Quebec. The ecofeminist praxis called for in *Comme une enfant de la terre* is in part ecological and Earth-centred, but it is also motivated by a nationalist appreciation of the political situation of Quebec in the 1970s.

Throughout the text, the narrator takes sensual pleasure in describing, through the use of mythical vocabulary, typical sights of Quebec's geography in minute detail. She "knows" her surroundings through her senses, assimilating her *terre de Québec* into her very being. Physical sensations such as touching, sucking, and tasting are privileged by the narrator, with special attention given to the sense of smell. Like the main character's experience with "la madeleine" in Marcel Proust's *A la recherche du temps perdu*, this narrator relies on her senses to provoke memories, and thus knowledge of the past (110). Immediate, direct experience, such as that derived from the contemplation of any living organism, is of far more importance than that derived from formal study. The ecofeminists' resistance to academic, institutional power is evident here: "La vie ainsi vécue est bien plus précieuse, bien plus universelle que tout ce qu'aurait pu m'apporter de longues années d'emprisonnement dans les universités de la mort" (122). In fact, this narrator's celebration of Quebec as Earth Mother is made possible because she has been able to avoid the indoctrination practised by the patriarchal, rational, hegemonic discourse of educational systems in the West. Her lack of formal schooling, her love of travel, her Amerindian heritage, and her wide range of varied experiences have enabled her to reconnect to ancient Amerindian mythologies and to Goddess worship. Stephanie Lahar argues that the central theme of most versions of ecofeminism is "the interrelationship and integration of personal, social, and environmental issues and the development of multidirectional political agendas and action" ("Ecofeminist Theory," 30). Marchessault's singular novel strongly underlines the interrelationship of feminism, ecology, and the narrator's personal concerns with nationalism and the Québécois and Amerindian ways of life. Surprisingly, Marchessault produced this novel in 1975, years before the popularity of ecofeminism in popular and academic discourses. Through ecofeminism, the narrator celebrates her sensuality and her sexuality, her people and her *pays*.

The second major aspect of feminine symbolism explored in Marchessault's text is the concept of the non-rational: those means of acquiring knowledge that defy the "empirical basis of the humanist and positivist concepts of knowledge – trust in observation and experiment" (Hutcheon, *Poetics of Postmodernism*, 167). Dreams, coincidences, and strong emotional experiences can all form part of the non-rational. In this novel, criticism of the rational is centred mainly on a refusal of accepted ways of acquiring knowledge. The narrator questions the logical, scientific approach to fact gathering that has dominated in the West since the Enlightenment ("les Lumières") and reflects the ecofeminists' attitude toward the traditional masculine philosophy of dominance over nature: "Que ceux qui examinent tout à la lumière de la science se moquent de ma naïveté! Nous sommes l'espèce, le type dominant du moment mais nous pourrions être remplacés" (42). In her worldview, direct experience is preferable to book-learning. Thus, she reproaches Francine for staying in her room to read about the ancient civilizations of Mexico when she could be learning by accompanying the narrator on a visit to the pyramids of Tenochtitlan (76). According to the narrator, the historical knowledge contained within most books is worthless. Searching for those books that would truly communicate direct knowledge of the past to her, she can find only insufficient texts that are "à deux doigts du néant, de la mort, dans l'épaisseur du temps historique" (126).

However, the paradoxes we saw in the contradictory ascent/descent movement in chapter 3 are repeated in the narrator's varying opinion of the utility of books and their relationship to knowledge of the past. At times, she does admire certain books – books that are free from the limitations of chronological time (125). They have significance because they are "en marge d'un temps historique et morne, en marge des livres scolaires, des livres officiels" (58). These books place an emphasis on direct communication, and their authors are praised in terms of life, of *speaking* (128). Most books, however, are condemned by the narrator because they try to impose "reasonable" boundaries on alternative ways of coming to knowledge of the past (127). Barbara Godard has undertaken a narratological analysis of Marchessault's first novel. She too notes Marchessault's strong desire to affect change, to "exposer les stratagèmes du récit afin de produire du *nouveau*" ("En mémoire de l'avenir," 100). While I agree with Godard that this novel provides an enumeration of texts and authors who have practised "le vécrire" (vie + écrire) in the desire to illustrate that it is possible to "effectu[er] des transformations dans l'ordre symbolique afin de réaliser un changement social," I propose that Marchessault's narrator is less devoted to the *writing project* than Godard suggests: "s'écrire construit et maintient une vie" (107). I argue instead that the narrator's ambivalent attitude toward books and learning is tied to her valorization of *la parole* and her problematization of the relationship between orality and the written text.

The narrator's shifting attitude toward books may be seen in her use of intertextuality. She cites passages from sources as diverse as travelogues, encyclopedias, the *Popol Vuh*, and the writings of Malcolm Lowry, delimiting them textually with italicis, but giving no sources whatsoever. She then undercuts this citational process by laying bare her technique. For instance, she quotes a passage, most probably taken from a history text, that portrays Christopher Columbus as a mythic, legendary, courageous personage (82–3). Commenting in detail and in her own words on Columbus's cruelty towards the Indians, she then deflates the Eurocentric myth of the beneficent explorer and sympathizes with the Amerindians in her account of the past. The juxtaposition of these two passages is a good illustration of the sometimes contradictory retelling that is typical of New World Myth historiographic fictions. In her story, the narrator produces alternative "facts" to those usually found in textbooks, such as the one referred to above: "[Les Indiens] qui furent pris vivants furent envoyés en Espagne comme esclaves. Des quatre cents esclaves entassés sur les caravelles qui retournèrent sous Antonio de Torres le 24 février 1495, deux cents mourrurent entre Madère et Cadix. Les autres périrent de maladie peu de temps après avoir été vendus par l'archidiacre Fonseca sur le marché de Séville" (79–80). This portrayal of both the European colonizers and the representatives of the Church in an uncomplimentary light is typical of New World Myth retellings of the historical past.

Although the above passage does relay dates and numbers, the general tone of the novel dismisses the need for accurate fact. The narrator proposes that those who do *not* subscribe to the idea of rigorous, detailed, scientific knowledge backed up by facts and statistics are better suited to acquire and to transmit the type of knowledge that she considers worthwhile. Her own development reflects this stance. In the first *chant*, she admits that her carefully accumulated knowledge is a dead end and has led only to the building of barriers between herself and the alternative knowledge of the past that she seeks (18). She gradually frees herself from the limitations of the rational (36), and allows herself to recreate an alternative worldview. A negative attitude toward the hard sciences is found in the narrator's condemnation of the "éminents médicastres" (an obvious play on *médecins* and *castrer*) who are unable to cure the sickness of silence that befalls her people (162–3).

Elsewhere in the text, in her retelling of the history of Montreal, the narrator proposes that rationality is detrimental to knowledge of the past. The tone of the following typical passage contrasts terms that are more traditionally associated with fairy-tales with terms from the political and ecclesiastical domains: "Montréal, abondance de temps et de lieux: à deux pas d'ici, dans une forêt qui borde le fleuve, vivent un cerf et une licorne ... La forêt où vivent ces animaux n'appartient à personne. En tout cas elle n'appartient pas au gouvernement provincial, ou au fédéral. Elle ne relève d'aucun ministère connu ou pratiqué. Cette forêt relève – si ma mémoire est bonne – de l'Empire suprême et supra-céleste et échappe de ce fait à tous ces malaises économiques qui ont jeté depuis toujours le désarroi dans toute la colonie du Canada" (206–7). The only "explanation" offered for this unusual history is a challenge to the reader – a challenge again couched in biblical and fairy-tale terms: "Et que ceux et celles dont le cœur et l'esprit ne s'illuminent pas en apprenant la bonne nouvelle, en lisant les mots cerf, licorne, carcajou, referment ce livre" (207). A refusal of book-learning, then, and a willingness to explore the non-rational as an alternative way of knowing the past, are components of the worldview that is explored in *Comme une enfant de la terre*.

Speech – *la parole* – is the third concept examined by the narrator in her particular poetic of the feminine. As a self-proclaimed goddess and an ecofeminist, the narrator frequently identifies herself and her powers of communication with certain animals, especially birds. The narrator's fascination with birds and snakes may be both an expression of her Amerindian heritage and a reflection of the ecofeminists' desire to blur boundaries between various worlds. According to Richard Cavendish, the "motif of the snake and the bird is one of the most ancient in Middle America, an expression of the lowly and the high, the sexual and the spiritual conjoined" (*Mythology*, 250). In her overview of the feminine in Aztec mythology, Susanna Rostas notes the importance of the snake/bird combination for the Aztecs. Generally, the bird was associated with the masculine, while the snake "represented the fertility of the earth and the female psyche." However, several important deities could be both masculine and feminine: Quetzalcóatl, the Plumed Serpent, "clearly represents both the masculine, the quetzal bird, and the feminine, the snake" ("Mexican Mythology," 371). Aztec-inspired mythological references to both snakes and birds are found in Marchessault's text, but there is a stronger privileging of the bird as a symbol of rejuvenation. This preference could signal Marchessault's recognition of the strength of this symbol in traditional Quebec social mythology, as well as a desire to reappropriate the power of the bird, which, as Rostas

explains it, is perceived to be the stronger of the two symbols:
another deity, Coatlicue, "combines the more aggressive male eagle
and the female snake; the two symbols which appear on the Mexican
flag."

At the beginning of the narrator's story, when she is ill at ease in
her body, she is "l'oiseau kiwi à la voix geignarde" (*Comme une
enfant*, 32). Once she has come to a definite decision to return home,
her self-image improves and she identifies with more beautiful and
progressively more vocal birds. Her ability to communicate develops
as she approaches her "quartiers d'hiver dans les demeures aquatiques de [ses] terres du Nord." She is now a "hirondelle de Chine,"
proclaiming, "je parlerai à la macreuse blanche qui ne parle jamais à
personne" (75). In the underground café, the bird imagery is even
more clearly associated with her capacity to speak and with the
importance of dispensing her particular knowledge. In the centre of
the sacred space, multicoloured birds surround her, forcing her to
open her mouth by tickling her lips with their feathers. She answers
to their urgings: "je reste bien tranquille ... à parler, à raconter ... Il
y a ... en moi, de vieux os, un vieux savoir" (101). A new-found
liberty comes from regaining control over two powers of expression:
la parole and *l'écriture*.

Much work has been done on speech and orality as privileged
means of communication.[2] Most studies presume, and therefore help
maintain, definite boundaries between primary orality, "the orality
of a culture which has never known writing" (Ong, *Interfaces*, 18),
and "secondary orality," post-writing orality that is "superficially
identical with that of primary orality but in depth utterly contrary,
planned and self-conscious ... totally dependent on writing and
print for its existence" (298). Underlying this binary division is the
presumption that "real" orality no longer exists – that as soon as
"primitive" peoples come into contact with "civilization," their orality is contaminated because it is less "real". Jacques Derrida, of
course, has argued that there is no such thing as "innocent" primary
speech that is somehow more authentic than the written word: he
questions the privileging of the oral over the written in his reread-
ings of Lévi-Strauss' work on "primitive" tribes in "The Violence of
the Letter." New World Myth novels self-consciously problematize
this oral/written polarization. They flaunt their thematization of
orality in their texts, thereby blurring the boundaries between oral
and written modes of communication, while mockingly maintaining
the inherent tensions in the primitive/civilized debate. Marchessault's novel does not ignore what Hutcheon has described as the
ironic struggle between oral and written modes of communication

being carried out "on the battlefield of the printed page" (Hutcheon, 'Postmodernist' Scribe," 289). The narrator obviously is aware of the metafictional quality of her text, but she nevertheless privileges the nonwritten aspects of this "resurrection of the feminine" (Godard, "Flying," 18) by her thematization of *la parole*. While the *author* Jovette Marchessault communicates with the general public through her novels, her artistic exhibitions, and performances of her feminist plays, it is through orality that this *narrator* reaches her public and transmits the historical and mythological knowledge that informs her New World view: "Je suis pressée de témoigner; je me torture avec cette pensée depuis ma première communion: comment dire? Comment exprimer l'ineffable? ... je veux prendre la parole" (105–6).

Given the shared Amerindian background of the author and the narrator of *Comme une enfant de la terre*, Barbara Godard's work on orality and native women, *Talking about Ourselves*, provides a useful backdrop to my discussion of orality in Marchessault's feminist novel. Arguing for the inclusion of native women's oral literary productions into the literary canon, Godard notes that such an adjustment requires a redefinition of the notion of text. Oral literature, she proposes, not only "stretch[es] the boundaries of literary study into the fields of history (oral history more precisely) and anthropology ... but it also underlines the dynamic nature of the text, which is not just an icon but a performance, not just a preconstituted meaning for easy consumption but an event in which meaning is actively negotiated" (1). *Comme une enfant de la terre* is a novel and not an example per se of oral literature. Marchessault's text, however, includes within its pages what Godard has determined to be the two characteristics of Native women's oral narrative, that is to say, autobiographical stories and shamanic myths of creation (*Talking about Ourselves*, 7). Long passages of *Comme une enfant de la terre* describe the narrator's childhood and her family history; equally long passages demonstrate her focus on creation myths. An understanding of the Indian copyright system, argues Godard, "makes clear to us why so many of the [women] storytellers insist on the fact that they are transmitters of tradition, or vehicles for the words of others to be put down in writing. In a very real sense the tales are not owned, but are communal property" (14).

In the retelling of native women's tales, the presence of the grandmother, or the old woman, is an important factor. Godard's research reveals that many native women narrators hesitate to tell their own life-stories and do so only to pass on the wisdom of their grandmothers (*Talking about Ourselves*, 18). The individual's life is seen as inseparable from the heritage of the group, and there is a strong link between the narration and the passing-on of knowledge. Indeed, the grandmothers' storytelling sessions are considered to be sacred rituals (19). Citing Carol Christ's argument in *Diving Deep and Surfacing* that many women's narratives effect entry into the sacred, Godard proposes that much of English Canadian women's fiction strives to attain to the spiritual quality of narrative, which, she says, is "characteristic of the native women's community" (*Talking about Ourselves*, 19). Marchessault's text is strongly marked by her desire for the sacred and one aspect of this desire is the text's underlining of the Amerindian respect for the grandmother figure. Marchessault herself has always credited her grandmother for her spiritual and artistic inspiration. In an interview with Donald Smith she says: "Les histoires de ma grand-mère, à mon tour je les transmets et c'est ce que les femmes font depuis le commencement du monde. Comme le dit si justement et si sensiblement Yolaine Simha, écrivaine française, nous sommes des 'passeuses de mémoire'" (Smith, "Jovette Marchessault," 54). Describing her family life, the narrator of Marchessault's novel insists on its communal aspect, on its matriarchal form, on the influence her grandmother exerted on her development, and on the long sessions of oral conversation that prompted her political awareness and her nationalist mission (*Comme une enfant*, 244). The narrator claims the authority of her grandmother as sufficient reason for passing on her knowledge through the retelling of story (98), and her own homeward trip has been presaged by the grandmother's heroic drive from the West to Quebec (290). Even in the sections of very personal her-story, the narrator's private life is linked to political history, and her highly ironic comments seem to suggest that there is no fundamental difference between the "circus" of the grandmother's life and the goings-on of important political personages of the past, such as William Lyon Mackenzie King's fascination with the occult (287–8). Indeed, the notion that stories are communal property is developed in this narrator's deliberate readjustment of the traditional political and historical systems of her *pays*.

Written history – usually a matter of who won which war – has traditionally ignored women's lives. Given the male dominance of history and historiography, the oral mode opens up new possibilities for womens' reclaiming of their stories. One articulation of this theory is found is Suzanne Lamy's concept of *bavardage* as a female method of communication ("Eloge du bavardage," 15–35). Lamy rejects the traditional definition of *bavardage* as women's idle gossip, as opposed to men's "important" discussions: "Bien que de genre masculin, [le bavardage] désigne une activité éminemment féminine ... Aux hommes – en sous-entendu – le privilège de dialoguer, de discuter, d'avoir des entretiens, de posséder et maîtriser la parole ... Parole sèche, prononcée généralement du bout des lèvres, le corps guindé de toutes les baleines de la respectabilité, coupé de l'émission de la voix" (17–18). In her effort to avoid prescriptive, dictionary-like definitions of *bavardage*, Lamy speaks in terms of coming-into-being and uses images of the womb and of birth – feminine images that are echoed in much of Marchessault's work. Lamy's theory of *bavardage* can shed light on the insertion of long, seemingly disconnected stories into the main body of Marchessault's text. The narrator's typically conversational, oral history passages, such as the long story about the construction of the Brooklyn bridge that begins the third *chant*, are atypical for history textbooks, which rely on governmental documents, newspaper accounts, and other written records. They are typical, however, of native women's oral narratives and an illustration of another way of transmitting knowledge of the past. Orality is a medium that provides for complicity between the narrator and her audience. As Lamy suggests, this language of friendship is also a language of intervention, and thus a medium capable of inspiring trust while intervening in – and adapting – a traditional patriarchal worldview.

Memory is the fourth element of Marchessault's poetic of the feminine. Video artist Lisa Steele has argued that "women have learned (and well-learned, to the point of truism) that history is not necessarily her story" ("Committed to Memory," 40). Remembering could be considered a particularly compelling component in the desire of Marchessault's narrator to tell her own story and other women's stories. According to Steele, in the early seventies, for feminists in English-speaking Canada and Quebec, "Remembering became an act of survival: remembering our own lives, our mothers' lives, our neighbourhoods, our jobs, the lives of others we knew. Remembering before it disappeared. No one else was talking about it: we had to. History is produced by whomever [*sic*] writes it down first. History should never be mistaken for truth ... Memory, if unrecorded or unspoken, dies ... Memory is not truth (or beauty, for that matter, since we are talking about art here). Memory is associative, sensual and illogical, it erupts and intrudes. History can be memorized; memory is added to by each who remembers" (41–2). In *Comme une enfant de la terre* the narrator's individual storytelling style, as we have seen, corresponds to Steele's description of memory: she frequently interrupts her own stories because of distractions provided by a sight, a smell, or an image. The characteristic blurring of genres within New World Myth is evident in the narrator's treatment of memory. Thus, autobiographical details, her grandmother's stories, her recollections of life in the sky, her historico-political reflections, and the fragments of mythical and historical knowledge that she has gleaned from various sources are all interwoven in this complex tale. Precision with regard to facts, dates, and places is not particularly important to this type of feminine memory, as is evident in the narrator's personal her-story. Her grandmother, she says, was born somewhere between Quebec, Rimouski, and Chicoutimi – an area of several hundred square kilometres (263).

The narrator retells the stories of the goddesses of some Amerindian tribes: "la Grand-Mère du maïs, la très vieille Ixmucane ... la Tortue-Immortelle et sa fille, la Mère-des-herbes, et celle qui porte une jupe de serpents, la vieille Coatlicue" (62). The narrator, herself an immortal goddess, remembers the reign of the sky-goddess, "la Grande-Oursonne" (13). The narrator's memories, then, are of a female-dominated community – in the sky and on earth. Part of the narratorial mission is clearly to promote the cause of women and to remake a mythological universe in their image. Most of the narrator's memories convey a positive portrayal of Woman, although an exception to this observation is found in the troubling memories of her education at the hands of the nuns within the patriarchal system of the Roman Catholic Church (105).

A second aspect of memory – collective memory – informs the other part of the narratorial mission: to free the telling of certain historico-political events from the dominance of the patriarchal Church and traditional European-inspired historiography. Although the narrator frequently reiterates her personal desire to facilitate this liberation, it is in the sections that recount the mission of her "apostolic" friends that the relationship of collective memory to political history is most clearly addressed. Speech, memory and the collectivity all intersect in the seventh *chant*, where the narrator praises the *voices* of these friends, who are representatives of a plurivocal community. The importance of the *oral* retelling of history to the development of nationalist sentiments is foregrounded in the opening paragraph of this *chant*: "Vos voix résonnent encore en ce pays de la Nouvelle-France, autrement nommé Amérique, autrement nommé Canada, en ce pays de la France subartique autrement nommé Québec" (*Comme une enfant*, 143).[3] As the narrator had done before them, these friends travel to every corner of *le pays*, and sometimes to areas outside the present-day borders of Quebec (but which formed part of New France), retelling Quebec's political history to its inhabitants. By means of oral delivery in a community setting, such as the *salle paroissiale* or around a campfire, the voices of these friends affect the historical memory of the collectivity: "Vous disiez notre histoire, les massacres, les répressions, le déclin de la race et sa descente circulaire, sanglante dans ce charnier que recouvre à peine quelques arpents de neige" (146). This last quotation is of course an ironic reference to Voltaire's infamous dismissal of New France and a precise example of what the narrator credits the voices with doing: playing with historical documents to *remake* myth. Although the friends, like the narrator, sometimes make use of facts and figures, they nevertheless maintain their distance from the sole tyranny of documents (149). Unusual, unverifiable and little-known "facts," such as the origins of the names "Canada" and "Québec," are transmitted by these voices – and thus by the narrator and, eventually, by this book. The boundaries between history and fiction are deliberately blurred, with historical personages such as Louis Riel and Sir John Colborne accorded the same attention as fictional characters such as Louis Hémon's Maria Chapdeleine. The voices' retelling of history is triggered by the same motivation that inspires the narrator: to free the inhabitants from the double yoke imposed by a colonial mentality and the authority of the clergy.

Hubert Aquin's well-known description of the colonial Québécois mentality is appropriate here: "The colonized are profoundly ambivalent: they hesitate, they waver and feel guilty for doing so, they always check anything that seems like impulsive behaviour, they are afraid of doing things they might regret and so find themselves constantly on the brink of paralysis ("Joual," 103). Marchessault's challenges to this mentality are most obvious in the passage that describes the colonial sickness of silence. This mysterious illness paralyses the larynx and the jaws of its victims, totally preventing speech. The British specialists from the famous institute Larnyx [sic] Incorporated of London (*Comme une enfant*, 162) diagnose the disease and offer a remedy: "nous connaissons cette maladie, dirent-ils, elle est sournoise, elle apparaît souvent dans nos colonies ... Il n'y a qu'une voie de guérison, qu'une solution: coupez la langue! ... God save the King!" (164). Neither the government nor the clergy can halt the epidemic, but the message of resistance preached by the voices takes hold in the imagination of the people and eventually eliminates the threat of mutism: "On parlait faiblement, on parlait à voix basse, comme des convalescents en utilisant précautionneusement le futur des verbes avoir et être" (165). The political allusions to the double colonial situation of Quebec and to the seemingly unending language issue are unmistakable here. The voices' mission, like the narrator's, is to decentre the traditional historical focus: to move away from Europe to the here and the now of Quebec. Whereas Christopher

Columbus and Jacques Cartier were supposedly seized by terror when they first saw what Cartier called "the land of Cain," this same New World geography extends a welcome to the voices (143–4). As was argued elsewhere, this readjusting of the centre is typical of the post-Europeanism of New World Myth narrators.

Like the narrator, the voices desire to promote political nationalism through a strong sense of communal identity. Thus, the voices always tell their stories in a community setting, while praising the birth of that new people, the descendants of an ancient European race and Amerindian tribes (*Comme une enfant*, 155–6). The people and the *pays*, however, like everything else in this New World Myth novel, have indeterminate, flexible boundaries. In the following passage, the blurring of symbols of various cultural entities (Amerindian, British, Québécois, and English Canadian) against governmental and clerical backdrops underlines a deliberate confusion regarding the cultural identity of this *nous*: "Nous nous sommes déguisés ... en premier ministre, en chapelet en famille, en gouverneur du Canada, en reine du Dominion. Nous avons couru le Derby ventre à terre en raquettes à queue de castor: nous avons joué au cricket avec des battoirs en tire de la Sainte-Catherine et des balles en poil de chien" (150–1). Thanks to the voices, this cultural confusion is transformed into a desirable quality: a *convergence culturelle* that works. Because they have been assimilated lovingly by the *terre amériendienne*, the people of this new race develop a sense of solidarity, which, the narrator prophetizes, will one day proclaim itself (184–5). The voices also have a protectionist attitude toward *le pays*, and part of their mission is to keep it from being overwhelmed by Anglo-American culture: "Vos voix arrivent à couvrir le bruit des claquettes de Fred Astair, les borborygmes d'Humphrey Bogart, le rire niais d'Errol Flynn" (183). This anti-Americanism (and implicit anticommercialism) is also shared by the narrator, who remarks that Americans are addicted to coke and ketchup and interested only in the commonplace. In contrast, her people are different; they are the real "enfants de l'Amérique" (132). The narrator uses biblical terms to signal their significance: "L'Ange Gabriel nous attend avec la bonne nouvelle au bout de la Panaméricana" (76). Finally, the voices' concern, like the narrator's, is to enter into another order: a mythological order. Their stories are meant to challenge the official versions of past events, as well as to instil pride and solidarity in their audience. Comparing the voices to salmon swimming upstream, the narrator praises their ability to rectify the subservient state in which the colonial situation had left them: "vous frappiez de vos queues les monuments officiels de nos deuils, usant, brassant l'argile friable des briques de nos parlements coloniaux" (149–50).

The narrator, like the voices, is interested in loosening the hold of traditional worldviews over the people's imagination. Her concern lies with *her pays* – and not with *all* the New World. She rejects Mexico, a country that she does not understand, and, as we have seen, an anti-American sentiment is present in the novel. Near the beginning of the novel, the narrator begins to realize that self-knowledge is important and that her self is somehow linked to the Québécois part of the New World, which she likens to the Promised Land (*Comme une enfant*, 65). In self-imposed exile in Mexico, her feelings of nostalgia permit her to recognize the close affiliation that exists between her self and her people. Like Christ, she *chooses* to come to earth for her particular Amerindian-Québécois people, to arrive "chez nous" – a politically invested term in Quebec – in "la géographie sacrée de la terre amérindienne" (347–8). In fact, the narrator and the *pays* are one and the same: "Mon pays est cet espace qui règne au-dedans de moi-même" (131).

The narrator works detailed historical and geographical lessons into her tale, mixing the personal with the political, the history with the place (*Comme une enfant*, 180). She also appreciates more modern aspects of her *pays*, such as its metropolis, Montreal. Describing the meetings of Jérome le Royer de la Dauversière and Jacques Olier concerning the establishment of a colony – the future Montreal – in the New World, the narrator first employs an informal, chatty delivery of historical data, and then subsequently negates its importance (191–4). Memories couched in mythical vocabulary are also a factor in the narrator's retelling of history. Standing at a busy intersection in downtown Montreal, the narrator remembers "l'ancien visage des choses" (208), as she incorporates various worldviews in her retelling of Montreal's foundation. Using the Amerindian mythology of Thunderbird and of the wind deities to change the accepted shape of white, male history, she also includes the women founders of Montreal in this potpourri of mythical systems: "Il vente! Par Jupiter, par Zeus, par le grand Manitou, par le Saint-Esprit, il vente! Il vente Jérôme, Jacques et Paul! Il vente! Il vente Père Lalemant! Il vente Jeanne-Mance! Il vente Marguerite Bourgeois! Il vente Madame de Bullion! Il vente les maraudeuses, les néophytes" (200).

The narrator implies that in her city – and, I would argue, in her nation – all is possible, including a readjustment of mythology and history that would permit women to inscribe themselves in an alternative knowing of the New World: "Il souffle ici, il se prononce ici, des mots qui redonnent envie d'essayer à nouveau, de se dépasser, de sortir du troupeau pour s'aérer la peau de l'âme ... Cette ville ... nous donne envie de recommencer à zéro" (199). The narrator of *Comme une enfant de la terre*, then, deliberately posits the lack of certainty in her stories about the past. Her retelling of history and of her story permits a recreation (through disruption) of history; this retelling makes room for an alternative, New World Myth view of feminine symbolism and mythology and feminist political history.

Joy Kogawa's *Obasan* also examines and contributes to the present-day uncertainty in the face of the collapse of a traditional mythological universe. Its narrator questions the traditionally accepted Christian religious system as well as the official versions of recent Canadian history. All of *Obasan* can be seen as a testimonial to the uncertainty that Kogawa describes here: "Life is a series of making and unmaking plans along a continuum of uncertainty. In North America and in the world we are a competing chaos of voices" ("Is There a Just Cause?" 20). No one conclusive history can be drawn from Kogawa's *Obasan*, as is evidenced by the sometimes contradictory appraisals of its "message." While one reviewer claims that the novel's "measured and sober prose ... rigorously avoids any expression of bitterness or resentment" (Stevens, "Kogawa," 416), another, giving an example of Kogawa's handling of the language, writes: "All the political tracts or speeches in the world cannot sum up the poignancy or bitterness that [this example] achieve[s]" (Richardson, "Ode to Joy," 5). As we have seen, on the mythical level no one system wins out. A similar lack of definitive resolution is found in the discussion of the political, personal, moral, and religious questions in this novel. Thus this text, which is generally said to contain a strong political indictment of the Canadian government and people, ends with an excerpt from a memorandum sent by the Cooperative Committee on Japanese Canadians to the House of Commons and the Senate of Canada. This memo, signed by James M. Finlay, Andrew Brewin, and Hugh MacMillan, is sympathetic to the experience of Japanese Canadians during and after World War II; it suggests, as King-Kok Cheung notes, the author's tacit acknowledgment of "the many political activists who have fought for the cause of justice" (*Articulate Silences*, 153). On the personal level, although the narrator of the text finally learns her mother's story, this does not permit her to regain all those years that were lost to her, because, for a child, "there is no presence without flesh" (243). The Christian religion, as we have seen, is presented as an inadequate belief system for dealing with the problems of the present and of the past. This lack of definitive conclusions, of tidy solutions to dilemmas on the personal, political, and mythical fronts is as characteristic of New World Myth historiographic novels as it is of many postmodern and postcolonial texts.

The protagonist of *Obasan*, Naomi, commenting on the subtleties of the Japanese language, says, "It is not a language that promotes hysteria" (60). Indeed, compared to the highly emotional, overly exclamatory style of Marchessault's narrator, Naomi's use of the *English* language could be said to avoid any suggestion of hysteria. Strong emotions from Marchessault; restrained poetry from Kogawa. As Suanne Kelman notes, "*Obasan* begins elusively ... [The characters] speak in a mixture of Japanese and English, mostly in two- or three-word sentences. Much of their speech is evasive, sliding away from questions ... Kogawa writes in nuance – little is stated directly" ("Impossible to Forgive," 39). In spite of the frequently distancing effect of Kogawa's poetic prose, I argue here that *Obasan*'s narrator also exemplifies that second stream of feminist writing discussed earlier: the poetic of the feminine. Although Kogawa's blending of historical fact and poetic expression does address at times the feminist deconstructionists' concern for the creation of reality through language, her narrator's main emphasis is not on language per se, but rather on "the cry, on a wealth of experience that has remained always on the other side of language" (Godard, "Flying," 20). Through her exploration of "wordlessness," silence, speech, and story in a matrilinear community of women, Naomi hesitantly explores her own capacity for expression. "Getting the story out" is essential to this narrator's efforts to reconcile the discomfort of her "disembodied voice," as Godard writes in another context (14). The strident feminist concerns that are proclaimed loudly by Marchessault's narrator are muted in Kogawa's story, in keeping with the gentler tone of her work. Both novels, however, are concerned with the personal, the political, and the spiritual. Kogawa's indictment of the Canadian government is highlighted in *Obasan*'s discussion of racial tension and political injustices, whereas the feminine concerns of the novel are less overt. Interestingly, several recent American readings of this novel occult the political dimensions of its criticism of Canadian policies, concentrating instead on the issue of silence,[4] on the "divided female subject" (Goellnicht, "Father Land," 119), and on the inaccurate thematic of the Japanese American experience, as is evident in, for instance, Shirley Geok-lin Lim's work (for example, "Women's Life Stories"). I examine *Obasan*'s retellings of the personal and political pasts here through an exploration of the same four concepts of feminine symbolism that concern Marchessault's narrator: sensuality, non-rationality, coming-to-speech, and memory. Similarities and differences are discernable in *Obasan*'s treatment of these elements.

The first difference lies in Naomi's attitude toward earthy sensuality, which is unlike the strong emphasis on the physical aspect of "woman" in Marchessault's text. In Kogawa's work, the *absence* of sensuality is inextricably connected with the concept of the difficulty of communication. Although the narrator remembers a comfortable childhood where all her physical and emotional needs were intuitively met by her "mother's and Grandma's alert and accurate knowing" (*Obasan*, 56), she feels uncomfortable in her adult body. This physical frustration is linked to her inability to communicate satisfactorily with others. Aunt Emily describes Naomi as being without "even a semblance of grace or ease" (50). She has, as she herself notes, a self-denigrating attitude (7). In speaking her story, Naomi must strive to overcome her awkwardness with her own femininity. Although she sometimes desires physical contact with her loved ones, she realizes that the pattern of corporeal separateness has been set and that she cannot give in to her urge to hold Obasan because the physical contact would startle her aunt (27). Body and mind are separate entities for this narrator. Informed of Uncle's death, and unable to speak, she notes that her mind "has separated and hovers above [her], ordering [her] to action from a safe distance, like a general" (9). The narrator's sensation of disembodiment originates in her mother's untimely disappearance shortly after Naomi's sexual awakening. As Gary Willis argues, Naomi's childhood silences are due in part to her unarticulated feelings of guilt about her enjoyment of Old Man Gower's sexual advances ("Speaking the Silence," 247). As a child, she perceived her mother's prolonged absence to be a punishment for her betrayal of her mother's love. As an adult, she ignores the memory of her sexual abuse. Willis suggests that in order to heal, Naomi must break the general taboo imposed upon the subject of sexual molestation: she must speak out because silence cannot heal her hurt. The sexual is linked to the political in Naomi's nightmares, which are haunted by terrifying images of white soldiers' aggressive sexual mistreatment of Japanese women whose only, ultimately futile, weapon is their sensuality. More positive dreams contain images of better communication. In her first recorded dream, for instance, Naomi is capable of wordless communication (*Obasan*, 29). Naomi's mother, too, communicates with her daughter through non-rational dreams, and maternal love is expressed in the physical terms of the senses, especially that of touch. This gentleness is contrasted with Naomi's nightmares, where the body is once again assaulted by the Grand Inquisitor, who pries her mother's mouth and her own eyes open.

Sensuality is not completely absent from the adult Naomi's waking life. She is aware that another, more physically expressive life exists somewhere: "I want to break loose from the heavy identity, the evidence of rejection, the unexpressed passion ... I am tired of ... [being] unable to shout or sing or dance, unable to scream or swear, unable to laugh, unable to breathe out loud" (183). Eventually the narrator comes to agree with Aunt Emily's position that "Health starts somewhere" and that her "body of grief" may give way to another, more physical self: "Let there be flesh. The song of mourning is not a lifelong song" (246). This biblically inspired language, of course, recalls Godard's portrayal of the feminine poetic, where, somewhat ironically, "the Word is made flesh of woman's body and the emphasis is on the surfaces of the body, on the cry" ("Flying," 20). It is Aunt Emily who insists on the cathartic effects of the "cry" and who helps the narrator realize that her disembodiment cannot be repaired until she expresses, through story, her personal and political pasts: "You have to remember ... You are your history ... Don't deny the past. Remember everything. If you're bitter, be bitter. Cry it out! Scream! Denial is gangrene" (49–50). Naomi's difficulty in articulating her story is illustrated by her use of negative birth imagery. For her, the requirement to remember and to tell is comparable to the pain of an abortion. In contrast to the generally positive birth-imagery of Marchessault's text, here we find: "Aunt Emily, are you a surgeon cutting at my scalp with your folders and your filing cards and your insistence on knowing all? The memory drains down the sides of my face, but it isn't enough, is it? It's your hands in my abdomen, pulling the growth from the lining of my walls, but bring back the anaesthetist turn on the ether clamp down the gas mask bring on the chloroform when will this operation be over Aunt Em?" (194). The narrator, of course, is telling her story even while she is proclaiming her reluctance to do so. In this postmodern telling, however, no neat conclusions are offered. Is the effort worth the pain? The narrator leaves us with the question: "are you thinking that through ... speech-making and story-telling, we can extricate ourselves from our foolish ways? Is there evidence for optimism?" (199).

A somewhat more positive sensuality is evident in the passages of *Obasan* that are more closely associated with its mythical aspects. Erika Gottlieb has pointed out that despite the numerous biblical allusions in *Obasan*, the novel draws heavily on a nature-centred, pantheist worldview ("The Riddle," 50). A strong bond exists between

Naomi and the earth, in particular that part of it that Uncle has chosen as the place of commemoration to honour her mother's death: the hill above the coulee under the prairie sky. The buffalo, we have seen, is the mythical animal par excellence in New World Myth novels, and the presence of buffalo bones at the foot of the nearby Indian buffalo jump implies that this spot has special, sacred significance. Here, Naomi feels at one with the earth: "My fingers tunnel through a tangle of roots till the grass stands up from my knuckles, making it seem that my fingers are the roots. I am part of this small forest" (*Obasan*, 3). The usual blurring of various mythical systems in New World Myth novels is evident here in that the biblical story of Moses is also used to describe the site: "The hill surface, as if responding to a command from Uncle's outstretched hand, undulates suddenly in a breeze, with ripple after ripple of grass shadows, rhythmical as ocean waves. We wade through the dry surf, the flecks of grass hitting us like spray" (1). In the same passage Uncle is compared not only to Moses parting the Red Sea but also to Chief Sitting Bull. Cultural blurring is evident in the passage that describes Uncle squatting on the virgin land of the prairie as "perfect for a picture postcard – 'Indian Chief from Canadian Prairie' – souvenir of Alberta, made in Japan" (2). B.A. St-Andrews has suggested that when Naomi thinks of Chief Sitting Bull while looking at her uncle, she is recalling "another man displaced by war and racial hatred" and that Kogawa here "unites the red and yellow-skinned peoples of Canada" who have suffered parallel "injustices" ("Reclaiming a Canadian Heritage," 31). Other critics, however, read this passage in the context of its mythologizing power: "In Naomi's eyes, Uncle ... is an icon of rugged endurance unto his last days: 'Uncle could be Chief Sitting Bull ... He has the same prairie-baked skin, the deep brown furrows like dry river beds creasing his cheeks' (Cheung, *Articulate Silences*, 141, quoting *Obasan*, 2).

Frank Davey has read the passage describing the coulee as an attempt to "'naturalize' the Japanese Canadians by associating them with organic signs familiar to readers of Western literature" – signs such as the North American Native and the natural landscape, and he argues that Naomi "repeats a persistent pattern in her life of retreat from the social to the natural" (*Post-National Arguments*, 105–6). Comparing Kogawa's text to other western Canadian novels, such as George Bowering's *Caprice* and Jeanette Armstrong's *Slash*, Davey condemns *Obasan* for its "endorsement of universal humanism" (112) and intimates that "Naomi's yearnings for a return to 'natural' unity" (109) and the relief she finds in the coulee are illustrative of that humanism, in that this coulee is a "natural landscape that transcends time and politics, [a] Wordsworthian refuge that compensates for social cruelties" (105). In a much earlier publication, Coral Ann Howells sees the prairie in *Obasan* as a wilderness site that offers a new way of seeing the world: there, "[p]romises of freedom are linked to an awareness of transgression, for boundaries assume a new importance when they have to be crossed, and dislocation with its attendant doubleness of vision is always a feature of wilderness narratives" (*Private and Fictional Words*, 106–7). This underlines Howells' basic argument that "the wilderness has provided a textual space for women writers' exploration of female difference and a site of resistance to traditional structures of patriarchy" (106). While I shall argue that the coulee in this novel is an important site in Naomi's personal mythology, I think that the overt references to other mythological systems in the pages that describe this coulee necessarily attenuate its potential as a wilderness site. This same foregrounding of other mythological systems, it seems to me, does not so much underline its "endorsement of universal humanism" (Davey, *Post-National Arguments*, 112), as point to an exploration of multiplicity in myth.

When she learns of the circumstances surrounding her mother's death, Naomi's efforts to make peace with "the facts" consist of visualizing death not as the beginning of the Christian afterlife but as a necessary part of the cyclical pattern of nature: "Father, Mother, my relatives, my ancestors, we have come to the forest tonight, to the place where the colours all meet – red and yellow and blue. We have turned and returned to your arms as you turn to earth and form the forest floor" (*Obasan*, 246). Returning to the coulee in the predawn hour, the narrator glories in the coming to life of her senses, ending the passage – and her story – by a celebration of her physical apprehension of her surroundings: the wet grass, the white moon, and the smell of wild roses (247). A muted sensuality in this novel, then, is associated with the powers of expression. As the narrator gradually assumes the burden of telling her stories, she experiences a feeling of sensual reunion with the earth, with nature, and with her family. Perhaps, eventually, the narrator's "woundedness may be healed and ... [her] limbs may learn to dance" (243). In any case, the partial healing of the "brokenness" (240) is expressed through the images of rebirth of the senses (243).

Marchessault's exploration of the second element of her feminine poetic – the non-rational – is paralleled in surprisingly similar ways in Kogawa's *Obasan*. Naomi gradually moves from a learned respect for books and their contents to a disregard for their ability to inform her about life. This paradoxical attitude toward books and academic knowledge is present in all six novels examined here and is probably a distinctive characteristic of post-European historiographic novels. When Naomi is a child, study is actively encouraged, both by her father's example and by the reverence given to the porcelain statue of "the great teacher, Ninomiya Sontaku of Odawara, Japan" (52). Bedtime stories entertain her and give her a sense of her "shadowy ancestry" (54). In the confusion of relocation in Slocan, she uses fairy tales to make sense of her world, comparing her surly injured brother Stephen to Humpty Dumpty and herself to Baby Bear. Confusion, however, has set in: is she, she wonders, Baby Bear or Goldilocks? Will she ever get out of the woods? Although her childhood "days and weeks are peopled with creatures of flesh and storybook and comic strip" (160), stories and fairy tales do not keep her from "the terror" (62). Old Man Gower carries her away under the pretext of telling her a story. When her family leaves Slocan, Obasan symbolically packs their belongings away in "layers of comics ... [of] Little Orphan Annie with ... her Daddy Warbucks who always rescues her" (174). Naomi is already learning that no one will rescue her. Books are not real life. Waking up in the hospital after nearly drowning, she dreams that she is "reading the careful table of contents of a book that has no contents" (150). A slightly older Naomi cynically recalls her childhood trust in fairy tales (and in her father): "'Tad' is what I think I'll call my frog – short for ... my father's name. There was a fairy tale I read in Slocan about a frog who became a prince. Hah!" (206). The adolescent Naomi does poorly in school, the red xs on her papers are "like scratches and wounds" (202). As an adult, she seems to have little love of learning; she is bored with her teaching job (7). Although she doubtfully supposes that she does need to be educated about the war experience, Naomi has acquired by now a thorough contempt for the dubious "knowledge" available to her. She implies that knowledge of the past is not only inexact but that it is useless. What's done is done, and "[d]ead bones do not take on flesh" (198).

The adult narrator challenges several "truths" about the past. In New World Myth novels, as in historiographic metafiction in general, history is not a unified linear story; *no one* holds the key to what really happened. The most obvious challenge to the unity of history in *Obasan* comes from the textual presence of three different stories: the child's story, the official version of events, and the war-time experience of the Japanese Canadians as described in Aunt Emily's diary. The narrator of *Obasan* constantly proclaims her own lack of certainty. As a child, she finds the answers to her questions "are not answers at all" (135); as an adult, she sees no escape from the still unanswered questions. Aunt Emily believes in the truth of the facts, but Aunt Emily, Naomi notes, sometimes gets the facts wrong. Whereas Naomi remembers as fact that in 1945 "the gardens in Slocan were spectacular" (183), Aunt Emily assumes that "it must have been hell in the ghost towns" (184). Naomi grows to mistrust all communication on paper: Aunt Emily's naïve pleas for information, governmental correspondence, her own unanswered letters to her parents, the photograph of the grinning and happy beet farmers, and even the photographs of her own family. In spite of the implied unity of the family portrait, Naomi, remembering a few things Obasan has told her, wonders "if the Katos were ever really a happy family" (20). Any document, then, can present only a partial view of personal and public history. Groping and sifting through "the facts," Naomi can only reconstruct "Fragments of fragments ... Segments of stories" (53).

While Marchessault's narrator searches out strong emotional experiences as an alternative to the rational, Kogawa's narrator invests as much energy in a futile search for peace. This peace is in part a refusal to know the past, but Naomi prefers to see it as respect for the dead. "Let the inquisition rest tonight. In the week of my Uncle's departure, let there be peace" (*Obasan*, 229). In spite of her wish to respect "the delicate ecology of this numb day" (45) by stopping the questions, the narrator does come to a partial knowledge of the past through an aspect of the non-rational – in her personal case, dreams. Naomi is well aware of the mythical aspect of dream: in her first described nightmare, a woman "recites an ancient mythical contract made between herself and the man so long ago the language has been forgotten" (30). Knowledge in dreams is shifting, hazy: "It is not yet known ... We do not know ... The mist is, is not, is a mist" (28–9). Nevertheless, Naomi welcomes the haze, the mist; she does not resist drifting "back down into white windless dream" (28), because non-rational knowledge comes to her through her dreams. As a child in Slocan she is "touched" by her mother on the day the bomb drops on Nagasaki: "She is reaching out to me ... and her hair falls and falls and falls from her head" (167). Much later, the adult Naomi is given all the clues to the healing knowledge of the past through another dream, where her mother dances "a slow courtly telling, the heart declaring a long thread knotted to Obasan's twine, knotted to Aunt Emily's package" (228). The package, of course, contains the letter that Naomi cannot read; it in turn contains the secret of her mother's silence. Although Naomi wonders if her mother "speak[s] through dream," she decides yet once again to bury the question; it is "an unseemly thing" (228–9). The non-rational, then, does reveal a part of the past to Naomi, but she does not always attend to its speech (241). That there is not one sole method of attaining knowledge of the past is triply underlined in Kogawa's work. First, Naomi is unsure of what she herself remembers (50). Second, Naomi is not fully open to the idea of learning from her dreams and from other non-rational ways of knowing. Third, she cannot fully learn of the past from documents, which present, as the entire novel suggests, only fragmented versions of the way things were.

The third and fourth aspects of the poetic of the feminine examined here – speech and memory – are so intertwined in Kogawa's work that they may best be studied together. "Story" is the point of conjuncture for these two concepts. Naomi, in her efforts to put the "living word" (*Obasan*, proem) into her life, must remember *and* articulate certain events of the private (personal) and public (political) past(s). The feminist Clio Collective notes that speaking out "is the first step to self-assertion. Speaking out means refusing to hide one's anger, fear or hope, expressing how you feel as a woman, making women's issues a subject of discussion for everybody, and describing the world from a woman's perspective" (*Quebec Women*, 372). Speaking from my own experience, I would say that this holds true for Quebec women and for Western women in general. It would be more than insensitive, however, to impose this obligation to speak out on all women of all cultures, as King-Kok Cheung notes in *Articulate Silences*, a lengthy study of silence in *Obasan* and in works by two women Asian American writers: "Whereas in English, 'silence' is often the opposite of 'speech,' the most common Chinese and Japanese ideogram for 'silence' ... is synonymous with 'serenity' and antonymous with 'sound,' 'noise,' 'motion,' and 'commotion.' In the United States silence is generally looked upon as passive; in China and Japan it traditionally signals pensiveness, vigilance, or grace. These differences are all too often eclipsed by a Eurocentric perspective; even revisionist critics may succumb to it" (127).

Kogawa, argues Cheung, has "a mixed attitude toward both language and silence," and the detailed study of *Obasan* in *Articulate Silences* explores Kogawa's portrayal of "protective, stoic, and attentive silence" (128). Cheung notes that most reviewers of the book agree with Emily's cry for action and "view Obasan and Naomi as passive and ineffectual" (133). My reading of Naomi's complex appreciation of silence and of speech, however, concurs on several points with Cheung's study: Naomi does indeed respect Obasan's attitude toward silence, and she definitely foregrounds her own "doubts [regarding] the very effectiveness of language" (*Articulate*

Silence, 138) and speech. While many reviewers of the novel unques-
tioningly assume a binary opposition between silence and speech in
their commentaries, this exceptional novel itself "absolutely forbids
it," as Leonard Cohen once said of his poems when refusing the
Governor General's Award for Poetry. In this novel, silence and
speech, history and theory, the past and the present are all subjected
to recent postmodern and postcolonial questionings of the notion of
truth. These questionings are foregrounded especially in Naomi's
complex attitude to narration, speech, and memory. As we have
seen, Marchessault's narrator, after an initial hesitation to undertake
her mission, joyfully welcomes speech and actively sets out to
answer her own question "Comment dire?" with a positive affirmation: "je veux prendre la parole" (*Comme une enfant*, 105–6). Naomi,
however, hesitates to confront the "silence that will not speak"
(*Obasan*, proem). Not only is she reluctant to explore the concept of
memory, but, during much of the novel, she actively resists speaking
the silence – "freeing [the] word."

As a very young child, even before she can speak, storytelling
sessions give Naomi a sense of being supremely safe inside her Vancouver home. Stories shape her worldview: years later, when her
brother leaves Alberta to pursue a musical career in Toronto, she
thinks of the boy Momotaro of the bedtime story, going off to con-
quer the world. Outside the home, however, the world is dangerous.
Naomi's initial confidence in story is soon betrayed, as Old Man
Gower uses the pretext of storytelling to lure her into his home. The
narrator's rhetorical question about the Old Man Gower episode, "Is
this where the terror begins?" (*Obasan*, 62), is connected not only to
her problems with sensuality and sexuality but also to her problems
with speech and memory. As a young child, the narrator equates
silence with safety: "If I speak [to Old Man Gower] I will split open
and spill out" (63). As an adult, finally remembering and telling this
taboo episode, the narrator describes the secret of Old Man Gower
as "a fiddlehead question mark asking with its unformed voice for
answers still hidden from me" (61). Gower's sexual abuse of Naomi
is therefore linked to her mistrust of story. After her mother's departure, Naomi becomes a voice asking for answers. Her questions,
however, like her memories, are always smothered in "a whirlpool
of protective silence" (21) by Uncle and Obasan. Consequently, the
narrator eventually becomes a solemn, silent child: Naomi = "Nomi"
= no "me." She is "consumed" (26) by her unanswered questions and
yet forced to adapt to the silence that will not speak.

One exception is provided to the bleak unknowing of Naomi's
childhood. Rough Lock Bill reintroduces Naomi to speech and story.

His tale about the etymology of Slocan, "slow can go," is referred to years later by the adult narrator as she follows Obasan to the attic. Like the Momotaro story, Rough Lock Bill's tales shape her worldview. He rescues Naomi from drowning (146–9); he also succeeds in getting her to talk. Robin Potter has criticized Rough Lock Bill's storytelling, arguing that it is "fragmented and has no ending, no sense of wholeness" ("Moral – In Whose Sense?" 135). In Rough Lock Bill's method, Potter claims, there "is no regeneration, no unifying force" (136). I would argue, however, that the very lack of cohesion in Rough Lock Bill's tale encourages Naomi to eventually accept fragmentation, writing, and open-ended "story." Another reading of *Obasan* also links this Rough Lock Bill episode to Naomi's powerlessness, arguing that "without the discursive power of language there can be no communication, no knowing, no identity, no self as a linguistically constituted subject" (Goellnicht, "Father Land," 125). However, Rough Lock Bill actually offers Naomi an alternative means of communication, getting her to write her name in the sand and encouraging her with his story of the Indian band whose journey across the mountains resembles both the Japanese Canadians' odyssey from Vancouver to the British Columbia interior and Naomi's gradual move from silence to memory and to the telling of these memories: "If you go slow, you can go" (*Obasan*, 146). As Gary Willis has posited, Rough Lock Bill is Old Man Gower's opposite, offering spiritual communion to replace Naomi's inner, lonely silences ("Speaking the Silence," 246). In spite of this respite from the terror that began with Old Man Gower's advances, however, silence and mistrust of story dominate much of the narrator's childhood and adolescence.

Although the adult narrator is aware that silence in the children she teaches is an indication of trouble, she has willingly accepted silence as appropriate behaviour for herself up until the time of Uncle's death. Fujita has argued that Naomi has learnt the value of quietude from Obasan and the other women of Japanese origin: this nonverbal "attendance" or "sensibility" is "rooted in Naomi's *nikkei* inheritance ("Attend," 34). Naomi's reluctance to remember and to tell her personal past also comes from her postmodern awareness of the impermanence of story: "All our ordinary stories are changed in time, altered as much by the present as the present is shaped by the past" (*Obasan*, 25). This reluctance also comes from her adherence, at the beginning of the novel, to Obasan's philosophy that in silence lies strength. Naomi cites Obasan when she tries to justify her rejection of painful memories: "Didn't Obasan once say, 'It is better to forget'? … What is past recall is past pain" (45).

Nevertheless, the narrator resents the lack of knowledge of the past imposed upon her by Obasan's silence (*Obasan*, 45). Informed of her uncle's death, Naomi realizes that she has become a prisoner of silence (9). Later, trying to comfort Obasan, she again runs into the wall of silence that she has slowly constructed: "I open my mouth to ask, 'Did he suffer very much?' but loud talking feels obscene" (11). Uncle's death acts as a catalyst for change. Encouraged by Aunt Emily, Naomi relives the major events of her personal life. She protests against the telling, but she does get her story out. Once her personal memories have been integrated through her act of retelling, she is prepared to hear eventually the oral delivery of the message of her mother's love: "Sensei pauses as he reads. 'Naomi,' he says softly, 'Stephen, your mother is speaking. Listen carefully to her voice'" (233). Speech has replaced the mother's "voicelessness" (241) and the rift in the narrator's body is somewhat healed. Whereas the child in the narrator's dreams has "a wound on her knee" (243) – a further reference to Old Man Gower – the adult, having heard of her mother's love, feels reunited to her mother's body: "Your leg is a tree trunk and I am branch, vine, butterfly. I am joined to your limbs by right of birth, child of your flesh, leaf of your bough" (242–3). The narrator's acknowledgment of culpability later on in this passage addresses the two silences of the prologue. At different points of their joint and then separated lives, both Naomi and her mother have been unable or unwilling to speak: "Gentle Mother, we were lost together in our silences. Our wordlessness was our mutual destruction" (243). Rough Lock Bill joined action to story by saving Naomi from drowning. Naomi must also act, joining memory to the telling of her stories. By finally "speaking the silence," Naomi is able to come to terms with the "stone," the silent word. At the end of the novel, speaking to her relatives and ancestors, she puts to rest the uneasiness of the years of noncommunication: "My loved ones, rest in your world of stone. Around you flows the underground stream" (246).

In *Comme une enfant de la terre*, Marchessault's narrator promotes the viewpoint of women through the textual use of *bavardage*-like exchanges. In Kogawa's text, these exchanges are generally signalled by a quiet togetherness of women, in the baths and at work: a peaceful, safe, intimately female territory. Marchessault's narrator promotes that alternate matriarchal tradition we saw earlier through her exploration of the grandmother figure, female goddesses, and a list of female heroines. A similar matriarchal lineage is proposed by Kogawa's narrator. Men are generally well-meaning but weak, broken, ill, or ineffectual presences in Naomi's universe. An exception

186 New World Myth

to this description is Rough Lock Bill. Although he is definitely a marginalized figure in white, middle-class English-speaking Canadian society, he helps Naomi toward the release of speech. In this, he resembles the male "voices" in Marchessault's text. The poetic of the feminine described here does not totally exclude men – nor does it deny them a place in the feminine symbolism in these novels. The narrators' emphasis, however, is on the description of the world from a woman's perspective and on their respective communities of women. In both novels, women are strong, resilient creatures. While her brother follows the war in the newspaper, Naomi peoples her imaginary world with mainly female heroines: Little Orphan Annie, Heidi of the mountains, the characters of the Louisa May Alcott stories. When war intrudes into her private world, in the form of "an ominous sense of cold and absence" (*Obasan*, 69), she wonders who could best resist torture, and her thoughts turn mainly to the *women* she knows. In traditional myth criticism, the male hero is, of course, the one who is tested; he must prove his courage in order to lead his people.[5] Here, the traditional male hero is replaced in the child narrator's private worldview by a world of courageous, flesh-and-blood women and by exemplary fairy-tale and storybook heroines. It is *women* who shape Naomi's perspective on the world.

The need for female lineage is strong in Naomi, most probably because the feeling of generational continuity has been destroyed by her mother's unexplained absence. The break in the female lineage makes Naomi feel incomplete. When she opens her Aunt Emily's diary, the sight of her mother's name still gives her, after all those years, "a peculiar sensation of pain and tenderness" (*Obasan*, 46). Reflecting on the fact that both she and her Aunt Emily have remained unmarried, she wonders if perhaps there is "something in the blood. A crone-prone syndrome" (8). She is aware that her own self-image is negative: "Personality: Tense. Is that past or present tense? It's perpetual tense. I have the social graces of a common housefly" (7). The matriarchal lineage will most probably end with Naomi. Knowledge of this ending haunts her and, perhaps, also acts as a catalyst in the telling of her story (21). At the end of the text, references to ancestors, to family, and to the nature cycle discussed above imply that Naomi has made peace with the rupture in the family line. The respective titles of both texts examined here honour the feminine: "*une* enfant de la terre" and "Obasan," the name of Naomi's surrogate mother and the Japanese word for aunt.

The particularities of feminine speech in *Obasan* show connections to Marchessault's and native women's motivations for overcoming their hesitancy to tell their own life stories: their desire to pass on and validate the wisdom of their grandmothers is primary in all. The grandmother, or the old woman, is an important presence in these retellings, and the passing-on of knowledge confers a sacred dimension upon the narrative. In Kogawa's text, Obasan is portrayed analogously as the mythical, universal old woman with special knowledge: "Squatting here with the putty knife in her hands, she is every old woman in every hamlet in the world ... Everywhere the old woman stands as the true and rightful owner of the earth. She is the bearer of keys to unknown doorways and to a network of astonishing tunnels. She is the possessor of life's infinite personal details" (15–16). Obasan's body is compared to the curves of the earth, and its eternal dimension is underlined: "I rub the washcloth over her legs and feet, the thin purple veins a scribbled maze, a skin map, her thick toenails, ancient rock formations ... Naked as prehistory, we lie together" (78). This last sentence underlines the special bond between Naomi and Obasan, who represents "the old woman of many Japanese legends" (54). However, because of her dual Japanese and Canadian heritages, Naomi's role as the "passeus[e] de mémoire" (D. Smith, "Jovette Marchessault," 54) is somewhat conflictual. The two aunts of the novel represent two different approaches to speech and to memory: "One [aunt] lives in sound, the other in stone. Obasan's language remains deeply underground but Aunt Emily, BA, MA, is a word warrior. She's a crusader, a little old grey-haired Mighty Mouse, a Bachelor of Advanced Activists and General Practitioner of Just Causes" (*Obasan*, 32). The first aunt, Obasan, accepts silence as a protection against the difficulties of life: her "land is impenetrable ... In her steadfast silence, she remains inviolate" (224–5). Aunt Emily, as was noted above, proposes the opposite: "Don't deny the past ... Cry it out! Scream!" (50). The narrator gradually changes allegiances in the novel; from staunchly supporting Obasan's point of view, she evolves into a willing storyteller of the personal and political past(s).

The coming-to-speech experience in Marchessault's novel parallels a coming-to-political-maturity experience in *Obasan*. Naomi, the reticent child narrator who is "filled with a need to hide" (*Obasan*, 72) and to keep speech within her, is still present in the adult narrator who wishes to establish "a comforting feeling of distance from all the things she [Aunt Emily] was saying" (184). Although the narrator humours her Aunt Emily, her personal inclination is to withdraw from the historico-political fracas her aunt stirs up: "People who talk a lot about their victimization make me uncomfortable" (34); "Crimes of history, I thought to myself, can stay in history" (41). Naomi's

amnesiac attitude draws sharp criticism from Aunt Emily, who interprets it as indecisiveness, which neutralizes concern and prevents
necessary action (35). Naomi has indeed "withdrawn": she has never
learned to read or write Japanese, and none of her friends are Japanese Canadians. As Aunt Emily points out, she "shuffl[es] back and
forth" (50) and belongs nowhere. In this, she perhaps represents the
reality outside the novel: Joy Kogawa herself has underlined the
absence of Japanese Canadian towns or even communities in Canada
since the Second World War.

The role of "the voices" in Marchessault's text, as we saw above,
is to give historico-political memories back to the people, freeing the
retelling of these events from the clutches of the "official" version of
what really happened. Aunt Emily partially fulfils this same role in
Kogawa's text. The documents in her package constitute a strong
indictment of the official government, along with a definite criticism
of God and the ministers of his churches. Her journal fills in the
necessary background information to the child narrator's story, and
permits Naomi, along with the reader, to piece together more of the
missing fragments of story. Naomi describes her Aunt Emily, as "the
one with the vision ...[who] believed in the Nisei, seeing them as
networks and streamers of light dotting the country" (*Obasan*, 31). It
is Aunt Emily who remembers the family as "the original 'togetherness' people" (20) and who attempts to regain a similar sense of
community. Thus, she attends conferences, corresponds with the
government, writes a sixty-page treatise entitled "The Story of the
Nisei in Canada: A Struggle for Liberty," and ceaselessly insists upon
the Canadian citizenship of the Nisei. Aunt Emily hopes that by
exposing the facts, injustices will be acknowledged and community
somewhat restored. To this end, she insists that Naomi feel pride,
and not confusion, with regard to her dual heritage: "'Milk and
Momotaro?' I asked. 'Culture clash?' 'Not at all,' she said. 'Momotaro
is a Canadian story. We're Canadian, aren't we? Everything a Canadian does is Canadian.'" (57). This blurring of boundaries between
various ethnic or racial groups is typical of New World Myth novels.
Aunt Emily, like the narrator's friends in Marchessault's text, sees
cultural multiplicity as a desirable quality.

Recalling those "friends," Aunt Emily devotes herself to curing the
sickness of silence that most Japanese Canadians willingly accepted:
"What a bunch of sheep we were. Polite. Meek. All the way up the
slaughterhouse ramp" (*Obasan*, 38). For Aunt Emily, "Reconciliation
can't begin without mutual recognition of facts ... What's right is
right. What's wrong is wrong" (183). However, as was the case in
Marchessault's text, the narrator's transformation of facts into story

makes a more vivid impression than the mere facts themselves. Thus, Aunt Emily's package contains documents such as the following letter from the governmental custodian, but it is the narrator's making of story out of this written document that makes a stronger impact here, on both the personal and political levels:

Dear Madam,

This will acknowledge your letter of the 31st ultimo.
This will also advise you that as Mrs T. Kato is a Japanese National living in Japan at the outbreak of war, all property belonging to her in Canada vests in the Custodian.

Yours truly,
B. Good.

A toneless form letter. I wondered what Aunt Emily's letter to the Custodian had been.
   "Tell me what happened to my mother's tiny house – the house where my sister was born ... Tell me what has happened."
   The Custodian's reply ... must have been the same to anyone else who dared to write. "Be good, my undesirable, my illegitimate children, be obe-dient, be servile, above all don't send me any letters of enquiry about your homes, while I stand on guard (over your property) in the true north strong, though you are not free. B. Good." (37)

The narrator goes on to emphasize the irony contained in the ono-mastics of the Custodian's name, B. Good, but she makes no overt reference here to her own obvious parody of the Canadian national anthem. As we shall see, her parodies of the anthem are related to "story" in this highly political text.

There are two major differences between Aunt Emily's concerns and those of Marchessault's "voices." First, the voices wish to move the centre away from Europe to the here and now of the New World. Aunt Emily's scapegoat, however, is not a colonial European "sys-tem," but the Canadian government, on whom she squarely places the blame for the dispersal. Aunt Emily's "facts" are all Canadian, and her package – and thus this book – contains excerpts from Par-liamentary speeches by politicians such as Stanley Knowles and Mackenzie King. A blurring of the boundaries between fiction and historical documents is typical of New World Myth novels. The main political criticisms of many New World Myth novels are directed at the enemies without – especially those of the distant past. Neverthe-less, as postmodern literature contains within itself its own theoretical commentary (see Hutcheon, "Challenging the Conventions," 34–8), so does New World Myth discourse dare to attempt its own political autocritique. *Obasan* is a particularly good example of New World Myth's explorations of cultural-national identity/ies. In this novel, the thrust to develop a New World Myth worldview is driven in part by the characters' puzzlement regarding this identity: this bewilder-ment is especially evident in those parts of the novel that discuss the "enemy/not enemy" dichotomy. This point is examined below.

The second difference between Aunt Emily and the "voices" con-cerns the latter's desire to enter into a mythological order, to mythol-ogize the past as they retell it. Aunt Emily is clearly lacking in the mythical quality that emanates from Obasan. She is too concerned with practicalities to be effective in terms of the collective memory of the community. Her voice is loud and strident; Naomi notes that the papers in her package are "fragile with old angers" (*Obasan*, 41). Naomi doubts the effectiveness of Aunt Emily's words, although she recognizes them as "the evidence of much activity" (189). The task of mythologizing this recent and much misunderstood political past falls upon *Naomi*'s ability to retell the story.

One tenet of the feminist movement is that the personal is political. In *Obasan*, Naomi's personal past is not separable from the more public past of the entire West Coast Japanese Canadian community. For instance, the seemingly personal story about Old Man Gower is read by Hilda Thomas on another, highly political level: he repre-sents the Canadian government, which, using the excuse that it was protecting the Japanese Canadians, uprooted them all and interned them in the ghost towns of the British Columbia interior ("A Time to Remember," 103–5). Sexual abuse and the victim's resulting shame and paralysis can also be read as a political allegory, as Gottlieb has argued ("Riddle," 45–6). Marilyn Russell Rose insists upon this point; for her the concept of rape is "the novel's central metaphor" and the silence of the Japanese Canadian community is linked to that of victims of rape. Using irony as a rhetorical tool, she suggests that "when violation is somehow deserved, it is shameful to speak about it. Japanese-Canadians, says Kogawa, like Naomi at the start of the novel, blame themselves and therefore choose silence and invisibility, and thereby slow death" ("Politics into Art," 223). Although I agree that Naomi's silence as a child is intended to symbolize, in part, the silence of the group, I would also agree with King-Kok Cheung's gentle criticism of Rose's comments here: although Rose is a "sophis-ticated critic keenly aware of the danger of Orientalist discourse,

[she] nevertheless places inordinate blame on the victims in *Obasan*." Reticence must not be presented only as "the internalization of Western stereotypes" (*Articulate Silences*, 128). Nonetheless, Naomi's political evolution is somewhat similar to the path followed by Marchessault's narrator: the development of a personal sense of identity is closely linked to an awareness of a group, and a willingness to bear witness for that group. In Naomi's case, the group consists mainly of the Japanese Canadian community, although she also develops a rather limited identity with the country, Canada.

At this point, more than halfway through this study, it is highly appropriate to note an aspect of New World Myth novels that has been inviting commentary: the relationships between what I call "cultural conflation," identity, the individual, and the community. Although an in-depth study of these terms is unfortunately beyond the scope of this work on New World Myth, I believe it imperative to briefly foreground what is frequently intimated by the novels themselves: these relationships are constantly shifting and changing, and New World Myth novels from English-speaking Canada and Quebec, like Leonard Cohen's saint who "rides the drifts like an escaped ski" (*Beautiful Losers*, 101), constantly adapt to these ever-changing notions. Key passages in the four novels studied so far underline these foci: Marchessault's novel speaks of a "nouvelle race"; Godbout's discussions of bicephalism in *Les Têtes* proclaim that it is time to stop navel-gazing; Rudy Wiebe successfully conveys the cultural conflation among the various groups living on the prairies at the end of the nineteenth century, and, as we shall see, Joy Kogawa dwells at length on the enemy/non-enemy confusion of her narrator. What is happening here? One notes the "bardic" (Rose, "Politics into Art," 219) function of the narrators of these novels, who are mythologizing, through their metafictional stories, their creation of a new way of dealing with cultural confusion. One also observes the blatant foregrounding of the narrator's desire for an end to clearly defined "group-isms" – be it through Marchessault's mythological reflections on "les enfants d'Amérique" or Kogawa's subtly portrayed identity issues in *Obasan*.

The importance of community to the postmodern world has been underlined by Benedict Anderson (*Imagined Communities*) and Zygmunt Bauman, who argues that it "is precisely because of its vulnerability that community provides the focus of postmodern concerns" (*Intimations of Postmodernity*, xix). Unhappily, Bauman's discussion of imagined communities is framed strongly in terms of power struggles between dissimilar groups. His vocabulary of confrontation in

the following sentences is typical of many theorists' appreciation of
the postmodern condition: "For whatever reason, we tend to believe
that men and women can only be goaded or cajoled, by superior
force or superior rhetoric, into peaceful coexistence ... Since no imagined community is alone in its struggle for public attention, a fierce
competition results that forces upward the stakes of the game" (xvii,
xx).

Happily, community can be understood in other ways. Heather
Zwicker is one of the very few critics of *Obasan* to grasp the shifting
quality of the relationships enumerated above. She too has difficulty
with the "new world trope," but finds it necessary to express the
differences she observes in contemporary women's fiction in Canada: "Making oneself at home in the new world necessitates a radical
rethinking of national identity, because the elements that convention-
ally constitute national identity – history, natality, family, and place
– no longer fall neatly into the territorial and historical entity that we
know as Canada" ("Canadian Women," 143). Zwicker notes the
importance of the notion of "transience" in any conceptualization of
new-world identity, even while acknowledging that the "idea of a
subject in continual transition works against an easy identity of self
with place in both the past and the future" (144). In the fictions she
studies, Zwicker celebrates the "struggle for community" with an
attitude that differs radically from that promoted by Bauman. Quoting from work by Biddy Martin and Chandra Mohanty, Zwicker
argues, "It is not by avoiding the struggles that inhere in a place, but
rather by taking part in them, that a meaningful home is created: the
safest community is 'that which is struggled for, chosen, and hence
unstable by definition; it is not based on "sameness," and there is no
perfect fit'" (144). Martin and Mohanty stress the importance of
"agency as opposed to passivity," underlining that "identity and
community are ... a constant recontextualizing of the relationship
between personal/group history and political priorities" ("Feminist
Politics," 208–10). Zwicker sums up her argument by underlining
that in contemporary fictions such as *Obasan*, the emphasis is on
mediation, not assimilation. Or as she puts it: "Metis and Creole, not
Indian or African, symbolize survival in the 'new world'" (151).

Naomi's multifaceted narrative exemplifies this kind of "struggle"
for community, with her gradual development of metaphors
and images illustrating her coming-to-story/coming-to-history/
coming-to-knowledge-of-Mother/coming-to-cultural-national identity.
For Zwicker, Naomi's metaphors of Canada (*Obasan*, 226) imply "an
ideal vision of Canada as a garden of many species, all of which

deserve to be tended," even though Naomi is conscious of the difficulties of the pluralist position of history/ies ("Canadian Women," 148). The novel, concludes Zwicker, "foregrounds as history the process of constructing history, the process of coming to hear its silences as well as its words" (150). This appreciation of the complexities of cultural-national identity in *Obasan* is rare among critics. New World myth novels themselves, however, clearly adopt an exploratory approach to what I have been calling alternately "cultural confusion" or "cross-cultural conflation."

As is the case with Marchessault's narrator, Naomi's political memories are fragmented at the beginning of the novel. Like a teacher using the occasional flash card, she briefly introduces bits and pieces of the political aspect of her story: Grandma Nakane in the Vancouver Hastings Park Prison, the RCMP officer driving off in Uncle and Mark's beautiful boat. On the whole, however, the narrator seems resigned to the dim memories she has of this personal and political past. Watching Obasan find Uncle's ID card in the attic, she reflects upon the end of story: "Everything, I suppose, turns to dust eventually. A man's memories end up in some attic ... His name becomes a fleeting statistic and his face is lost in fading photographs, the clothing quaint, the anecdotes gone" (*Obasan*, 25). Naomi pretends an interest in Aunt Emily's historical documents out of politeness but denies (to herself) any interest in the past. When urged by Aunt Emily to feel a sense of responsibility for the group, Naomi, siding with Obasan and Uncle, refuses to get involved: "If Aunt Emily with her billions of letters and articles and speeches, her tears and her rage, her friends and her committees – if all that couldn't bring contentment, what was the point?" (42). This question haunts the entire narrative. A postmodern lack of certainty is deeply entrenched in the narrator's worldview: although Aunt Emily lives "the truth" as she sees it, the narrator knows that her own "truth" is "more murky, shadowy and grey" (32). In the midst of her personal recollections, the narrator underlines her private doubts about her power to effect change through story: "'Life is so short,' I said sighing, 'the past so long. Shouldn't we turn the page and move on?'" (42). Elsewhere, she notes that racial tensions and fears remain with us still (78). After this resistance to story and just after this declaration of uncertainty, the narrator begins to read her aunt's journal.

It is at this point in the novel that a major shift occurs. Immediately following the chapter containing the journal entries, the narrator's "I" becomes the group's "we." Naomi determines to tell the group's story with her voice and her memories. The passage where this decision occurs is full of allusions to biblical and pagan mythology and to the narrator's own personal mythology, where silence is stone:

We are leaving the BC coast ... We are going down to the middle of the earth ... We are hammers and chisels in the hands of would-be sculptors, battering the spirit of the sleeping mountain. We are the chips and sand, the fragments of fragments that fly like arrows from the heart of the rock. We are the silences that speak from stone. We are the despised rendered voiceless ... We are those pioneers ... the fishermen who are flung from the sea to flounder in the dust of the prairies. (111–12)

Like Marchessault's narrator, Naomi accepts her task: to mythologize the story of a group. The above passage concludes: "We are the Issei and the Nisei and the Sansei, the Japanese Canadians. We disappear into the future undemanding as dew" (*Obasan*, 112). The following chapter of the novel describes a return visit to the British Columbia interior made by the narrator and her family in 1962. Again, the "we" is unmistakably collective: "We looked for the evidence of our having been in Bayfarm, in Lemon Creek, in Popoff ... Where on the map or on the road was there any sign? Not a mark was left" (117). Someone, the narrator implies, deliberately erased all evidence of the Japanese Canadians' stay. Unlike the prospectors who were there before them, the Japanese Canadians' presence has not been permitted to mix with the elements, to become a part of the local mythology: "The first ghosts were still there, the miners, people of the woods, their white bones deep beneath the pine-needle floor, their flesh turned to earth, turned to air ... But what of the second wave?" (117). In order to tell the story of the group, Naomi must retell their story, contradicting the "outright lies" (85) in the newspapers of the time: thus, her denial of the newspaper caption "Grinning and Happy," which accompanies Aunt Emily's index card entitled "Facts about evacuees in Alberta" (193). She begins to protest vehemently, and in her own name, against the political injustices visited upon her people. Naomi gradually takes over her aunt's expository function: she voluntarily integrates newspaper clippings into her own story, including titles, dates, and journalists' names. In this novel, then, there is a gradual evolution in the narrator's acceptance to retell the story of the group. Rose argues convincingly that because the narrator's "own experience is representative of a communal, racially shared past, Naomi's words about it, when she is freed into speech, will be *bardic* in the sense of giving voice to the experience of an entire people as narrator of her 'fiction'" ("Politics into Art," 219). Individuals from this "entire people" have been compared within the text to the Israelites: Stephen, riding his bike through the heat of Granton, Alberta, is "like one of the Israelite children moving unharmed through the fiery furnace" (*Obasan*, 205). This exile to Granton, argues Rose, is "a racially based diaspora like that of the Old Testament Jews" ("Politics into Art," 221).

Rose's strong argument for reading what was done to the Japanese Canadian community as a "kind of sociopathic rape" ("Politics into Art," 222) sets up a binary us/them opposition (white Canadians versus Japanese Canadians) that is echoed by many critics' readings of the novel. Thus, B.A. St-Andrews proposes that "Kogawa intertwines historical fact and often rhapsodic fiction to show how one little girl, Naomi Nakane, becomes aware of being an outsider, an enemy, an outcast in her homeland" ("Reclaiming," 226). Cheng Lok Chua's discussion of the novel ("Witnessing the Japanese Canadian Experience") also presents Naomi as a heroic representative of a *particular* group, the Japanese Canadians, who are set up in a binary opposition to those whom Chua, using an American construct, calls the "Caucasian Canadians" of the homeland. I would argue, however, that the us/them framework is not as unequivocal as that proposed by critics such as St-Andrews and Chua.

This point is best illustrated by the enemy/not-the-enemy discussion in the novel. Like the image of the yellow chicks or the image of violence in dreams, the image of "the enemy/not-the-enemy" is foregrounded as problematic throughout the novel. For the *Nisei* generation (Aunt Emily and Naomi's father), the situation is clear: "Are we [Japs]?" Naomi asks her father. "'No, Father says. 'We're Canadian'" (*Obasan*, 70). Aunt Emily's diary contains several condemnations of those who treated Japanese Canadians as the enemy. It also adopts an "inside/outside discourse" that problematizes the question. Thus, in an imaginary dialogue with her sister Emily writes: "But over here, they say, 'Once a Jap always a Jap,' and that means us. We're the enemy. And what about you over there? Have they arrested you because you're a Canadian?" Elsewhere in the diary, Emily refers to a suspect use of vocabulary: "There is something called a Civilian Labour Corps and Mark and Dan were going to join ... but now will not go near it as it smells of a demonic roundabout way of getting rid of us. There is a very suspicious clause "within and *without*" Canada, that has all the fellows leery" (*Obasan*, 85). For Emily, the situation is clear. "What this country did to us, it did to itself," she states (33). Despite all the struggles Emily goes through during the war, she answers a rhetorical question about being Canadian years later with a strong affirmative: "*Is* this my own, my native land? The answer cannot be changed. Yes. It is. For better or worse, *I am Canadian.*" (40).

For the *Sansei* generation (Naomi and Stephen), however, the question of the enemy/not the enemy and Canadian/not Canadian is not as easily solved. As children, they see being "both the enemy and not the enemy" as a riddle (*Obasan*, 70). As an adult, Naomi is still confused by the question: "It was hard to think of Uncle as anyone's enemy. On Sunday when Uncle went to church, the clergyman turned him away from the communion rail. But there was no enemy there" (38). Elsewhere, the adult Naomi dryly notes: "Given a yard full of enemies, the most familiar enemy is a friend" (60). The question of the enemy/not-the-enemy is linked in the text to the related questions of community and of being Canadian. Naomi recognizes that Emily is strong in her sense of community, of belonging: "When she [Emily] is called like Habakkuk to the witness stand, her testimony is to the light that shines in the lives of the Nisei, in their desperation to prove themselves Canadian, in their tough and gentle spirit. The truth for me is more murky, shadowy and grey" (*Obasan* 32).

What *is* Naomi's position regarding Canada? How does she resolve the enemy/not-the-enemy confusion? The novel offers no easy interpretation of the question. As we have seen, critics' discussions of difficult issues presented in this novel, such as, for instance, speech and silence, are far-reaching and sometimes contradictory. Although many studies of Kogawa's novel discuss at length Naomi's role as spokesperson for the Japanese Canadian community, far fewer studies discuss the similar complexities of her "Canadianness." Mason Harris' argument is typical: he argues that Naomi feels "no real sense of membership in Canadian society" ("Broken Generations," 43). I believe, however, that the national identity question in this novel is in some ways as complex as the speech-and-silence issue, in part because of the strong presence of irony as a rhetorical tool in the text. Chua notes the importance of irony to readings of the text's subversion of Christian motifs, but it is imperative equally to grasp the use of irony in Naomi's initial appreciations of belonging, community, and "Canada."

As a child, Naomi must first deal with the culture clash of being both Japanese and Canadian. The lunches she and her brother take to school are symbolic of the everyday struggle taking place between the two heritages: Stephen's lunch box contains peanut-butter sandwiches while Naomi carries two moist and sticky rice balls. The Canadian symbols – coronation mugs and so on – that the child narrator refers to are in fact British artifacts, ironically reflecting the general patriotism toward Britain in English-speaking Canada during the Second World War – a patriotism shared by the Japanese Canadian characters. Thus, those King George or Queen Elizabeth coronation mugs are taken on every move, and Naomi, in Slocan, makes a scrapbook of the Royal Family. Upon their forced evacuation from Slocan, the irony of the minister's prayer, "save and defend ... Thy servant George, our King: that under him we may be godly and quietly governed" (*Obasan*, 176), seems to be lost on the child narrator, but in her hospital dream, the doctor is "angry and British" (158). An older, more cynical Naomi notes the irony of the unpacked coronation mugs on the beet farm (197). As an adult, Naomi can still feel confusion about the British/Canadian split. The Old World system of her childhood resurfaces in her dream of the British martinet. In her waking life, her images are taken from both cultures. Thus, meeting her Aunt Emily at the Lethbridge airport, she describes her as "a woman with a Winston Churchill stoop" (33) who, with "her mind and her hair leaping wildly in the gusts ... [is] Stephen Leacock's horseman riding off in all directions at once" (33).

As the story evolves, Naomi, following her aunt's lead, takes more direct aim at the "system" of the here and now of the New World: the Canadian government and, less directly, the Canadian people. The political allegory contained in the Old Man Gower story is echoed in a similar image that runs through all of *Obasan*: the chicken and hen episodes. As we saw in chapter 3, the child Naomi equates Japanese Canadians with these powerless little yellow chicks whose necks all crook at the same angle, watching the dangers that come from above. The episode of the white mother hen and the little yellow chicks is usually read as a metaphor for the treatment meted out to the Japanese Canadians by "white" Canadian society and government. Naomi herself, while clearly advancing this comparison, problematizes any exclusively binary us/them argument. The description of the initial encounter between the hen and the chicks is indeed brutal: the hen's "sharp beak jabs down on the chick" (59). Naomi indirectly compares the action of the hen to the displaced anxieties of an over-protective mother (country): "Mrs. Sigumoto reminds me of the white hen, always fussing over her boys, telling them to put sweaters on even when the weather is warm (59–60). These criticisms of the white hen, however, are countered in this puzzling passage: "With swift deft fingers, Mother removes the live chicks first, placing them in her apron. All the while that she acts, there is calm efficiency in her face and she does not speak. Her eyes are steady and matter of fact – the eyes of Japanese motherhood.

They do not invade and betray. They are eyes that protect, shielding what is hidden most deeply in the heart of the child. She makes safe the small stirrings underfoot and in the shadows ... There is no blame or pity. *I am not responsible. The hen is not responsible*" (60; my emphasis). If, as has been repeatedly argued, the hen represents "white Canada," this last sentence refutes the argument that Naomi's narrative represents an outright and unmitigated condemnation of Canada; rather, the narrative, through its multifaceted presentation of this and other images, sets out to challenge, question, and explore the identity issue.

As a child, Naomi quickly learns to deny her Japanese heritage in the interests of survival: "To be yellow in ... [her brother's 'made in Canada'] Yellow Peril game is to be weak and small. Yellow is to be chicken. I am not yellow" (*Obasan*, 152). Aunt Emily, however, underlines the impossibility of denying the collectivity: "None of us, she said, escaped the naming. We were defined and identified by the way we were seen. A newspaper in B.C. headlined, 'They are a stench in the nostrils of the people of Canada'" (118). For Aunt Emily, anger comes easily: like "one of the world's white blood cells," she reacts strongly and definitely to "any injustice." (34) For Naomi, anger is much harder. At first, that anger comes out as being ill at ease, both in her body and in feeling that she is faced with "crimes of history" (41). It is wordless and is seen as a nameless longing: "Here, in this familiar density, beneath this cloak, within this carapace, is the longing within the darkness" (111). As an adult, nearing the end of her story and provoked by a comment by Mr Barker, Naomi can cry out in her own name against this collective suffering: "Ah, here we go again. 'Our Indians.' 'Our Japanese.' 'A terrible business.' It's like being offered a pair of crutches while I'm striding down the street" (225). Usually, though, Naomi reverts to irony to express her anger against injustice.

Ironic references to strictly Canadian emblems, such as the Mounties, the flag, and the national anthem are fairly frequent in this text. M. Jeanne Yardley, in her discussion of literary emblems in Canadian literature, such as Falardeau's horizontal and vertical axes (*Notre Société et son roman*, 58) or Stratford's double spiral (*All the Polarities*, 6–8), suggests that "the only good emblem is a dead emblem" (Yardley, "The Maple Leaf, 255). Decrying the nationalistic quest of critics such as Margaret Atwood, Laurie Ricou, and Northrop Frye, Yardley writes, "Understanding the infiltration of politics into literary study, critics must subvert this nationalistic project and find an approach that is both more self-conscious and less predetermined" (259–60).

Interestingly, in Kogawa's highly political *Obasan*, the *narrator's* approach to emblem is similar to that prescribed here by Yardley for the *critic* of Canadian literature. For instance, this narrative overtly flaunts its self-conscious political and literary use and abuse of the Canadian anthem. As a child, Naomi refrains from singing the national anthem in the Slocan school, which she hates to attend. Excerpts from the anthem, however, are ironically incorporated into her story; others sing as she and her companions, arriving late, "scuttle into place like insects under the floorboards" (*Obasan*, 156). As an adult, in the following parodic reworking of the anthem, Naomi criticizes her country's inhospitality and its refusal of her story: "Where do any of us come from in this cold country? Oh Canada, whether it is admitted or not, we come from you we come from you ... We come from the country that plucks its people out like weeds and flings them into the roadside ... We grow where we are not seen, we flourish where we are not heard ... We come from our untold tales that wait for their telling" (226). This lengthy, accusatory, and highly political passage closes with a curious remark. Canada, says the narrator, is "filled with the wise, the fearful, the compassionate, the corrupt." This is one of the last overt references in the text (with the exception of the memorandum) to "Canadian-ness"; the remaining pages discuss the resolution of Naomi's personal quest, her mother's story. The tolerance shown in this quotation creates the same effect as the appendix-like inclusion of the pro–Japanese Canadian memorandum at the end of the text: the author, like the narrator, does not appear to be totally one-sided in her political condemnations.

Solving the puzzle of the narrator's mother's story is linked to the question of national identity through the image of the Canadian maple tree that grows on mother's grave, "utter[ing] its scarlet voice in the air," its leaves "scratching an empty sky" (*Obasan*, 241). It is as though Naomi asks, through image, how God and Canada could cause this to be – with the "this" an umbrella covering the injustices of the entire period. Although I would not go as far as Gottlieb, who argues that Naomi has made her peace with Canada ("Riddle," 43), I would suggest that a limited resolution to her personal and political turmoil is found in her development of her own mythology – a mythology that finds its expression in an exploration, through nature and through story, of her feminine being. The mistreatment and dispersal of the Japanese Canadians was not officially acknowledged until September 1988, when the Canadian government formally apologized and offered a financial settlement to the survivors of the wartime treatment. During the war, writes Aunt Emily, the "pure hell" that resulted from the bureaucrats' decisions was "kept 'hush

hush' from the public" (*Obasan*, 92). All signs of the Japanese Canadians' life in the ghost towns were carefully removed. It was not
until the 1990s that the Nikkei Internment Memorial Centre was
opened on the site of an internment camp in New Denver, in the
Slocan Valley of British Columbia's interior, so that the experience of
the thousands of Japanese Canadians evacuated to that area could
become part of the place – could leave, as Naomi put it, "a sign …
a mark" (*Obasan*, 117). Indeed, the publication of *Obasan* is generally
hailed as having contributed to the government's addressing of the
concerns of the redress movement. Aunt Emily's summing-up of the
dispersal – "It's as if we never existed" (88) – is countered in the text
itself by Naomi's dual accomplishment.

First, Naomi finds a physical place to leave her memories of the
dead – "those who refuse to bury themselves" (*Obasan*, 26). This
sacred place is her uncle's spot by the coulee. The mythical aspects
of this site have been noted previously: Naomi's feeling of oneness
with that particular section of earth and the fact that this virgin prairie is the site of an annual pilgrimage. It is the spot where the remains
of her loved ones, like those of the miners of Slocan, can finally
become one with the elements. References to biblical and Buddhist
mythologies in the passages that describe this section of prairie
underline its transformation into a sacred place, while equally striking references to its New World aspects – such as the nearby presence
of buffalo and Amerindian bones – emphasize that the sacredness of
the place is the result of an alternative mythologization.

Naomi's second accomplishment lies in her striving to adjust to
both personal and political turmoil through growth in terms of the
four elements of the feminine poetic I have been discussing: an
acceptance of sensuality, an exploration of non-rational knowledge
of the past, and a willingness to remember and to get the personal
and political stories out. In the last chapter of *Obasan*, Naomi sadly
asks, "After the rotting of the flesh, what is the song that is left?"
(245). Although the telling of "story" cannot restore Naomi's innocence or the Japanese Canadian community, the power of telling is
sufficient to give Naomi some control over the hold the past has had
on her: "Let there be flesh. The song of mourning is not a lifetime
song" (246). It is in full recognition that "All our ordinary stories are
changed in time, altered as much by the present as the present is
shaped by the past" (25), that Naomi Nakane speaks out. In spite of
her doubts about the utility of story, her "tales that [waited] for their
telling" (226) affirm the power of narrative to alter her – and perhaps
our – worldview.

Louise Dupré writes that from the early 1970s onward "Modernity has had to reckon with the fact that women writers are committed to seeking an identity ... Never again to be alone writing, reading, thinking, remembering the past. To inscribe oneself as a woman in History. But also in the everyday reality ... [to] write what has till now not been lofty enough to be written" ("From Experimentation to Experience," 356–7). Through their exploration of the four major elements of their feminine poetic the narrators of Jovette Marchessault's *Comme une enfant de la terre* and Joy Kogawa's *Obasan* put forth their identities as women in history. Discussing women's writing in Quebec, Patricia Smart makes a statement that can be equally applied to historiographic texts by women from English-speaking Canada: their writing "is a writing of resistance, insisting on a simple but radical truth: that it is possible, it has to be possible, to live and to write in a relationship to reality other than that of domination" ("My Father's House," 29–30). The narrators of both novels discussed here neither negate injustices of the past nor create political utopia in the present. However, their courage to articulate story permits them to discover ways of being women in history. Both narrators challenge what Linda Hutcheon has called "such previously unassailable and solidly centred entities as continuous History and the rational Cartesian cogito." ("Shape Shifters," 219). These narrators' questionings of the traditional or official version(s) of our historico-political past(s) and their explorations of alternative feminine mythologies allow both for New World Myth's celebration of indeterminacy and for women's tellings and retellings of their stories.

5 Magic Realism and Postcolonial Challenges to History: George Bowering's *Burning Water* and François Barcelo's *La Tribu*

The current popularity of fictionalized history, suggests Eva-Marie Kröller, is the result of a thrust of former colonies to reclaim their past ("Postmodernism," 56). Much historiographic metafiction has indeed been produced by New World authors, from Gabriel García Márquez to Alejo Carpentier and from Timothy Findley to Victor-Lévy Beaulieu. George Bowering's *Burning Water* (1980) and François Barcelo's *La Tribu* (1981) overtly foreground the uncertainty of knowledge of the past in this postmodern age. These novels nonetheless retell *particular* (hi)stories. Why? One can problematize history in fictional works without making blatant use of such well-known historical personages as George Vancouver (Bowering) – or without reviewing, yet once again, the failures and successes of military strategies during the Battle of the Plains of Abraham (Barcelo). The didactic urge in English Canadian and Québécois fiction to retell major historical events in a new light suggests the presence of a postcolonial thrust in several postmodernist texts. Kröller argues that this postmodern/postcolonial link is obvious in Québécois postmodernists' interest in Latin American novels such as García Márquez' *One Hundred Years of Solitude* and Julio Cortázar's *Rayuela*. In francophone postcolonial countries, she states, "postmodernism becomes intimately linked with postcolonialism; its assaults on the concepts of progressive history and geometrically ordered space are attacks on the perceptual patterns of the European conqueror" ("The Politics of Influence," 120). While theories of postcolonialism are infrequently raised in discussions of contemporary Quebec,[1] arguments over the postmodern/postcolonial rapport have raged in the English-speaking world of theory and criticism in the 1980s and 1990s. These arguments are far-reaching, sometimes contradictory, and as yet unresolved.[2]

Some non-Occidental researchers see postcolonial studies as their exclusive domain and hope that postcolonial theories will serve to invert what James Clifford has called the "the West [and] the rest" paradigm (*Predicament of Culture*, 273). Arif Dirlik notes that "Unlike other 'post' marked words, postcolonial claims as its special provenance the terrain that in an earlier day used to go by the name of Third World" ("The Postcolonial Aura," 329). Dirlik, however, goes on to argue that postcolonialism is a child of postmodernism, that it is of First World origin, and that it permits what is frequently called "the new global capitalism" to thrive on "Third World terrain" (348). There is, then, a high degree of confusion at the present time regarding who can be postcolonial, what postcolonial studies are, how they can be carried out, and what elements constitute the defining differences between postmodernism and postcolonialism.

Even the chronology of the two "isms" can be problematic. For instance, in his comparative study of "Self-projection" in George Bowering's *Burning Water* and *All Visitors Ashore* by the New Zealander C.K. Stead, Reginald Perry implies that postcolonial cultures are to be congratulated for finally *becoming* postmodern: "when a post-colonial literary culture begins to see the publication of fictions which conscientiously (and consciously) go about dismantling the central notion of modernist fiction, that is, when the *non-existence* of the writing self in the text is replaced by the *performing self*, then post-modernism has really arrived, fictionally, in that culture" ("A Deckchair of Words," 312). Elsewhere, he underlines this surprising suggestion that postcolonialism predates postmodernism: in Bowering and Stead, "we have here two writers (representative of their literary cultures, I would suggest) who can assume that their postcolonial national literary cultures have become post-modern" (314).

On the other hand, and at the other end of the spectrum, Helen Tiffin argues against the cultural imperialism of postmodernism: "the label of 'post-modern' is increasingly being applied hegemonically, to cultures and texts outside Europe, assimilating post-colonial works whose political orientations and experimental formations have been deliberately designed to counteract such European appropriation ("Post-Colonialism," 170); postcolonial cultures, she suggests, should actively resist such appropriation. Tiffin, Bill Ashcroft, and Gareth Griffiths devote an entire section of their *Post-colonial Studies Reader* to the frequently occurring conflation of these two discourses, noting that "the intensification of theoretical interest in the post–colonial has coincided with the rise of postmodernism in Western society and this has led to both confusion and overlap between the two" ("Postmodernism and Post-colonialism," 117). Within this section are reprinted edited articles by Hutcheon ("Circling") and Brydon ("The White Inuit Speaks"); both critics note, albeit from different perspectives, the complexities of the overlap and of the differences between postmodernism and postcolonialism within "Canada." In the longer, unedited versions of these articles, both critics also raise, again from different angles, the representation of the Amerindian in contemporary fictions, noting that it is fraught with difficulties. Thus, Brydon: "When directed against the Western canon, postmodernist techniques of intertextuality, parody, and literary borrowing may appear radical and even potentially revolutionary. When directed against native myths and stories, these same techniques would seem to repeat the imperialist history of plunder and theft" (140). In this chapter and the following one, I investigate manifestations of New World Myth in Bowering's *Burning Water* and Barcelo's *La Tribu*. Part of my discussion necessarily dwells on the uses of that postmodernist technique of parody in these texts, especially with regard to the figure of the Amerindian.

While these texts are marked by the deconstructionist techniques of postmodern fiction, they are also engaged in the postcolonial questioning of "givens" such as European-inspired history. My discussion therefore also investigates the postcolonial thrust behind these texts' investigations of history. Historical fictions, because they purport to retell the past, can be apt illustrations of a certain tension between fiction, "myth," and "reality." This tension is particularly evident in postmodern historiographic texts, which are already engaged in a process of deconstruction and alteration. The fictional retellings of historico-political events in François Barcelo's *La Tribu* and George Bowering's *Burning Water* thematize postcolonial worldviews: their narrators examine alternative modes of knowing these events.

Chapter 6 analyses *Burning Water*'s metafictional challenge to realistic narrative, which constitutes a large part of its reaction against Old World literary modes and of its refusal to understand history as a past interpreted once and for all. The focus of this chapter is on the particular use the narrator makes of some aspects indicative of a postcolonial worldview: a recreation of history that seeks to destabilize the fixity of the traditional story; a deliberate tension between magic realism, history, and "myth"; a didactic urge to retell events of the past that nonetheless acknowledges the impossibility of fully knowing the past from the standpoint of the present; the somewhat problematic yet extensive use in the text of parody and humour and its blurring of the political concerns of the distant and near historical past(s).

Stephen Slemon notes that the concept of magic realism "is a troubled one for literary theory" ("Magic Realism," 9).[3] As Cecilia Ponte has remarked, the terminological debate surrounding magic realism, marvellous realism, the marvellous real, and so forth, frequently means that "le problème s'est déplacé du niveau analytique au niveau terminologique" ("Carrefour," 105). Slemon puts forth a similar argument: "In none of its applications to literature has the concept of magic realism ever successfully differentiated between itself and neighbouring genres such as fabulation, metafiction, the baroque, the fantastic, the uncanny, or the marvellous" ("Magic Realism," 9). In contemporary critical practice the term "marvellous realism" is most frequently used to designate literary texts from the Caribbean.[4] The appellation "magic realism" tends to dominate in discussions of texts from Latin America and has appeared more recently in discussions of non-Caribbean post-European works by writers from English-speaking Canada and India.[5]

This geographically determined terminology is far from definitive in contemporary critical practice. I would argue, however, that another important difference is apparent between works of magic realism and those of marvellous realism. J. Michael Dash argues that a fundamental dialogue with history is to be found in works of marvellous realism. However, "this dialogue with the past essentially consisted of a continuous and desperate protest against the ironies of history. They [the Third World writers] adhered to the view of history as fateful coincidence and tragic accident, and saw their function as artists in terms of their attitude to the past, that is, either in terms of a committed protest against the past which would give birth to a new humanism, or were so overwhelmed by the "fact" of privation or dispossession that they withdrew to a position of cynicism with regard to their peoples (V.S. Naipaul the Trinidadian novelist is often quoted as typical of this attitude)" (Dash, "Marvellous Realism," 65). Works of marvellous realism appear to embody a worldview that is concerned with *de*colonization, where the primary attitude toward the dominant historical discourse remains one of mistrust and wariness. Whether one protests against events of the past or adopts a cynical attitude because of feelings of dispossession, one is still in reaction to history. Magic realist works, however, bear witness to their liberation from a teleological and homogenous historical discourse and to an acceptance of postcolonial heterogeneity with regard to historiography and to myth. Magic realist works present clearer examples of *post*colonial worldviews.

Because of the controversy surrounding the definition of the term "magic realism," a brief overview of its characteristics – as described by various critics of New World writing – is in order here. Angel Flores proposes that the "amalgamation of realism and fantasy" is the principal unifying element of Latin American magic realist texts ("Magic Realism," 189). Slemon notes that the term "magic realism" is an oxymoron – as is the term "New World Myth" – which opposes the "representational code of realism and that, roughly, of fantasy" ("Magic Realism," 10). A distinctive tone is evident in magic realist works: here, "reality is stranger than fiction; things occur unexpectedly; absolute truth or reality is impossible for mortal man to grasp" (Menton, "Jorge Luis Borges," 416). Carpentier's argument in the preface to *El reino de este mundo* is that the cultural diversity of the Latin American heritage permits what Slemon calls its "uniqueness or difference from [the] mainstream" ("Magic Realism," 9). Carpentier also posits, according to Robert Rawdon Wilson, that an unquestioning faith and a certain credulity, along with an oral tradition of a pretechnological peasant class, create the inherent "marvellousness" of South American reality (Wilson, "The Magic and the Real," 41). Carpentier's emphasis, claims Wilson, is on "the typical South American fusion of geographical, historical, mythological, cultural, political and linguistic diversity." Magic realism frequently works within a "pre-technological, even pre-literate, perspective" (42), where any imaginable thing is possible, largely because of the oral tradition and the presupposed faith of the peasant discussed by Carpentier. Jack Hodgins has remarked on the sense of community and of the author's enjoyment in magic realist texts (Hancock and Hodgins, "Jack Hodgins," 56). The potential of magic realism as a vehicle for expressing a postcolonial worldview has been noted by Keith Maillard: "The spirit of fabulation is something like this: Nothing important can be said, so why not have fun? The spirit of magic realism, in contrast, is: Something tremendously important *must be* said, something that doesn't fit easily into traditional structures, so how can I find a way to say it?" ("'Middlewatch' as Magic Realism," 12).

The juxtaposition or the conflation of "reality" and "fantasy" in magic realist texts frequently produces a feeling of strangeness. Carpentier proposes that this strangeness – the marvellousness of the real – is the natural heritage of America. In the preface to *El reino de este mundo*, he emphasizes both the mythical and the historico-political qualities of New World cosmogonies: "esa presencia y vigencia de lo real maravilloso ne era privilegio único de Haití, sino patrimonio de la América entera, donde todavía no se ha terminado de establecer, por ejemplo, un recuento de cosmogonías. Lo real maravilloso se encuentra a cada paso en las vidas de hombres que inscribieron fechas en la historia del Continente ... ¿Pero qué es la historia de América toda sino una crónica de lo real-maravilloso?" ("The presence and functioning of the marvellous real are not the unique privilege of Haiti, but belong to all of America, which has not yet finished making its list of cosmogonies. The marvellous real is encountered at each step in the lives of the men who inscribe dates on the history of the Continent. Because what is the history of all of America if it is not a chronicle of the marvellous real?" [55–7, my translation]). Carpentier also suggests that "America is far from having used up its stock of mythologies" (56) and insists on "an inhabitual illumination of the unnoticed riches of reality" (53; my translation) in his discussion of magic realism. Carpentier thus ties the making of new mythologies to the historico-political happenings of the New Continent. Geoff Hancock, in his reflections on magic realism in English Canadian and Québécois texts, also sees a strong link between magic realism and political history. Among some features of magic realism he notes: "an absurd re-creation of 'history'; a parody of government and politicians ... [and] a collective sense of a folkloric past" ("Magic or Realism," 28).

Discussing the potential for political postcolonial discourse in magic realist writing, Stephen Slemon writes, "it seems, in a literary context, to be most obviously operative in cultures situated at the fringes of mainstream literary traditions. As Robert Kroetsch and Linda Kenyon observe, magic realism as a literary practice seems to be closely linked with a perception of 'living on the margins' [Kenyon, "A Conversation with Robert Kroetsch," 15], encoding within it, perhaps, a concept of resistance to the massive imperial centre and its totalizing systems" ("Magic Realism," 10). Slemon addresses three characteristics that allow a postcolonial magic realist work to address the social relations of postcolonial cultures. These are, first, a "transformational regionalism" (12), whereby the site in the text acts as a microcosm of the entire postcolonial culture; second, the telescoping of historical events; and, third, a preoccupation with gaps, silences, and disjunctive narration in the text. This third element is evident, according to Slemon, in the textual preponderance of images of borders and centres – boundaries that are constantly being destabilized within the text (12–13). All three characteristics are present in La Tribu. Barcelo's use of parody and of reversal techniques lays bare the inherent tensions regarding historiography that is characteristic of New World Myth narrative. Through its use of magic realist techniques in its particular reworking of events of the Québécois past, Barcelo's novel resists and challenges European-inspired totalizing systems of history.

François Barcelo was born in Montreal in 1941. Although he published some short stories in literary journals during his late teenage years and had had two longer unpublished manuscripts short-listed for the prize of the Cercle du livre de France, he was not acknowledged as a writer of fiction in Quebec's literary community until the 1980s. Like Jacques Godbout, he worked for many years in advertising before returning to the writing of fiction, which he did shortly before his fortieth birthday.[6] His impressive literary production consists of a dozen published novels and several short stories, most of which make substantial use of humour and parody in their investigations of what might be called social concerns. Several of his stories have been anthologized in English, Dutch, and Chinese collections. Although his novels have not been translated into English, some of his work is being translated into Spanish and published in Mexico.

The literary establishment in Quebec appears to have had some difficulty in categorizing or, more appropriately perhaps, "labelling" Barcelo and his work in the 1980s. One senses that Quebec's mainstream critics, used to novels to which the grilles d'analyses of the structuralists could be successfully applied, were somewhat mystified by Barcelo's work. For instance, his novels were frequently reviewed by Michel Lord in his science fiction and fantastic literature column in Lettres Québécoises in spite of their strong social commentary. However, in Imagine, a journal devoted to Québécois science fiction, Michel Bélil, while praising Barcelo's versatility and calling La Tribu "un livre important, qui plonge profondément dans notre imaginaire collectif," concludes that it is not a work of "science-fiction ou de fantastique ... C'est plutôt une fable ou une allégorie réussie" ("Barcelo et Beauchemin," 56). Elsewhere, Lord cites another mainstream critic's puzzled reaction to Barcelo's work: "Thomas Pavel avait déjà noté que le système narratif chez Barcelo ne renvoie pas à un réseau référentiel bien défini" ("Aaa! Aâh! Ha!" 32). According to Jacques Michon, La Tribu tells "la saga fantaisiste et désopilante d'une tribu imaginaire," and although he notes in passing the novel's obvious parody of Quebec's history and politics, his emphasis is on its "ton ... léger, enjoué, drôle et souvent émouvant" ("Romans," 337). Very few mainstream critics note what Pierre Hébert characterizes as the "sérieux humoristique" aspect of Barcelo's work ("A l'impossible certains sont tenus," 194), although a few ecstatic reviewers have acclaimed him as a "Messie ignoré" (for example, Lefèbvre, "J'ai Barcelo dans la peau," 16). In an interview,

Barcelo himself underlined that critical analyses of his novels are usually limited to discussions of structure and humour and that they usually occult the political and social foci of his texts: "je crois que tous mes romans sont des critiques sociales, mais pas déguisées. Il me semble facile de reconnaître dans *Agénor* ... une œuvre pacifiste. *La Tribu* est un roman indépendantiste. *Ville-Dieu* serait plutôt social-iste. *Aah, Aâh, Ha* ... est antinucléaire et xénophile ... Pourtant je crois être la seule personne à être totalement consciente de ce con-tenu politique. Aucun critique, à ma connaissance, ne l'a clairement souligné – sauf peut-être Réginald Martel dans le cas de *Ville-Dieu*. Pour le reste, les spécialistes ont plutôt parlé de la forme ou du côté divertissant de mes romans" ("Je suis un écrivain," 64). The critical reception of Barcelo's fictions can be in some ways compared to reac-tions to *Burning Water*: the political import of Bowering's work is often ignored, and he has been castigated for his irreverent and inac-curate treatment of historical facts – which he "made strange," as we shall see below.

In *La Tribu* strangeness is evident in the unusual and often unbe-lievable adventures of its characters and in the gradual development of what Pavel calls "un système de transpositions" ("*Agénor*," 35) whereby the narrator skilfully weaves the major events of Quebec's political history into his "fantastic" tale. *La Tribu*'s dedication is indicative of the political dimension of Barcelo's work, in that it is addressed to nine Amerindian tribes of Quebec: "Aux Cris et aux Montagnais, aux Algonquins et aux Hurons." The Québécois too are a tribe here: "aux Mohawks, aux Québécois et à toutes les tribus du monde qui tardent à succomber aux tentations de la liberté." This dedication also intimates the textual parody of some Franco-Euro-pean approaches to "primitive myth" and the postcolonial challenge to the notion of the Québécois as a homogeneous collectivity. *La Tribu* consists of twenty-one chapters of relatively equal length, an epi-logue, a "point final" and a postscript. Ten of the chapters are simply entitled in the style "Chapitre I," whereas ten others are presented as the story of a particular character, for example, "Histoire de l'amiral Le Corton," "Histoire de Grand-Nez." Interspersed within these two sets of chapters – themselves mixed according to no fixed system – are three others entitled "Parenthèse contemporaine," where the narrator tells stories of his obviously twentieth-century personal life. These sections, together with the "point final," are qualified within the text as optional reading.

The story begins with the arrival of two "vieux-pays" ships on the coast of the New World and the exploration of the virgin forest by the ship's captain and crew. The ship's cabin boy, Jean-François, is inadvertently left behind. A small Amerindian tribe, the Clipocs, adopts him, changing his name to Jafafoua and adapting their language and customs to suit his needs. The focus of the story, if there is one, is the erratic evolution of this tribe and the description of its members' extraordinary lives. For instance, Grand-Nez, an old wise man, is immortal, having arrived on the "Nouveau Continent" centuries ago, following the migration of the reindeer across the ice (71). As is common in postcolonial fictions that parody historiographical techniques, the notion of historical truth is constantly installed and then subverted by narratorial interventions. Thus, although we are told that Grand-Nez's faulty memory makes it impossible for him to "raconter fidèlement le récit qui suit" (59), the narrator implies that *his* "Histoire de Grand-Nez" is exact in every respect. However, in true *conteur populaire* style, he asserts his power to construct the past by modifying basic facts at the very beginning of his tale: "Grand-Nez, qui ne s'appelait pas encore Grand-Nez mais que nous appellerons Grand-Nez pour simplifier les choses, était un jeune chasseur" (59).

Due to his frequently problematic immortality, Grand-Nez witnesses the various adventures of the nomadic tribe over the centuries. He observes how Jafafoua's daughter, Mahii, eventually becomes the leader of the small band. In the short space of twenty years under her leadership, the tribe goes through a rapid scientific and technological expansion, inventing everything from the hockey puck to toothpaste to automatic guns. The younger members of the tribe use some newly invented weapons to attack and to annihilate a neighbouring tribe, the Niox. Mahii, ashamed of the progress that she had advocated, orders the destruction of all recent inventions. She then leads the tribe toward the North, and the Clipocs, once again "primitives," live like precontact Inuit for a while. One day while ice-fishing, the Clipocs realize that their section of ice has become detached from the mainland and that they are stranded on a drifting iceberg. Here, Mahii decides to have a child, and every man of the tribe ceremoniously copulates with her in a hollowed-out ice cave. This "enfant de la tribu," ironically named Notregloire, is born just as land is sighted and the iceberg melts away. Amazingly, the tribe is returned to land at exactly the same spot they had abandoned many years before. Now, however, the area is populated not only by "Vieux-Paysans" but also by "les Zanglais." The tribe gradually becomes more and more involved in the politics and the religious practices of "les Régions du Haut" (197) – a term that obliquely refers to specific areas of rural Quebec. At the end of the story the tribe's movements have been limited by the terms of a contract signed with "la Société d'exploitation de la Grande Baie du Nord," an obvious ironic reference to the James Bay developments in northern Quebec (298). Nonetheless, against all odds the tribe survives, and the immortal Grand-Nez, in conversation with one of the magic realist characters of the novel, a talking garter snake, proclaims that "[l]es tribus ont le devoir de vivre" (299).

This principal narrative about the Clipocs is interspersed with several other stories that permit the narrator to further develop his parodic transpositions in the retelling of past events. For example, in the "Histoire d'Amédée Demers" are found these unusual political observations about the European reactions to the fall of Balbuk (Quebec City) during the Seven Years War: "Ce n'était pas la première fois que Balbuk tombait aux mains des Zanglais ... Mais, chaque fois, les rois vieux-paysans et les rois zanglais finissaient éventuellement, après la guerre, par s'entendre sur des échanges compliqués, les rois zanglais rendant Balbuk aux rois vieux-paysans parce qu'ils ne savaient pas quoi en faire, et les rois vieux-paysans étant forcés de la reprendre parce qu'ils avaient eu la bêtise de perdre la guerre" (197). Narratorial play with fantasy and history in this novel can be explored in the context of its use of magic realist techniques, which here ultimately serve to emphasize various multifaceted aspects of Québécois history. Although many studies of Québécois literature concentrate on le merveilleux and on le fantastique – especially with regard to their presence in the genre of le conte, magic realism as a postcolonial device – or even as a genre – has not received much critical attention in Quebec. Barcelo's first novel, Agénor, is dedicated to Gabriel García Márquez, among others – a sign of his interest in the South American magic realists.

Carpentier contrasts the European "marvellous," which he qualifies as literary and artificial, to the superstitions and collective fears and beliefs of the inhabitants of the New World (for a discussion and references, see Weisberger, "Le Réalisme magique," 41–2). The narrator of La Tribu ironically foregrounds certain aspects of this New World vision du monde – aspects such as orality, timelessness, and folklore – in his parodic portrayal of the Clipocs as "des primitifs" (25). My use of quotation marks around the word "primitive" signals both accurate citation and parodic distancing, as Barcelo plays with the usually oppositional primitive/civilized dichotomy throughout his text. His flaunting of the term "primitive" and the concepts it represents, which are somewhat different from the essentialist argument usually attached to the English-language use of the term, constitutes a parodic commentary on traditional Franco-European studies of philosophy, literary history, and myth criticism, as we shall see in chapter 6.

In *Parody/Meta-Fiction* and *Parody: Ancient, Modern, and Post-Modern*, Margaret Rose has written extensively about parody, both as a term in use since ancient Greek times and in the context of twentieth-century literature. In the latter half of the twentieth century, as she notes in her introduction to the latter work, structuralist analyses tended to discuss parody in negative and dismissive terms, but "with the rise of what has been called 'postmodernist' literature and theory, parody has seen something of a revival in contemporary theory and artistic practice" (1). In her study of parody in twentieth-century art forms, Linda Hutcheon notes that many "historians of parody agree that parody prospers in periods of cultural sophistication that enable parodists to rely on the competence of the reader (viewer, listener) of the parody" (*Theory of Parody,* 19). As with any discussion of a long-existing but renewed technique – or, as Hutcheon prefers, "genre" (19) – historians and theorists of parody tend to divergent definitions and positions. It is not my purpose to dwell on the many interpretations of parody or to enter into the debates that strive to distinguish parody from related forms, such as pastiche and burlesque. Instead, I offer a brief discussion of contemporary appreciations of parody, followed by my analyses of parody in the context of Bowering and Barcelo's historiographic fictions.

Parody has frequently been equated with the comic (Rose, *Parody/Meta-Fiction,* 59) and with humour, but the title of Hutcheon's earlier publication, "Parody without Ridicule," indicates that she does not relegate parody only to the ludic sphere. Hutcheon defines parody as "repetition [of the parodied object] with critical difference [which] would allow for the range of intent and effect possible in modern parodic works." She sees parody as "operating as a method of inscribing continuity while permitting critical distance. It can, indeed, function as a conservative force in both retaining and mocking other aesthetic forms; but it is also capable of transformative power in creating new syntheses" (*Theory of Parody,* 20). While Hutcheon points to the possibility of parody serving to reinscribe conservative practices, she insists on its pragmatic aspect, suggesting that in the twentieth century, parody "marks the intersection of creation and re-creation, of invention and critique" (101). In other words, she opposes the more structuralist Euro-American approach to parody, which would deny it any connection with "the real world." This approach, she suggests, is perhaps represented by Jonathan Culler, who insists that parody is unrelated to mimesis – to "a serious statement of feelings about real problems or situations" (*Structuralist Poetics*, 153). For Hutcheon, parody does indeed have a connection with "the world," and one must be aware of its complexities: parody's "appropriating of the past, of history, its questioning of the contemporary by 'referencing' it to a different set of codes, is a way of establishing continuity that may, in itself, have ideological implications" (*Theory of Parody*, 110). Nonetheless, for Hutcheon, in the contemporary situation parody "is endowed with the power to renew" (115).

Hutcheon's insistence on the pragmatic functions of parody differs from the views generally held in the Euro-American sphere of influence, which continue to dwell on the ludic function of the technique and to offer, following Rose, an apolitical appreciation of the term. Indeed, the assumptions underlying Hutcheon's argument that parody is "an important way for modern artists to come to terms with the past" (*Theory of Parody*, 101) has been criticized by Rose: "some late-modern theorists of parody following Hutcheon who have denied it its comic functions have also implicitly extended its critical and ridiculing functions in attributing to it new and often unrealistic political powers" (*Parody*, 240). These different ways of reading parody correspond perhaps to the differences I have been alluding to regarding Euro-American and postcolonial approaches to contemporary fictions. While the Euro-American approach, as represented by Rose and Culler, pursues a rather distanced investigation of parody as part of the structure of the novel, postcolonial fictions frequently use parody as an *engagé* – if sometimes problematic – technique. It is my belief that New World Myth fictions such as *La Tribu* strongly insist upon parody's power to contribute to postcolonial challenges to history, historiography, myth, and the political present.

To understand Barcelo's parody in *La Tribu*, a brief summary of the European-inspired tenets regarding "primitive thought," such as the one Georges Gusdorf provides in *Mythe et métaphysique*, is useful. According to Gusdorf, in the primitive worldview "le mythe correspond à ... l'unité ontologique ... [où toute] la réalité s'inscrit dans un seul ordre" (65). It is impossible for the primitive mind to accommodate the notion of history, Gusdorf argues, because it knows only "le Grand Temps initial" (76). Space, too, is conceived of differently by the primitive: the only acknowledged space is that of the immediate surroundings (102). Ritual celebrations are an essential component of the primitive worldview, and the tribal cosmology is collectively constituted (98–9). This description of primitive thought is parodically echoed in *La Tribu*, where all of "reality" – no matter how bizarre – is unquestionably accepted by the Clipocs. The tribe has no way of measuring time; it operates according to a collective instinct (52). The tribal concept of history is vague: its four wise men vaguely remember earlier events, but no one is interested in retaining facts and figures. Thus, when Ksoâr reinvents writing in order to keep records of the tribal hunt, his invention is received with total indifference by the tribe (56). The concept of a particular delimited space is equally unfamiliar to the tribe. When the Vieux-Paysans begin to encroach on the tribe's territory, the Clipocs simply pick up and move north because in their worldview hunting territories and living space are limitless (211).

The Clipocs, then, seem to be portrayed by the narrator as a primitive tribe, living in harmony with Nature, evolving slowly through a timelessness far removed from the political situation of present-day Quebec: "Les Clipocs faisaient bien ce qu'ils faisaient, mais semblaient vouloir se contenter toujours de ce qu'ils avaient" (72). Jean-François's first sighting of the Clipocs at first reinforces the traditional image of a primitive tribe, complete with huts and shamanic wise man. However, as the narrator informs us, his characters' observations may be "en deçà de la vérité" (27). And indeed, the Clipocs soon belie the supposed accuracy of Jean-François' description. Frequent narratorial interventions, along with the narrator's highly unusual handling of topical and historical events, foreground the constant unsettling of expectations hinted at here in Jean-François' incorrect appraisal of the tribe. Thus, on one level the Clipocs are presented as primitive Amerindians. On another level this small tribe can most definitely be seen as a microcosm of the Québécois people. The Clipocs' territorial area, with its Grand Nord and its cities of Ville-Dieu (Montreal) and Balbuk (Quebec City) strategically located on the Grand Fleuve (40–1), is similar to Quebec's geography. The technological explosion, where the Clipocs invent not only mechanical aids, but also social systems such as "les allocations familiales" and "l'assurance-chômage" (121) further blurs the divisions between primitive Amerindians and twentieth-century Québécois. La Tribu's unsettling of accepted expectations in many arenas, from history and culture through storytelling to myth, constantly lays bare and then subverts both the characters' and the reader's possibly unexamined worldviews. It also disallows an us/them critique, because the "other" is not Other but part of "us"; in other words, the parody works both ways.

While the blurring of the Clipocs and the Québécois provides the forum for a postcolonial reexamination of Franco-European approaches to precontact cultures, La Tribu also opens up a space to discuss Quebec's struggle with internalized historico-political myths. This struggle is largely ignored in comparative Canadian or English-language postcolonial studies, where it is assumed that the question of national identity in Quebec has long been resolved. The Quiet Revolution in the 1960s did bring about social, cultural, and literary reforms, and the nationalist concerns of most Québécois literature of the early period of *la modernité* (1960–75) were relatively homogenous, as Micheline Cambron has argued in *Une société, un récit* (1989). Contemporary Québécois texts published after the referendum of 1980, however, address the social and ideological heterogeneity of contemporary Quebec, as Sherry Simon proposes: "Si au Québec la culture a longtemps désigné le lieu d'un consensus identitaire, l'expression d'une appartenance collective totalisante, elle est aujourd'hui de plus en plus marquée du signe de l'hétérogène. C'est le caractère organique à la fois du domaine culturel et de son lien à la communauté qui est aujourd'hui mis en question" (Simon, L'Hérault, et al., *Fictions de l'identitaire*, 9). In his contribution to the same volume, Pierre L'Hérault suggests that from the 1980s onward, "la littérature québécoise s'articule désormais sur la tension de l'identitaire et de l'hétérogène" (56).

As we saw in the preface to this study, an interesting argument was put forth by Arun Mukherjee in Victoria in 1990 in a significantly entitled talk, "Whose Post-colonialism and Whose Postmodernism?" Mukherjee notes that postcolonial constructions of a centre-periphery discourse prohibit any exploration of what I might call power struggles *within* postcolonial communities. Binary oppositions such as centre-periphery or colonized-colonizer tend to overlook "the cultural work that a post-colonial text does on its home ground" (6). Current postcolonial theory privileges parodic texts, arguing that parody is the tool par excellence with which to undercut imperial textuality. Mukherjee, however, argues against the predominant assumption that postcolonial texts are fundamentally engaged in writing back to the centre and warns against limiting postcolonial studies to those parodic texts that correspond to what the theory calls for: "despite its best intentions [this restriction] ends up homogenizing and assimilating" (7).

James Clifford has argued that in the West the approach to ethnographic allegory is often one of salvaging – that is to say, "The other is lost, in disintegrating time and space, but saved in the text" ("On Ethnographic Allegory," 112). The "slippage" among what has traditionally been perceived as separate or separable groups in Barcelo's fictional allegory, however, provides a textual space in which to explore various manifestations of cultural representation. (By "slip-page," I mean a back-and-forth movement between groups that produces a constantly shifting, blurring, blending, conflation and reconfiguration of the group(s).) Signalling a postcolonial acceptance of heterogeneity, the novel's reexamination of many givens (among them Franco-European thought, the history of New France, the nationalist assumptions of the 1960s) also makes room for *other* ideologies, decrying what has recently been described as the wish to proclaim oneself "Québécois-francophone-de-souche" (Godbout, "Qu'est-ce qu'un Québécois?" 236). This slippage is an important technique of postcolonial fiction, in that it permits an examination of the home-ground issue of identity or, to use the Québécois neologism, *l'identitaire*. A slippage among previously separable groups is linked to magic realist techniques and is more closely affiliated with Latin American and Brazilian fiction than with Euro-American manifestations of contemporary writing, as Antón Risco argues: "ce qui importe dans le cas présent c'est de signaler la volonté pure et simple des critiques de la littérature latino-américaine, de lire le corpus touchant le fantastique ou le merveilleux d'une façon particulière, pour ainsi dire *autochtone*" ("Le Postmodernisme latino-américain," 71).

In contemporary Québécois literature, the previously sacrosanct concept of the *collectivité* has begun to be the focus of a postmodern and postcolonial thrust to disunity. The utter lack of *any* fixed racial, linguistic, or religious boundaries in *La Tribu* permits this novel's retelling of conflicts of the past to offer ongoing commentary on the social issues of the present. This post-European text demonstrates an openness toward cultural multiplicity by underlining the constantly changing nature of the Clipocs: are they "primitives"? Inuit? Amerindians? Québécois? Something else? Postcolonial cultures, as Brydon points out, are more receptive to heterogeneity than the European cultures that have dominated cultural theory to the present day ("Myths," 7). The characteristic postcolonial insistence on cross-cultural awareness has become practice in this text. *La Tribu*, then, through its frequently parodic retellings of past events, promotes a heterogeneous approach to political history and to society. The use of Amerindian and non-Amerindian figures in the novel, along with the novel's deliberate installation of a continual but erratic slippage regarding *l'identitaire* of those figures, permits an examination of the issues that are foregrounded in much postcolonial literature. Among other techniques, the use of parody opens up space in the text for various colonial and postcolonial relationships to be explored.

However, this novel's retelling of problematic linguistic and cultural relations between Amerindians, Inuit, European colonizers, and Québécois touches on several issues, including that of the image of the Amerindian in non-Amerindian Québécois fiction. As I mentioned in the foreword, it has been argued that the term postcolonial can hardly be applied to Québécois, given their confrontations with Natives at Kanesatake (Oka) during the summer of 1990. Quebec's position, proposes Caroline Bayard, "made the formerly colonized 'Nègres Blancs d'Amérique' (see Vallières) look like the colonizers in their turn" ("From *Nègres blancs d'Amérique*," 21).[7] In chapter 3 I proposed that there may be basic differences in how the two major literatures of English-speaking Canada and Quebec incorporate the figures of the Amerindian and Métis into their textual discussion of postcolonial issues, differences that are rooted in part in the historically divergent relationships to Amerindians in the two linguistic groups. These relationships are important, in that some fictional writings of the years 1975–85 reflect and embody them and in that unspoken attitudes underlie the image of the Amerindian in contemporary Québécois novels. Because of the multi-tiered historico-colonial relationships between various cultural groups in what is now called Quebec, it is important to discuss, albeit briefly, recent studies of historical Franco-Amerindian relations.

The historical French-Amerindian rapport and the intermingling of races in New France lead francophone cultural commentators in Quebec to link its situation to that of Latin America. In "Ne sommes-nous pas tous des Amérindiens?" Pierre-André Julien cites a respected ethnologist's estimate that 60 percent of the Québécois population have "du sang indien," and he argues that it is important to "bien distinguer les politiques des pays latins de ceux des anglo-saxons envers les Amérindiens tout au long de leur histoire." Whereas the Latins of North and South America formed alliances that blended Europeans and Amerindians, causing *métissage*, the English created reserves, and, as Julien sees it, "La culpabilité envers les Amérindiens que l'on retrouve en filigramme dans les journaux canadiens (ou américains) ... relève de cet esprit des réserves créées par les gouvernements anglophones" (13). Julien proposes that closer attention be paid to *métissage*, a practice that has been receiving much critical attention in the writings on hybridity and *mestizaje* in Latin American discourse (Chanady, *Latin American Identity*, xvi). Julien argues that historically, there are closer links between French-speaking North Americans and Amerindians than between the latter and their English-speaking counterparts. This argument is supported by recent nonfrancophone historical studies, such as Richard White's *The Middle Ground*, which "steps outside the simple stories of Indian-white relations – stories of conquest and assimilation and stories of cultural persistence." White argues that the encounter between Europeans and Indians changed from an initial meeting of two groups who each regarded the other as alien and "virtually nonhuman" to "a search for accommodation and common meaning." These two groups, according to White's voluminous research, "constructed a common, mutually comprehensible world in the region around the Great Lakes that the French called the *pays d'en haut*. Here the older world of the Algonquians and of various Europeans overlapped, and their mixture created new systems of meaning and of exchange" (foreword).

Barcelo's blurring of the Clipocs and the Québécois in *La Tribu* uses this usually unarticulated cultural *métissage* as its backdrop and explains the ease with which its many characters highlight cross-cultural conflation. While the subject of Franco-Amerindian relations is far too complex to be examined in great detail here, the work of the well-known Amerindian historian Denys Delâge provides a brief summary of its main points. Delâge argues that the history of francophone North Americans "s'est construite en relation avec les premières nations et leur identité y a également beaucoup emprunté" ("Les Amérindiens," 15), although he notes that the strong and fruitful alliances between "autochtones" and "colons" have sometimes receded from collective memory. In his diachronic survey, Delâge first underlines that the historical cross-cultural interaction was "étroite, soutenue, prolongée" (18). He traces in some detail the complex alliances between the First Nations and French-speaking Europeans and argues that, strategically, these alliances benefited both sides. Delâge's research underlines that the "autochtones étaient des alliés, non des sujets" and gives a succinct overview of military collaboration and interaction that is frequently occulted from current accounts of history. He then distinguishes among three subgroups of non-Amerindian settlers: the first group consisted of those "qui se sont intégrés aux sociétés amérindiennes et s'y sont assimilés" (mainly those involved in the fur trade); the second group was composed of those who also lived in "pays amérindien," but who retained more of their European culture. In both cases *métissage* was important, but to different degrees. The third group, downstream from Montreal, the "habitants canadiens," had less direct interaction with Amerindians, but even this group "emprunte aux autochtones de nombreux traits de leur culture" (18–19). Delâge discusses at some length the influence of Amerindian culture on the

Franco–North American, as opposed to European, identity: "Dans l'ensemble, ces emprunts créent une différence entre les Français métropolitains et ceux d'ici, ils servent bientôt de repères à la creation d'une identité nouvelle ... Par opposition au Français le Canadien habite le pays, a côté de ses premiers occupants. La naissance d'une identité canadienne résulte donc de l'implantation d'immigrants dans une terre nouvelle parmi des peuples non européens (20). Although Delâge does not wear rose-coloured glasses, noting in passing the many negative effects of the arrival of the Europeans, he does suggest the importance of the extended Franco-Amerindian relations: "Le va-et-vient continuel entre la société coloniale française et les sociétés autochtones, les emprunts mutuels, le métissage ont pour effet d'estomper les frontières, de les rendre floues, sans bien sûr les effacer" (23). Addressing himself to readers of today, he then raises an important question: "Comment avons-nous pu en perdre la mémoire? Une longue série de ruptures en sont la cause." The British conquest, he proposes, marks "la fin de l'alliance franco-amérindienne." In the second half of the nineteenth century, the creation of reserves and the withdrawal of civil rights "ajouteront encore à l'isolement des Amérindiens par rapport à la population eurocanadienne. De surcroit, sur de nombreuses réserves indiennes du Québec, l'enseignement en anglais contribuera à l'isolement avec les francophones" (25).

Delâge also advances the hypothesis that, while a close association with Amerindians helped the Canadiens to distinguish themselves from the metropolitan French, this closeness disadvantaged them in the eyes of the British after the Conquest and that they therefore chose to distance themselves from their former associates: the British "jugeaient donc que les Canadiens étaient métissés biologiquement et qu'ils étaient culturellement ensauvagés. Du coup, ils plaçaient donc les Canadiens du côté de la barbarie. Ceux-ci cherchèrent à se démarquer des 'Sauvages' pour se rattacher à un pôle de civilisation" (26). Delâge supports this idea by revealing little-known facts, such as the suppression of thousands of Amerindian place-names from the map of Quebec after 1912. He argues that the nationalist impulse behind the Quiet Revolution constituted an additional rupture in the history of Franco-Amerindian relations, as historians turned their attention to the *habitant-cultivateur* and away from the Amerindian (28). Recently, suggests Delâge, both Amerindians and non-Amerindians in Quebec have "un intérêt nouveau et une volonté commune de se redéfinir en dehors des vieux paradigmes ... Sur le plan politique, ... le Québec assume ses responsabilités auprès des autochtones dans les secteurs jusque-là occupés par le gouvernement fédéral a marqué un premier rapprochement, qui se poursuivit avec la reconnaissance des dix nations autochtones du territoire québécois" (28).

Georges E. Sioui, in *Pour une autohistoire amérindienne*, cites Delâge, Rémi Savard, Bruce G. Trigger, and other Amerindian historians who have noted the long-standing closeness of Franco-Amerindian relationships and the importance of *métissage* to New World living. Indeed, the reflective tone adopted throughout Sioui's philosophical work stands in sharp contrast to Amerindian commentators from the English Canadian sphere, as shall be seen in the discussion of Bowering's work. Sioui argues that the Amerindian, far from "disappearing" as some postcolonial theorists would have it, can strongly influence the world as we know it today. He proposes that as a society we abandon the myth of evolutionism and adopt those aspects of the Sacred Circle of Life that will enable transcultural harmony. To this end, he directly addresses and assuages the notion of guilt, and gives detailed and transhistorical summaries of Franco-Amerindian transcultural interactions, not limiting these to the history of his Huron/Wendat nation. The following typical statement embodies the entire tone of the work, in that it emphasizes intercultural work within one society: "La technique d'autohistoire est aussi une tentative pour susciter des stratégies d'action interculturelle qui donneraient à *notre société, considérée dans son ensemble*, le pourvoir d'utiliser l'immense richesse que recèle la connaissance de l'histoire et de la philosophie amérindiennes" (51, my emphasis).

The historical Franco-Amerindian *métissage* is behind much of the use of the Amerindian or Métis figures in contemporary fictions in Québec. I agree with Gilles Thérien, who proposes that the Métis presence is demonstrably linked to explorations of cross-cultural representations in contemporary Québécois society ("L'Indien du discours," 365–6). In cultural discourse, the term "Métis" has a wider acceptation in French than it does in English. Of course, some Amerindian scholars and writers do not adopt Sioui's philosophy of shared culture(s). For instance, Diane Boudreau, in her *Histoire de la littérature amérindienne au Québec*, finds little common ground between *l'indianité* and *québécitude*, except for "la force de l'affirmation identitaire" (15). Her tone is more oppositional; although she too qualifies Amerindian literature as "métissée," she does not so much see it as transcultural but as fragmented: "La littérature écrite amérindienne est actuellement une littérature de survie (pour les nations) et de 'résistance' (aux Blancs). Comme d'autres littératures issues de sociétés orales, elle est polymorphe et 'métissée': l'écriture relève de la volonté de survivre, et les formes qu'elle revêt correspondent à la réalité amérindienne" (15). And of course the stormy confrontations between Amerindians and non–Amerindians at Kanesatake and Kahnawake in the summer of 1990 (which are addressed in detail in works mentioned above, and whose historical and federal/provincial/municipal complexities are explained in English by Lisa Austin and Christina Boyd in *The Oka Crisis*), belie the harmonious historical and present-day relationships favoured by Sioui and others.

Nonetheless, I would argue that Barcelo's *La Tribu*, in spite of the fact that it predates the crises at Kanesatake and Kahnawake by almost a decade, does address certain postcolonial concerns of contemporary Quebec. It is indeed in the *slippage* among the various characters and cultural groups that the postcolonialism of this text is most clearly evident. Because of the constant foregrounded blurring of demarcation lines, for want of a better expression, the parody works both ways, with the constantly changing foci permitting the text to parody many aspects of contemporary Quebec worldviews, including those inherited from Franco-European philosophy and those held by Amerindians and non-Amerindians alike. Historical *métissage* and the constantly-coming-into-being aspect of New World Myth is underlined by this technique.

Language issues are often thematized in postcolonial fictions, given that the act of colonization frequently involved the imposition of a foreign language upon an indigenous people (Slemon, "Magic Realism," 12). There are differing colonial situations – and therefore different linguistic struggles – as D.E.S. Maxwell points out in this discussion of two major categories in Commonwealth countries: "In the first, the writer brings his own language – English – to an alien environment and a fresh set of experiences: Australia, Canada, New Zealand. In the other, the writer brings an alien language – English – to his own social and cultural inheritance: India, West Africa. Yet the categories have a fundamental kinship. Viewing his society, the writer constantly faces the evidences of the impact between what is native to it and what is derived from association with Britain, whatever its form" ("Landscape and Theme," 82–3). Postcolonial theorists such as Diana Brydon distinguish between the literatures of India and African countries – where "the lines between colonised and coloniser were more clearly drawn" – and settler colonies like Australia, where "the English language and culture were transported (whether by settlers, convicts, or slave-masters) to a foreign territory … [and where] it was much more difficult to eradicate an internalised Englishness that militated against developing an indigenous identity" (Brydon, "Myths," 3). English-speaking Canada is usually defined as a settler colony in postcolonial practice, although as Hutcheon points out, "the pluri-ethnic (and lately more multiracial) nature of Canadian society" further condition "the use of the term post-colonial in a Canadian context" ("Circling," 159).

The situation in Quebec is not as clear-cut. There, post-European writers such as Barcelo must constantly address the shifting dynamics of language politics. In New France, despite the eventual integration of Amerindian vocabulary into Canadian French, the French colonists did impose their European language upon some indigenous peoples – a linguistic imposition that was continued by the British and then by the English Canadians, to the point that the first nonnative language of many Inuit and Amerindians living in Quebec today is still English (Delisle, "Les langues autochtones," 3). The French speakers, however, were colonized linguistically in their turn by the British, and the survival of French as a living language is an ongoing concern in Quebec. Writers of francophone fiction in Quebec face a challenge similar to the one posed to writers from settler colonies such as English-speaking Canada: "the importation and modification of a language and literary conventions from elsewhere" (Brydon, "Discovering 'Ethnicity,'" 95). The rage to write in *joual* during the Quiet Revolution was in part a response to this unarticulated linguistic and literary pressure to conform to French standards. In this sense, joual may be seen as the language of decolonization: a "socio-linguistic form of protest akin to Caliban's interjectory 'Uhuru' in Césaire's *Une Tempête*" (Zabus, "A Calibanic Tempest," 48). Barcelo's post-European novel, like most Québécois fictions of the 1980s, is not written in joual; instead, its postcolonial approach to linguistic battles involves a blurring of the boundaries between linguistic/cultural groups and a humourously parodic look at Quebec's history of passionate debates around language, culture, and identity.

The first indication of the *québécitude* of the tribe is that its members *choose* to speak *vieux-paysan* instead of Clipoc. One of the many complex cultural subversions in this novel is evident here: instead of portraying the linguistic colonization of the Clipocs by the Vieux-Paysans – the usual *colonisé* argument – the narrator describes the willingness of the tribe to absorb Jafafoua's language and customs. This parodic and unusual treatment of the rapport between language and colonization is sometimes received with puzzlement; Christian Bouchard's review of the novel qualifies it as "un phénomène pour le moins étrange" (*"La Tribu,"* 24). Barcelo's handling of this sensitive issue is effective because it constantly slips between previously inseparable "groups." Thus, the Clipocs are not just representative of the Amerindians but also of francophone Québécois, and this passage parodies the multilayered linguistic impositions in Quebec, including "la facilité avec laquelle les Québécois de Montréal ont appris l'anglais de leurs patrons" (personal interview with the author, n.p.).

In *La Tribu* language temporarily becomes a political issue for the Clipocs when Ksoâr proposes that the Clipocs learn the language spoken by the Reverend Nelson Golden, a "zanglais" missionary who tries unsuccessfully to convert them to Christianity. The humorous descriptions of the tribe's arguments for and against the project recall the periodic heated debates about bilingualism in Quebec (152–3). Some Clipocs argue for the intellectual stimulation provided by a bilingual or multilingual society, whereas others oppose bilingualism on the grounds that language is not just a method of communication but the very *soul* of the tribe. Barcelo's ironic descriptions of these debates manage to convey a certain 1980 postreferendum ennui; all the over-used clichés used here underline the fact that the tribe is tired of discussing language rights.

In another bizarre cultural reversal, Jafafoua wants to "se faire plus clipoc que les Clipocs" (*La Tribu*, 51) – an inversion of the case when some Québécois, particularly those in academic circles, used to be accused of wanting to be "plus français que les Français."[8] In his desire to become a real man of the tribe, Jafafoua quickly forgets what life was like in the old country. He regresses (in the European worldview) or progresses (in the tribal worldview) to a state of primitive space and time, where "les images de son ancien pays étaient de plus en plus vague en sa tête, de plus en plus lointaines, de plus en plus dépourvues d'intérêt" (52). Eventually his assimilation (another politically weighted term in Quebec) is complete: watching a naval battle between Old World factions, he realizes that he no longer feels any affinity to the miserable country where he was born (79). Jafafoua, formerly Jean-François, has *chosen* to evolve into a typical member of a New World collectivity, no longer influenced by any allegiance he might have had to his distant roots in the Old World.

Cultural tensions typical of New World Myth narrative arise from the deliberate allegorical blurring of the linguistic boundaries between this "primitive" tribe and the Vieux-Paysans. Toward the end of the novel, the Clipocs have a problematic identity: they speak the same language and practice the same religion as the Vieux-Paysans (265) and appear to be aligned with the latter in their ongoing cultural struggles against a large and powerful country to the south. They are nonetheless distinct from the Vieux-Paysans, and sometimes scorned by them, as is evident in several exchanges between the two groups toward the end of the novel. At other times, parodically echoing the Franco-Métis-Amerindian collaboration during the Riel uprisings, the two groups work as a unit. This episodic blurring of cultural and linguistic boundaries appears to constitute, at least in part, a postcolonial exploration of heterogeneity in Barcelo's work – an example, perhaps, of Jacques Brault's theory of nontranslation, which proposes "ne pas annexer l'autre, [mais] devenir son hôte" ("Nontraduire 1," 15).

The narratorial play with history in *La Tribu* is another technique that foregrounds the novel's postcolonial slant. The text presupposes a general knowledge of the traditional version of the history of the New World. This in turn presupposes a tacit acknowledgement that the traditional version of events needs to be re-examined in the here and now – that is to say, an acknowledgment that there may well be a need and a place for an alternative apprehension of past events. By placing a "primitive" people who closely resemble the Québécois in the foreground of the story, the narrator first emphasizes the histories of the peoples of the New World and jolts the traditional focus on the historical voyages of the Old World European explorers. It is easy to discern the symbolism of the political message in the first chapter, where the Clipocs skilfully and deliberately explode the explorers' boat and kill all Europeans on board. By parodically disguising the history of the Québécois collectivity in stories about a primitive tribe where anything – no matter how unbelievable – is possible, Barcelo's narrator seems to suggest that the history of the Québécois part of the New World is also "una crónica de lo real-maravilloso" where, indeed, "no se ha terminado de establecer ... un recuento de cosmogonías" (Carpentier, *El reino de este mundo*, 55, 57). This emphasis on the marvellous, however, does not keep the text from critically examining the political behaviour of the Québécois government and people. The detailed stories of the poor treatment meted out to the Clipocs by the Vieux-Paysans at the end of the novel constitute a narratorial criticism of the Québécois policy toward the Amerindian peoples who live within Quebec's boundaries today, as well as a comment on the historical French colonization of the New World Amerindian tribes. Some of the inequalities of the present-day sociopolitical situation in Quebec are attributed here to the political actions of the Québécois instead of to "autrui."

At times, the cultural distinctions are maintained among the three main cultural groups in the text – the Vieux-Paysans, the Zanglais, and the Clipocs – and it is well-known historical events that are

subjected to the postcolonial technique of *slippage*. A detailed examination of the story of the great debates provides an illustration of the
deliberate conflation of fantasy, language, history, and politics in this
New World Myth text. As background to this story, the narrator
explains that an agreement had existed between the conquering
Zanglais and the Vieux-Paysans. The latter could keep their language,
their religion, and their traditions, as long as they did not ally themselves to the rebellious colonies farther south. This obvious reference
to the Quebec Act of 1774, which was intended to keep the French
colonists in British North America from participating in the American
Revolution, is immediately followed by an allusion to the repatriation
of the Constitution of 1982:

> Pour faire accepter le nouveau traité, qui d'ailleurs ne serait pas à propre-
> ment parler un traité puisqu'il serait comme le précédent tout bonnement
> imposé à la population vieux-paysanne, on tenta de faire croire à celle-ci que
> l'objectif unique de la manœuvre était de ramener le traité dans des Régions
> du Haut, au lieu de le laisser à Lugdune où il n'avait aucune raison d'être.
>
> Quelques Vieux-Paysans tombèrent dans le panneau, d'autant plus facile-
> ment que ce nouveau traité leur était proposé par quelques-uns des leurs,
> enflammés pas les idées de l'époque qui proclamaient que tous les peuples
> devaient disposer d'eux-mêmes. (*La Tribu*, 262)

The use of the literary past tense in the above quotation, as well as
phrases that imply a great distance in time, such as "les idées de
l'époque," creates a sense of distance from the Constitutional debate,
a political event whose outcome was being debated even as the novel
was being written. The adaptation of an *indépendantiste* slogan ("tous
les peuples ont le droit de décider de leur avenir") and the allusion
to the francophone federalists working with Pierre Trudeau in
Ottawa further conflate political issues and historical periods in this
magic realist story.

In the paragraphs following the above quotation, the narrator
describes the formation of two opposing camps. Their members are
supposedly for and against the treaty, but, in fact, this issue has been
dropped from the constantly changing story. The names of the two
groups, les Fils de la Patrie and les Enfants de Dieu (*La Tribu*, 262),
parodically recall – and confuse in terms of language and religion –
the citizens' groups that existed during the Rebellions of 1837–38 in
Lower Canada: l'Association des Fils de la Liberté and the Doric
Club. Because the Vieux-Paysans in the neighbouring village of les
Ricochets are loyal to les Fils de la Patrie, the Zanglais send a punitive expedition against them composed of the First Regiment of

Giants' Cove Grenadiers from l'Anse-aux-géants (263). This linguistic confusion appears to be a humoristic narrative device, but it is also a reflection of the linguistic tension produced by the sometimes confusing typology of Quebec.[9] Again, through the use of parody, Barcelo integrates minute details of everyday life in Quebec into his text. In the same way, he also foregrounds more important cultural conflations – known to all but rarely articulated.

In the village of les Ricochets, the notary and the doctor, concerned about their lack of resources to fend off the attack, visit the Clipocs in the hope of persuading them to become allies of their cause. The Clipocs then engage in a debate that has many similarities to the prereferendum discussions of the late 1970s. The supporters of the "Yes" vote force themselves to use rational arguments to convince the rest of the tribe to engage in battle, although they know, deep down, that a "Yes" vote is an emotional declaration: "une façon de montrer que les Clipocs existaient encore et voulaient exister toujours" (La Tribu, 265). In contrast, the supporters of the "No" vote are older, cautious, and concerned about the financial future of the tribe. And, finally, given Barcelo's humour, there is a third group, the undecided voters, who enjoy being won over repeatedly by the arguments of the two opposing camps (265–6). When it is time to vote, the "No" vote wins with a three-to-two margin – a well-known 1980 referendum statistic.

The slippage between historical periods in this novel is obvious at the conclusion of this tribal debate, where a reference to the expatriation of the rebels to a distant colony takes the narrative back to historical events in Quebec after the Rebellions of 1837–38. However, in a later chapter, the story of Cheval Rétif and his tribe, the Siffleux, foregrounds once again the issue of the referendum. Cheval Rétif, who resembles René Lévesque, decides to hold a referendum on political sovereignty. Rich merchants, "des zanglais," spread rumours about economic hardship if the "Yes" vote wins. When the votes are counted, half of Cheval Rétif's tribe has voted "No," and a few "zanglais" votes are sufficient to turn down Cheval Rétif's project (La Tribu, 283–4). In an obviously parodic reference to René Lévesque's text, Option Québec, the narrator manages to mock the literary industry, oppose literacy to aurality, and through his use of parodic humour, pose and then challenge the question of political independence: "Cheval Rétif organisa des réunions publiques, des manifestations, écrivit même un livre qui fut le premier livre écrit en siffleux, et qui s'intitulait Je veux un pays pour les Siffleux, parce que tant que les Siffleux n'auront pas leur pays à eux seuls, ils devront se soumettre à la volonté des Zanglais qui sont bien plus nombreux. Personne ne lui avait jamais dit qu'un titre de livre devait être court, mais cela n'empêcha pas son livre de lui valoir l'estime de tous les Siffleux qui savaient lire – et de tous ceux qui savaient écouter ceux qui savaient lire" (282). *La Tribu*, then, retells – sometimes more than once – a selected number of significant political events of the near and distant past of Québec, thinly disguising these events in bizarre stories about encounters between primitive tribes from a mythical past and non-indigenous peoples. This reworking of Quebec's political history illustrates the flexibility of New World Myth. The narrator adopts and then adapts Québécois history in his fictional move to reclaim the past: the "history," such as it is, is integrated into the stories about "primitive" Clipocs.

Carpentier's insistence on the marvellousness of New World history-in-the-making is echoed in *La Tribu*'s opening story about Admiral Le Corton. The narrator begins by underlining, over several paragraphs, the unreliability of historical records about this character's name and then proposes to "laisser le lecteur juger de l'hypothèse qu'il préfère retenir – ou même toutes les rejeter, ce qui n'aurait d'ailleurs aucune influence sur la compréhension du reste de ce récit" (32). Having thus posited the superiority of story over historical records, the narrator recounts Le Corton's extreme disappointment when he first sights the New World and the effect the hostile coast has on the imagination of this usually rational explorer, whose principal desire is supposedly to seek out truth (37). The land he sees before him does not correspond to the descriptions in other explorers' journals, and Le Corton begins to doubt the reliability of these documents. Soon, however, he too begins to imagine strange creatures: huge birds, enormous trees, and even four-legged human beings in the undergrowth (12–13). The narrator explains how Le Corton finally decides to stick to the "truth," so that he will be the first to be cited in history books for his honest descriptions of the New World (13). Subverting this explanation, the narrator then gives examples of the Le Corton's textual embellishment of his journals and of his constant temptation to alter the facts (15). Le Corton's prolific memoirs are ridiculed by his contemporaries because they are considered far too factual, and they are in fact forgotten at the time of his death. Four centuries later, they are published, and the reviewers reproach Le Corton for his exaggeration of the facts (42–3). This story, then, fulfils a double function: it casts doubt on the authenticity and the credibility of historical records, and it also underlines the magical difference of this bizarre, unusual New World, and the effects of its strangeness on rational European thought. Fantastic elements in the text, such as various characters' metaphysical conversations with a common garter snake and Indians paddling out of the fog to the tune of a French/Québécois folk-song, "A la claire fontaine," lend an aura of make-believe to the novel. At the same time, the insertion of real-life historical events into the narrative suggests that these events are in some way not mere history but are imbued with that same aura of the magical.

In *La Tribu*, the narrator flaunts his blatant claim to the right to reinvent the past, even while underlining that it is impossible for *any* historian or storyteller to know and tell completely "what really happened." For instance, in the following parodic retelling of the deaths of characters who parody Wolfe and Montcalm, the narrator first implies that he is only repeating "historic" words supposedly uttered by the generals, and then implies that, since historians invented them anyway, he has every right to change them if he so desires:

Blessé à mort par un boulet de canon, [le marquis-général de Trompart] eut quand même une bonne heure pour songer à une parole historique à prononcer avant de rendre l'âme. Peu imaginatif, il ne put trouver mieux que:
   "Je meurs heureux, car même si je sais que les Zanglais vont prendre la ville, ils ne l'ont point encore prise. Et si mes hommes doivent se rendre, ce n'est point moi que les aurai alors commandés."
   Pendant ce temps, au pied des remparts, touché lui aussi à mort mais par une balle perdue, l'amiral Blackburn disait dans son dernier souffle:
   "Comme il est dommage que Balbuk ne tombe que lorsque je serai mort. Mais il est heureux que je sache avant de mourir que Balbuk tombera."
   Il est surtout heureux que les historiens écrivent mieux que les militaires ne parlent. (204)

These fictional renditions of the leaders' dying words are in fact deliberately awkward and lengthy adaptations of the "historically authentic" phrases contained in standard history texts. Thus, informed of his imminent death, Montcalm is quoted as saying, "Tant mieux! Je ne verrai pas les Anglais dans Québec." Wolfe supposedly said, "Now, God be praised. Since I have conquered, I will die in peace."[10] The fictional retelling, then, foregrounds the narratorial manipulation of what may well be, after all, phrases invented by historians to import glory to dying European generals. *La Tribu*'s narrator, while casting doubt here on the authenticity of historical records, paradoxically implies that he is perhaps only setting the record straight.

This passage, which parodies the Battle of the Plains of Abraham, refers to the British presence in North America. Curiously, very few passages of *La Tribu* dwell on the colonization of the francophone *Canadiens* by the British. Indeed, the effects of the British presence are minimized: "Quant à la tribu, ayant peu de contacts avec les Vieux-Paysans des villages voisins, elle en eut encore moins avec les rares Zanglais de la contrée, et ne fut aucunement consciente de la conquête" (211). *La Tribu's* narrator appears to be more interested in the French/Québécois/Amerindian link than in the British/English Canadian/Québécois link. In a sense, this interest underlines the need in Québécois New World Myth to rework *French*-shaped history – to rewrite the traditional *patrie*-centred historical myths that have outworn their utility, in short, to decolonize the mind.

Another postcolonial element in this text is its use of humour in its discussions of Québécois history – humour that is suggestive of a certain political maturity. As Steve Linstead has noted, humour can constitute a challenge to traditional myths about our past(s). He suggests that myth forms are so familiar in everyday society that they are easily maintained. To challenge traditional myths, however, requires much energy and creativity ("'Jokers Wild,'" 127). Deliberate humour is one method of provoking that challenge, because, as Mary Douglas argues, jokes, by their very nature, imply that all ordering of experience is discretionary and arbitrary (*Implicit Meanings*, 90–114). Rick Salutin, discussing what he perceives to be the marginal situation of Canadian culture and politics, proposes that "the place where marginality inevitably aches is politics" (*Marginal Notes*, 5). *La Tribu's* humorous approach to recognizable political (especially "nationalistic") foibles, however, is indicative of its deliberate *non*-marginalization of Québécois history and politics. A nation's ability to laugh at its own political history and aspirations, is, I would suggest, part of the distancing process necessary to the development of a postcolonial state of mind.

The narrator of *La Tribu* revels in his capricious treatment of the vicissitudes of Québécois history. The flaunting of political humour in this New World Myth text may well be indicative of a significant change in contemporary Québécois society. In a special number of *Thalia* devoted to Québécois humour, Pierre Hébert argues that until quite recently the "peuple [canadien-français] ... a converti sa situation de dominé et de dépossédé en vocation messianique" ("Le *Journal d'un Inquisiteur* de Gilles Leclerc," 7) and that this worldview was an impediment to a humorous, and therefore mature, self-evaluation: "Résumons-nous. Le peuple canadien-français, bafoué par l'histoire, s'est cru élu de Dieu, et s'est donné de son destin une image à ce point vaniteuse qu'elle a déclenché le rire de tout son entourage, sauf de lui-méme, crispé, tendu, réducteur. Le sens de l'humour n'est donc pas son fort" (10). Barcelo's humorous historiographic novel, which also contains a strong New World Myth parody of the Christ figure and of biblical mythology, flaunts its rejection of the traditional "givens" discussed in chapter 1. Self-critical political humour and postcolonialism go hand-in-hand here. Beverly Rasporich writes: "Struggling to release himself from colonial forms, literary or cultural, in order to realize his own identity, the continental Canadian gravitates to parody. What is continually parodied in Canadian literary humour is the New Eden, New World dream of common immigrant experience which, historically, has been fostered by the religious and romantic visions of many of Canada's colonizers" ("Literary Humour," 38). In its particular humorous rewriting and reclaiming of traditional (hi)stories, *La Tribu*'s humourous parodies of historical events are indicative of a strong postcolonial slant. Its narrator, while mocking the seriousness of those whose messianic drive was to be the "élus de Dieu" or, later, those who wrote in order to "nommer le pays," flaunts the indeterminacy of history and foregrounds both his playful adaptation – and serious undercutting – of "primitive" myth in his overt construction of a postcolonial worldview.

In addition, *La Tribu*'s fictional representation of the past incorporates a reflection on sociopolitical concerns of the decade in which the novel was published. The narrator not only comments ironically on the former patronizing attitude of the Europeans vis-à-vis the New World but also satirizes the New World's equally patronizing treatment of its own indigenous peoples, of its immigrants, and of Third World nations. Thus, in a parodic reference to the Canadian gift of indigestible food to famine-stricken areas of Africa, Mahii proposes "qu'a tout le moins on offrit aux Niox ... des surplus de lait en poudre lorsque la faim les tenaillerait" (129). Other current sociopolitical issues, such as anti-Semitism, religious fundamentalism, immigration, and feminism are ironically signalled in various stories here. As we have seen, this New World Myth text demonstrates an openness toward cultural multiplicity by underlining the constantly changing cultural identity of the Clipocs. Elsewhere in the text, in a "parenthèse contemporaine," the narrator – whose name is similar to that of the author – insists on the diversity of his own ethnic, linguistic, and religious background: "je ne pus refréner un léger frisson (de fierté peut-être?) de me sentir à la fois espagnol, canadien-français et juif" (170). This insistence on cross-cultural awareness is characteristic of New World Myth.

La Tribu, then, through its frequently parodic retellings of past events, promotes a heterogeneous approach to sociopolitical history and constantly blurs events of the past with those of the present. This novel also foregrounds the themes which Slemon and Hancock have posited as characteristic of a magic realist postcolonial work: the language issue; the foreshortening of history; the group as representative of a whole; parodies of government and politicians; and absurd re-creations of history which seek to destabilize the fixity of any one point of view.

George Bowering's oxymoronically entitled *Burning Water* also offers a postcolonial challenge to traditional versions of our historical past(s). This narrative, which draws on magic realist conventions, retells the adventures of the European explorer George Vancouver and his charting expedition along the West Coast of the New World in the late eighteenth century. Bowering was born in the Okanagan Valley of British Columbia; he is a prolific Vancouver-based poet, novelist, and critic. In *George Bowering: Bright Circles of Colour*, Eva-Marie Kröller, following Bowering, outlines overlapping critical phases that can serve as loose guidelines to his work (114–15).[11] Bowering, unlike many other English-speaking Canadian writers of fiction, is often perceived as being highly controversial, as Kröller notes: "Bowering has persistently subjected his literary and personal reputation to the same deconstruction as his work" (112). Discussing the portrayal of the author on the jacket of *Mirror on the Floor* (1967), she notes that Bowering "appears less as a detached creator of his work than as a fragment contained in it" (113). Bowering has metafictively described himself as "an ongoing verb" (*Errata*, 7). He is well known for his opposition to the power wielded by the literary establishment in Eastern (really, Central) Canada and for his enthusiastic admiration of American experimental poets, especially Charles Olson. Although sometimes disparaged by academic critics, Bowering is very active in literary circles and has even infiltrated – a word he would probably appreciate – "the very academic institution that he often professes to despise," teaching at Simon Fraser University and lecturing in many other academic institutions (Kröller, *Bright Circles*, 121).

Bowering's sense of humour, his love of play, his explorations of postmodernist techniques, his use of pseudonyms, and his constant adaptations of his own life-story have been extensively reviewed, condemned – and appreciated. His frequent use of parody and humour, especially in his revision of history, has sometimes been seen as problematic, and his tendency to downplay the "seriousness" of his work has probably added to the mixed reception he and his work have received. In his investigation of parody in Bowering's *A Short Sad Book*, Martin Kuester associates Bowering's ludic postmodernism with a lack of seriousness: "Although the metafictional comments about the writing of a novel and the metahistorical comments about the writing of history go in the same direction as some of the conclusions drawn from Timothy Findley's writing, there does not seem to be the same kind of commitment and seriousness behind the persona of Bowering's narrator. This may well be due to the different – more ludic – attitude that a confessed post-modernist such as Bowering has towards questions of history and historicity" (*Framing Truths*, 105). Kuester concludes his work on parody in *Burning Water* by insisting that Bowering's strength lies "in the admirable structural acrobatics of parody rather than in the political arguments that are the intention behind these parodies" (123).

Other critics, however, take an opposite stance. Glenn Deer advances the notion that "Bowering is unmistakably a highly playful and intertextually sophisticated creator of postmodern works. Yet there are deeper political and ethical components in his writing as well, even though he is reluctant to be explicit on these matters: his writings can be read as often giving voice to those groups that have traditionally been marginalized or disempowered in the popular literary forms – women, ethnic minorities, and natives in the Western in *Caprice*, for example – and often imply that the violence, competition, ethnocentrism, and misogyny inherent in popular forms can be challenged and subverted through comedy" (*Postmodern Canadian Fiction*, 97). And Russell Brown argues that Bowering's jokes do not refute the seriousness of the joker: "the truth about Bowering is contained at the beginning of his essay on David McFadden: 'He was joking, but he was not kidding'" (Brown, "Words, Places, Craft," 47; Bowering, "Proofing the World," 184). Bowering himself has reflected on the uneasy relationship between the reading public and the popularity of historiographic fictions in Canada, although he tends to maintain a third-person stance when it comes to commenting about his own position in the parody/history/fiction debate: "Canadians intent on discovering themselves and exploring their time have been slow to welcome the unreliable and the capricious in their writing, to respect the author who invents rather than obeying" ("A Great Northward Darkness," 2).

Many initial English Canadian reviews of *Burning Water* strongly criticized its author's inventions and lack of "obedience," targeting the novel's humour, its irreverence, its historical inaccuracies, and its attempts to set up a dialogue about the act of novel writing. It was not taken seriously because it was felt that it did not take itself seriously. Kuester remarks that "Bowering's novels did not receive very much critical attention before *Burning Water* won the 1980 Governor General's Award, and a fellow writer of historical fiction, Chris Scott, even denied this latter work the status (if there be any attached) of being a historical novel" (Scott, "A Bum Rap," 96). The outrage the novel provoked, however, was most probably due to an attack on the establishment at a deeper, mythological level, as Kröller has observed: "A text such as *Burning Water* is suspected, and rightly so, of sabotaging the enterprise of a cohesive Canadian mythology, hence a cohesive national identity, a concern much fueled by the activities of the Centennial decade" (*Bright Circles*, 118). Thus, the critics' indictment of the novel is a reaction, suggests Kröller, to "an act of treason against an episode in Canadian history which, together with other voyages and explorers' tales, doubles as a founding myth" (117).

The initial francophone and postcolonial receptions of *Burning Water* were more enthusiastic, perhaps because their authors were less implicated culturally and mythologically. In Quebec, Michel Beaulieu ("Le Canada existe-t-il?" 47, 49) praised Bowering's innovative versatility, and René Lapierre's review of the French version, *En eaux troubles*, was enthusiastic. The very title of Lapierre's review, "Appelez-moi George," contains an overt reference to "Appelez-moi Lise," the highly influential, highly political television talk show hosted on Radio-Canada during the turbulent 1970s by Lise Payette, a former minister of the Parti Québécois cabinet. Lapierre, then, noted the strong political dimension of Bowering's work. And Kuester notes that in New Zealand, "a country that shares some important postcolonial features with Canada … the reception of *Burning Water* was quite positive" (*Framing Truths*, 107). The fact that several in-depth critical studies of *Burning Water* have appeared in the 1990s, more than a decade after the novel was published, points to its importance as a text in which, as Kröller suggests, "postmodernist scepticism toward the mimetic ability of language has been placed at the service of defining the role of fiction in a post-colonial context" (*Bright Circles*, 92).

In *Burning Water* it is often the Amerindian presence that, somewhat ironically, provides a forum for those aspects of magic realist, postcolonial works discussed above. Margery Fee argues that nationalism is the "major ideological drive behind the use of the Indian" in contemporary English Canadian literature, and she links this use to Romanticism as a literary movement and to "its related political ideology," nationalism. Fee notes that the "many New World colonial and post-colonial writers who work within this theory ... find themselves hampered by the bad fit between Old World Romantic theory and the New World situation" ("Romantic Nationalism," 17). At the time of publication of *Burning Water*, Bowering had distanced himself from the kind of writing that articulates a "national identity" and that seeks to create heroes out of figures from the past: "I am utterly bored by ... all that business of saying, 'Let's go and find a Canadian hero like Riel and write a play or an opera or a long poem or a novel about him.' All you had to do to have a hit Canadian play during the past five years was to have a one-word title and that one word would be the name of some famous priest or RCMP officer or politician or Indian or whatever" (Leitch, "Interview," 30). As Kröller notes, "Bowering resists the 'culture-fixing'[12] which often accompanies attempts at national self-definition, and his text sabotages the easy equations he found offensive in Northrop Frye and Margaret Atwood's criticism ... The obsessive search for a cultural identity and a unifying myth which characterizes Canadian thematic criticism becomes a futile endeavour indeed if the subject itself cannot be trusted to remain stable" (*Bright Circles*, 56). Although Kröller's remarks here concern Bowering's *A Short Sad Book*, they are equally applicable to *Burning Water*.

In what he himself calls his historical novel, Bowering's use of the Amerindian figure as an element of postcolonial discourse is problematic (Leitch, "Interview," 30). On the one hand, the conversations among "Indians" in *Burning Water* subvert the European clichés of the monosyllabic savage; mock the Eurocentric, anthropological image of the myth-laden primitive; disrupt the notion of the progressive flow of historical time; and upset the colonizer/colonized dichotomy. On the other hand, while Bowering's play with language in the novel does indicate his interest in the problematics of communication and translation between different linguistic and cultural groups, the Indian figure is used to illustrate mainly non-Amerindian points of view. Indeed, Bowering's choice of vocabulary may itself constitute part of his extended parody, given the frequently negative connotations associated with the very term Indian in Canada. Thus, Daniel Francis: "Indians, as we think we know them, do not exist. If fact, there may well be no such thing as an Indian.... The Indian began as a White man's mistake, and became a White man's fantasy" (*The*

Imaginary Indian, 4–5). Terry Goldie has outlined the difficulties of vocabulary – and ideology – when it comes to representing the "Indian" in (English) Canadian literature ("Getting It Right," 80). Goldie argues that the "literary Indian is not the Indian. [Edward] Said makes the point, however, that while the image is not 'real,' the value of the image has a 'reality' in its reflection of the cultural values both of the writers and of the cultures in which the writers live" (Goldie, "Signs of the Themes," 84–5). Bowering's use of parody further complicates his fictional representation of the Amerindian. As Hutcheon has noted, there are inevitable complicities and complexities in the use of parody: while the postmodern period, like that of the sixteenth century, is marked by a "sense of ideological instability, of a challenging of norms ... parody today can be both progressive and regressive" (*Theory of Parody*, 82). I return to Bowering's parodic use of the Amerindian below, in my further discussion of language and postcolonialism.

Although *Burning Water* is not primarily a magic realist text, as its emphasis lies more heavily on historiography and metafictionality, its narrator does make extensive use of several magic realist techniques. Vancouver's explorations of the marvellous New World, as described by Bowering's narrator, provide a forum for contrasting Western rationality, inherited from eighteenth-century European thought, with the "magic worldview" of the Amerindians (Pache, "Fiction Makes Us Real," 73). As we have seen, Carpentier's concept of myth in the New World is that it is in flux – being created in the here and now – and that it is linked to historico-political reality (*El reino*, 55).

Bowering's reflections on myth support the flexibility of myth in a New World setting. In an early article, cited below, he divides Canadian poets into the "Fryed" and the "raw," parodically echoing the title of Claude Lévi-Strauss's study *The Raw and the Cooked*. Bowering's criticism of Northrop Frye's literary theories permits the novelist to formulate his *own* concept of the relationship of myth, literature, and life: "As a poet, I feel it impossible to agree with Frye that my writing looks either up toward heaven or down to hell, never horizontally at life ... Myth is the imaginative base of culture, and culture is not alive if it is not being formed with the materials and shapes available to the senses. The literary mind thinks about past culture, but to copy the modes of past culture is to give oneself over to time, where gods and giants are only reported, never met. They must be met in the here and now" ("Why James Reaney," 45–6). Rejecting the history/real world/myth separation, Bowering praises James Reaney for making myth from local materials (48). He then cites a poem of Reaney's for its discussion of the onomastics of the Avon River: "What did the Indians call you? / For you do not flow / With English accents" (Reaney, "To the Avon River," 1). Bowering comments: "I find two things important here – the *personal* pronoun and the determination to find myth with the senses, the taste of water in cupped hands, not the idea of a sacred Greek or English stream … Not Noah of the book, but Reaney of the river, is the prototype of this myth's beginning (and middle, anyway)" (49). This is New World discourse. In New World Myth, there is no such thing as an ultimate, teleological goal; the myth has a beginning and a middle, but no end. Bowering's concept of myth, as early as 1968, concerns the writer's personal need to recreate the world, to move the setting from England or Greece to the here and now, to lay bare the deliberate construction of New World Myth, and to foreground a postcolonial worldview.

Burning Water begins with a page of acknowledgments where Bowering gives sources for quotations in the text, a dedication, "if he does not mind," to George Whalley, and a prologue in which the speaker ties his subject matter, Vancouver's navigational voyage, to himself, to George Bowering, and ultimately, to *us*, the readers of the text. The novel is divided into three parts, of almost equal length, and consists of fifty-eight short chapters: 1–59. As in his other works, due to his superstitious dislike of the number 52, there is no chapter 52 in *Burning Water*, a fact that seems to excessively perturb many of Bowering's critics. The speaker in the prologue insists upon the communal effort of this recreation of the past: "We are making a story, after all, as we always have been, standing and speaking together to make up a history, a real historical fiction." The ambiguous "I" of the prologue becomes the ambiguous "he" of the text. In the following discussion, I maintain the distinction between George Bowering, the author, and the ambiguous I/he narrator. This is not because of the influence of what Bowering has called, again in reaction to Frye's theories of literature and myth criticism, the "closet fiction of the New Criticism, the idea that the poem is entirely self-contained" ("James Reaney," 45), but because this study explicitly explores the *narratorial* manipulations of history and myth. In the same way, the "Vancouver" and other characters referred to here are Bowering's fictional creations, except when I make explicit reference to the historical figures he parodies.

In the first chapter of *Burning Water*, two Indians sight Vancouver's ships off the coast and start a debate as to whether they are facts or visions. The fact/fancy/imagination debate, which recalls a well-known passage in Samuel Taylor Coleridge's *Biographia Literaria*

(1817), is thematized throughout the text, emphasizing the narrator's control over his particular recreation of this (hi)story. Vancouver's mission is to "chart the coast, be friendly but firm with the Spanish, and if he had any time left over, keep an eye open for gold and the Northwest Passage" (26). His crew is hand-picked, with the exception of Archibald Menzies, the civilian botanist who is imposed on him by the British Royal Society and whose presence is a source of constant torment to the captain. Vancouver is proud of being a representative of the British crown, settling disputes among the Indians by imposing British justice on them. Above all else, he is proud of the precision and beauty of his cartography: "Map making, one would assume on hearing his tone, perfectly combined the vocations of making high art and saving souls" (77).

According to treaties signed in Europe, Vancouver is to take over the command of Nootka and all the Pacific Coast to the north. During his sojourn, Vancouver meets Don Juan Bodega y Quadra, the naval commander-in-chief of the Spanish forces. Quadra becomes his lover and gradually replaces Sir James Cook as Vancouver's mentor and spiritual father. Vancouver's health grows progressively worse as the voyage continues, and he has increasing difficulty maintaining control over his temper and his frail body. The strong dislike he feels for Menzies, the aggressiveness of some of the Indians, and the news of Quadra's death all contribute to his sense of isolation and his lack of decorum at the fictional version of the end of his explorations. Vancouver's increasingly erratic behaviour prompts Menzies and the crew to question his mental stability. Finally, Menzies has a tremendous argument with Vancouver, on whom he blames the destruction of his extensive botanical collection. The novel ends with Menzies' shooting of the captain; in the last sentence of the text, Vancouver seems "to be lifted by some strength unwitnessed, over the rail and into the unsolicitous sea" (258).

Practically every review of *Burning Water* has noted that the historical Vancouver did not die at sea but in his own bed in England. Other inaccuracies are the homosexual relationship between Quadra and Vancouver and a lack of correspondence between historical dates. Aritha van Herk notes that *Burning Water* "distorts the facts of Vancouver's life so much that when the book appeared, there was a minor uproar, with historians and biographers falling over themselves to prove how wrong Bowering was" ("Mapping as Metaphor," 82). Kuester suggests that Bowering's rearranging of the "original order of [his] source material" (which consists of the historical Vancouver's journals and those of his crew) makes "his readers lose any sense of chronology based on the European calendar, a standard foreign to the regions Vancouver explored" (*Framing Truths*, 106). Historical inaccuracies, sometimes pointed out by ironic narratorial commentary, lead the reader to be wary of all "history" in this book. Magic realist happenings, such as the "flight of fancy" in the central chapter of the novel where Vancouver, his men, and his ships, searching for the elusive Northwest Passage, fly over the Rockies and land in Hudson's Bay, provoke a similar wariness regarding this retelling of Vancouver's explorations. The textual incorporation of passages "borrowed" from the writings of the historical George Vancouver and other officers of his expedition creates the tension inherent in New World Myth texts by contrasting historically authentic documents with historically impossible facts. *Burning Water*'s use of fantasy corresponds to Slemon's comments ("Magic Realism," 10–11) regarding the realism/fantasy opposition in a postcolonial magic realist work: in such a text, a battle occurs between two opposing systems of narration, with each system striving to create a different fictional world. In Bowering's story, those passages that appear to contain historically authentic documents and those that describe Vancouver's voyage in realistic terms are engaged in a battle with the more fantastic elements such as the Hudson's Bay "flight."

Through their thematization of cartography, Bowering's and Barcelo's novels mock the European explorers' efforts to impose order on the New World. Narratorial play with the concept of cartography foregrounds the text's play with the notion of borders and centres (Slemon, "Magic Realism," 13). In *La Tribu*, the young Le Corton draws a map of the world based on the travels of his sailor-uncle. When he realizes that his uncle is inventing his stories, he destroys this map, although according to the narrator it was almost the equal of those of the talented geographers of the time – that is to say, scarcely more fanciful (34). Le Corton then begins another map, based on the records of the explorers of the period. He quickly realizes that these explorers contradict one another and that they are as untruthful as his uncle (35). In any case, that section of the New World where Admiral Le Corton drops anchor many years later, north of the areas plotted by "les Zespagnols" and "les Zanglais," has never been mapped. The narrator implies that to the European explorer the New World is threatening because of the fearful uncertainty it represents. To New World peoples, however, freedom is implicit in the notion of unmapped territory.

Noting that mapping as a motif occurs repeatedly in English Canadian literature, Aritha van Herk proposes that cartography, like language, is "creation more than representation … The only way a country can be truly mapped is with its stories" ("Mapping," 77).

Burning Water's narrator does indeed privilege the literary imagination over the "facts" of cartography: "It was only because I had put
my own eyes into the poem and its story that those rocks and shoals
were actual enough to make exploration worthwhile" (prologue).
His constant play with the various locations of the Strait of Anian in
his own text is one way in which he foregrounds the unreliability of
maps. The narrator finds this body of water on a painted sixteenth-
century map in the old palace in Trieste (36); he then claims that it
is mentioned in an "untowardly ribald passage," which, we are
given to understand, is in Vancouver's journals (52); finally, he presents it as the Indians' "holy Strait of Anian, which no invader has
ever been able to find" (94). In other words, this strait of water can
be anywhere the narrator wants it to be.

The tension between fiction and reality inherent in New World
Myth texts is also evident in the fictional Vancouver's treatment of
cartography. First, it is ironic, as van Herk points out, that in spite of
his self-proclaimed ability to trace the North Pacific coast "true," the
historical Vancouver did not find the mouths of the Columbia and
the Fraser Rivers, either of which could have provided him with the
Northwest Passage he sought ("Mapping," 82). Second, although we
are told in *Burning Water* that Vancouver "loved the simple, the neat,
the straightforward" (58) and that he was capable of charting the
twisty edge of the North Pacific "as no more even and no more odd
than it was" (59), the novel also underlines Vancouver's admitted
ideological manipulation of geographico-political "facts" in the passage about the location of Los Mojos – a group of islands supposedly
"discovered" by the Spanish before Vancouver's voyage. When Menzies' calculations reveal that Los Mojos are most probably the British
Sandwich islands, Vancouver, that official cartographer and lover of
facts, responds to Menzies' query in this way: "If Los Mojos are not
there [that is, a few hundred miles east of the Sandwich Islands],
then the Spaniards were visitors to the Sandwich Islands before
James Cook landed there, and that would not be an acceptable fact
in my view of history" (202).

Maps, then, can be adapted to fit any number of "factual" versions
of political history. Narratorial play with the concept of mapping
here thematizes both the unreliability of so-called authentic historical
documents and the resistance of the New World to any efforts to
impose a systematic grid on it. Thus, in a passage reminiscent of the
Clipocs exploding the *vieux-paysan* ship, a Capilano, mocked by a
crew member as a "noble savage" allowed to have "one boom
boom," fires a European musket and shoots "the table that Puget's
chart was on, and the chart along with most of the table was blown

into shreds" (*Burning Water*, 131). *Burning Water*'s rejection of the eighteenth-century Europeans' admiration of order and rationality, then, supports van Herk's notion that the imagination plays a role in cartography: human beings do not transcribe only the world they see but also the work their imagination performs on that "reality." In the following passage, *Burning Water*'s narrator notes the effect of the New World's marvellous reality on the civilized European explorer, who cannot totally adjust to what is, to him, the fantastic geography of this strange place: "A sailor from Britain must always know that experience [of seeing the New World] as the resolute image of the foreign. Coming from a civilized arrangement of chalk cliffs to mark an edge, and the flat greenery with reasonable fences, and trees grouped around church or house, a greenery that stretched inward from that white edge, a Briton comes to mountains miles high as if to islands on the moon. Might as easily conceive the sails as wings, and fly to a meeting on the moon" (106–7).

We have seen how the retelling of the Wolfe/Montcalm conflict in *La Tribu* highlights the narratorial urge to rework the story in order to jar conventional acceptance of traditional versions of history. *Burning Water* reexamines – and reworks – the same episode. In Bowering's anachronistic story, Vancouver's anger toward the French supposedly stems from the fact that they killed his friend, James Wolfe, during the Franco-British conflict over Quebec City. The historical George Vancouver, however, was two years old at the time of the Battle of the Plains of Abraham, and could not have met Wolfe. The following passage, where Quadra is consoling Vancouver over Wolfe's death, refers in the future tense to events of the more recent past, such as Benjamin West's artistic rendering of the death scene on the battlefield and once-famous ballads about the exploits of "England's greatest military commander" (29). Even if the parody contained in Quadra's reassurances about the "secure place in history" that Wolfe will occupy is lost on the average reader – possibly because of a lack of "historical" knowledge – the implied narratorial address to the reader ("You") and Quadra's apparent ignorance of the time preceding Wolfe's death lay bare the precise lack of security that historiographic texts such as *Burning Water* occasion:

"He died on the ground, on *their* Goddamned ground … "
You can see what kind of state he was getting into …
"But try to look at it this way, George. He will have a secure place in history. They will paint pictures of his triumphant death, with his body fully-clothed in the colours of his homeland. They will write great poems and

perhaps songs about him. His name will live forever in that land. Have they decided on a name for it yet?" (29)

Of course, in the preceding historical period "that land" had a name – la Nouvelle France – and a historico-political past. Furthermore, the presence of the Indians in the text is a constant reminder of yet another unrecorded past: the Amerindian one. Both Bowering's and Barcelo's texts, then, overtly foreground their narrators' manipulation of "the facts" regarding this significant New World conflict between Montcalm and Wolfe, and both passages emphasize the blurring of time-frames between the eighteenth and twentieth centuries.

A slippage between historical time periods, which allows for polit-ical commentary on events of the present day in a supposedly his-torical narrative, is foregrounded in *Burning Water*, especially in the ubiquitous contrast between the fictional portraits of eighteenth-century historical figures and the twentieth-century narrator and Amerindians. Trading with a white man, two Indians refuse whiskey and guns, and are then asked, "You want to trade some waterfront property for some mirrors and necklaces?" (200) – an overt reference to the expensive waterfront properties of the city of Vancouver owned by First Nations today. As is the case in *La Tribu*, this text incorporates a reflection on the political concerns of the present age in its fictional representation of its past. A foreshortening of history is one way texts mediate the social relations of postcolonial cultures. The blurring of historical periods and the blatant and parodic adap-tations of the "traditional" stories about this event also mediate a need to imaginatively lay claim to the past from a postcolonial point of view.

Whereas *La Tribu*'s primary narrative recounts the adventures of an indigenous group, *Burning Water*'s narrator appears to focus mainly on the experiences of Old World explorers and *their* perceptions of the geography and the indigenous populations of the New World. How then can this text thematize a postcolonial retelling of history? A surprising number of passages in *Burning Water* contain stories about the New World's indigenous peoples. As is the case with *La Tribu*, these stories parody traditional clichés about "primitive" Amerindians, poking fun at supposedly elementary motivations, such as the desire to become "a full man of the tribe" (15) and upset-ting the colonizer/colonized dichotomy. Together with the obviously twentieth-century narratorial commentary, these passages ensure a reworking of history from a contemporary New World viewpoint. For instance, in this passage describing a "friendly meeting, more or less" (140) between Vancouver's party and an Indian tribe, the Indian's query may well be a parodic rendering of the Freudian question regarding women's needs and also, and more relevantly, a parody of the frequent prereferendum question "What does Quebec really want?"

"What does the white man want?" asked the first Indian [...]
Vancouver did not want to place his contingent higher than the Red Men. He was a little surprised when Tyee Cheslakees arranged things so that the Indians were seated a little higher up the slope.
"They haven't said yet," said the second Indian. "So far they have just been going through their elaborate greetings and ceremonial preparations. We have learned not to rush them directly into business or they would feel insulted." (140)

This cultural reversal, with the Indians adopting the paternalist attitudes historically attributed to Europeans' first contacts with Amerindians, is typical of the many Amerindian/non-Amerindian encounters in the text. Although the wording of the first sentence of the above passage points to the "intertext" of Québécois politics, and although there are a few allusions to Québécois in the text, *Burning Water*'s story is much more focused on its reshaping of the British-inspired history of the West Coast than it is on the English Canadian/Québécois polarity. In this it resembles *La Tribu*, whose story focuses primarily on the retelling of the history of francophones in North America, only infrequently referring to the English Canadian presence in Quebec. Both texts, then, are rewriting traditional nation-centered founding myths in their efforts to decolonize the mind.

Language issues, which frequently are thematized in postcolonial works, are underlined doubly in *Burning Water*. Vancouver is portrayed as an imperialist explorer, capable of mastering "a naked foreigner's tongue" (42) in order to establish some form of control or government but incapable of grasping the idea that "languages have purposes beyond allowing one man to tell the other his demands upon his behaviour" (42). Even Menzies, that paradigmatic eighteenth-century man, recognizes in Vancouver's lack of appreciation of totem poles that his grasp of the indigenous "languages" is limited to a useful imperialist tool. The second and perhaps stronger thematization of the language issue is the Indians' anachronistic flaunting of twentieth-century psychological jargon and contemporary obscenities. As Susan Lynne Knutson points out in her study of communication strategies in *Burning Water*, Bowering's portrayal of Menzies' fluent Nootka and of the Amerindians' elegant English prose and twentieth-century vernacular is as "nonrealistic, in its own way, as is Vancouver's vision of sailing across the Rocky Mountains" ("Bowering and Melville on Benjamin's Wharf," 75). Most conversations among Amerindians or between Amerindians and non-Amerindians not only subvert the cliché of the unsophisticated and uneducated "savage" but parody "truths" of the non-indigenous colonizers:

"There you go, speaking out of some habitual framework of guilt. I think you *want* to be punished. I think you enjoy your private sins so much that you desire some confirmation of them, and so you walk around all the time with your shoulders hunched and your eyes looking up guiltily, waiting for Koaxkoaxanuxiwae to poke his beak into the top of your head."

"Okay, not to punish us. Maybe to bring us news of a wonderful new life? ... "

"There is an old Haida saying I have heard ... that says, history will repeat its unhappiest hours upon those who do not remember what happened the first time." (92–4)

The reference to Spinoza's famous saying about history repeating itself is attributed here to the Haida, thus undercutting Western philosophy and the notion of teleological history. While this passage's ironic mixing of the popular psychology of the 1980s with a revision of philosophy may constitute a "way of casting off identity clichés imposed from outside" (Pache, "Fiction," 74), it also undercuts the notion of the superiority of white, European men over "primitive," indigenous peoples. The Indians speak more like twentieth-century Vancouverites than "primitives." By contrasting their agreeable, idiomatic, and familiar conversations with stilted passages supposedly taken from eighteenth-century journals – whose authors, the narrator notes, "were fond of nouns and Latinate abstractions" (101) – this text installs a linguistic tension between "them" (the eighteenth-century British) and "us" (people who sound like twentieth-century inhabitants of the New World). This opposition, of course, is ironic – and political – in that the "us" are Amerindians who have almost lost their voice in "our" New World culture.

Many readings of *Burning Water* simply occult any discussion of the presence of the Indian figure within the text, choosing rather to explore the novel's strong metafictional aspects. Others, perhaps more politically engaged, do address the novel's use of the image of the Amerindian, with varying results. Does Bowering's use of the

Indian construct continue Western imperialist practices with their ideological implications, or is it rather "endowed with the power to renew" (Hutcheon, *Theory of Parody*, 110, 115)? Much depends on the difficulty of determining "Bowering's idiosyncratic way of expressing his opinions and defining his own version of postmodern narrative" (Pache, "Fiction," 73). Whereas Goldie claims that in the context of non-Amerindian English Canadian literature, "the semiosis in which native peoples are presented is under the control of the white signmakers" ("Signs," 86), Kuester argues that it is in their very blatancy that Bowering's parodies critically foreground the usual deficient treatment of indigenous peoples in Canadian historical fiction (*Framing Truths*, 118). Knutson also sees Bowering as engagé: "Bowering indicates his awareness of the problems surrounding communication and translation at a critical point in history; and he employs a variety of strategies intended, I think, to undercut racist stereotypes, and to indicate the complexity surrounding the real possibilities of transcending them" ("Bowering and Melville," 68). As does Kuester, Knutson argues for the importance of reading Bowering's parodies in the context of the parodied texts, such as Melville's *Moby Dick*, and of comparing Melville's textual "erasure or repression" of, for instance, homosexuality, with the "playful parody [with which] Bowering's text seems to confront Melville's evasions" (69). According to Knutson, "Bowering shows a greater awareness of political reality than Melville ... Whereas Melville portrays perfect understanding, Bowering depicts countless misunderstandings, which aggravate the actual conflict of interests that exists. Whereas Melville idealizes a few isolated islanders, Bowering portrays ordinary guys who are always making silly jokes about becoming a full man of the tribe" (73).

Whether one sees parody as "capable of transformative power in creating new syntheses" (Hutcheon, *Theory of Parody*, 20) or as exploitative and demeaning also depends on the point of view of the reader. Thus, Marcia Crosby, writing as a Haida/Tsimpsian and as a woman, argues that in the case of Bowering's work, "[o]ne can only parody something that is shared .... For me [Crosby] as a native reader, Bowering's approach is not radical, but a continuation of the West's assumed right to use native figures ... in a search for its own 'roots'" ("Construction of the Imaginary Indian," 271–2). Her criticism centres on Bowering's undermining of one of the novel's characters, Menzies–that otherwise perfect "eighteenth-century man" – by its portrayal of Menzies' sexual use of an unnamed Amerindian woman. Crosby argues that although "the ideological dimension of Western discourse has changed to one of self-criticism, in this case it is still about a particular 'self,' and not about First Nations People" (271). Bowering's construction of the "Imaginary Indian," which exploits stereotypes to subvert eurocentric attitudes, is perhaps not as accommodating of various levels of cross-cultural representation as is Barcelo's text. This may well be because, in spite of the use of the Indian construct to foreground postcolonial concerns in *Burning Water*, there is (with the possible exception of Quadra) no portrayal of *métissage* in this text. Indeed, cultural commentators, from Goldie through Crosby to Lenore Keeshig-Tobias, tend to the binary division contained in the following cryptic pronouncement: "The indigene is Other and the white signmaker, the self, must find some means of dealing with Other, by denying or embracing" (Goldie, "Getting It Right," 65). Many cultural commentators from within and without the First Nations uphold the binary point of view when it comes to discussing the rapport between Amerindians and non-Amerindians in English Canadian fiction; *métissage* is not central to the relationship among these groups, and it is therefore difficult, as Barbara Godard says in a somewhat different context, "to elaborate alternate practices" ("The Politics of Representation," 194).

While there are undoubtedly complexities in Bowering's use of parody, Bowering's sophisticated play with language in *Burning Water* does indicate his interest in the problematics of communication and translation between groups with different worldviews. It may well be through his play with language that Bowering intimates "alternate practices." His interest is signalled in his awareness of the theories of the American linguist Benjamin Whorf, who is obliquely referred to in *Burning Water* (143). Whorf and his colleague Edward Sapir based their theory of linguistic relativity on studies of Nootka and other American Indian languages. According to W.D. Ashcroft, "Sapir proposed the exciting and revolutionary view that what we call the 'real' world is built up by the language habits of a group, and that the worlds in which different societies live are quite distinct, not merely the same world with different labels attached" ("Constitutive Graphonomy," 65). Translation and communication between Europeans and indigenous New World peoples here are not simply a matter of learning new words for taken-for-granted objects or concepts but a realization of the complexities of transcending different ways of seeing. Thus, Whorf: "What surprises most is to find that various grand generalizations of the Western world, such as time, velocity, and matter, are not essential to the construction of a consistent picture of the universe" (Whorf, "Science and Linguistics," 216).

The thematization of the complexities of worldviews is expressed through varied versions of the English language in *Burning Water*.

Indians who can discuss "relative concepts" and "unsubstantiated rumours" with sophistication in English respond to Vancouver's rudimentary Nootka with English of another type: "Many portage. Many days eating chickens on the flat land past the highest mountains" (144). Knutson underlines Bowering's accurate representation of the grammatical structures of Nootka (described by Whorf as a "polysynthetic language," in which "the sentence without subject or predicate is the only type" [Whorf, "Languages and Logic," 237, 242]) and argues that Vancouver utters sentences that attempt to represent the grammatical structures of Nootka in English, such as "How through forest it days with canoes many is?" (*Burning Water*, 143). Knutson also points to *Burning Water*'s insistence "on parodic play and the repetitious overturning of stereotypes as a kind of challenge to the stiff prejudices which otherwise reign unchallenged" in the English language ("Bowering and Melville," 79). In his development of a postcolonial theory of literary writing, W.D. Ashcroft argues that postcolonial literature's "appropriation of English, far from inscribing either vernacular of 'standard' forms, creates a new discourse at their interface" ("Constitutive Graphonomy," 61). Bowering's flaunting of different linguistic norms, which parody both linguistic and racial stereotypes, is an example, albeit a problematic one, of this type of postcolonial writing.

Very little of the growing body of criticism of Bowering's work addresses his extensive use of humour. Even if we remain within the loose "primitive" framework that best illustrates the New World Myth challenge to European-inspired religious and historical "givens," we find many examples of this humour. Along with parody, humour can allow for the reexamination of a familiar text in an unfamiliar way. By introducing an element of unfamiliarity or uncertainty into the traditional historical "text," humour acts as a catalyst for change: it questions the hegemony of European-dictated history, and it allows for the alternative versions of "what really happened" that are characteristic of New World Myth texts. The familiar "text," that is to say, the traditional European-inspired versions of Vancouver's explorations, Wolfe's death, the "primitives'" behaviour, and so on, are forcibly reexamined here because of the New World Myth challenge *Burning Water* issues in its unconventional and funny retellings of these historical events.

For instance, when Vancouver's sailors set out a seine net, parodying the image of Christ as the fisher of men's souls, the Indians are invited to observe the harvest. When the net comes up "plain empty," the white men's curses in reaction to the lack of fresh fish for dinner are repeated by the Indians: "understanding that the imprecation was an essential part of a ceremony having to do with assuring the Great Spirit that one was thankful for His care despite a disappointment this time ... [a]ll the Capilanos, about fifty of them, stood up in their dugout canoes as only they could do and shouted in unison, so that their deep Indian voices resounded from a curved rock-face a mile away: 'Aeh, shitt!'" (128). The Indians then make their own seine of hemp, and fish with far better results. The narrator's comment – "The Indians were always doing that to white men" (130) – reflects what he is doing to us: subverting the expectations of success aroused by the use of the Christ motif, which is associated with "technologically advanced" Europeans. The passage, of course, is also an illustration of Old World attitudes being subverted: while the Indian understanding is way off the mark, European technology does not baffle the supposedly primitive Indians.

Bowering's continual punning is evident in the following passage, which also illustrates the mockery of academia typical of New World Myth texts. A native has just stolen five knives from Vancouver's ship:

"That thief has five of our best *coltelli*," hollered Mr Gransell, who was under the impression that he had uttered a French plural, and thought that the occasional such borrowing gave class to his galley ...

"You'll be wanting the cutter, sir?" suggested the sailor ...

"Of course, we shall employ our one cutter to retrieve our other five," said Vancouver ...

"Droll," said Menzies ... taking his pipe in his hand and looking for all the world like an approving university professor. (68)

At times, humour is as problematic a component of Bowering's textual construction of a postcolonial worldview as is his use of parody. Russell Brown notes that Bowering's extended use of puns makes his readers wary: "Why, of all forms of humour, is it only the pun that we greet with a groan? Because such word-play is dangerous ... The pun threatens communication, because for language to be efficient its meanings need to be single and understood singly" ("Words," 46). Bowering frequently undercuts his own comic writings, juxtaposing humourous passages with others that expose unequal power relationships. For instance, in an initial exchange between the two Indians and the Yankee trader Magee, the latter walks up to the Indians and says "How!" Believing his greeting to be another ceremonial word, the two Indians make their faces "look patient," and one of them raises his hand in his best imitation and says "Aeh, shit!" (199).

Commenting on this passage, Knutson notes that "Bowering's play with stereotypes and misunderstandings is very funny, but our laughter is checked when Magee reappears later," having killed some Amerindians and stolen their medicine bundles ("Bowering and Melville," 76–7). Magee's language in this second passage refers to the Amerindians he has violated as "specimens" and "meat" left for the coyotes; even the strongly Eurocentric officer, Peter Puget, reacts in anger and disgust. The juxtaposition of parodic humour with criticism of imperialist attitudes in related passages may well be Bowering's way of challenging hierarchically ordered thinking and attitudes inherited from the eighteenth century, although, as we have seen, his techniques may be read as problematic. As Crosby has argued, there "is a difference between using a theoretical critique and being used by it" ("Construction of the Imaginary Indian," 271).

A strong narratorial sense of humour in *Burning Water* undercuts "another of the Indian standard commodities, mysticism" (Goldie, "Getting It Right," 75), by portraying Indians who forget the names of their gods and who mock their own religious rituals and sacred places. The narrator frequently signals his puzzlement regarding the obvious rapprochement between European Catholics and Amerindians, especially in matters concerning gods and mysticism: "The Iroquois and the Aztecs became part of the global village that is the Catholic church at its rites, but one would look far and wide before coming upon a Redskin who professed to be a Nonconformist, much less an Anglican" (*Burning Water*, 167). Vancouver's lack of respect for the Indians' religious practices and his crew's ignorance of their languages bring about a misunderstanding with a local Indian chief, who is initially denied permission to board the *Discovery*. The *only* "indigenous" non-Amerindian character in *Burning Water*, the Peruvian-born Quadra, explains the eighteenth-century European "rational" mentality to the chief, Maquinna: "They are without gods, and therefore ignorant when it comes to conversing with those into whose heads the gods still speak" (168). Whereas Goldie credits what he calls Quadra's "highly developed European sophistication" (75) for his understanding of both worldviews here, it is Quadra's definitely New World outlook that allows him to bridge conflicting cosmogonies. He understands all "languages" and interprets cultural behaviour for all: "Quadra, as was his wont, told Maquinna as much as he could about the English, to explain to him why he had been treated as he had; then he told Vancouver what a mistake had been made aboard his ship. He told him further how to patch things up" (168–9). Quadra's New World origins are strongly underlined in

Bowering's text (27–9). Thus, while Vancouver, "could not, as a European, renounce his feelings of superiority over a man who had been born in South America" (*Burning Water*, 159), the text itself suggests that it is in Quadra, who understands magic, gods, and languages and who actively practices intercultural translation, that a New World understanding might be found. The novel also intimates, as Leslie Monkman has suggested, that "perhaps the most that the contemporary explorer-artist can hope for is the role of the shaman-artist who 'puts white paint next to red paint so that one cannot help seeing the red paint'" ("Visions and Revisions," 92; see *Burning Water*, 240). The artist-figures in both *Burning Water* and *La Tribu* can effectively jar traditional views of history and myth and underline an important function of New World Myth texts: the "imaginative projection" (Pache, "Fiction," 76) of admittedly alternative histories. The emphasis on the liberation of the creative imagination in this postmodern and post-European projection constitutes the subject of the next and final chapter of this book.

6 Imagining Myth in the New World: George Bowering's *Burning Water* and François Barcelo's *La Tribu*

In "The Creative Imagination in Fiction and History," Mark Weinstein proposes that to "'show how it really was' is not to produce a photographic copy of an objective reality but to make a leap of creative imagination" (264). The creative imagination and its relationship to knowledge of the past are thematized in George Bowering's *Burning Water* and François Barcelo's *La Tribu*. Contrary to Weinstein's statement that the narrator in William Faulkner's *Absalom, Absalom!* cannot give the true history because he does not know it (272), however, the narrators of the two texts examined here strongly suggest that there is no *one* truth of the past to know.

Walter Pache has linked the development of postmodernism in English Canadian literature to post-Europeanism; he posits that in the Canadian perspective "the liberation of the creative imagination runs parallel with the emancipation from foreign literary models" (71–2). The expression "creative imagination" can, of course, be a red flag to postmodern and postcolonial writers and theorists, especially those who decry the ideological pressure of any residual nationalist stance in post-European literatures. These texts by Barcelo and Bowering, however, overtly foreground their ironic use of the traditional notion of the artist as an inspired creator and transmitter of cultural and historical myths; they also undercut this notion in their challenge to the Romantically inspired relationships between art, myth, and the imagination. Pache refers to contemporary authors' use of "a-logical, a-realistic, incoherent and non-hierarchical qualities of mythical narrative" in texts that foreground the "productive force of the creative act itself" ("Fiction," 76–7). Ginette Michaud refers to many of the same characteristics of postmodernism as those cited by Pache, but in a Québécois context: "la réactualisation de genres 'anciens' (conte, allégorie, fable, etc.), le retour à des schémas narratifs mythiques ... la métafiction autoréflexive, la présentation régulière de ses propres procédures, la coexistence de l'histoire officielle et des péripéties picaresques, de personnages réels et fictifs, [et] l'ironie métaphysique" ("Récits postmodernes?" 71). These characteristics are present in *La Tribu* and *Burning Water*, two New World Myth texts where narratorial recreations of the past encourage imaginative, self-conscious reconstructions of history. By "imaginative" I mean here the formulation of ideas about historico-political events of the past which involves an acceptance of *ambivalence* in creative reworkings of what is generally termed reality or characterized as "what really happened."

Metafiction, "a term given to fictional writing which self-consciously and systematically draws attention to its status as an artefact in order to pose questions about the relationship between fiction and reality" (Waugh, *Metafiction*, 2), is the most obvious of the techniques used by the narrators of *La Tribu* and *Burning Water* to thematize the power of the creative imagination. Waugh's enumeration of the basic concerns and characteristics of metafiction echoes those described by Michaud: a flaunting of the power of the creative imagination, an extreme self-consciousness about language and the writing of fictions, and parodic, playful, or deceptively naïve styles of writing. Given that this study focuses on the narratorial blurring of fiction and history in the creation of New World Myth, the metafictional passages that are considered here are mainly those where the narrators make explicit their manipulation of the "facts" of the past in their (hi)stories. These metafictional aspects, of course, underline the fragility of any retelling of the past and the impermanent and flexible nature of New World Myth.

Barcelo's and Bowering's novels overtly refute what Hayden White has described as the nineteenth-century opposition between history and fiction and the twentieth-century distinction between myth and fiction (*Tropics of Discourse*, 121–34). In the eighteenth century, according to White, the writing of history was regarded as a literary art. In the nineteenth century, history became a distinct scholarly discipline in the West, and the transformation occurred in part because of a strong reaction against "mythic thinking," which was considered to be the cause underlying the excesses and failures of the French Revolution. Consequently, in the nineteenth century, it was felt that the study of history had to be demythified. Eventually, a further distinction was made: history came to be opposed to fiction as "the study of the real versus the study of the merely imaginable" (124). Barcelo's and Bowering's novels show more affinity to the eighteenth century's appreciation of history as literary art than to the nineteenth and twentieth centuries' subsequent divisions of the scholarly fields. While challenging what White calls "the Western prejudice for empiricism as the sole access to reality" (122), these two texts propose that a reworking of the dynamics of fiction, history, and myth leads to a relative and adaptable apprehension of historico-political events. Carla Visser proposes that *Burning Water* addresses two central concerns of many contemporary fiction writers: an awareness of the difficulties involved in "the narrativization of history," and a further awareness that any discourse has the power to shape our perceptions of reality ("Historicity in Historical Fiction," 90). These two concerns are also addressed in *La Tribu*. In both texts, the narrators' manipulations of historical "facts" are tied to an imaginative reworking of events they describe. These novels not only promote self-conscious awareness of the conventions of narrative and of historiography; they also challenge the European-inspired stories of our historico-political past(s).

Through its debate on fact, fancy, and the imagination, *Burning Water*, a twentieth-century story of eighteenth-century voyages, explores the acquisition of knowledge of the past. The opening paragraphs of its first chapter address this debate by admitting the ambiguous nature of visions and subverting the importance of factual knowledge, such as places and dates: "Whatever it was, the vision, came out of the far fog and sailed right into the sunny weather of the inlet. It was June 10, 1792. It could have been June 20 for all the two men who watched from the shore could care" (13). A later reference ties this passage to the narrator, whose idea of going to Trieste to write his novel "was probably informed by the malaise that had been responsible for a decade of waiting around for a shape to appear out of the fog" (17). The Indians, the narrator, Vancouver, and Menzies all refer frequently and overtly to the tension between fact, fancy and/or the imagination. Expressions such as "in fact," "as a matter of fact," and "if the truth be known," are overused in the novel. In the Prologue, the author/narrator, flaunting his role as a reteller of history, discusses his plans for a novel "about the strange fancy that history is given and the strange fact that history is taken. Without a storyteller, George Vancouver is just another dead sailor." He proposes, then, that the role of the storyteller is crucial to the transmission of knowledge of the past, but that this knowledge may be taken and given – changed and adjusted – at the whim of the narrator's imagination. Vancouver, accused later on in the novel of being unimaginative, responds: "You speak of it [the imagination] as if it were the opposite of facts, as if it were perhaps the enemy of facts. That is not true in the least, my two young friends. The imagination depends upon facts, it feeds on them in order to produce beauty or invention, or discovery ... The true enemy of the imagination is laziness, habit, leisure. The enemy of imagination is the idleness that provides fancy" (155).

The intertext here is the brief but important passage in Coleridge's *Biographia Literaria*, in which a distinction is made between fancy and the imagination (167). Coleridge defines the "primary imagination" as "the living power and prime agent of all human perception, and as a repetition in the finite mind of the eternal act of creation in the infinite I AM." The secondary imagination, says Coleridge, is "an echo of the former ... differing only in degree." The imagination "dissolves, diffuses, dissipates, in order to re-create" (167). "Fancy, on the contrary ... [plays] with fixities and definites. The fancy is indeed no other than a mode of memory emancipated from the order of time and space." Kathleen M. Wheeler's gloss of Coleridge's definitions is useful in a reading of Bowering's text. She comments that "[f]ancy and memory cannot make new materials, they can only juggle existing elements into different positions relative to each other. Imagination is the faculty which rejuvenates these proxies [of the 'everyday' world] into fresh acts of perception" (*Sources, Processes, and Methods*, 138–9). Bowering's retelling of Vancouver's historical voyage in a highly self-conscious text – which blatantly emphasizes the "I AM" – allows for that imaginative "dissolving, diffusing, dissipating" of the past. The free play given to the imagination in Bowering's novel leaves room for the possibility of other equally acceptable stories about past events, resulting in a rejuvenated, alternative history. These rejuvenating activities create a fresh perspective on those histories that have traditionally been accepted as unquestionably true.

In his reading of *Burning Water*, Edward Lobb argues that when he wrote his novel, Bowering had in mind both Coleridge's "The Rime of the Ancient Mariner" and George Whalley's essay on Coleridge's work, "The Mariner and the Albatross" ("Imagining History," 114). Lobb discusses the thematic of the imagination in the light of these two works. He characterizes the two main eighteenth-century characters, Vancouver and Menzies, in rather rigid terms. Thus, Menzies is a gatherer and classifier of facts who is hostile to the imagination, as is shown by his shooting of the albatross. Vancouver, too, is a "figure of failed or false imagination" (120). Moving on to discuss the narratorial interventions, Lobb raises the possibility that Bowering is a hero of imagination. He notes, however, that Bowering has contradictory goals, in that he wants his work of art to be both "historically accurate and novelistically alive" and that he is frustrated in his attempts to animate the historical figure. Lobb concludes that the "novelist is omnipotent and unaccountable, and therefore runs the risk of becoming as rigid, arbitrary and self-absorbed as Vancouver" (125). In fact (!), however, Bowering's tampering with historical dates and events and his use of twentieth-century idioms refute Lobb's statement about Bowering's desire to create a historically accurate novel. Contrary to what Lobb argues, neither Vancouver nor Menzies *totally* represents anything in this fiction. They illustrate, by their inherent contradictions and by the tension produced by their existence as both historical and fictional characters, the impossibility of knowing the past in one determinate manner. Lobb's gloss of *Burning Water* does not appear to appreciate fully this novel's problematization of the imagination in the apprehension of historical knowledge – a problematization that focuses on the flexibility of our modes of knowledge of the past and their adaptability to circumstances.

Jerry Varsava calls this "the knowledge problem," that is, "the contemporary preoccupation with what constitutes 'truth' in the late twentieth century" ("History and/or His Story?" 217). Bowering's treatment of Vancouver, suggests Varsava, "repudiates a well-established tenet of traditional historiography – the notion of historical truth as an essential, substantial entity" (215). Varsava suggests that historians "have typically viewed Vancouver as a staid, meticulous fellow … doing some very important work that happened to be desperately dull." In Bowering's novel, however, "Vancouver becomes a complex man. He is no longer seen as a caricature of the Apollonian ideal of the Age of Enlightenment. In claiming for him imagination, deviant sexual appetites, and even a touch of madness, Bowering makes of Vancouver a living rebuke to the moral and epistemological norms of the age" (216).

This typical New World Myth tension between a real person and a fictional character is first established in the prologue, where the author/narrator conflates himself, the explorer Vancouver, and an English king named George. Feeling as if "current history and self were bound together," George begins to plan a novel: "So of course that book had a lot of myself mixed up in it, though it had to be objective if it was to be any good." The irony contained in the preceding metafictional sentence mocks the notion of objective historiography by presenting the author/narrator's contradictory urges to write a personal yet objective (hi)story. Other similar metafictional passages in *Burning Water* blur the boundaries between reality and fiction and between "truth" and the imagination. The narrator's preoccupation with the imagination in the production of story is thematized in his many overtly self-conscious evaluations of the progress of his work – his retelling of the Vancouver story. Having "set up in an utterly foreign and rather dull north coast city," he finds that "the story was less real than it would have been otherwise, that only the distractions were real and seized upon. The imagination, too, fails. Or it finds it very difficult to find footing where the fancy has sent it sailing" (26). By showing the reader his struggles to overcome the limitations of fact and fancy and his ironic pursuit of the imagination, the narrator engages the reader in the ongoing debate about the importance of these three elements in any re-creation of the past. Indeed, the narrator deliberately foregrounds his shaping of the Vancouver/Menzies story (while paradoxically underlining the fragility of his tale) in the following reflection on "truth": "If the truth be known, and of course we are in a position to know it, or whatever purchase one makes on the truth in a work of imagination, if that is what we are engaged in, that being the entire issue we test here, Vancouver did not really have anything against Dr Menzies" (84). A single, unified "truth" of the past – a "given," as discussed in the introduction to this study – does not exist here. In the New World Myth novels examined in this study, knowledge of the past is in a constant state of flux.

The narrator's foregrounding of the fact/fancy/imagination debate undercuts the traditional myth of the European explorer as conquering hero and proposes that all knowledge of the past is adaptable, flexible, and constantly changing. The typical drawings of the claiming-the-land scene in English Canadian history textbooks are parodied in *Burning Water*: "Vancouver loved to jump out of a boat, stride a few paces up the beach, and announce: 'I claim this newfound land for his Britannic Majesty in perpetuity, and name it New Norfolk!' – Usually the officers and men stood around fairly alertly, holding flags and oars and looking about for anyone who did not agree" (26–7).[1] The narrator's descriptions of the complicated eighteenth-century politics of European nations underline the tension between fiction and reality produced by this text's manipulation of the facts. On the one hand, the narrator adopts a deliberately casual tone in his retelling by his use of familiar interjections such as "well" and "of course": "The relationship between Captain George Vancouver and, well, Don Juan Francisco de la Bodega y Quadra, should have been a simple one ... But it was not as simple as George Vancouver wanted it to be, of course" (58–9). On the other hand, the narrator frequently and deliberately complicates "the facts" of history by creating, for instance, a homosexual relationship between Vancouver and Quadra – a relationship that, as Aritha van Herk notes, does not at all adhere to known fact ("Mapping as Metaphor," 82). Tension between Bowering's "imagination" and Vancouver's "reality" is evident here, as this homosexual relationship is most probably Bowering's literalization of the following sentence taken from the historical George Vancouver's journals: "In our conversation whilst on this little excursion, Senr Quadra had very earnestly requested that I would name some port or island after us both, to commemorate our meeting and *the very friendly intercourse* that had taken place and subsisted between us" (Vancouver, *Voyage of Discovery*, 1:397; emphasis added). The narrator also admits to inventing past events: Vancouver and Menzies "did not often have such quiet conversations, and usually one just had to imagine them" (108).

This last narratorial reflection on the invention of the past casts doubt on the authenticity of the historical documents – excerpts from travel journals – that are included within the text. Bowering does refer to the "obvious passages from the writings of George Vancouver and other officers of his expedition" in his acknowledgments, but, as Russell Brown notes, Bowering's love of play with regard to facts (he himself has, to date, at least three different "official" places of birth) is always a consideration in a reading of his work ("Words," 45). For instance, Martin Kuester notes that chapter 23 of *Burning Water* "is an almost literal transcription of a letter that [the historical Vancouver] sent to Admiral Stephens on 6 December 1793, and which summarizes events …that took place in the month of August of that year" (*Framing Truths*, 119). However, by the time the reader reaches this chapter, Bowering's parodic flaunting of eighteenth-century syntax and vocabulary would have destroyed any faith the reader might have had in his historical accuracy, and, ironically, the "historical" passage would not be taken for what it "truly" is. The juxtaposition of the eighteenth-century texts with the narrator's twentieth-century story stresses the latter's creative, playful production of history.

As we saw in the last chapter, Bowering's fictional Vancouver adapts the facts of cartography to fit his vision of the political situation. The narrator has a similar approach to the facts of history. His frequent metafictional commentary stresses his omniscience and his total control of the retelling: "'And certainly (for novelists have the privilege of knowing everything) [Vancouver] thought a great deal about readers far in the future" (*Burning Water*, 63). The odd punctuation used in this anachronistic commentary, the "fact" that chapter 52 is missing and that the flight of fancy to Hudson's Bay is thus the central chapter of the text are all metafictional techniques that underline the narrator's flaunting of the textuality of *Burning Water* and his control over its production. Elsewhere in the text, in a chatty, informal tone, the narrator tells us that he "got as far south as he was going to go that winter – the National Museum of Costa Rica, which is all about Indians and Spaniards and the great question of religion – before Vancouver did, or before he allowed him to" (192). This story of Vancouver, then, appears at times to be under the control of the narrator's imagination. However, the narrator underlines his research – his own seeking out of the facts – in this fictional recreation of the past. He visits this museum because of his need for "a bit of fact here and there" (192). Having discovered a fact – various Spanish names for Vancouver's hat – he flaunts the unresolved tension between facts and imagination by ending this passage with "Imagine that" (192).

A similar blurring of boundaries is signalled in the following quotation:

Two nights ago, he'd [the narrator] told a student of literature that he thought that imagination implied a travelling, or a trip ...

He said that a passive leaning on a rail and seeing what the coast provides for one's gaze is linear, foppery and fancy. Going there and looking, turning over a rock or a clam, that is what is meant by the imagination. The ship is the vessel of metaphor, a carrying across as they say. (*Burning Water*, 166)

Punning here on the Greek meaning of *metaphora* (carrying across), the narrator implies in this passage that history has more need of the imagination than of fancy to carry across the story of a past event. Indeed, the many references to fact, fancy, and the imagination in this novel suggest that its narrator considers the imagination to be superior to fact, fancy, and a related term: "truth." With Coleridge's work in the not-so-distant background, Varsava wonders if the author will be able to accomplish his goal: "For Coleridge, the true artist is able to fashion from the discrete a new, vital, organic whole. He calls this syncretizing capacity *imagination* and contrasts it to *fancy* which achieves a mere mechanical compilation of given thematic and formal elements. The novel represents a test for the author. Will he be able to conjure up an integrated, living portrait of Vancouver or will his 'Vancouver' be a mere juxtaposition of the documentary and the fictitious, of the empirical and the intuitive?" (218). Varsova's choice of vocabulary – "organic whole", "integrated ...

portrait," "mere juxtaposition" – would seem to indicate his desire for a totality that is far from Bowering's goal. While the author may indeed see *Burning Water* as a test of his capacity to produce a work of totality, that is to say, the novel itself, his narrator indubitably flaunts the continual precariousness of his undertaking by strongly underlining the relativity of the antinomious imagination.

The narrator suggests that he himself comes to knowledge of the past through nonscientific, haphazard means, such as chance encounters and intuitive hunches. Visiting the old palace in Trieste, he finds that, as usual, he is following the tour suggested in the guidebook backwards, and he does not quite know where he is when he spies a map of the very area that is preoccupying his thoughts, the Stretto di Annian (*Burning Water*, 36). A coincidence? And what to make of the mysterious "she," who appears very realistically in his dreams, giving him "the idea he needed right there, but it didn't sink in for a while" (23)? A third passage, which describes his bizarre encounter with a seagull, seems to have no connection whatsoever to the telling of the story, and yet it illustrates the narrator's attitude about how we come to knowledge of the past: "a sheet of intuition fell over him. He felt a pressure of memory. Of his earlier life as a seagull" (38). This last passage ends with both an affirmation and a denial of any particular significance to the episode: "But it was very authentic, the apprehension, and soon it went away. It did not change his life in any way." By ironically foregrounding alternative ways of knowing, such as the coincidences, dreams, and the intuitive memory prized by the Romantics, the narrator underlines the flexible quality of all imaginative projections of the past – including his own. *Burning Water*'s narrator suggests, then, that fact, fancy, and the imagination are all necessary elements in the acquisition of knowledge of the past. Assuming for the moment that Bowering's narrator works within the framework of Coleridge's problematic definitions of "fancy" (fixity, memory) and "imagination" (rejuvenation, recreation), *Burning Water* privileges the imagination over both fact and fancy. It is the one element that permits a rejuvenating perspective on events of the past. It is also, however, the element that most strongly destabilizes the notion of *one* truth of the past. Certitude in the present with regard to our knowledge of "what really happened" in the past keeps sliding away.

Whereas the narrator of *Burning Water* thematizes the power of the creative imagination in the acquisition of knowledge of the past through the Coleridgian fact/fancy/imagination debate, the narrator of *La Tribu* addresses the same issue through the use he makes of the

Cartesian *cogito*. Ksoâr, the poet-historian of the tribe, reinvents writing in order to record the statistics of the hunt. Faced with the tribe's rejection of recorded knowledge, Ksoâr, like other writers in a similar situation, begins to write for himself, recording the fruits of his fertile imagination on a piece of birch bark (56). One result of his "useless" texts is a poem entitled "Je pense," whose final line is a parodic adaptation of *cogito ergo sum*: "Je me dis que je pense, et je sais que je suis" (57).

In francophone cultures, and more generally, in the Western world, René Descartes' *Discours de la méthode* has long been regarded as the seminal work emphasizing the need for rational thought in the acquisition of knowledge. Barcelo's narrator constantly challenges the status accorded to rationality in a typical French Canadian classical education through parodic passages that concern a French Québécois folk song, "A la claire fontaine," and with the poem "Je pense." Ksoâr, in conversation with the illiterate Jafafoua, puts forth a technical critique of his own poem, thereby poking fun at the traditional *exposé de texte*. In this critique, Ksoâr emphasizes that imbedded version of the *cogito* by insisting twice on the surprise of the final line of the poem (57). Following his literary exposition of rhyme and technique, Ksoâr asks Jafafoua if he would like to hear the poem again. "Ksoâr relut le poème" is the last line of printed text of page 57; at the top of page 58 the poem "Je pense" is reprinted in its entirety. Metafictional repetition, of course, signals the narrator's control of the text as artifact: he chooses which elements he will include (and how often) within his story.

The third printing of "Je pense" illustrates the New World Myth blurring of fiction and reality and its challenge to rationality. Laval Lavigueur, a European sailor, has become a coureur de bois. Inexperienced, he eats mushrooms to survive in the wilderness. When he comes upon some Clipocs singing "A la claire fontaine" around a campfire, he blames the mushrooms for what he believes to be a hallucination (104). The talking garter snake then explains the truth to him by recapitulating Jafafoua's life story. Laval accepts this logical explanation and moves through the snow toward the group, but is brought up short by Ksoâr's recital of "Je pense," which is reprinted differently here in one paragraph of prose. Unable to accept that an Amerindian might be capable of reciting metered poetry, Laval again blames what he is hearing on the mushrooms. Because he denies "reality," Laval dies of exposure in the snow. Textual play with the rational *cogito* underlines the problematization of reality in this New World Myth text. Thus, within the confines of the story, Laval Lavigueur's apprehensions of reality are correct,

although he believes them to be false. The sophistication of the Clipocs is bizarre to a character used to "savage" Indians in the New
World and "civilized" people from the Old Continent. This passage
and others in a similar vein strongly refute European positivistic
models of thinking.

Earlier in the story, this same Laval is misled in a similar way in
his efforts to remain "rational" by the Clipoc folk song routine.
Having fallen overboard during a naval battle, Laval is awaiting
rescue when he hears his preferred verse of "A la claire fontaine"
(81). He thinks sailors have come to help, but instead, he sees the
singing Clipocs paddling out of the fog toward him. Blaming this
"vision" on delirium, Laval faints away. He is eventually rescued
and hospitalized, but it is the folk song – not the "rational" science
of medicine – that saves his life. Unconscious, Laval appears to be
dead, and the doctor orders that his body be thrown into the
common grave. Laval, however, hums "A la claire fontaine," and the
doctor is forced to accept that he is still alive. The frequent textual
use of this Québécois nationalist folk song implicitly links various
episodes in the novel and underlines yet once again the textual parallels between the Clipocs and the Québécois.

The fourth and final printing of "Je pense" is contained in Ksoâr's
written history of the tribe, which he buries in a cookie tin just before
committing suicide. This unusual history contains Ksoâr's reflections
on his tribe's future:

> Peut-être la tribu n'est-elle pas perdue comme je le crois. Peut-être celui
> qui me lira sera-t-il un jour membre de la même tribu, redevenue florissante,
> forte et indépendantes [sic].
>
> Mais je ne le crois pas.
>
> Je crois plutôt que ces feuillets seront le dernier souvenir laissé par un
> peuple qui disparaît de la face de la terre. (253)

At the end of Ksoâr's history, the narrator calls attention to this passage by noting that in his own rereading of his text, Ksoâr corrects
his grammatical error – the "s" of "indépendantes." The probable
metafictional reference in the above passage to the closing pages of
García Márquez's *One Hundred Years of Solitude* – in which Aureliano
Babilonia learns his own history and that of his people, through his
reading of the self-destructing manuscripts – draws attention once
again to the New World Myth tension between "reality" and rationality, on the one hand, and the imagination and fiction, on the other.
One of the narrator's children finds Ksoâr's document while out
walking along the top of the cliff with his father. While the child

examines the tin box and its contents, the father reflects on the permanence of the site and the continuity of "le pays" (258). The narrator briefly holds Ksoâr's text – his own text's competition, given that they both tell the history of the Clipocs – in his hands, but the parchment accidentally falls over the cliff and is destroyed by the waves. It is then dismissed by the narrator as "des vieux bouts de papier" (260). Although Ksoâr's "history" and his favourite poem have been destroyed in the narrator's parenthetical interjection, they do of course exist in the story of the novel. The partial allegorical conflation of the Clipocs and the Québécois provides for a possibly more optimistic scenario than the one in the last sentence of García Márquez's text. The Québécois who holds Ksoâr's text within his hands – who has in fact retold Ksoâr's story – is perhaps, as Ksoâr predicted, that future member of the same tribe. The narrator's musings on the cliff seem to uphold this idea, as does the fact that near the end of the story Mahii, defying death by singing "A la claire fontaine," is proud that her tribe has survived (295). *La Tribu*'s narrator has indeed retold Quebec's history, but his text's deliberate blurring of the "tribal" identities of the Clipocs and the Québécois precludes any definite conclusions to that history. It is evident, however, that the narrator's reworkings of linear history and the rational Cartesian *cogito* problematize the use of the creative imagination while using it in re-creations of the past.

The narrator of *La Tribu* self-consciously flaunts the power of his creative imagination, while making blatant use of metafictional techniques to insist upon the flexibility of his narrative and the indeterminacy of truth in his story. Thus, in a parodic move reminiscent of John Fowles' *The French Lieutenant's Woman*, he provides four different endings to a story, and then leaves a blank space for the potentially dissatisfied reader to make up his or her own conclusion (294). Elsewhere in the text, we are told that two different characters had exactly the same childhood and that the environmentally conscious narrator will tell their story once only, thereby saving printing paper and the electricity needed to read his book. As is the case with Bowering's novel, Barcelo's text makes frequent references to the tension between memory and the imagination. Another similarity is in overused clichés such as "en réalité" (176) and "en fait" (138) in clearly fictional contexts, which foreground the truth/imagination tension. The chapters entitled "Parenthèse contemporaine" serve the same purpose as Bowering's anachronistic intrusions: they purposely subvert the illusion of historical time. It is particularly in these chapters that *La Tribu*'s narrator foregrounds the contribution of *his* imagination to his text's recreation of the past. The narrator claims that *his* history makes up for the glaring deficiencies in all other historians' work. Paradoxically, the text also posits the superiority of story over historical records. Because its narrator blurs the borders of the real and the fictive and those of truth and the imagination, this text produces tension between ways of knowing the past.

In many cultures, the imagination is strongly associated with the creative arts. Gaile McGregor posits that "the figure of the *artist*, in all his guises, is one of the most important problems posed by the Canadian œuvre" (*The Wacousta Syndrome*, 280). The artist's presence in our literature(s), according to McGregor, is related to our uncertainties about our national self-image. She gives examples of "the Canadian doomed artist figure" (282), who, she says, is consumed by two fears, namely, "the fear of being dehumanized and diminished by a commitment to art" and "the fear not of destroying but of being destroyed [by art]" (281). New World Myth texts, however, adopt a different approach to art; they self-consciously thematize the artist figure in a celebratory manner. Their investigations of a creator who has at least partial control of a particular retelling of history do not reveal artists who, as McGregor would have it, react in fear to creative art or to the past. There is another reason for the foregrounding of artist figures in *Burning Water* and *La Tribu*, namely, the postmodern challenge to liberal humanist ideas of art as original and unique and to the modernist notion of art as autonomous and separate from the world.[2] Frank Davey also decries "the humanist argument that art is the sign of ... the triumph of humanity over time" (*Reading Canadian Reading*, 36). The humanist's "conflict-free and cheerful view of history" (36), according to Davey, reveals an emphasis on the shaping imagination as something that gives lasting form and meaning to historical events (37). In *La Tribu* and *Burning Water*, the narrators do *not* uphold the imagination as a tool whereby the artist gives such lasting form and meaning to significant events of the past. They do uphold, however, the power of the creative imagination over specific facts: these narrators valorize the imagination. However, the self-consciousness of their comments about the role of the artist's imagination – and its product, the work of art – underlines their awareness that their art does not seek to impose one eternal form and universal meaning – *one* truth of the past.

The artist figure is triply present in *La Tribu*, represented by Ksoâr, the narrator, and Mahii. Ksoâr creates his poems and stories to serve the tribe's needs – but the tribe has no need whatsoever of them. This insistence on the *utility* of art is typical of New World Myth texts; it runs counter to the liberal humanist notion of art existing eternally as a Keatsian thing of beauty for its own sake. Ksoâr's preferred artistic work, the poem "Je pense," is printed four times *within* the narrator's text, even if, paradoxically, it is destroyed in a *parenthèse contemporaine* before that narrator can read it. The scribe's ironic statement that the beauty of his poem resides in that original "surprise de la dernière ligne" (57) parodies the notion of the originality of a work of art: this line, taken from Descartes, is anything but original. Furthermore, Ksoâr's artistic writing does not at first appear to contribute to the needs of the tribe. Its members express no interest whatsoever in his long historical chronicles, his bizarre poems, and his works of science fiction. Ksoâr founds a literary club, but no one joins. Asked by Mahii to teach some moral history to the younger members of the tribe, Ksoâr writes a long epic poem on the subject that his bored students are incapable of understanding (123). And yet, the narrator notes, Ksoâr has an influential role within the tribe, even if it is not understood. The very irrationality of his literary activity influences the Clipocs. Because of his artistic endeavours, each member of the tribe begins to view the world differently (77). Ksoâr serves as an obvious foil to *La Tribu*'s narrator. Both characters artistically recreate the histories of their people. Ksoâr's voluminous historical and artistic writings do affect the worldview of the Clipocs. By implication, the narrator's recreation of the past might also affect the worldview of his "tribe." However, Ksoâr's history and poem were destroyed before they could be read in the present of the text. The narrator's sometimes deprecatory attitude toward his own work suggests that *his* text may also not earn the traditional humanist attitude of respect for a completed literary work of art, seen as eternal and universal: it too may not last. Utility, not eternity, is the focus here, and even the utility of the narrator's own work is presented as debatable.

The narrator nonetheless insists upon the power of his own creative imagination and upon the facility with which his writing gains direct access to the reader's imagination. Thus, having created in Mahii the most beautiful woman of all time, with a simple stroke of the pen, he notes the superiority of writing over all other artistic genres (*La Tribu*, 108). In the "Point final" of the novel, the narrator again insists upon the effortless creativity of his writing: "c'est l'art idéal pour les paresseux. En écrivant, on peut créer n'importe quoi sans se casser la tête" (302). However, a few lines before this, he defends *l'écriture* from those who would suggest that the apparent facility with which he creates a story makes of his work "un art facile et méprisable" (301). This artist's contradictory attitude toward his own work reflects the tension in the relation between art, reality, and the imagination in

New World Myth texts. For instance, the narrator blurs the boundaries between reality and fiction in a discussion with his artist friend
Angèle: "Je n'ai, par exemple, qu'à décider qu'il y aura un milliard
de personnes devant la fenêtre de ce restaurant. Et quelques lignes
plus loin, il y aura effectivement un milliard de personnes devant la
fenêtre" (302). And, of course, a few lines later, Angèle looks out the
window and sees a billion dissimilar figures. This metafictional
flaunting of the power of the narrator's creative imagination, which
can cause multitudes to exist at will, does not overly impress the artist
Angèle, who can also portray reality as she so desires. Her reaction
to the narrator's feat is thus not as laudatory as he wishes it to be.
The final line of the text poses an unresolved question about the role
of the artist in the postmodern age, while underlining the narrator's
ambivalent attitude toward his art: "Enviait-elle mes pouvoirs ou me
méprisait-elle de savoir si mal les utiliser?" (303). This contradictory
attitude permeates the text: the novelist first proclaims his creative
power as an artist and then underlines his own limitations in the
production of art.

The tension between art and reality is further thematized in *La
Tribu* by narratorial devices that render the real unreal. The narrator
installs a tension about what really happened in the past in those
passages that retell Quebec's political history through stories about
characters who are obviously fictional inventions and yet whose life
stories resemble those of well-known political leaders. If the artist
can cause a billion people to exist at will, then he can also create facts
of the past to suit his whim. The narrator only contributes to the
tension caused by the conflict between real and imagined history
when he stresses his knowledge of potentially embarrassing historical facts that have not yet been brought to life: "De plus, leur pen-
daison [à Mahii et à Mogo] aurait pu attirer l'attention sur la bataille
du chemin des Ricochets, dont on interdit toute mention dans les
journaux et dans les livres d'histoire" (272). In his retelling of the
past, the narrator also implies that this text is sometimes a collective
effort. Thus, he does not describe certain episodes, preferring to
leave the details to the experience and the imagination of his readers
(47). *La Tribu*'s narrator, then, flaunts the artist's imaginative production of story in the retelling of history, and yet, paradoxically, he
undercuts this same imagination by noting its insufficiencies and by
questioning its function and utility.

Mahii best illustrates this text's parody of the notion of "pure" art
that has its own autonomous existence, divorced from the real world.
The narrator first insists upon his own contribution here: he has not
only created the most beautiful, most intelligent, most moral and,

especially, most sexy woman in the world, he has also made of her the greatest artist of all time (*La Tribu*, 138). His reason for this excess, he ironically notes, is to "revaloriser les artistes" including himself and thus, perhaps, the author of the text. Having accidentally discovered the visual arts, Mahii quickly learns that, given the lack of artistic appreciation in the tribe, her art can exist only for herself. (139) The suggestion here of the purity, the originality, and the inviolacy of her art is immediately undercut by the narrator's description of Mahii's artistic development. He draws deliberate and ironic parallels between her and the acknowledged artists of Western civilization. Like Michelangelo, she builds special scaffolding that permits her to paint the ceiling of her hut while lying on her back (139). Like da Vinci, she pulls out of her imagination the future mechanical inventions of her people (140). Like Picasso, she privileges certain colours over others and has her own grey period (142).

Mahii eventually perfects her technique and stops to reflect on the role of the imagination in her work. She concludes a discussion with the talking garter snake about the relationship of art to reality by painting scenes of her own life that allow her to finally establish a balance between her own internal world and the external one (144). Due to the massacre of the Niox, which leads to the Clipoc's obliteration of all signs of progress, Mahii's masterpieces are destroyed just as she is about to show them to the tribe. Only the garter snake sheds a tear as he listens to Mahii's artistic works burn. She herself gracefully accepts the destruction of her work and never paints again. In the passage describing Mahii's death, the narrator implies that she should have felt frustrated by her failure to satisfy her artistic ambitions in her life's work. Indeed, he states: "si on le lui avait demandé, elle aurait fini par reconnaître qu'elle regrettait beaucoup de choses" (295). However, he eventually admits that she never regretted anything (296). The destruction of her work, it would seem, leaves this artist figure cold. In a final artistic parody, Mahii dies with Edith Piaf's words on her lips "non, je ne regrette rien."

The artist figures in *La Tribu*, then, reflect the tension that is characteristic of New World Myth texts in their investigations of the imagination. On the one hand, the artists celebrate the power of the creative imagination in the retelling of history. In so doing, they of course provoke doubt about what really happened in the past. On the other hand, the artists downplay the notion of the originality of all art forms – especially creative writing – by dwelling on the intertextual nature of all art. They refute the liberal humanist argument that pure art is important in and of itself and that it will endure as a sign of human domination over time, by insisting on the questionable utility and on the impermanence of their artistic productions. Flaunting the precarious existence and the dubious validity of their work, these artists undermine the traditional humanist respect for a "thing of beauty" – a work of art.

The contradictory attitude of New World Myth to the role of the artist's imagination in the retelling of the past is equally evident in Bowering's *Burning Water*, where the artist figure is especially present in three figures: the narrator, William Blake, and the younger Indian. Discussing his own difficulties with the progress of his book, the narrator's typical cryptic statement foregrounds the issues of art, life, fact, and the imagination without resolving the tension caused by their juxtaposition and conflation: "So: art and life again. Or at least life and literature. Or if not granting that, fact and imagination" (66–7). As is the case with *La Tribu*, Bowering's text both celebrates and mocks the liberal humanist notion of the special or gifted quality of the artist's imagination in the telling or retelling of story. Because of the strong metafictional component in this novel, the narrator's self-conscious comments in the passages about the artist William Blake point indirectly to his *own* artistic approach to facts and the imagination and to his contradictory attitude regarding the power and influence of the artist figure. When Blake's drawings deeply disturb the King's equilibrium, causing the monarch to expel him from court, Blake's traditional "superior artist" reaction is deliberately annoying to the friend who had accompanied him to court: "Blake smiled the kind of smile a person who is supposed to be a sage or artist will smile when he wants to indicate that he himself has been reminded of a knowledge he has long retained though it might still stay hidden from you" (*Burning Water*, 160). In sharp contrast to the sentiment of artistic superiority attributed here to Blake, the narrator is self-conscious about the difficulties he experiences in creating his own text. His pretended nostalgia for the "good old days" (23) of the realist novel, his forays into Vancouver's journals for appropriate words (145), and his repeated statement about his artistic work – "this all seemed crazy" (15, 80) – underline his struggle to retell history creatively. The self-consciousness of these episodes also constitutes "a representation of the producer at work" (Hutcheon, *Canadian Postmodern*, 63). By *showing* the reader how the haphazard workings of the imagination eventually lead to story, the narrator undercuts – but does not deny – the usual notions of poets' inspiration and muses (145). Bowering challenges here the convention of the modern realist novelist: "One writes a book & then tries to make the reader agree that he is not reading a book" (Bowering,

The Mask in Place, 20). The narrator's direct addresses to the reader and his implication of that reader in the imaginative process that will lead to the recreation of Vancouver's story also challenge the notion that history consists of chronological, objective facts that the narrator needs only to lay before the passive reader. The success of this particular creative retelling of the past depends in part upon the reader, to whom the narrator dares to show his vulnerability: "He [the narrator] did not know, to be sure, why all this, but he trusted it, though as the voyage grew longer and the book got thicker he felt himself resting more and more on his faith in the readers: would they carry him, keep him afloat? He thought so" (*Burning Water*, 173). This story of the past, then, has need of the imaginations of both the storyteller and of the reader.

Burning Water's narrator also plays up the traditional notion of the artist as a marginalized and under-appreciated purveyor of eternal god-given myths. This notion is first installed and then parodied in *Burning Water*. The younger Indian, criticized by his older companion for his inability to be practical, replies, "I am an artist ... what do I know about swimming?" (14). Artists, the older Indian implies, only "[t]alk talk talk" (14); together with "designers and sometimes teachers," they are frequently homosexuals: this makes of them "a minority, an exception to our ways" (148). The Indian artist wishes to gain acceptance and to contribute to the welfare of the tribe through his visions and songs. The laconic sneers of the older Indian at the artist's ambitions, however, underline the ambivalent attitude of New World Myth to art. The Indian artist relies on the Great Spirit to give shape and meaning to his song, which in turn will guarantee his acceptance and welcome as a full man of the tribe (15). This traditional attitude, which attributes shamanic qualities to the poet as the revealer of gods to humans, is mocked at various points in the story by the older, more experienced Indian: "That is your fancy speaking. That can be very dangerous for people such as us. You must never believe that you have seen a god when you have seen a man on a large boat" (17).

The narrator metafictionally stresses his own existence as a solitary and misunderstood artist: "here he was an ocean and a continent away, and one could expect something at least novel. To tell the truth, it *was* different. It was lonelier alone in the damp" (44). Most of the examples the narrator gives to illustrate this clichéd notion are ludicrous. They involve eating *salsicce con krauti* (recalling, of course, Vancouver's daily ration of sauerkraut) and reflections that when "one is a continent and an ocean from one's own refrigerator one uses a thing like eating to fill one's time" (66). The very banality of these observations parodies the traditional portrait of the dedicated young artist starving in a garret in order to create a masterpiece. *This* narrator flies to Trieste, Italy and to South America to do research, making no bones about the governmental subsidies that aid his *production* of art (18).

Patricia Waugh has remarked that "metafiction rests on a version of the Heisenbergian uncertainty principle: an awareness that 'for the smallest building blocks of matter, every process of observation causes a major disturbance,' and that it is impossible to describe an objective world because the observer always changes the observed" (*Metafiction*, 3). The narrators of *Burning Water* and *La Tribu* foreground their personal artistic contributions to – and their metafictional presence in – their (hi)stories and thus signal the impossibility of their producing objective or definitive versions of past events. Thus, when we read in *Burning Water*, "Well, then was then and now was now. [And now *is* now, but we're forgetting that for the moment.]" (21), it becomes obvious that the present (of writing, and also of reading) *is* present in this tale of the past. This passage, as Smaro Kamboureli argues in her initial, positive review, "asserts the ontology of the novel … It is the writer, his voice bracketed, who reminds us that certain texts do not exist until we read them" ("*Burning Water*," 92). *Burning Water*'s narrator – a solitary being who always seems to be "at some geographical or marine end of something" self-consciously portrays his *struggles* with his re-creation of the past within his text (*Burning Water*, 217). Near the end of the novel, the narrator shows himself to be striving to "bring Captain Vancouver to being as alone as he had made himself." Shortly thereafter, the character of the narrator quietly disappears from the story, without saying goodbye to what he himself has presented as his imperfect work of art. The narrator's very presence within his own story reflects Heisenberg's uncertainty principle. Through his critical examination of his own production of Vancouver's story, the narrator suggests that every story is inevitably a product of a particular time and place, and not a disinterested, objective chronicle.

In *La Tribu*, the narrator/artist, as we saw above, is ambivalent about his creative talent, acknowledging his inadequate use of his powers and yet celebrating his participation in this recreation of the past. When he learns of his own mixed heritage in the first "Parenthèse contemporaine" (168), he affirms that his own genealogy does not interest him, even if he is fascinated by "l'origine des hommes" (170). In an apparently contradictory statement, he then places the blame – or the praise – for the possible inadequacies of his work on this mixed cultural baggage: "Que je sois bourreau ou victime, génie universel ou déchet de l'humanité, voleur, ivrogne ou curé, un biographe si jamais j'en ai un trouvera sûrement dans cette triple origine de quoi expliquer toutes les tares comme tous les talents" (170). Even if, as he self-deprecatingly says, he thinks slowly and ponderously, this imperfect story about the past is what it is because *he* is who he is. Just as Heisenberg established that the observer always changes the observed, so these two narrators propose that their unavoidable presence in their retellings of history make it impossible for them to describe objectively *one* world of the past.

Many twentieth-century works of myth criticism posit a connection between the imagination and "primitive" notions of gods, religion, and myth. From Sir John Frazer through René Girard to Northrop Frye, the study of myth and the imagination has been linked to religions as they were thought to be practised by pre-contact indigenous peoples from outside the European continent. In his discussion of Edward Said's *Orientalism*, James Clifford notes that Said's argument "reinforces Stanley Diamond's contentions that Western culture can conceive of itself critically only with reference to fictions of the primitive" (*The Predicament of Culture*, 272). It is perhaps because of these European-inspired fictions of the primitive that studies of myth, religion, and the imagination – including many from the twentieth-century – often are more strongly linked to anthropology, ethnology, and ethnography than they are to literature. These fields of enquiry have been strongly challenged in the later part of the twentieth century, as Clifford notes in his introduction to the collection *Writing Culture*: "In popular imagery the ethnographer has shifted from a sympathetic, authoritative observer (best incarnated, perhaps, by Margaret Mead) to the unflattering figure portrayed by Vine Deloria in *Custer Died for Your Sins*" (9). Clifford foregrounds the complexities of ethnographic work, including that of indigenous ethnographers, suggesting that it is now situated somewhere between these two approaches. Today, he argues, anthropology "no longer speaks with automatic authority for others defined as unable to speak for themselves ('primitive,' 'pre-literate,' 'without history')" (10). Nonetheless, in his own contribution to this collection of essays, "On Ethnographic Allegory," Clifford argues "that the very activity of ethnographic *writing* – seen as inscription or textualization – enacts a redemptive Western allegory" (99). In this, he reflects many theorists' concerns with the difficulty of apprehending the subaltern or the "indigenous colonized" without this apprehension being filtered through the European-inspired gaze.

Both *Burning Water* and *La Tribu* ironically highlight some ethnographic practices in order to foreground New World Myth's challenge to traditional, European-inspired ethnography. Because of
these texts' differing degrees of conflation of Amerindians and non-
Amerindians and because of the use they make of allegory, parody,
irony, and *métissage* in their problematizations of the creative imagination and myth, it is important to return briefly to what is called
primitive myth in European-inspired investigations of pre-contact
cultures.[3]

In the Anglo-American sphere of influence, the very term "primitive mentality" is strongly rejected today for its overtones of imperialist colonialism. However this same term, "la mentalité primitive,"
has been used by French philosophers, anthropologists, and structuralists throughout the nineteenth and twentieth centuries; it was used
as recently as the 1989 Paris retrospective of Claude Lévi-Strauss'
work. In much French European thought, the idea of teleological
evolution underlies the use of the term *la mentalité primitive*. Even
those European thinkers who object to the use of the term itself, such
as Lévy-Bruhl, conceptualize thought in terms of change and
improvement through time and civilizations, and maintain the
notion of "the primitive": "il n'y a pas une mentalité primitive qui
se distingue de l'autre par deux caractères qui lui sont propres (mystique et prélogique). Il y a une mentalité mystique plus marquée et
plus facilement observable chez les 'primitifs' que dans nos sociétés,
mais présente dans tout esprit humain" (Lévy-Bruhl, *Carnets*, quoted
in P. Hébert, "Un Problème de sémiotique," 219–20). All of *La Tribu*
is an extended parody of this way of thinking, which still appears in
many texts of late twentieth-century French writers and philosophers. This belief in cultural evolutionism is strongly opposed by
contemporary Amerindian historians such as Georges Sioui, of the
Huron/Wendat Nation near Quebec City; he proposes abandoning it
in favour of "le Cercle sacré de la vie qui s'oppose à la conception
évolutionniste du monde selon laquelle les êtres sont inégaux, souvent méconnus, constamment bousculés et remplacés par d'autres
qui semblent adaptés à l'"évolution'" (*Pour une autohistoire amérindienne*, 3). While the use of parody directed against Amerindian
myths and stories can sometimes be problematic, there is no doubt
that cultural evolutionism – another "given," in my sense of the term
– is challenged and frequently undercut through the use of parody
in New World Myth fictions.

In *Victorian Anthropology* the well-known historian of anthropology, George Stocking, has studied the gradual construction of the
European-inspired myth of the primitive. He lays bare the usual

assumptions regarding the "primitive's" sexuality, promiscuity, simplicity, timelessness, ahistoricity, animistic religiosity, folklore, oral traditions, myth and legends, limited vocabulary, and lack of higher intelligence. Stocking's summary of primitive thought as discussed by Herbert Spencer reveals the typical "superior European" approach: "'Lacking words even for low generalities and abstractions, it is utterly impossible that the savage should have words to frame a conception uniting high generality with high abstractness.' There was no such thing as a primitive 'mythopoeic tendency.' It was rather that lacking imagination, and 'having only rude speech' which was, of necessity, 'full of metaphor,' the savage created the marvelous 'unawares'; from there he gradually progressed toward factual narrative by a 'slowly increasing ratio of truth to error.'" (Stocking, *Victorian Anthropology*, 308; Spencer, *The Principles of Psychology*, 1: 831–3, 837, 841). As we saw in chapters 1 and 5, this attitude corresponds to the notion of *la mentalité primitive*, as formulated by Georges Gusdorf and criticized by Georges Sioui.

Although this anthropological eurocentrism has been strongly criticized in the latter half of the twentieth century, as is evident in the collected essays in Stocking's *Observers Observed*, literary studies of myth frequently tend to trace the evolution of myth in literature from "primitive orality" to "sophisticated civilizations." While Kenneth Bourke suggests that confusion occurs between religious and literary discourse because the two "involve intense symbolic activity" ("Doing and Saying," 101), Richard Chase argues that myth and religion were once indistinguishable, with myth being a kind of religious philosophy ("Myth as Literature," 127). Chase further proposes that the origins of myth lie in the "primitives'" fear and adoration of nature. A similar attitude is found in the writings of many myth critics, including Franz Boas, whose anthropological approach to myth led him to study the indigenous peoples of Northwestern Canada. Boas declares: "Songs and tales are found all over the world. These are the fundamental forms of literature among primitive people" (quoted in Chase, "Myth as Literature," 129). Even in the latter half of the twentieth century, some myth critics perpetuate this teleological evolutionism; Colin Falck sees myth as having its roots in "primitive cultures":

Myth, and the mythic mode of apprehension of reality, seems in actual historical and prehistorical fact to be a universal stage through which the developing human linguistic consciousness passes, and the mythic mode of awareness can perhaps best be understood as another aspect or dimension of the corporeally based awareness of our own powers and agency ... The

seeming universality of myth and of mythic consciousness in primitive cultures must on its own be a *prima facie* justification for supposing that these
corporeally based and pre- or incompletely conceptual modes of awareness
may be not merely a universal, but also a necessary, aspect of human existence on which our fully articulated and discursive conceptual language has
its experiential foundation. (*Myth, Truth and Literature*, 116)

In both *La Tribu* and *Burning Water*, albeit with varying degrees of
sensitivity, the narrators parodically foreground some widely held
assumptions regarding traditional studies of myth and its role within
and without pre-contact societies. By the very blatancy of their ironic
portrayals of some traditional tenets of myth criticism, the narrators
hold these assumptions up for closer critical examination. In both
novels, there is a deliberate narratorial unsettling of the types of
assumptions found in many studies of myth criticism that discuss
the artistic concerns of "primitive cultures."

The use of allegory and *métissage* in *La Tribu* highlights some complexities of the New World challenge to traditional myth-criticism:
its narrator flaunts the use he makes of the image of the Amerindian
to parodically and allegorically represent, respectively, the *pure laine*
Québécois and an Amerindian tribe from pre-contact times. Paul
Smith has noted that many recent studies have remarked on the
resurgence of allegory in the second half of the twentieth century,
from Paul de Man's *Allegories of Reading* to Gayatri Spivak's articles
on the subject ("The Will to Allegory in Postmodernism," 105). Like
parody, allegory is usually seen as "doubling or duplicating extra-
textual material ... with the allegorical sign refer[ing] always to a
previous or anterior sign" (Slemon, "Post-Colonial Allegory," 158).
Slemon, however, has a very interesting perspective on allegory that
corresponds in large part to the way I see New World Myth operating in contemporary texts. He argues that "post-colonial allegorical
writing is engaged in a process of destabilizing and transforming our
fixed ideas of history, and [that] this process demonstrates ... the
inadequacy of the critical position that perceives allegory as a mode
of writing that is limited in scope and mechanically determined by
the historical or literary 'pretext' upon which it is based" (164). For
Slemon, the practice of allegory in postcolonial texts is different from
that prescribed for it in mainstream criticism: "despite this renewal
of interest in allegorical practice, significant discrepancies exist
between the various theories of allegory now in critical currency and
the kind of allegorical writing and reading that is currently being
practised in post-colonial cultures – which is perhaps not entirely

surprising given the fact that mainstream allegorical theory is based almost exclusively on art and intellectual traditions of European and United States provenance" (157). Slemon sees postcolonial allegory as a practice that opens up previously cut-and-dried issues such as history and "pretexts." For him, postcolonial allegory sets up multiple tensions between fiction and history, and postcolonial allegories "are concerned with neither redeeming nor annihilating history, but with displacing it as a concept and opening up the past to imaginative revision" (165). Slemon's proposal here could be equally applied to New World Myth: "post-colonial allegorical writing not only constitutes a challenge to prevailing theoretical assumptions about what kind of cultural grounding is required for allegorical communication to take place, but also ... it is helping to change our received ideas of history" (158).

La Tribu is a postcolonial text that seeks through its work on myth to destabilize the fixity of history and of the present. New World Myth opens history and the present up to the type of imaginative revision that Slemon privileges here. The *métissage* that underlies Barcelo's use of allegory constitutes both a foregrounding and a challenge to accepted notions of this cultural grounding. In previous discussions of *métissage*, I argued that it is an aspect of reality in Quebec that is largely ignored in academic and cultural circles. It is indeed highly ironic that Jacqueline Peterson and Jennifer Brown, in their introduction to *The New Peoples: Being and Becoming Métis in North America*, foreground the "composite 'mestizo' populations" of Latin America, while downplaying the importance of the *métissage* population in Quebec:

despite Latin America's continued domination by Euro-American financial interests and ethnic minorities, the future identity and direction of many of its post-colonial and post-revolutionary nations belong to the "new peoples." In North America, by contrast, both the historical process of mixing and the resultant peoples themselves have been obscured ... The word *métis* was rarely applied, on an individual basis, to persons of English-Indian or non-French and Indian ancestry, nor was it generally extended in its collective usage to mixed populations outside western Canada or those with no historical connection with the Red River group. Even in its Manitoba heartland, the term was rarely used by English speakers before the 1960s. In the United States, the word itself was virtually unknown. (4–5)

Peterson and Brown go on to note that the term *métis*, from the 1970s onward, has had a much wider usage in certain parts of Canada and in the northern border states of the United States, but, regrettably, they make no serious investigation of *métissage* in Quebec. Pierre-André Julien, however, in his previously cited article, "Ne sommes-nous pas tous des Amérindiens?" sees the *mestizo* population of Brazil as comparable to *métissage* in Quebec. He decries the federal interventions: "L'anglicisation d'un grand nombre de bandes indiennes ... dans un Québec francophone, tout aberrant que ce soit, découle de cette politique [de réserves amérindiennes]. He suggests that it would be advisable to "sortir de la logique anglo-saxonne, par exemple en revenant à l'esprit de nos coureurs des bois et des Métis de l'Ouest." (13). Underlying Julien's proposals for a better relationship with Amerindians is a firm acceptance of the transcultural heritage of many Quebecers, including that of his own relatives. My point here is that the strong *métissé* background of a very impressive number of francophone Quebecers provides a basis for the narrator's easy slippage between various cultural groups in *La Tribu*. The usual cultural grounding, in which "a fairly common assumption seems to be that allegorical modes of reading and writing are concerned with redeeming or recuperating the past" (Slemon, "Post-Colonial Allegory," 158) is challenged by the continual coming and going between these groups in the novel.

Slemon notes that postcolonial writings may not adhere to the "traditionally past-to-present direction of allegorical signification" ("Post-Colonial Allegory," 162), and may thus subvert what Paul de Man calls "the rhetoric of temporality" (de Man, "Rhetoric," 173). By challenging the order of who/what "allegorizes" who/what, by disrupting the usual order of the past allegorized in the present, postcolonial texts can change accepted versions of allegory *and* history: "allegory can itself be used to dismantle the system of allegorical thinking that underwrites the act of colonisation" (Slemon, "Post-Colonial Allegory," 163).

La Tribu's narrator asserts that *his* primitive tribe makes no use whatsoever of the imagination to produce what Boas called the fundamental forms of literature among primitive people: "Personne dans la tribu n'avait songé à sculpter des totems. Personne n'avait pensé qu'il serait agréable de tailler un personnage mythique dans un bout de bois ou un caillou mou ... Non, la tribu avait les pieds sur terre. Elle n'avait ni dieux, ni religions, ni croyances, ni superstitions. Elle n'avait pas la moindre chanson, à l'exception de celles que Jafafoua avait apportées du Vieux-Pays et leur avait apprises ... [Elle] n'avait en fait ni musique, ni art, ni poésie, ni légendes" (138). This potentially problematic passage illustrates at least three concerns of postcolonial writing: first, it so blatantly foregrounds the superior

European/primitive native construct that it undercuts it, especially as this type of foregrounding is omnipresent throughout the text. Parodic repetition of this construct highlights it *as* construct and weakens its force. Second, the passage outrightly contradicts the European-inspired anthropological emphases on tribal myths, tribal culture, tribal works of art: this tribe has none. Third, and most fundamentally, to parodically mock the traditional *mythes de l'identité* of the pre-1960s Québécois society, it uses the *slippage* technique against a backdrop of *métissage* practice. The Clipocs are/are not Amerindians; they also are/are not twentieth-century Quebecers. Thus, this passage and others like it constitute an obvious mockery of the Québécois' self-image as a struggling people whose cultural and religious heritages have been preserved through the centuries in the face of great obstacles – a myth perpetrated and reinforced by fictions from *Les Anciens Canadiens* to *Prochain Episode*. The passage is doubly ironic. The Clipocs' only "culture" consists of songs from the "Vieux-Pays," just as old French songs gradually became the nationalist folk songs of Quebec. The passage first underlines this irony, and then rejects those traditions formerly prized in Quebec for their ability to maintain "l'héritage du peuple": the Catholic religion and the "peuple élu de Dieu," the protectionist attitude of the "collectivité," and a belief in the inviolability of popular cultural practices such as the folk songs of "la soirée canadienne."

With a tabula rasa in matters of myth, art, religion, and the imagination, the narrator suggests, the Clipocs can get *on* with things. Like the new generation of Québécois entrepreneurs who were beginning to wield political power in the years 1975–85, Mahii is fed up with the status quo, and in particular with Pogo and Togo (or Sogo and Wogo – the first letters of their names change constantly) who while away their time by imagining winter games such as hockey and curling (*La Tribu*, 113). Under Mahii's leadership, scientific and industrial expansion leaves no room for "idle" activities such as creative art. Thus, the younger Clipocs, returning home from their punitive expedition against the Niox with small works of primitive art as war trophies, know that these objects prove beyond any doubt that "les Niox étaient barbares car ils occupaient leur temps libre à fabriquer des choses inutiles" (131). As we have seen, the tribe's "progress" culminates in the massacre of the Niox. The subsequent destruction of all forms of progress makes the tribe "primitive" again (134), but its members are no more accepting of art than before. This "primitive" tribe is not a typical one, as the narrator frequently points out – nor are the Québécois, he also intimates through this *métissage(d)* allegory, a typical colonized people. In the igloos of the Inuit, Wogo is puzzled by the carved soapstones, and although Mahii explains that they are only statuettes, he persists in the perfectly useless activity of finding a use for them (151).

Religion is equally problematic for the Clipocs. They do not understand the importance of the religious myths and artistic statuettes of neighbouring tribes. The parodies of all religious expression and theocratic societies in this text foreground the massive rejection of Catholicism in Quebec in the 1960s and '70s. Thus, the narrator's story of the Reverend Nelson Golden retells the persecution of the "Rahélites" (Jews), parodically mocking various Christian religions' interpretations of God (166). The immortal Grand-Nez, who believes that *all* the indigenous peoples of the New Continent are his descendants (this certainty is undercut elsewhere in the novel), realizes the ridiculousness of some tribes' practice of attributing their origins to invented gods (71). Indeed, the absence of gods, religion, art, and myth among the Clipocs attracts Grand-Nez, because, as he laconically notes: "[une] tribu aussi ennuyeuse, aussi casanière ... est incapable du moindre mal" (138). Such a comment again uses allegory and *métissage* to upset, as Slemon describes it, the "traditionally past-to-present direction of allegorical signification" ("Post-Colonial Allegory," 162), and to subvert de Man's "rhetoric of temporality." It is not so much the tribe as the twentieth-century Québécois who are being parodied here. As long as the Clipocs are in opposition to those expectations aroused by the traditional notions of the myths of primitive tribes and/or the heritage of the French Canadian people, they flourish. Indeed, it is when the tribe temporarily becomes more like the European concept of what constitutes a primitive tribe – choosing a leader, Notregloire, making him into a god and practising the rites of his pagan religion (which constitute a pronounced parody of the Catholic mass) – that things begin to fall apart for them.

Again, the Clipocs do not have that communion with nature that, according to anthropologists and ethnographers, all primitives are supposed to enjoy. The myth of the Canadian North as a spiritual place of purity, renewal, and freedom is a tradition in both English and French Canadian culture.[4] In *La Tribu*, this specific myth is ironically reversed. Although Mahii does lead the Clipocs toward the purity of the great white North after the episode with the Niox, the tribe soon discovers that *everyone* is heading north (172). It is back in the *South* that the tribe eventually makes that fresh start, although no one but the narrator notices the irony of the situation (207).

One final myth of the primitive is parodied in *La Tribu*: the notion of communal storytelling sessions that teach history. In his seminal work on history and metahistory, *Comment on écrit l'histoire*, Paul

Veyne notes that primitive peoples' histories are passed on to future generations through storytelling sessions (27–8); Jean-François Lyotard also uses the Cashinahua storyteller to illustrate the importance of narrative to pre-contact cultures (*La Condition postmoderne*, 39). *La Tribu* contains an extended parody of the traditional notion of myth as a story containing great wisdom handed down through the generations and capable of imparting the truth to those who can decipher it. For instance, Grand-Nez's great age and accumulated wisdom should make of him a shamanic wise man. Not wanting to be taken for "un vieux menteur" (71), Grand-Nez is discreet about his origins and his immortality. Nonetheless, he decides to impart the true story of his past to Jafafoua. The latter, however, falls asleep of boredom in front of the fire instead of listening and learning. Grand-Nez, deeply hurt, changes tactics. He becomes one of the tribe's most preferred distractions, telling newly invented stories. When the wonder-child of the tribe, Notregloire, asks Grand-Nez to recount "des histoires d'autrefois" (212), the old man chooses once again to tell only what he has seen and heard in the past, but the incredulous Notregloire learns nothing from history, because he considers the tales to be ludicrous. This tribe's lack of appreciation for its past would seem to support the notion that the past is useless and that the Clipocs – like the Québécois – should release their "légendes vieillotes" into the past and gladly embrace the present. The narrator of this novel, however, chooses to retell (together) the distant and recent past of both the Clipoc tribe and the Québécois people. On the one hand, the obvious parodies of "primitive" and / or Québécois myths of the past seem to be an invitation to escape from the stasis of a mythology into a praxis of the here and now. On the other hand, that praxis involves the retelling of historico-political events, thereby positing a need for that past, along with an acknowledgment that there are alternative versions of that past. The narrator, then, through his allegoric storytelling, installs and maintains the tension of the imagination that is characteristic of New World Myth.

George Bowering's *Burning Water* also explores this tension of the imagination. In passages that foreground the narrator's struggle with narrative and others that highlight the "Indians," Bowering ironically challenges certain accepted truisms about "primitive" myth and discusses the related notions of the creative imagination, madness, "primitives", and gods. Where Barcelo's allegories mock the European-inspired construct of the myth of the primitive, which underlies much of evolutionist French philosophy and the *histoire des religions*, Bowering's target is closer to home. As we saw in the preceding chapter, Bowering makes it clear that he is in opposition to much of the myth theory of Northrop Frye, including Frye's Christian/Western conception of the artist as one who imposes his desires on the world of nature. In her overview of Bowering's development as a writer and critic, Eva-Marie Kröller proposes that Bowering's stay at the University of Western Ontario in the late 1960s brought him into contact with a creative and influential group of writers with whom he disagreed on one important point: regionalism. As Kröller notes, Bowering "suspected 'regionalism' of perpetuating the grid-system that had dismayed him in Alberta, for both imply man's ascendancy over nature. He particularly blamed Northrop Frye for promoting poetry with a mythopoeic direction" (*Bright Circles*, 49). Challenging Frye's idea that all literature is in some way an imitation of earlier literature, Bowering declares that a "real" encounter with myth would take place in the here and now ("Why James Reaney," 46). Poets, he writes: "do not get their forms from literary code alone. Literature is not myth with belief removed" (43). Given Bowering's obvious interest in myth and the vehemence with which he refutes much of the myth criticism of Northrop Frye, it is not surprising that an ironic subtext of myth is found in many allusions to the "primitives" in *Burning Water*.

Irony, like allegory and parody, often depends on the viewer/hearer/reader. Linda Hutcheon argues that irony, "a trope that works from within a power field but still contests it, is a consistently useful strategy for post-colonial discourse" (*Splitting Images*, 80). Homi Bhabha takes a different stance, condemning the figures of farce, such as "*trompe l'œil*, irony, mimicry and repetition" as tools with which colonialism exercises its authority (*Location of Culture*, 85). W.H. New sees irony as allowing a discussion of the issues that the irony is directed at: "Though dualities abound in the ironist's world, the stances he may take range from parody and innuendo through sarcasm and self-disparagement to absurdity and nihilism ... At its best, the ironic stance provokes a serious deliberation into the problems that led to dualities in the first place" (*Among Worlds*, 3). Bowering's ironic play with Frye's theories of myth-criticism constitute a locus for a critical look at traditional myth-criticism.

In *The Educated Imagination*, Frye comments on the following passage from Shakespeare's *Midsummer Night's Dream*: "The lunatic, the lover, and the poet / Are of imagination all compact" (5.1.102). According to Frye, "the lunatic and the lover are trying to identify themselves with something, the lover with his mistress, the lunatic with whatever he's obsessed with. Primitive people also try to identify themselves with totems or animals or spirits ... The poet, too, is an identifier: everything he sees in nature he identifies with human life. That's why literature, and more particularly poetry, shows [an] analogy to primitive minds" (31). The following parodic passage from *Burning Water* plays satirically with the above notions of lunatics, poets, gods and poetry:

Dr. Menzies patched [the sailor] up and told him he was a fool.

"I *am* a fool," said the sailor. "I am a poet, too."

"Oh well, I am a god from the sun," muttered Menzies, tearing the bandages and tying the ends.

"I am preparing a long poem about our search for El Dorado and the Strait of Anian," said the youth.

"I am preparing a long poem, too," said Menzies ... "It uses as its central metaphor the flora of newly discovered lands."

"An interesting fancy," said the bandaged sailor.

"Get out of my sight, you idiot," said Menzies. (225)

In this passage, the sailor is called Delsing, a name that has served Bowering as an alter ego in many of his texts; he is, according to Bowering, "a projection of myself more than anyone else is" ("Delsing and Me," 46). Through metafictional references, then, this passage sends up the myth of the inspired poet, as well as touching ironically on a Canadian genre, the long poem, and on the textual deconstruction of European myths in the New World. It also mocks the common assumption in myth studies that one of the first gods of any "primitive" collectivity is the sun-god. This assumption is played on elsewhere in *Burning Water* when an Indian, referring to Vancouver's flight of fancy over the Rockies, discusses the possible divinity of the white men in a tone that mocks anthropological studies: "There are stories that our great grandfathers saw them. At least that is the most common interpretation these days of their stories about flame-bearded gods who sailed here from the sun" (146). The Indian artist at first believes that the white men fulfil a "primitive" need: "these persons may be gods and they may be men, but ... in either case they came to us from the sun" (91). The Indians then realize that the white men do not quite have the specialness of gods: they are "very rich, not quite gods, but certainly permitted by the gods a favoured position in life" (146). Toward the end of the voyage, the British are attacked by unfriendly Indians. They try to deflect the attackers' wrath by declaring themselves to be invincible gods, but the Indians' derisive reactions reveal their disbelief: "'Aeh, shit!' ... 'They say that you should go and be gods in your own land. They say you are not permitted to step your sacred *Mamathni* feet upon their mother'" (231). This last reference to the "primitive" myth of the Earth-Mother is of course misunderstood by the British: "'We don't care about their old women' ... 'By their mother they mean the continent,' said the guide" (231–2).

The notion that all primitives have a sacred place is also parodied in the following conversation, which itself arises out of a discussion among the Indians as to whether the invading white men are gods:

We will fall back upon the people's secret ... One night, as if rising to an undescribed instinct, all our people will quit the victors' sight and vanish into the mist. An unstated number of days later we will have established our dwelling in the holy Strait of Anian, which no invader has ever been able to find ... When the danger has passed, we will say a prayer of gratitude to our holy place and return to our workaday world, there to put our minds and bodies to the task of feeding the people at home. A simple life, but one that leaves a lot of time for thinking about things such as gods and men. (94)

The notion of a relatively fixed mythology known to all adult members of a primitive collectivity, whose lives are regulated by known ritual and by what they perceive to be the desires of their gods, is mocked in the opening chapter of *Burning Water*. This European-inspired construct is the target here: *this* Indian artist incorrectly takes the white men's ships for visions and shows his cheerful ignorance of the names of his own Amerindian gods. The commonly accepted notion that every collectivity has certain basic myths such as those of a life-destroying flood and a migration is also parodied in *Burning Water*.[5] The ironic tone of scholarship employed by the Indians in their responses to Menzies' queries about cannibalism foregrounds this novel's parody of the European-inspired myth of the primitive: "It seems as if I did hear something once about our forefathers eating people long ago before the time of the Great Flood ... There is a rumour, unsubstantiated, that a remnant of that ancient people-eating society survives" (112). Textual capitalization of such myths also parodies this accepted notion of myth criticism: "the Great Uprising of the People," "the Great Going Away" (94). Indeed, it is possible that the oxymoronic title of this novel makes reference not only to Coleridge's rewriting of the journals of Captain Cook but also to an Amerindian myth. Kuester points to John Livingston Lowes's work on Coleridge, which argues that Coleridge based his lines about burning water on Cook's writings. The multiple parody signalled here by Kuester traces both a European genealogy and a postcolonial reaction to it: "So we are here confronted with a complex network of parodic relationships: Coleridge artistically re-works (parodies, in one sense of the word) Cook's writing; the real George Vancouver, who had been Cook's apprentice on his expeditions, rewrites what had been erroneous statements in the journals of Cook ... Here we have a good example of what Helen Tiffin calls 'canonical counter-discourse': This strategy ... is one in which a post-colonial writer takes up a character or characters, or the basic assumptions of a British canonical text, and unveils those assumptions, subverting the text for post-colonial practices" (*Framing Truths*, 117; see also Tiffin, "Post-Colonial Literatures," 22). It is also possible that Bowering, who has frequently indicated his interest in demythologizing European-inspired myths, had in mind an intertext more specific to the Americas. As Laurette Séjourné points out in her work on Nahuatl myths, *Burning Water: Thought and Religion in Ancient Mexico*, the burning water myth is central to this Amerindian mythology. It involves creativity: "the divine spark is freed only when matter is burned up ... The construction of the temple [the Great Temple at Tenochtitlan] on the site of the fountain from which the blue and red water flowed is also significant, and shows that the gods ruling over it symbolized the mystic formula of 'burning water'" (108–10).

Another way in which *Burning Water*'s narrator undercuts the European-inspired myth of the primitive is by mockingly presenting the storytelling sessions in which myths of wisdom are handed down from one generation to another: "The second Indian loved being middle-aged. It meant that he could be the one who passes on the stories from the old people to the young people ... One was also credited with a certain store of wisdom" (147). However, the second Indian's "wisdom" is off the mark: when his younger companion points out to him a surprising "fact" that he has not considered, the older and supposedly wiser Indian is taken aback, or as the narrator puts it, he is "a truly disoriented middle-aged man for the moment." We are a long way from Paul Veyne's storytelling sessions – or Lyotard's Cashinahua storyteller.

   The concept of the Indian as a myth-ridden creature easily dominated by European technology is also parodied – and frequently inverted – in Bowering's novel. The European literary myth of the noble savage is ridiculed here: "Before the white 'settlers' arrived there were lots of impatient Indians. It's only in the last two hundred years that Indians have been looking patient whenever there were any white men around" (*Burning Water*, 92). Elsewhere, the narrator writes, "The third Indian shifted uncomfortably, despite all the people who think Indians are always fully comfortable in their natural environment" (93). Although the British explorers use disparaging terms to describe the Indians – "wily aborigines" (21); "monkeys"; "mouse-eating savages" (119); "regular heathen[s]" (168) – the narrator's tale often has the white man acting in a "primitive" manner:

Magee stepped out of the nearby copse with a donkey loaded down with supplies. He held his hand up, palm forward.

"How!" he said, in a deep voice.

The two Indians made their faces look patient.

"What is this 'How'?" asked the first Indian of his companion.

"Search me," said the second Indian. "But we may as well go along with him." (199)

The "primitiveness" of the white man's perspective and behaviour are underlined frequently in this text. Menzies suggest that Vancouver's fear and misunderstanding of the New World stems from his personal mythological universe: "It is because you take a mountain for a god and a god for a father" (108). In contrast, Menzies suggests, Indians are not prisoners of a myth-ridden worldview and, consequently, are more able to accept reality: they "deem the mountains to be mountains, that and whatever advantage they can make of that. They are true Western man" (108). The longer passage from which the preceding quotation is taken inverts the assumption that Western [European, white] man is a rational, civilized human being and the Indian a superstitious primitive dominated by natural phenomena.

Vancouver, as the leader of possibly divine beings, is closely scrutinized by the Indians for any sign of divinity. However, as the Indian artist regrettably concludes, Vancouver "lacked one quality that would have made him a god ... he had no madness in him, none at all" (*Burning Water*, 240). A concern with madness permeates this novel. This recurring theme foregrounds the fact/fancy/imagination debate and highlights the eighteenth-century preoccupation with rationality and the nineteenth-century Romantic interest in creative madness. Near the end of the novel, Menzies, the "good eighteenth-century man" (96), determines through careful observation that Vancouver *is* crazy (211); shortly thereafter, he shoots the captain. However, the Europeans' dislike of madness is countered by the Indians' admiration of it. In their worldview, lunacy appears to be the magic ingredient that can turn a human being into a god. Curiously, while this text undercuts the usual precepts of myth-criticism, its narrator underlines the traditional linking of madness to artists, deities, and the creative imagination. Thus, Blake's friend wonders "whether Blake were mystifying the occasion, averring something about a world we normal eighteenth-century souls could not follow, or whether he were as mad as a button maker" (160). Vancouver often wonders if he himself is mad, but never reaches a definitive conclusion. Neither the narrator nor Vancouver has *one* determinate approach to madness and its relationship to gods and creativity. Bowering's Vancouver does have a desire for divinity and posterity. If, as is suggested traditionally, a myth is a story about a god, then Vancouver has aspirations to be the subject of such a story: he "wanted to be a famous story very much, the kind of story that is known before you read it. He wanted his name and his exploits to be a part of the world" (62–3). In the end, Vancouver relies on his artistically rendered scientific work to make him known to posterity – to history. The theme of gods from the sun occurs even here – evoked not by "primitives" but by an eighteenth-century character longing for recognition for his perfect maps: "If strangers were to come from the sun they could scan these hard-won facts and journey wide of peril" (242).

Like his Vancouver, Bowering's narrator is preoccupied with madness. He repeatedly suggests that his own work – the creative and self-conscious retelling of the Vancouver story – is crazy (15, 80). The emphasis on madness and divinity in the artist-writer-explorer Vancouver points to similar questions about the narrator. Is *he* mad? Will his work last? Will his story "mythologize" Vancouver? Or does he, like Vancouver, lack what Lobb characterizes as "the divine madness of the visionary or the poet" ("Imagining History," 117n6)? Although the textual conflation of the narrator and Vancouver (and, occasionally, Blake) insists that these questions should be posed, the narrator's disappearance from the text leaves them unresolved. He leaves the question of his *own* contribution to a New World mythology dangling, unsettled, in front of the reader. In this ending is *Burning Water's* beginning: we "are making a story, after all, as we always have been, standing and speaking together to make up a history, a real historical fiction" (prologue).

Both Bowering's and Barcelo's texts, then, foreground the problematic use of the creative imagination in the retelling of history. By emphasizing the indeterminate nature of the "truth" of the past, and by parodically illustrating, through self-conscious metafictional examples, that Romantic image par excellence, the artistic imagination at work, these narrators issue a challenge to traditional assumptions about the nature of a work of art and the relationship between rationality and historical facts, on the one hand, and fiction and myth on the other. The textual use of irony, parody, allegory, and *métissage* issues an invitation to the reader to participate in the perpetual coming-into-being of New World Myth.

Afterword

Nowhere is the process of what Foucault once called "the interrogating of limits that is now replacing the search for totality" (Hutcheon, *The Politics of Representation*, 9) more evident than in these contemporary historiographic novels that retell events of the political past. Several narrative techniques contribute to this process: self-conscious narration that emphasizes that the tale varies according to teller; alternative – even contradictory – versions of one event of the past; and the dismantling of traditional literary and historical worldviews through reworkings of myth in narrative. New World Myths are not timeless, eternal, transhistorical tales about gods and goddesses from other worlds but rather stories grounded in historico-political realities that signal their flexibility and their awareness of the mutability of *all* story. The metafictional nature of the six New World Myth texts discussed here, working in conjunction with their investigations of history and historiography, installs a postmodern tension about knowledge of the past in these post-European texts from English-speaking Canada and Quebec.

The narrators of these "not always fictional fiction[s]" (Thiher, *Words in Reflection*, 190), like Joy Kogawa's narrator, Naomi, are fully aware that "stories are changed in time, altered as much by the present as the present is shaped by the past" (*Obasan*, 256). And yet, paradoxically, the didactic urge is strong in New World Myth: the narrators do address specific events of the historical past in their stories. Their postmodern and postcolonial retellings of these events install the tension between fiction and reality that is typical of New World Myth texts.

In-depth analyses of six selected texts have permitted the investigation of various manifestations of New World Myth: among them, the narrator as self-conscious myth-maker, the deliberate problematization of traditional cosmogonies, the foregrounding of some aspects of feminine symbolism, the use of magic realist techniques, the problematization of community, the foregrounding of *métissage*, and the use of parody, irony, and allegory to challenge accepted tenets of myth criticism in literary studies. Many other novels published in English Canada and Quebec – some in languages other than English and French – could provide equally interesting analyses of or different manifestations of New World Myth.

Is the work on myth begun in these historiographic fictions going to evolve *eventually* into a codified, fixed mythology such as that described by Frye in "Literature and Myth"? Frye states: "It is rare for a society to realize that its myths are its own creations ... what the myth presents is not what happened in the past, but what is said to have happened in the past in order to justify what is in the present. Such myth has the social function of rationalizing the status quo: it explains, not merely why we do the things we do, but why we ought to go on doing them" (27–8). Although it is impossible to predict where the New World challenges to Old World concepts will lead with time, the very nature of New World Myth belies the suggested prognosis that it will eventually become a fixed and immutable element. The narrators of the six texts studied here not only realize but also flaunt the idea that their New World Myths are their own creations. Assuming that the status quo consists of Old World givens, especially regarding history and religion, New World Myth subverts the status quo: it questions precisely *whether* we ought to go on doing, believing, practising them. Accompanying these narratorial challenges, however, is a persistent tension, occasioned by the narrators' sense of driving mission to posit a flexible and adaptable alternative mythology composed of New World (hi)stories that are *not* that definitive, canonic group of stories proposed by Frye. While the ramifications of this tension are not always clear, this study has shown the need to acknowledge the coexistence of the narratorial desire to mythologize and the desire to expose the mythologization process.

Ginette Michaud, discussing the difficulties inherent in trying to define the term postmodernism, remarks that this term should be redefined in the present of each (different) situation ("Récits postmodernes?" 68). The same remark might well be applied to the concept of New World Myth. The narrators' self-consciousness about their retellings of history and their deliberate maintenance of the political, historical, and fictional tensions that are typical of New World Myth create a mythology that is fluid, adjustable, and continually shifting. Thus, future manifestations of New World Myth will indeed need to be defined in the future present of each situation. Because of its inherent nature, New World Myth is constantly adapting to ever-changing notions; it is in a perpetual state of coming-into-being.

From a comparative point of view, this study has not dwelt on those similarities and differences between the French- and English-language literatures in Canada, as Philip Stratford does in *All the Polarities*, but rather on the manifestations of New World Myth in selected historiographic fictions published between 1975 and 1985 in English-speaking Canada and Quebec. In these texts, New World Myth is clearly a response to a need to reimagine the past in a post-colonial, postmodern, and post-European manner.

Notes

PREFACE

1 See, for instance, Patai, *Myth and Ideology*; González Echevarría, *Myth and Archive*; Calviño, *Historia, Ideologia y Mito*; Webb, *Myth and History in Caribbean Fiction*; and Hestetun, *A Prison-House of Myth?*
2 See, for instance, Foucault, "Nietzsche, Genealogy, History"; and Clifford, *Predicament of Culture*.
3 See Simon et al., *Fictions de l'identitaire au Québec*.
4 See Bayard, "From *Nègres blancs d'Amérique*," 21.

CHAPTER ONE

1 See Frazer, *Sir James Frazer*.
2 One example of this type of research is Eastman, "Myth and Fate," which compares D.H. Lawrence's characters to Apollo, Dionysus, and others, in order to show how the lack of absolute parallels between the classical and modern figures liberates the latter from the stereotypical.
3 See for example Bonnard, *Les Dieux de la Grèce*.
4 See Eliade, *Le Mythe de l'éternel retour, Images et symboles*, and *Aspects du mythe*.
5 Similar work was done in English by Andrew Lang in *Magic and Religion*.
6 Two exemplary works would be Albouy, *Mythes et mythologies*, and Prémont, *Le Mythe de Prométhée*.

7 Lévi-Strauss himself did not have much contact with those peoples whose customs he described in detail in his massive four-volume *Mythologiques*.

8 For instance, the Swiss psychoanalyst Carl Jung's theories of archetypes and the collective unconscious (based in part of the theories of Lévy-Bruhl, who associated myth with mystical and prelogical thought) have had a bearing on many twentieth-century studies of myth in literature. The French philosopher Georges Gusdorf's *Mythe et métaphysique*, first published in 1953, resembles Frazer's *Golden Bough* in its theory of the evolution of "primitive" thought, but Gusdorf's ideas were not taken up by French and Québécois literatures in the way that Frazer's work influenced Anglo-American literature. And several anthropologists, sociologists, and historians of religion, such as Eliade, Mauss, the functionalist Bronislaw Malinowski ("Myth in Primitive Psychology"), and Georges Dumézil (*Mythe et épopée*) did interesting work on the relationship between myths and the maintenance of society as a system – work that undoubtedly influenced cultural and literary productions of the mid-twentieth century. Ernst Cassirer (*Language and Myth, Mythical Thought*) discussed the importance of *language* to the making of myths, while Vladimir Propp's work on the basic elements of folktales (*Morphologie du conte*) led to a corresponding search for predictable sequences in myth.

9 Examples of this type of myth criticism are provided by Lauter and Rupprecht, *Feminist Archetypal Theory*, which criticizes the masculine bias in Jung's work and sets out to redefine basic concepts like archetypes and the unconscious, and by Wall, *The Callisto Myth*, which investigates patriarchal perceptions of female sexuality.

10 Two notable exceptions are Mailhot, "Romans de la parole," and Fee, "Howard O'Hagan's *Tay John*," both of which are discussed in greater detail below.

11 See Hamilton, *Northrop Frye*; Hart, *Northrop Frye*; and the collected essays in Lee and Denham, *The Legacy of Northrop Frye*. Even negative appraisals of his work, such as Wimsatt's critique of his theories ("Criticism and Myth") or even Powe's humorous and ironic "Fear of Fryeing" add to his stature as an international critic.

12 Buss's article, which addresses sexual behaviour in Laurence's women characters in the light of a "Hephaestus-Aphrodite-Ares triangle" is typical of the genre ("Margaret Laurence's Dark Lovers," 97).

13 See, for instance, the panel discussion on postcolonialism and postmodernism in Mukherjee, King, and Bayard, "Post-colonialism and Postmodernism."

14 See Simon, *Fictions de l'identitaire*; and Lacroix and Caccia, *Métamorphoses d'une utopie*.

15 Ashcroft, Griffiths, and Tiffin, *Empire*, 24; see also Tiffin, "Post-Colonialism," 180.
16 A very selective list of such works might include the following: the somewhat straightforward histories of Louis Caron contained in his *Fils de la Liberté* series (*Le Canard de Bois*, 1981; *La Corne de brume*, 1982) or Orlo Miller's *Death to the Donnelleys* (1975) and Heather Robertson's *Willie: A Romance* (1983); more experimental narratives such as Timothy Findley's *The Wars* (1977) or Claire de Lamirande's *Papineau ou l'épée à double tranchant* (1980); novels that address a specific event, such as Bruce Allen Powe's *The Aberhart Summer* (1983) or Evelyn Dumas' *Un événement de mes octobres* (1979).
17 The use of "indigenous" can be problematic, as Goldie suggests in "Signs of the Themes," 85–6. Fee is not referring here to the more usual acceptation of "indigenous" as representing Amerindians but to the concept of a non-European mythology.
18 See Said's discussion in "Representing the Colonized," 207.

CHAPTER TWO

1 See Barthes' discussion in "L'Effet de Réel."
2 As is noted in Smith's interview, the publicity passage was written by Godbout ("Jacques Godbout," 55).
3 Various versions of this popular song exist in print: see Falcon, "La Bataille des Sept Chênes," 246–7; "La Grenouillère," 15–17; and "La Chanson de la Grenouillère," 128–9.
4 See Fraser's portrayal of this aspect of Quebec society in *Quebec Inc.*
5 The two folk songs referred to here are the well-known "Alouette" and "V'là l'bon vent": "[Le fils du roi] visa le noir, tua le blanc / O fils du roi tu es méchant!" See Daigneault, *Vive la compagnie*, 139–40, 161.
6 Des Ruisseaux, *Le Livre des expressions québécoises*, 240, as cited by Bellemare, "*Les Têtes à Papineau*," 162n3.
7 The diaries were published under the title *l'Ecrivain de province* in 1991.
8 Cantin here quotes from Dumont, "La représentation idéologique," 20–1.

CHAPTER THREE

1 From the early *Tryptique lesbien* and *La Saga des poules mouillées*, both published in 1980, to the more contemporary *Anaïs, dans la queue de la comète* (1985) and *Le Voyage magnifique d'Emily Carr* (1991), Marchessault has explored the conditions of women's lives and, especially, the conditions under which creative women from the historical past produced their work. *Saga*, for instance, is typical of Marchessault's strong dramatic style and her subversive play with historical and biographical

"facts"; it presents a mythical encounter between four women writers from Quebec – women who would never have met in chronological time: Laure Conan, Germaine Guèvremont, Gabrielle Roy, and Anne Hébert. Another play, *Alice et Gertrude, Nathalie & Renée et ce cher Ernest* (1984), signals in its very title another dramatic grouping of disparate creative personages.

2 See Rosenfield, "The Development of a Lesbian Sensibility," 227.

3 It received *Books in Canada*'s First Novel Award and the Canadian Authors' Association Book of the Year Award, and it was selected for the Literary Guild Book Club and the Book of the Month Club of Canada.

4 A different, more complete, version of the arguments presented at the conference is found in Koh's subsequent publication, "Speculations and (Dis)identification."

5 See, for instance, Assiniwi, *Il n'y a plus d'Indiens*, and *l'Odawa Pontiac*; and Durand, *Atiskenandahate ou Voyage au pays des morts*.

6 Other examples are Francis, *The Imaginary Indian*; New, *Native Writers and Canadian Writing*; and King, Calver, and Hoy, *The Native in Literature*.

7 Therien, *Les Figures de l'Indien*, "L'Indien imaginaire: une hypothèse"; Boudreau, *Histoire de la littérature amérindienne au Québec*.

8 For a development of this argument, see Linteau, Durocher, and Robert, *Histoire du Québec contemporain*, 233.

9 See, in particular, Frye, conclusion to *Literary History of Canada*, 2d ed., 328–30; and Jones, *Butterfly on Rock*, 15–32.

10 Out of respect for possibly different Amerindian traditions with regard to copyright, I refer those who would learn the story in its entirety to Brant, *Food and Spirits*.

11 See "C'est l'aviron" and "V'là l'bon vent" in Daigneault, *Vive la compagnie*, 39, 139–40; and du Berger, "Le diable et la chasse-galérie," in *Les Légendes d'Amérique française*, 19.

12 See Adachi, *The Enemy That Never Was*; Sunahara, *The Politics of Racism*; and Broadfoot, *Years of Sorrow*, an oral documentary history. See also Wheeler's film *The War between Us*.

13 For a discussion of the practices of the Eastern Woodlands peoples, see Smith, "Native People, Religion," 1458.

CHAPTER FOUR

1 See Marron, *Witches, Pagans and Magic* or Guiley, "Witchcraft as Goddess Worship."

2 See, for instance, Lord, *The Singer of Tales*; McLuhan, *The Medium is the Massage*; Ong, *Orality and Literacy*, and *Interfaces of the Word*.

3 Interestingly, this politically significant sentence, and others like it, has been omitted from the English translation: *Like a Child of the Earth*, 73.
4 See Fujita, "To Attend the Sound of Stone."
5 This point is explored in Campbell, *The Hero with a Thousand Faces*, and in Eliade's work.

CHAPTER FIVE

1 See Kröller, "Postmodernism"; Bayard, "From *Nègres blancs d'Amérique*"; and my "Les Métarécits."
2 This is frequently noted in the collection of theoretical essays in Adam and Tiffin, *Past the Last Post*.
3 In literary practice the term "magic realism" has, until quite recently, been associated mainly with Latin American literature published during what is commonly called the "boom" of the 1950s, '60s, and '70s. García Márquez's *One Hundred Years of Solitude*, first published in 1967, is perhaps the best known example of a magic realist work. The origin of the term "magic realism" is sometimes credited to Carpentier, who used the expression "lo real maravilloso" in the prologue to his novel *El reino de este mundo* (1949). The term, however, was first coined by the German art critic Franz Roh. In his book *Nach Expressionismus (Magischer Realismus)* (1925) Roh described as magic the act of perception in postexpressionist German painting. When Ortega y Gasset had this work translated into Spanish as *El realismo mágico*, the expression began to circulate in Spanish literary circles (see Imbert, "Magic Realism," 2). Carpentier's theory of "lo real maravilloso," however, has strongly marked theoretical studies of magic realism, and Angel Flores contributed to the popularity of this last term in a frequently cited article "Magic Realism in Spanish American Fiction" (1954). The analogous term "marvellous realism" is attributed also to Carpentier.
4 See Alexis, "Prolégomènes"; Des Rosiers, "Les Fruits piqués"; Laroche, *Contributions*; and Ponte, "Au Carrefour" and *Le Réalisme merveilleux*.
5 See Chanady, *Magic Realism*, "Origins"; Durix, "Magic Realism"; Hancock, "Magic or Realism"; Ricci Della Grisa, *Realismo Mágico*; and Slemon, "Magic Realism."
6 *La Tribu*, "la suite qui précède," is the second novel of a trilogy, although, chronologically, its action takes place before the events described in the first novel of the series, *Agénor, Agénor, Agénor et Agénor*, published in 1980 (Grégoire, "Les Détours de l'imagination," 65). The third novel is *Ville-Dieu* (1982). Since the publication of the trilogy, Barcelo, an avid runner, has written a guide for runners to the city of Montreal, as well as a highly personal introduction to the photographic collection, *Montreal: Mia et Klaus*, 1983.

7 Criticisms of this sort were vehemently countered by cultural commentators such as Jeanne Morazain, Gilles Lesage, Pierre-André Julien, and Delisle in the pages of *Le Devoir* in the summer of 1992. Longer works, from the passionate and polemical *Oka: dernier alibi du Canada anglais*, by Robin Philpot (1991), to the curt and definitive statements in *Oka: la hache de guerre*, by François Dallaire (1991) or the more reasoned rendition of "only the facts" in *L'Eté des Mohawks* by Jacques Lamarche (1990) also refute some English-speaking Canadians' appreciations of the events at Oka.

8 This last phrase constitutes a good example of what appears to be a characteristic of New World Myth novels: parodic adaptations of political clichés.

9 For instance, la Malbaie is also known as Murray Bay and Sainte-Catherine-de-Hatley is referred to locally, in both English and French, as Katevale.

10 For Montcalm, see Casgrain, *Montcalm et Lévis: les héros de Québec*, 222; for Wolfe, see Hibbert, *Wolfe at Quebec*, 157.

11 The "lyric phase" covers the early period, from the publication of *Sticks and Stones* (1963) to the poetry produced during the years he spent in Montreal (1967–71). The "symphonic phase" follows, with an emphasis on the long poem, from approximately the mid-sixties to the late seventies; during this period Bowering wrote *Vancouver, a Discovery Poem* (written 1967, published 1970). The third phase, from 1977 to the present, dates from the publication of his parodic novel dealing with Canadian history, *A Short Sad Book*, and is marked by the publication of poetry (*Kerrisdale Elegies* [1984]), fiction (*Burning Water* [1980], *Caprice* [1987], *Harry's Fragments* [1990]), and works of criticism such as *The Mask in Place* (1982), *A Way With Words* (1985), and *Imaginary Hand* (1988).

12 The term "culture-fixing" is Frank Davey's; see "Surviving the Paraphrase," 5.

CHAPTER SIX

1 Interestingly, *La Tribu*'s narrator also parodies this claiming-the-land scene by undercutting the colonial drive to acquire territories in the name of Old World monarchs. For instance, after the Vieux Paysans leave, the Amerindians dismantle the crosses the foreigners had planted and use them to build benches for their community huts (41).

2 For a discussion of these points, see Hutcheon, *The Canadian Postmodern*, 7–10.

3 See my initial discussion of the European construction of the myth of the primitive in chapter 1, in my references to the work of Sir James

Frazer, Andrew Lang, Mircea Eliade, Lucien Lévy-Bruhl, and Georges Gusdorf.

4 See Margaret Atwood's comments in her interview with Davidson (204); See also Dobbs, "Canada's Regions," 64–8. Jack Warwick examines the same attraction for this myth in *The Long Journey*, 1968.

5 See Frye's discussion of this point in *Anatomy* (198).

Bibliography

Abrams, M.H. *The Mirror and the Lamp: Romantic Theory and the Critical Tradition.* New York: W.W Norton 1953.

Accardi, Bernard, David J. Charlson, Frank A. Doden, Richard F. Hardin, Sung Ryol Kim, Sonya J. Lancaster, and Michael H. Shaw, comp. *Recent Studies in Myths and Literature, 1970–1990: An Annotated Bibliography.* New York: Greenword Press 1991.

Adachi, Ken. *The Enemy That Never Was: A History of the Japanese Canadians.* Toronto: McClelland and Stewart 1976.

Adam, Ian, and Helen Tiffin, eds. *Past the Last Post: Theorizing Post-Colonialism and Post-Modernism.* Calgary, AB: University of Calgary Press 1990.

Albouy, Pierre. *Mythes et mythologies dans la littérature française.* Paris: Armand Colin 1969.

Alexis, Jacques-Stéphen. "Prolégomènes à un manifeste du réalisme merveilleux des Haïtiens." *Présence Africaine* 8–10 (June–November 1956): 245–71.

Alter, Peter. *Nationalism.* Trans. Stuart McKinnon-Evans. London: Edward Arnold 1985.

Andersen, Marguerite. "Subversive Texts: Quebec Women Writers." *Studies in Canadian Literature* 13.2 (1988): 127–41.

Anderson, Benedict. *Imagined Communities: Reflections on the Origin and Spread of Nationalism.* London and New York: Verso 1991.

Angelo, Ivan. *The Celebration.* Trans. Thomas Colchie. New York: Avon 1982.

Appiah, Kwame Anthony. "Is the Post- in Postmodernism the Post- in Postcolonial?" *Critical Inquiry* 17.2 (winter 1991): 336–57.

Aquin, Hubert. "L'art de la défaite." In *Blocs erratiques*. Montreal: Quinze 1977, 113–22.

– "Joual: Haven or Hell?" In *Writing Quebec*. Ed. and intro. Anthony Purdy; trans. Paul Gibson, Reva Joshee, Anthony Purdy, and Larry Shouldice. Edmonton, AB: University of Alberta Press 1988, 100–6.

– "Le joual-refuge." In *Blocs erratiques*. Montreal: Quinze 1977, 137–42.

– *Prochain Episode*. Ottawa: Le Cercle du livre de France 1965.

Arès, Richard. "L'Evolution de l'Eglise au Canada français de 1940 à 1975: survivance et déclin d'une chrétienté." In *Idéologies au Canada français 1940–1976*. Vol. 3. Les Partis politiques – l'Eglise. Eds. Fernand Dumont, Jean Hamelin, and Jean-Paul Montminy. Quebec: Les Presses de l'Université Laval 1981, 267–97.

Arguin, Maurice. *Le Roman québécois de 1944 à 1965: symptômes du colonialisme et signes de libération*. Montreal: l'Hexagone 1989.

Ariel 20, no. 4 (October 1989). Special Issue on Post-Colonialism and Post-Modernism.

Arthur, Kateryna Olijnyk. "Between Literatures: Canada and Australia." *Ariel* 19. no. 1 (January 1988): 3–12.

Ashcroft, Bill, Gareth Griffiths, and Helen Tiffin. *The Empire Writes Back: Theory and Practice in Post-Colonial Literatures*. London: Routledge 1989.

– eds. *The Post-Colonial Studies Reader*. London and New York: Routledge 1995.

Ashcroft, W.D. "Constitutive Graphonomy: A Post-Colonial Theory of Literary Writing." *Kunapipi* 11 (1989): 58–73.

Assiniwi, Bernard. *Il n'y a plus d'Indiens*. Montreal: Leméac 1983.

– *L'Ondawa Pontiac: l'amour et la guerre*. Montreal: XYX 1994.

Atwood, Margaret. Interview with Jim Davidson. *Meanjin* 37.2 (July 1978): 189–205.

– *Survival: A Thematic Guide to Canadian Literature*. Toronto: Anansi 1972.

Austin, Lisa, and Christina Boyd. *The Oka Crisis*. Peace Research Reviews 13.1. Dundas, ON: Peace Research Institute 1993.

Bachelard, Gaston. *L'Eau et les rêves: essais sur l'imagination de la matière*. 1942. Paris: J. Corti 1993.

– *La Psychanalyse du feu*. 1949. Paris: Gallimard 1985.

Bakhtin, Mikhail. *The Dialogic Imagination*. Trans. Caryl Emerson and Michael Holquist; ed. Michael Holquist. Austin, TX: University of Texas Press 1981.

Barcelo, François. *Aaa, Aâh, Ha ou les amours malaisées*. Montreal: l'Hexagone 1986.

– *Agénor, Agénor, Agénor et Agénor*. Montreal: Quinze 1980.

– Introduction to *Montreal. Mia et Klaus*. Montreal: Libre expression 1983.

– "Je suis un écrivain, un point c'est tout." Interview with Claude Grégoire. *Québec français* 78 (summer 1990): 63–4.

– *La Tribu*. Montreal: Libre expression 1981.

- *Ville-Dieu*. Montreal: Libre expression 1982.
Barth, John. "The Literature of Exhaustion." *Atlantic* 220.2 (August 1967): 29–34.
- "The Literature of Replenishment: Postmodernist Fiction." *Atlantic* 245.1 (January 1980): 65–71.
Barthes, Roland. "L'Effet de Réel." *Communications* 11 (1968): 84–9.
- "Eléments de sémiologie." [1965]. In *Roland Barthes: Œuvres complètes*. Paris: Seuil 1993.
- *Mythologies*. Paris: Seuil 1957.
Basile, Jean. "Le Crachat scolaire de Jovette Marchessault." *Le Devoir*, 18 October 1975, 14.
Bauman, Zygmunt. *Intimations of Postmodernity*. London and New York: Routledge 1992.
Bayard, Caroline. "From *Nègres blancs d'Amérique* (1968) to Kanesatake (1990): A Look at the Tensions of Postmodern Quebec." In Mukherjee, King, and Bayard, "Post-Colonialism and Postmodernism," 17–29.
- *The New Poetics in Canada and Quebec: From Concretism to Post-Modernism*. Toronto: University of Toronto Press 1989.
Beaudet, Marie-Andrée. Review of *Comme une enfant de la terre*, by Jovette Marchessault. In *Dictionnaire des œuvres littéraires du Québec*. Ed. Maurice Lemire. Vol. 5 (1970–75). Montreal: Fides, 1987, 167–70.
Beaulieu, Michel. "Le Canada existe-il?" *Nuit blanche* 11 (December 1983–January 1984): 40–50.
Beaulieu, Victor-Lévy. "La Grande Leçon de Jose Donoso et G.G. Márquez aux romanciers québécois." *Le Devoir*, 8 Septermber 1973, 15.
- *Monsieur Melville*. Montreal: VLB 1978.
Beckman, Susan. "The Place of Experiment." Review of *Magic Realism*, by Geoff Hancock. *Canadian Literature* 89 (summer 1981): 152–5.
Begnal, Michael. "James Joyce and the Mythologizing of History." In *Directions in Literary Criticism*. Eds. Stanley Weintraub and Philip Young. University Park, PA, and London: Pennsylvania State University Press 1973, 211–19.
Bélil, Michel. "Barcelo et Beauchemin: romanciers de la littérature générale." *Imagine … Revue de science-fiction québécoise* 3.3 (spring 1982): 55–6.
Belleau, André. *Le Romancier fictif: essai sur la représentation de l'écrivain dans le roman québécois*. Sillery, QC: Presses de l'Université du Québec 1980.
Bellemare, Yvon. *Jacques Godbout, romancier*. Montreal: Parti Pris 1984.
- "Les Têtes à Papineau." *Canadian Literature* 96 (spring 1983): 157–62.
Belsey, Catherine. *Critical Practice*. London and New York: Methuen 1980.
- "Towards Cultural History – In Theory and Practice." *Textual Practice* 3.2 (summer 1989): 159–72.
Belyea, Barbara, and Estelle Dansereau, eds. *Driving Home: A Dialogue between Writers and Readers*. Waterloo, ON: Wilfrid Laurier University Press 1984.

Bennett, Donna. "Criticism in English." In *The Oxford Companion to Canadian Literature.* Ed. William Toye. Toronto: Oxford University Press 1983, 149–66.

Bergman, Brian. "Rudy Wiebe: Storymaker of the Prairies." In Keith, ed., *Voice,* 163–9.

Berry, Reginald. "A Deckchair of Words: Post-Colonialism, Post-Modernism, and the Novel of Self-Projection in Canada and New Zealand." *Landfall 159* 40.3 (September 1986): 310–23.

Bersianik, Louky. *Le Pique-nique sur l'Acropole: cahiers d'Anycl.* Montreal: VLB 1979.

Bersianik, Louky, Nicole Brossard, Louise Cotnoir, Louise Dupré, Gail Scott, and France Théoret. *La théorie, un dimanche.* Montreal: Les Editions du remue-ménage 1988.

Berthoff, Warner. "Fiction, History, Myth: Notes toward the Discrimination of Narrative Forms." *The Interpretation of Narrative: Theory and Practice.* Ed. Morton W. Bloomfield. Harvard English Studies 1. Cambridge, MA: Harvard University Press 1970, 263–87.

Bessette, Gérard. *Les Anthropoïdes.* Montreal: Editions La Presse 1977.

Bhabha, Homi K. *The Location of Culture.* London and New York: Routledge 1994.

La Bible de Jérusalem. Paris: Editions du Cerf 1974.

Bilan, R.P. "Fiction I. Letters in Canada 1981." *University of Toronto Quarterly* 51.4 (summer 1982): 315–18.

Blodgett, E.D. "Canadian Literature is Comparative Literature." *College English* 50.8 (December 1988): 904–11.

– *Configuration: Essays in the Canadian Literatures.* Toronto: ECW Press 1982.

– "The Canadian Literatures as a Literary Problem." In his *Configuration,* 13–38.

– "The Writer's Job." In Belyea and Dansereau, eds., *Driving Home,* 9–26.

– "European Theory and Canadian Criticism." *Zeitschrift der Gesellschaft für Kanada-Studien* 6.2 (1986): 5–15.

Blumenberg, Hans. *Work on Myth.* Trans. Robert M. Wallace. Cambridge, MA, and London: MIT Press 1985.

Bolen, Jean Shinoda. *Goddesses in Everywoman: A New Psychology of Women.* New York: Harper and Row 1984.

Bolle, Kees W., and Richard G.A. Buxton. "Myth and Mythology." In *The New Encyclopedia Britannica.* Chicago: Encyclopedia Britannica 1989.

Bonnard, André. *Les Dieux de la Grèce: mytholoige classique illustrée.* Lausanne: Gonthier 1944.

Bouchard, Christian. "Review of *La Tribu,* by François Barcelo." In *Livres et auteurs québécois 1981.* Quebec: Presses de l'Université Laval 1982, 24–5.

Boucher, Denise. *Les Fées ont soif.* Montreal: Les Editions Intermède 1978.

Boudreau, Diane. "L'écriture appropriée." *Liberté 196–97* 33.4–5 (August–September 1991): 58–80.

– *Histoire de la littérature amérindienne au Québec*. Montreal: l'Hexagone 1993.

Bourke, Kenneth. "Doing and Saying: Thoughts on Myth, Cult, and Archetype." *Salmagundi* 15 (1971): 100–19.

Bowering, Angela. *Figures Cut in Sacred Ground: Illuminati in the Double Hook*. Edmonton, AB: NeWest Press 1989.

Bowering, George. *Burning Water*. [1980]. Toronto: General Publishing 1983.

– *Caprice*. Markham, ON: Penguin 1987.

– "Delsing and Me." *Open Letter* 2.1 (winter 1971–72): 45–7.

– *En eaux troubles*. Trans. L.-Philippe Hébert. Montreal: Quinze 1982.

– *Errata*. Red Deer, AB: Red Deer College Press 1988.

– "A Great Northern Darkness: The Attack on History in Recent Canadian Fiction." In Bowering, *Imaginary Hand*, 1–21.

– *Harry's Fragments: A Novel of International Puzzlement*. Toronto: Coach House Press 1990.

– *Imaginary Hand*. Edmonton, AB: NeWest Press 1988.

– *Kerrisdale Elegies*. Toronto: Coach House Press 1984.

– *The Mask in Place: Essays on Fiction in North America*. Winnipeg: Turnstone Press 1982.

– *Mirror on the Floor*. Toronto: McClelland 1967.

– "Modernism Could Not Last Forever." *Canadian Fiction Magazine* 32–3 (1979–80): 4–9.

– "Proofing the World: The Poems of David McFadden." In Bowering, *A Way with Words*, 184–99.

– *A Short Sad Book*. Vancouver: Talonbooks 1977.

– *A Way with Words*. Ottawa: Oberon 1982.

– "Why James Reaney is a Better Poet (1) Than Any Northrop Frye Poet, (2) Than He Used to Be." *Canadian Literature* 36 (spring 1968): 40–9.

– *George, Vancouver: A Discovery Poem*. Toronto: Weed/Flower Press 1970.

– ed. and afterword. *Sheila Watson and the Double Hook*. Ottawa: Golden Dog Press 1985.

Brandt, Di. "Tenderness and Rage." *Books in Canada* (June–July 1989): 23, 25.

– *Wild Mother Dancing*. Winnipeg: University of Manitoba Press 1993.

Brant, Beth. "This Is History." In *Food and Spirits: Stories by Beth Brant (Degonwadonti)*. Vancouver: Press Gang Publishers 1991.

Brault, Jacques. "Nontraduire 1." In *Poèmes des quatre côtés*. Saint-Lambert: Noroît 1975.

Brennan, Anthony S. Review of *Burning Water*, by George Bowering. *Fiddlehead* 131 (January 1982): 85–7.

Broadfoot, Barry. *Years of Sorrow, Years of Shame: The Story of the Japanese-Canadians in World War II*. Toronto: Doubleday 1977.

Brooke, Rupert. *Letters from America*. New York: Charles Scribners and Sons 1916.

Brown, Russell M. "Critic, Culture, Text: Beyond Thematics." *Essays on Canadian Writing* 11 (summer 1978): 151–83.

- "Words, Places, Craft: Bowering's Critical Voice." *Essays on Canadian Writing* 38 (summer 1989): 30–52.

Bruffee, Kenneth. *Elegiac Romance: Cultural Change and Loss of the Hero in Modern Fiction.* Ithaca, NY: Cornell University Press 1983.

Brydon, Diana. "The Myths That Write Us: Decolonising the Mind." *Commonwealth* 10, no. 1 (autumn 1987): 1–14.

- "Re-writing *The Tempest.*" *World Literature Written in English* 23.1 (winter 1984): 75–88.

- "The White Inuit Speaks." In Adam and Tiffin, eds. *Past the Last Post,* 191–203. Reprinted and edited in Ashcroft, Griffiths, and Tiffin, eds., *The Post-Colonial Studies Reader,* 136–42.

Brydon, Diana, and Helen Tiffin. *Decolonizing Fictions.* Sydney: Dangaroo Press 1993.

Bucher, Bernadette. "Sémiologie du mixte et utopie américaine: l'hybride et le métis indien dans l'imaginaire européen." In Thérien, ed., *Figures de l'Indien,* 307–22.

Buss, Helen M. "Margaret Laurence's Dark Lovers: Sexual Metaphor and the Movement toward Individualization, Hierogamy, and Mythic Narrative in Four Manawaka Books." *Atlantis* 11:24 (spring 1986): 96–107.

Calvino, Italo. "Myth in the Narrative." Trans. Erica Freiberg. In *Surfiction: Fiction Now ... and Tomorrow.* Ed. Raymond Federman. 2d ed. Chicago: Swallow Press 1981, 75–81.

Calviño, Julio. *Historia, ideologia y mito en la narrativa Hispanoamericana contemporanea.* Madrid: Ayuso 1987.

Cambron, Micheline. *Une Société, un récit: discours culturel au Québec (1967–1976).* Montreal: l'Hexagone 1989.

Cameron, Anne. "Why I'm Not an Ecofeminist." *BC Bookworld* 5.2 (summer 1991): 12.

Cameron, Barry, and Michael Dixon. Introduction to "Mandatory Subversive Manifesto: Canadian Criticism vs. Literary Criticism." *Studies in Canadian Literature* 2.2 (1977): 137–45.

Cameron, Donald. *Conversations with Canadian Novelists I.* Toronto: Macmillan 1973.

Campbell, Joseph. *The Hero with a Thousand Faces.* 1949. Princeton, NJ: Princeton University Press 1968.

Cantin, Serge. "La Fatigue culturelle de Jacques Godbout." *Liberté* 206 35.2 (April 1993): 3–37.

Caron, Louis. *Le Canard de bois.* Paris: Seuil 1981.

- *La Corne de Brume.* Montreal: Boréal 1982.

Carpentier, Alejo. Prologue to *El reino de este mundo.* 1949. Buenos Aires: Libreria del Colegio 1975.

- *Explosion in a Cathedral.* Trans. John Sturrock. London: Victor Gollancz 1963.

Carrier, Roch. *Il n'y a pas de pays sans grand-père.* Montreal: Stanké 1977.

Carroll, John B., ed. *Language, Thought, and Reality: Selected Writings of Benjamin Lee Whorf*. Cambridge, MA: MIT Press 1956.

Casgrain, H.R. *Montcalm et Lévis: les héros de Québec*. Tours: Maison Alfred Mame et Fils, n.d.

Cassirer, Ernst. *Language and Myth*. Trans. Susanne Katherina (Knauth). New York and London: Harper and Brothers 1946.

– *Mythical Thought*. Vol. 2 of *The Philosophy of Symbolic Forms*. Trans. Ralph Manheim. New Haven, CT: Yale University Press 1955.

– *The Myth of the State*. New Haven: Yale University Press 1946.

Cavendish, Richard, ed. *Mythology: An Illustrated Encyclopedia*. New York: Rizzoli 1980.

Chamberlin, J.E. *The Harrowing of Eden: White Attitudes toward Native Americans*. New York: Seabury Press 1975.

Chanady, Amaryll Beatrice. *Magical Realism and the Fantastic: Resolved versus Unresolved Antinomy*. New York: Garland 1985.

– "The Origins and Development of Magic Realism in Latin American Fiction." In Hinchcliffe and Jewinski, eds., *Magic Realism*, 49–60.

– ed. *Latin American Identity and Constructions of Difference*. Minneapolis, MN: University of Minnesota Press 1994.

Charest, Gilles. *Le livre des sacres et blasphèmes québécois*. Montreal: l'Aurore 1974.

Chase, Richard. "Myth as Literature." In *Myth and Method: Modern Theories of Fiction*. Ed. James E. Miller Jr. N.p.: University of Nebraska Press 1960, 127–43.

Chauveau, Pierre-Joseph-Olivier. *L'Instruction publique au Canada: précis historique et statistique*. Quebec: A. Coté 1876.

Cheung, King-Kok. *Articulate Silences: Hisaye Yamamoto, Maxine Hong Kingston, Joy Kogawa*. Ithaca, NY: Cornell University Press 1993.

Christ, Carol P. *Diving Deep and Surfacing: Women Writers on Spiritual Quest*. Boston: Beacon Press 1980.

Chua, Cheng Lok. "Witnessing the Japanese Canadian Experience in World War II: Processual Structure, Symbolism, and Irony in Joy Kogawa's *Obasan*." In Lim and Ling, eds., *Reading the Literatures of Asian America*, 97–108.

Clifford, James. "On Ethnographic Allegory." In *Writing Culture: The Poetics and Politics of Ethnography*. Eds. James Clifford and George E. Marcus. Berkeley: University of California Press 1986, 98–121.

– *The Predicament of Culture: Twentieth-Century Ethnography, Literature, and Art*. Cambridge: Harvard University Press 1988.

Clio Collective (Micheline Dumont, Michèle Jean, Marie Lavigne, Jennifer Stoddart). *Quebec Women: A History*. Trans. Roger Gannon and Rosalind Gill. Toronto: Women's Press 1987.

Cohen, Leonard. *Beautiful Losers*. [1966.] New Canadian Library no. 153. Toronto: McClelland & Stewart 1989.

Coleridge, Samuel Taylor. *Biographia Literaria*. Ed. and intro. George Watson. New York: Dutton 1975.

– *The Rime of the Ancient Mariner*. Ed. Alexander S. Twombly. New York: Silver, Burdett 1899.

Collard, Andrée, with Joyce Contrucci. *Rape of the Wild: Man's Violence against Animals and the Earth*. Bloomington, IN: Indiana University Press 1989.

Collectif Clio (Micheline Dumont, Michèle Jean, Marie Lavigne, Jennifer Stoddart). *L'Histoire des femmes au Québec depuis quatre siècles*. Montreal: Quinze 1982.

Colombo, John Robert, and Michael Richardson, eds. *We Stand On Guard: Poems and Songs of Canadians in Battle*. Toronto: Doubleday 1985.

Cook, David. *Northrop Frye: A Vision of the New World*. Montreal: New World Perspectives 1985.

Cook, Ramsay. *The Maple Leaf Forever: Essays on Nationalism and Politics in Canada*. New ed. Toronto: Macmillan 1977.

Cortázar, Julio. *A Manual for Manuel*. Trans. Gregory Rabassa. New York: Pantheon 1978.

– *Rayuela*. Buenos Aires: Editorial Sudamericana 1966.

Coulter, John. *Deidre of the Sorrows: An Ancient and Noble Tale Retold by John Coulter for Music by Healey Willan*. Toronto: Macmillan 1944.

Creighton, Donald. *John A. Macdonald: The Old Chieftain*. Toronto: Macmillan 1955.

Crosby, Marcia. "Construction of the Imaginary Indian." In *Vancouver Anthology: The Institutional Politics of Art*. ed. Stand Douglas. Vancouver: Talonbooks 1991, 267–91.

Cuddon, J.A. "Historical Novel." In *A Dictionary of Literary Terms*. Harmondsworth, England: Penguin 1979.

Culler, Jonathan. "Beginnings." *Modern Language Review* 73 (July 1978): 582–5.

– *Structuralist Poetics: Structuralism, Linguistics and the Study of Literature*. London: Routledge & Kegan Paul 1975.

d'Allemagne, André. *Le Colonialisme au Québec*. Montreal: Editions RB 1966.

Daigneault, Pierre. *Vive la compagnie*. Montreal: Les Editions de l'homme 1979.

Dallaire, François. *Oka: la hache de guerre*. Ste-Foy, QC: Editions La Liberté 1991.

Daly, Mary. *Gyn/Ecology: The Metaethics of Radical Feminism*. Boston: Beacon Press 1978.

Dash, J. Michael. "Marvellous Realism: The Way Out of Négritude." *Caribbean Studies* 13.4 (January 1974): 57–70.

Davey, Frank. *From There to Here: A Guide to English-Canadian Literature since 1960*. Erin, ON: Press Porcépic 1974.

– *Post-National Arguments: The Politics of the Anglophone-Canadian Novel since 1967*. Toronto: University of Toronto Press 1993.

– *Reading Canadian Reading*. Winnipeg: Turnstone Press 1988.

– "Surviving the Paraphrase." In his *Surviving the Paraphrase: Eleven Essays in Canadian Literature.* Winnipeg: Turnstone Press 1983, 1–12.

Davidson, Arnold E. "History, Myth, and Time in Robert Kroetsch's *Badlands.*" *Studies in Canadian Literature* 5.1 (spring 1980): 127–37.

Davidson, Jim. Interview with Margaret Atwood. *Meanjin* 37.2 (July 1978): 189–205.

Davies, Alan, ed. *Antisemitism and the Foundations of Christianity.* New York: Paulist Press 1979.

Davis, N. Brian, ed. "The Battle of Seven Oaks [La Bataille des Sept Chênes]." *The Poetry of the Canadian People 1720–1920: Two Hundred Years of Hard Work.* Toronto: NC Press 1976, 246–7.

Daymond, Douglas, and Leslie Monkman, eds. *Canadian Novelists and the Novel.* Ottawa: Borealis 1981.

d'Eaubonne, Françoise. *Le Féminisme ou la mort: femmes en mouvement.* Paris: Pierre Horay 1974.

de Grandpré, Chantal. "La canadianisation de la littérature québécoise: le cas Aquin." *Liberté* 159 (June 1985): 50–9.

de Lamirande, Claire. *Papineau ou l'épée à double tranchant.* Montreal: Quinze 1980.

de Man, Paul. *Allegories of Reading: Figural Language in Rousseau, Nietzsche, Rilke, and Proust.* New Haven, CT: Yale University Press 1979.

– "The Rhetoric of Temporality." In Singleton, C.S., ed., *Interpretation: Theory and Practice,* 173–209.

Deer, Glenn. *Postmodern Canadian Fiction and the Rhetoric of Authority.* Montreal and Kingston: McGill-Queen's University Press 1994.

Delâge, Denys. "Les Amérindiens dans l'imaginaire des Québécois." *Liberté* 196–7 33.4–5 (August–October 1991): 15–28.

Delisle, Norman. "Les langues autochtones se portent mieux au Québec que partout ailleurs au Canada." *Le Devoir,* 12 August 1992, 3.

Deloria, Vine. *Custer Died for Your Sins.* New York: Macmillan 1969.

Derrida, Jacques. "The Violence of the Letter: From Lévi-Strauss to Rousseau." In his *Of Grammatology.* Trans. Gayatri Chakravorty Spivak. Baltimore and London: Johns Hopkins University Press 1976, 101–40.

Derrière la charette de Pélagie: lecture analytique du roman d'Antonine Maillet. Pointe-de-l'église, Nova Scotia: Presses de l'Université Sainte-Anne 1984.

Descartes, René. *Discours de la méthode et autres textes.* [1637]. Presentation, chronology, and notes by Jacques Morissette. Montreal: l'Hexagone 1981.

Des Rosiers, Joël. "Les Fruits piqués du réalisme merveilleux." *Vice Versa* 21 (November 1987): 57–8.

DesRuisseaux, Pierre. *Le Livre des expressions québécoises.* Montreal: Hurtubise/HMH 1979.

D'haen, Theo, and Hans Bertens, eds. *History and Post-War Writing.* Amsterdam: Rodopi 1990.

– *Postmodern Fiction in Europe and the Americas*. Amsterdam: Rodopi 1988.

Diamond, Stanley. *In Search of the Primitive: A Critique of Civilization*. New Brunswick, NJ: Dutton 1974.

Dirlik, Arif. "The Postcolonial Aura: Third World Criticism in the Age of Global Capitalism." *Critical Inquiry* 20.2 (winter 1994): 328–56.

Dobbs, Kildare. "Canada's Regions." In *Profile of a Nation*. Ed. Alan Dawe. Toronto: Macmillan 1969, 64–8.

Donaldson, Gordon. *Battle for a Continent: Quebec 1759*. Toronto: Doubleday 1973.

Dorsinville, Max. *Caliban Without Prospero: Essay on Quebec and Black Literature*. Erin, ON: Press Porcépic 1974.

Douglas, Mary. *Implicit Meanings: Essays in Anthropology*. London: Routledge and Kegan Paul 1975.

du Berger, Jean. *Les Légendes d'Amérique française, premiere partie: textes*. Quebec: Presses de l'Université Laval 1973.

Dueck, Allan. "Rudy Wiebe's Approach to Historical Fiction: A Study of *The Temptations of Big Bear* and *The Scorched-Wood People*." In *Here and Now*. Ed. and intro. John Moss. The Canadian Novel, vol. 1. Toronto: NC Press 1983, 182–200.

Duffy, Dennis. "Losing the Line: The Field of Our Modernism." *Essays on Canadian Writing* 39 (fall 1989): 164–90.

– *Sounding the Iceberg: An Essay on Canadian Historical Novels*. Toronto: ECW Press 1986.

– "Wiebe's Real Riel? *The Scorched-Wood People and Its Audience*." In M.L. Friedland, ed., *Rough Justice*, 200–13.

Dumas, Evelyn. *Un événement de mes octobres*. Montreal: Biocreux 1979.

Dumézil, Georges. *Mythe et épopée*. 3 vols. Paris: Gallimard 1968–78.

Dupré, Louise. "From Experimentation to Experience: Québécois Modernity in the Feminine." Trans. A. J. Holden Verburg. In Neuman and Kamboureli, eds., *A Mazing Space*, 355–60.

Durand, Gilbert. *Figures mythiques et visages de l'œuvre: de la mythocritique à la mythanalyse*. Paris: Berg International 1979.

– *Les Structures anthropologiques de l'imaginaire: introduction à l'archétypologie générale*. [1960]. Paris: Bordas 1979.

Durix, Jean-Pierre. "Magic Realism in *Midnight's Children*." *Commonwealth* 8.1 (Autumn 1985): 57–63.

Dybikowski, Ann, Victoria Freeman, Daphne Marlatt, Barbara Pulling, and Betsy Warland, eds. *In the Feminine: Women and Words/Les Femmes et les mots*. [Vancouver 1983]. Edmonton, AB: Longspoon Press 1985.

Eagleton, Terry. *Literary Theory: An Introduction*. Minneapolis, MN: University of Minnesota Press 1983.

Eastman, Donald R. "Myth and Fate in the Characters of *Women in Love*." *The D.H. Lawrence Review* 9 (1976): 177–93.

Eliade, Mircea. *Aspects du mythe*. Paris: Gallimard 1963.
– *Images et symboles: essais sur le symbolisme magico-religieux*. [1952]. Paris: Gallimard 1979.
– *Myth and Reality*. Trans. Williard R. Trask. New York: Harper and Row 1963.
– *Le Mythe de l'éternel retour: archétypes et répétition*. Paris: Gallimard 1949.
Eliot, T.S. "*Ulysses*, Order and Myth." In *James Joyce: Two Decades of Criticism*. Ed. Seon Givens. New York: Vanguard Press 1948, 198–202.
Emond, Maurice. *La Femme à la fenêtre: l'univers symbolique d'Anne Hébert dans Les Chambres de bois, Kamouraska, et Les Enfants du sabbat*. Quebec: Les Presses de l'Université Laval 1984.
Falardeau, Jean-Charles. *Notre Société et son roman*. Montreal: HMH 1967.
Falck, Colin. *Myth, Truth and Literature: Towards a True Post-Modernism*. [1989]. Cambridge: Cambridge University Press 1994.
Falcon, Pierre. "The Battle of Seven Oaks [La Bataille des Sept Chênes]." In *The Poetry of the Canadian People 1720–1920: Two Hundred Years of Hard Work*. Ed. N. Brian Davis. Toronto: NC Press 1976, 246–7.
– "La Chanson de la Grenouillère." In *Anthologie de la poésie franco manitobaine*. Ed. J.R. Léveillé. Saint-Boniface, MB: Les Editions du blé 1990, 128–9.
– "La Grenouillère." "p.o.s. by Pierre Falcon." *White Pelican* 1.3 (summer 1971): 15–17.
Faulkner, William. *Absalom, Absalom!* New York: Random House 1936.
Fee, Margery. "Howard O'Hagan's *Tay John*: Making New World Myth." *Canadian Literature* 110 (fall 1986): 8–27.
"Romantic Nationalism and the Image of Native People in Contemporary English Canadian Literature." In King, Calver, and Hoy, eds., *The Native in Literature*, 15–33.
Fennario, David. *Jos Beef (A History of Pointe Saint Charles)*. Vancouver: Talonbooks 1991.
Ferron, Madeleine. *Sur le Chemin Craig*. Montreal: Stanké 1983.
Findley, Timothy. *Famous Last Words*. Toronto: Clarke and Irwin 1981.
– *The Wars*. Markham, ON: Penguin 1977.
Fink, Cecelia Coulas. "'If Words Won't Do, and Symbols Fail': Hodgins' Magic Reality." *Journal of Canadian Studies* 20.2 (Summer 1985): 118–31.
Fischman, Sheila. Jack Hodgins, Sandra Martin, and John Richardson. "Ode to Joy." *Books in Canada* 11.4 (April 1982): 4–5.
Fitz, Earl E. *Rediscovering the New World: Inter-American Literature in A Comparative Context*. Iowa City, IA: University of Iowa Press 1991.
Flores, Angel. "Magic Realism in Spanish American Fiction." *Hispania* 38.2 (May 1955): 187–92.
– ed. *El Realismo mágico en el cuento hispanoamericano*. Mexico: Premià 1985.
Fogel, Stanley. *A Tale of Two Countries: Contemporary Fiction in English Canada and the United States*. Toronto: ECW Press 1984.

Foucault, Michel. "Nietzsche, Genealogy, History." In *Language, Counter-Memory, Practice: Selected Essays and Interviews*. Trans. Donald F. Bouchard and Sherry Simon. Ithaca, NY: Cornell University Press 1977.

Fournier, Marcel. *L'Entrée dans la modernité: science, culture, et société au Québec*. Montreal: Les Editions Saint-Martin 1986.

Fowles, John. *The French Lieutenant's Woman*. London: Jonathan Cape 1969.

Francis, Daniel. *The Imaginary Indian: The Image of the Indian in Canadian Culture*. Vancouver, BC: Arsenal Pulp Press 1992.

Fraser, Matthew. *Quebec Inc.: French-Canadian Entrepreneurs and the New Business Elite*. Toronto: Key Porter Books 1987.

Frazer, Robert, ed. *Sir James Frazer and the Literary Imagination*. London: Macmillan 1990.

Frazer, Sir James George. *The Golden Bough: A Study in Magic and Religion*. 1 vol., abridged ed. New York: Macmillan 1951.

Frédéric, Madeleine, and Jacques Allard, eds. *Modernité/Postmodernité du roman contemporain*. Les Cahiers du département d'études littéraires, 11. Montreal: Université du Québec à Montréal 1987.

French, William. "Bowering Novel Entertains, History Takes the Hindmost." Review of *Burning Water*, by George Bowering. *Globe and Mail*, 4 September 1980, 17.

Freud, Sigmund. *Nouvelles conférences sur la psychanalyse*. Trans. Anne Berman. Paris: Gallimard 1971.

Friedland, M.L., ed. *Rough Justice: Essays on Crime in Literature*. Toronto: University of Toronto Press 1991.

Frye, Northrop. *Anatomy of Criticism: Four Essays*. Princeton, NJ: Princeton University Press 1957.

– *The Bush Garden: Essays on the Canadian Imagination*. Toronto: Anansi 1971.

– Conclusion to *Literary History of Canada: Canadian Literature in English*. [1965]. Ed. Carl F. Klinck. Toronto: University of Toronto Press 1966, 821–49.

– Conclusion to *Literary History of Canada: Canadian Literature in English*. Ed. Carl F. Klinck. 2d ed. 3 vols. Toronto and Buffalo: University of Toronto Press 1976, 3: 319–32.

– *The Educated Imagination*. The Massey Lectures. Second Series. Montreal: CBC Enterprises 1983.

– *Fearful Symmetry: A Study of William Blake*. Princeton, NJ: Princeton University Press 1947.

– *The Great Code: The Bible and Literature*. Toronto: Academic Press Canada 1982.

– "Literature and Myth." In *Relations of Literary Study: Essays on Interdisciplinary Contributions*. Ed. James Thorpe. New York: Modern Language Association of America 1967, 27–41.

– "Myth as the Matrix of Literature." *The Georgia Review* 38.3 (fall 1984): 465–76.

– "New Directions from Old." In his *Fables of Identity: Studies in Poetic Mythology.* New York: Harcourt 1963, 52–66.

– *The Secular Scripture: A Study of the Structure of Romance.* Cambridge: Harvard University Press 1976.

– *Words with Power: Being a Second Study of "The Bible and Literature."* Markham, ON: Viking 1990.

Fuentes, Carlos. *Terra Nostra.* Trans. Margaret Sayers Peden. New York: Farrar, Straus, Giroux 1976.

Fujita, Gayle K. "'To Attend the Sound of Stone': the Sensibility of Silence in *Obasan.*" *Melus* 12.3 (fall 1985): 33–42.

Fuss, Diana. "Getting Into History." *Arizona Quarterly* 45.4 (winter 1989): 95–108.

Gaboriau, Linda. "Jovette Marchessault: A Luminous Wake in Space." *Canadian Theatre Review* 43 (summer 1995): 91–9.

Galloway, Priscilla Anne. "Sexism and the Senior English Curriculum in Ontario Secondary Schools." PHD diss., University of Toronto 1977.

García Márquez, Gabriel. *One Hundred Years of Solitude.* Trans. Gregory Rabassa. New York: Avon Books 1971.

Garrod, Andrew, and Joy Kogawa. "Joy Kogawa." *Speaking for Myself: Canadian Writers in Interview.* Ed. Andrew Garrod. St John's, NF: Breakwater Books 1986, 139–54.

Gibbs, Lee W. "Myth and the Mystery of the Future." In Gibbs and Stevenson, eds., *Myth*, 19–33.

Gibbs, Lee W., and W. Taylor Stevenson, eds. *Myth and the Crisis of Historical Consciousness.* Missoula, MT: Scholars Press 1975.

Godard, Barbara. "En mémoire de l'avenir: les stratégies de transformation dans la narration de Jovette Marchessault." *Voix et Images* 49 (autumn 1991): 100–15.

– "Feminist Critical Theory in English Canada and Quebec: Present State and Future Directions." *Tessera* 11.2/3 (spring–summer 1988): 10–14.

– "Flying Away with Language." Introduction to *Lesbian Triptych*, by Jovette Marchessault. Trans. Yvonne M. Klein. [1980]. Toronto: Women's Press 1985.

– "The Politics of Representation: Some Native Canadian Women Writers." In New, ed., *Native Writers: Canadian Writing*, 183–225.

– "Re: Post." in "Symposium: Feminism and Postmodernism in Quebec: The Politics of the Alliance." *Québec Studies* 9 (fall/winter 1989–90): 131–43.

– Review of *Configuration: Essays in the Canadian Literatures*, by E.D. Blodgett. *Ariel* 16.3 (July 1985): 108–12.

– "Structuralism/Post-Structuralism: Language, Reality, and Canadian Literature." In Moss, ed., *Future Indicative*, 25–51.

– *Talking about Ourselves: The Literary Productions of the Native Women of Canada.* Ottawa: CRIAW/ICREF 1985.

– ed. *Gynocritics/La Gynocritique.* Toronto: ECW Press 1987.

Godbout, Jacques. "Le Chevalier errant." *Actualité* 15.19 (December 1990): 100–1.

– *L'Ecrivain de province: Journal, 1981–1990*. Paris: Seuil 1991.

– "Les Ecrivains sont souverains." *Liberté 203* 34.5 (October 1992): 39–42.

– "Novembre 1971/Ecrire." In Godbout, *Le Réformiste*, 147–57.

– "Novembre 1964/Faut-il tuer le mythe René Lévesque?" In Godbout, *Le Réformiste*, 69–73.

– "Qu'est-ce qu'un Québécois?" *Actualité* 13.11 (October 1988): 236.

– *Le Réformiste : textes tranquilles*. Montreal: Quinze 1975.

– *Salut Galarneau!* Paris: Seuil 1967.

– *Le Temps des Galarneau*. Paris: Seuil 1993.

– *Les Têtes à Papineau*. Paris: Seuil 1981.

Goellnicht, Donald C. "Father Land and/or Mother Tongue: The Divided Female Subject in Kogawa's *Obasan* and Hong Kingston's *The Women Warrior*." In Morgan and Hall, eds., *Redefining Autobiography*, 119–34.

Goldie, Terry. "Getting It Right: The Image of Indigenous Peoples in Canadian Fiction in the Eighties." *English Studies in Canada* 14.1 (March 1988): 64–81.

– *Fear and Temptation: The Image of the Indigene in Canadian, Australian, and New Zealand Literatures*. Montreal and Kingston: McGill-Queen's University Press 1989.

– "Signs of the Themes: The Value of a Politically Grounded Semiotics." In Moss, ed., *Future Indicative*, 85–93.

Goldie, Terry, and Daniel David Moses, eds. *The Oxford Anthology of Canadian Native Literature in English*. Toronto: Oxford University Press 1992.

González Echevarría, Roberto. *Myth and Archive: A Theory of Latin American Narrative*. Cambridge: Cambridge University Press 1990.

Gottlieb, Erika. "The Riddle of Concentric Worlds in *Obasan*." *Canadian Literature* 109 (summer 1986): 34–53.

Gould, Eric. *Mythical Intentions in Modern Literature*. Princeton, NJ: Princeton University Press 1981.

Grace, Sherrill. "A Portrait of the Artist as Laurence Hero." *Journal of Canadian Studies* 13.3 (fall 1978): 64–71.

Grand'Maison, Jacques. "L'Eglise et les idéologies au Québec." *Relations* 343 (November 1969): 293–6.

Grégoire, Claude. "Les Détours de l'imagination." *Québec français* 78 (summer 1990): 65–6.

Groult, Benoîte. *Ainsi-soit-elle*. Paris: Grasset 1975.

Groulx, Lionel. "Why We Are Divided." Trans. Gordon O. Rothney. In *French Canadian Nationalism*. Ed. Ramsay Cook. Toronto: Macmillan 1969, 237–56. Originally published as *Pourquoi nous sommes divisés*. Montreal: l'Action Nationale 1943.

Guiart, Jean. "A l'Occasion de l'exposition Les Amériques de Claude Lévi-Strauss." *Le Petit Journal du Musée de l'Homme*. Paris (1989): 1.

Guiley, Rosemary Ellen. "Witchcraft as Goddess Worship." In Larrington, ed., *The Feminist Companion*, 411–24.

Guillot, M. "Godbout le réducteur de têtes." *L'Education* 478 (21 January 1982): 24–7.

Gusdorf, Georges. *Mythe et métaphysique.* [1953]. Paris: Flammarion 1984.

Hallen, Patsy. "Making Peace with the Environment: Why Ecology Needs Feminism." *Canadian Woman Studies* 9.1 (spring 1988): 9–12, 14–18.

Hamilton, A.C. *Northrop Frye: Anatomy of His Criticism.* Toronto: University of Toronto Press 1990.

Hancock, Geoff. Introduction to *Magic Realism.* Ed. Geoff Hancock. Toronto: Aya Press 1980, 7–15.

– "Magic or Realism: The Marvellous in Canadian Fiction." *Canadian Forum* 65.755 (March 1986): 23–36.

– "Magic Realism, or the Future of Fiction." *Canadian Fiction Magazine* 24/25 (spring/summer 1977): 4–6.

– "Vancouver's Founder Gets a Drubbing." Review of *Burning Water*, by George Bowering. *Toronto Star*, 13 September 1980, F9.

Hancock, Geoff, and Jack Hodgins. "Jack Hodgins." *Canadian Writers at Work: Interviews with Geoff Hancock.* Toronto: Oxford University Press 1987, 51–78.

Harris, Mason. "Broken Generations in *Obasan*: Inner Conflict and the Destruction of Community." *Canadian Literature* 127 (winter 1990): 41–57.

Harrison, Dick, ed. *Crossing Frontiers: Papers in American and Canadian Western Literature.* Edmonton, AB: University of Alberta Press 1979.

Hart, Jonathan. *Northrop Frye: The Theoretical Imagination.* London and New York: Routledge 1994.

Hatch, Ronald. "Narrative Development in the Canadian Historical Novel." *Canadian Literature* 110 (fall 1986): 79–96.

Hébert, Anne. *Les Fous de Bassan.* Paris: Seuil 1982.

Hébert, Pierre. "A l'impossible certains sont tenus." *Voix et images* 37 (autumn 1987): 192–4.

– "Le *Journal d'un Inquisiteur* de Gilles Leclerc: réflexion sur les conditions sociales de l'humour québécois." In O'Neill-Karch, ed., "Humour Québec," 6–14.

– "Un Problème de sémiotique diachronique: norme coloniale et évolution des formes romanesques québécoises." *Recherches sémiotiques/Semiotic Inquiry* 2.3 (1982): 211–39.

– "Le Roman québécois depuis 1975: quelques aspects saillants." *The French Review* 61.6 (May 1988): 899–909.

Hémon, Louis. *Maria Chapdeleine.* [1916]. Montreal: Fides 1970.

Hénaut, Dorothy Todd. *Les Terribles Vivantes.* 84 min. Office national du film du Canada/National Film Board. 1986.

Herz, Micheline. "A Québécois and an Acadian Novel Compared: The Use of Myth in Jovette Marchessault's *Comme une enfant de la terre* and

Antonine Maillet's *Pélagie-la-Charette.*" in Lewis, ed., *Traditionalism, Nationalism, and Feminism,* 173–83.

Hestetun, Øyunn. *A Prison-House of Myth? Symptomal Readings in Virgin Land, The Madwoman in the Actic, and The Political Unconscious.* Uppsala, Sweden: Uppsala University Press 1993.

Hibbert, Christopher. *Wolfe at Quebec.* London and New York: Longmans, Green 1959.

Hill, Douglas. "Ethnic Fiction: The Dispossessed Japanese, a Reactionary Transylvanian, and a Clever but Tedious Run at the Royal Family." Review of *Obasan,* by Joy Kogawa (among others). *Books in Canada* 10.8 (October 1981): 31–2.

Hinchcliffe, Peter, and Ed Jewinski, eds. *Magic Realism and Canadian Literature.* Waterloo, ON: University of Waterloo Press 1986.

Hodgins, Jack. *The Invention of the World.* Toronto: Macmillan 1977.

Hodgson, Richard. Review of *L'Ecrivain de province. Canadian Literature* 137 (summer 1993): 84–5.

Homer. *The Odyssey.* Trans. Robert Fitzgerald. Garden City, NY: Anchor Press 1961.

Howells, Coral Ann. *Private and Fictional Words: Canadian and Women Novelists of the 1970s and 1980s.* London and New York: Methuen 1987.

– "Rudy Wiebe's Art and Acts of Narrative in *The Scorched-Wood People.*" In Nicholson and Easingwood, eds., *Cnadian Story and History,* 19–26.

Hoy, Helen. "Fiction I." In "Letters in Canada 1981." *University of Toronto Quarterly* 51.4 (summer 1982): 318–34.

Hutcheon, Linda. "Canadian Historiographic Metafiction." *Essays on Canadian Writing* 30 (winter 1984–85): 228–38.

– *The Canadian Postmodern: A Study of Contemporary English Canadian Fiction.* Toronto: Oxford University Press 1988.

– "Challenging the Conventions of Realism: Postmodernism in Canadian Literature." *Canadian Forum* 66.758 (April 1986): 34–8.

– "'Circling the Downspout of Empire': Post-Colonialism and Postmodernism." *Ariel* 20.4 (October 1989): 149–75.

– "Colonialism and the Postcolonial Condition: Complexities Abounding." *PMLA* 110.1 (January 1995): 7–16.

– "Frye Recoded: Postmodernity and the Conclusions." In Lee and Denham, eds. *The Legacy of Northrop Frye,* 105–21.

– "Parody without Ridicule: Observations on Modern Literary Parody." *Canadian Review of Comparative Literature* 5.2 (spring 1978): 201–11.

– *A Poetics of Postmodernism: History, Theory, Fiction.* New York and London: Routledge 1988.

– *The Politics of Representation in Canadian Art and Literature.* Working Paper Series 88-F01. North York, ON: Robarts Centre for Canadian Studies, York University, 1988.

- "The Post Always Rings Twice: The Postmodern and the Postcolonial." *Textual Practice* 8 (1994): 205–38.
- "The 'Postmodernist' Scribe: The Dynamic Stasis of Contemporary Canadian Writing." *University of Toronto Quarterly* 53.3 (spring 1984): 283–95.
- "'Shape Shifters': Canadian Women Novelists and the Challenge to Tradition." in Neuman and Kamboureli, eds., *A Mazing Space*, 219–27.
- "Someday." Review of *Itsuka*, by Joy Kogawa. *Canadian Literature* 136 (spring 1993): 179–81.
- *Splitting Images: Contemporary Canadian Ironies.* Toronto: Oxford University Press 1991.
- *A Theory of Parody: The Teachings of Twentieth-Century Art Forms.* New York and London: Methuen 1985.
- Ignatieff, Michael. *Blood and Belonging: Journeys into the New Nationalism.* Toronto: Viking 1993.
- Imbert, Enrique Anderson. "'Magic Realism' in Spanish-American Fiction." *International Fiction Review* 2.1 (January 1975): 1–8.
- Jameson, Fredric. Foreword to *The Postmodern Condition: A Report On Knowledge*, by Jean-François Lyotard. Trans. Geoff Bennington and Brian Massumi. Minneapolis, MN: University of Minnesota Press 1984, vii–xxi.
- *The Political Unconscious: Narrative as a Socially Symbolic Act.* Ithaca, NY: Cornell University Press 1981.
- "Postmodernism, or the Cultural Logic of Late Capitalism." *New Left Review* 146 (July–August 1984): 53–92.
- Jardine, Alice A. *Gynesis: Configurations of Woman and Modernity.* Ithaca, NY, and London: Cornell University Press 1985.
- Jones, D.G. *Butterfly on Rock: A Study of Themes and Images in Canadian Literature.* Toronto and Buffalo: University of Toronto Press 1970.
- Jordan, David. *New World Regionalism: Literature in the Americas.* Toronto: University of Toronto Press 1994.
- Joyce, James. *Ulysses.* [1922]. New York: Random House 1961.
- Julien, Pierre-André. "Ne sommes-nous pas tous des Amérindiens?" *Le Devoir*, 5 August 1992, 13.
- Juneja, Om P., M.F. Salat, and Chandra Mohan. "'Looking at Our Particular World': An Interview with Rudy Wiebe." *World Literature Written in English* 31.2 (1991): 1–18.
- Kamboureli, Smaro. "*Burning Water*: Two Stories/ One Novel: Narrative as Exploration." Review of *Burning Water*, by George Bowering. *Island* 10 (1981): 89–94.
- "A Window onto George Bowering's Fiction of Unrest." In Moss, ed., *Present Tense*, 206–31.
- Katz, Ephraim. *The Film Encyclopedia.* New York: Thomas Y. Crowell 1979.

Keeshig-Tobias, Lenore. "The Identity of the Native Voice." Presentation at conference, Postcolonialism: Theory and Practice, Programme in Comparative Literature, University of British Columbia, March 1992.

Keith, W.J. *Epic Fiction: The Art of Rudy Wiebe*. Edmonton, AB: University of Alberta Press 1981.

– ed. *A Voice in the Land: Essays by and about Rudy Wiebe*. Edmonton, AB: NeWest Press 1981.

Kelman, Suanne. "Impossible to Forgive." Review of *Obasan*, by Joy Kogawa. *Canadian Forum* 61.715 (February 1982): 39–40.

Kenyon, Linda, and Robert Kroetsch. "A Conversation with Robert Kroetsch." *The New Quarterly* 5.1 (spring 1985): 9–19.

Kerouac, Jack. *On the Road*. 1955. New York: New American Library 1957.

King, Thomas. "Godzilla vs Post-Colonial." In Mukherjee, King, and Bayard, "Post-Colonialism," 10–16.

King, Thomas, Cheryl Calver, and Helen Hoy, eds. *The Native in Literature*. Toronto: ECW Press 1987.

Kinsella. W.P. *The Fencepost Chronicles*. Burlington, MA: Houghton-Miffin 1987.

Klinkenberg, Jean-Marie. "Schizobout le Papineauphrène–identité, narcissisme et postmodernisme dans *Les Têtes à Papineau*." In Frédéric and Allard, eds., *Modernité/Postmodernité* 111–18.

Knutson, Susan Lynne. "Bowering and Melville on Benjamin's Wharf: A Look at Indigenous-English Communication Strategies." *Essays on Canadian Writing* 38 (summer 1989): 67–80.

Kogawa, Joy. "Is There a Just Cause?" *Canadian Forum* 63.737 (March 1984): 20, 21, 24.

– *Itsuka*. Toronto: Penguin Books 1992.

– *Naomi's Road*. Toronto: Oxford University Press 1986.

– *Obasan*. 1981. Markham, ON: Penguin 1985.

– *The Rain Ascends*. Toronto: Alfred A. Knopf 1995.

Koh, Karlyn. "Speculations and (Dis)Identification: Notes on Asian Canadian Women Writers. *New Scholars, New Visions in Canadian Studies* 1.1 (summer 1996): 3–30.

Kortenaar, Neil ten. "The Trick of Divining a Postcolonial Canadian Identity: Margaret Laurence between Race and Nation." *Canadian Literature* 149 (summer 1996): 11–33.

Krieger, Murray, ed. *Northrop Frye in Modern Criticism: Selected Papers from the English Institute*. New York and London: Columbia University Press 1966.

Kroetsch, Robert. *Badlands*. Toronto: New Press 1975.

– "Beyond Nationalism: A Prologue." *Mosaic* 14.2 (Spring 1981): v–xi.

– "A Canadian Issue." *Boundary* 2 3.1 (fall 1974): 1–2.

– "Disunity as Unity: A Canadian Strategy." in Nicholson and Easingwood, eds., *Canadian Story*, 1–11.

- "Myth." In Kroetsch, Neuman, and Wilson, eds., *Labyrinths*, 85–136.
- *The Studhorse Man.* Toronto: Macmillan 1969.
- "Unhiding the Hidden: Recent Canadian Fiction." In Daymond and Monkman, eds., *Canadian Novelists*, 239–43.
- *The Words of My Roaring.* Toronto: Macmillan 1966.

Kroetsch, Robert, and Reingard M. Nischik, eds. *Gaining Ground: European Critics on Canadian Literature.* Western Canadian Literary Documents Series 4. Ed. Shirley Neuman. Edmonton, AB: NeWest Press 1985.

Kroetsch, Robert, Shirley Neuman, and Robert Wilson. *Labyrinths of Voice: Conversations with Robert Kroetsch.* Edmonton, AB: NeWest Press 1982.

Kroker, Arthur, and David Cook. *The Postmodern Scene: Excremental Culture and Hyper-Aesthetics.* Montreal: New World Perspectives 1986.

Kröller, Eva-Marie. *George Bowering: Bright Circles of Colour.* Vancouver: Talonbooks 1992.

- "The Politics of Influence: Canadian Postmodernism in an American Context." In *Inter-American Literary Relations.* Vol. 3. of *Proceedings of the Tenth Congress of the International Comparative Literature Association in New York, 1982.* Ed. Mario J. Valdés. New York and London: Garland Publishing 1985, 118–23.
- "Postmodernism, Colony, Nation: The Melvillean Texts of Bowering and Beaulieu." *Revue de l'Université d'Ottawa/University of Ottawa Quarterly* 54.2 (April–June 1984): 53–61.
- "Two Heads." Review of *Les Têtes à Papineau*, by Jacques Godbout. *Canadian Literature* 96 (spring 1983): 111–13.

Kuester, Martin. *Framing Truths: Parodic Structures in Contemporary English-Canadian Historical Novels.* Toronto: University of Toronto Press 1992.

Lacroix, Benoît. "La Mythologie religieuse traditionnelle des Canadiens français." *Revue de l'Université d'Ottawa/ University of Ottawa Quarterly* 55.2 (April–June 1985): 63–75.

Lacroix, Jean-Michel, and Fulvio Caccia, eds. *Métamorphoses d'une utopie.* Montreal: Triptyque 1992.

Lahar, Stephanie. "Ecofeminist Theory and Grassroots Politics." *Hepatia* 6.1 (spring 1991): 28–45.

Lamarche, Jacques. *L'Eté des Mohawks.* Montreal: Stanké 1990.

Lambertson, Michiko. "Obasan." Review of *Obasan*, by Joy Kogawa. *Canadian Woman Studies/Les Cahiers de la femme* 4.2 (winter 1982): 94–5.

Lamy, Suzanne. "Eloge du bavardage." In her *d'elles.* Montreal: l'Hexagone 1979, 15–35.

Lang, Andrew. *Magic and Religion.* New York: Longmans, Green 1901.

Langer, Beryl Donaldson. "Women and Literary Production." In McDougall and Whitlock, eds., *Australian/Canadian Literature*, 133–50.

Lapierre, René. "Appelez-moi George." Review of *En eaux troubles*, by George Bowering. Trans. L.-Philippe Hébert. *Le Devoir*, 22 May 1982, 20.

Laroche, Maximilien. *Contributions à l'étude du réalisme merveilleux.* Sainte-Foy, QC: GRELCA 1987.

– *Le Miracle et la métamorphose: Essai sur les littératures du Québec de d'Haïti.* Montréal, Editions du jour 1970.

Larrington, Carolyne, ed. *The Feminist Companion to Mythology.* London: Pandora Press 1992.

Laurence, Margaret. "The Black Celt Speaks of Freedom." Interview with Donald Cameron. In Cameron, ed., *Conversations,* 96–115.

– *The Diviners.* 1974. Toronto: McClelland & Stewart 1993.

– "Ivory Tower or Grassroots? The Novelist as Socio-Political Being." In New, ed., *A Political Act,* 15–25.

Lauter, Estella, and Carol Schreier Rupprecht, eds. *Feminist Archetypal Theory: Interdisciplinary Re-visions of Jungian Thought.* Introduction and conclusion by Lauter and Rupprecht. Knoxville, TN: University of Tennessee Press 1985.

Lecker, Robert, ed. *Canadian Canons: Essays in Literary Value.* Toronto: University of Toronto Press 1991.

Lee, Alvin A., and Robert D. Denham, eds. *The Legacy of Northrop Frye.* Toronto: University of Toronto Press 1994.

Lee, Dennis. "Cadence, Country, Silence: Writing in Colonial Space." *Boundary 2* 3.1 (fall 1974): 151–68.

– *Savage Fields: An Essay in Literature and Cosmology.* Toronto: Anansi 1977.

Lefèbvre, Jean. "J'ai Barcelo dans la peau!" *Nuit blanche* 10 (autumn 1983): 16–19.

Leitch, Linda M. Interview with George Bowering. *Books in Canada* 9 (November 1980): 30–1.

Lemire, Maurice, ed. *Dictionnaire des œuvres littéraires du Québec.* 5 vols. Montreal: Fides 1978–87.

Lentricchia, Frank. *After the New Criticism.* Chicago: University of Chicago Press 1980.

Lesage, Gilles. "Bonne note pour la politique autochtone québécoise." *Le Devoir,* 24 July 1992, 1, 4.

Lévesque, René. *Option Québec.* Montreal: Editions de l'homme 1968.

Levine, Marc, Louis Balthazar, and Kenneth McRoberts. "Symposium. Nationalism in Quebec: Past, Present, and Future." *Quebec Studies* 8 (1989):119–29.

Lévi-Strauss, Claude. *Mythologiques* 4 vols. *Le Cru et le cuit* 1964; *Du miel aux cendres,* 1966; *L'Origine des manières de table,* 1968; and *L'Homme nu,* 1971. Paris: Plon.

– *The Raw and the Cooked.* Trans. John and Doreen Weightman. New York: Harper and Row 1969.

– *Tristes Tropiques.* Paris: Plon 1955.

– *La Voie des masques.* Vol. 1: Geneva: Editions d'Art Albert Skira 1975; Vols. 1 and 2: Paris: Plon 1979.

Lévy-Bruhl, Lucien. *Carnets*. Paris: Presses Universitaires de France 1949.
- *La mentalité primitive*. Paris: Félix Alcan 1922.
Lewis, Paula Gilbert. "Literary Relationships between Québec and the United States: A Meagre Reciprocity." *Essays on Canadian Writing* 22 (summer 1981): 86–110.
- ed. and intro. *Traditionalism, Nationalism and Feminism: Women Writers of Quebec*. Westport, CT: Greenwoood Press 1985.
L'Hérault, Pierre. "Figures et langage(s) de l'ethnicité dans le théâtre québécois." Presentation to the Association for Canadian Studies in the United States, Seattle, WA, November 1995.
- *Jacques Ferron: cartographe de l'imaginaire*. Montreal: Presses de l'Université de Montréal 1980.
Lim, Shirley Geok-lin. "Japanese American Women's Life Stories: Maternality in Monica Sone's *Nisei Daughter* and Joy Kogawa's *Obasan*." *Feminist Studies* 16.2 (summer 1990): 289–312.
Lim, Shirley Geok-lin, and Amy Ling, eds. *Reading the Literatures of Asian America*. Philadelphia, PA: Temple University Press 1992.
Linstead, Steve. "'Jokers Wild': Humour in Organisational Culture." In *Humour in Society: Resistance and Control*. Eds. Chris Powell and George E.C. Paton. Houndmills and London: Macmillan 1988, 123–48.
Linteau, Paul-André, René Durocher, and Jean-Claude Robert. *Histoire du Québec contemporain: de la Confédération à la crise (1867–1929)*. Ville Saint-Laurent: Boréal Express 1979.
Lobb, Edward. "Imagining History: The Romantic Background of George Bowering's *Burning Water*." *Studies in Canadian Literature* 12.1 (1987): 112–28.
Lord, Albert Bates. *The Singer of Tales*. Cambridge: Harvard University Press 1960.
Lord, Michel. "Aah! Aâh! Ha! que de belles catastrophes narratives!" *Lettres québécoises* 45 (spring 87): 32–3.
Loriggio, Francesco. "Myth, Mythology and the Novel: Towards a Reappraisal." *Canadian Review of Comparative Literature/ Revue canadienne de littérature comparée* 11, no. 4 (December 1984): 501–20.
Lowes, John Livingston. *The Road to Xanadu*. Boston: Houghton Mifflin 1955.
Lyotard, Jean-François. *La Condition postmoderne: rapport sur le savoir*. Paris: Minuit 1979.
- *Le Différend*. Paris: Minuit 1983.
- *The Postmodern Condition: A Report on Knowledge*. Trans. Geoff Bennington and Brian Massumi. Minneapolis, MN: University of Minnesota Press 1984.
Maclulich, T.D. "Our Place on the Map: The Canadian Tradition in Fiction." *University of Toronto Quarterly* 52.2 (winter 1982–83): 191–208.
Mailhot, Laurent. "Romans de la parole (et du mythe)." *Canadian Literature* 88 (spring 1981): 84–90.

Maillard, Keith. "'Middlewatch' as Magic Realism." *Canadian Literature* 92 (spring 1982): 10–21.

Malinowski, Bronislaw. *Myth in Primitive Psychology*. [1926]. Westport, CT: Negro Universities Press 1971.

Mandel, Eli. *Criticism: The Silent-Speaking Words*. Toronto: Canadian Broadcasting Corporation 1966.

– "Imagining Natives: White Perspectives on Native Peoples." In King, Calver, and Hoy, eds. *The Native in Literature*, 34–49.

– *The Family Romance*. Winnipeg: Turnstone Press 1986.

Mandel, Eli, and Rudy Wiebe. "Where the Voice Comes From." In Keith, ed., *Voice*, 150–5.

Marcato-Falzoni, Franza. *Du Mythe au roman: une trilogie ducharmienne*. Trans. Javier García Méndez. Montreal: VLB 1992.

Marcel, Jean. *Jacques Ferron malgré lui*. Montreal: Parti Pris 1978.

Marchessault, Jovette. *Alice & Gertrude, Nathalie & Renée et ce cher Ernest*. Montreal: Editons de la Pleine Lune 1984.

– *Anaïs, dans la queue de la comète*. Montreal: Editions de la Pleine Lune 1985.

– *Des Cailloux blancs pour les forêts obscures*. Ottawa: Leméac 1987.

– *Comme une enfant de la terre*. Vol. 1, *Le Crachat solaire*. Montreal: Leméac 1975.

– "Il m'est encore impossible de chanter, mais j'écris." *Jeu* 16 (1980): 207–10.

– *Lesbian Triptych*. 1980. Trans. Yvonne M. Klein. Toronto: Women's Press 1985.

– *Like a Child of the Earth*. Trans. Yvonne M. Klein. Vancouver: Talon Books 1988.

– *La Mère des herbes*. Montreal: Quinze 1980.

– *La Saga des poules mouillees*. Montreal: Editions de la Pleine Lune 1980.

– *Tryptique lesbien*. Montreal: Editions de la Pleine Lune 1980.

– *Le Voyage magnifique d'Emily Carr*. Montreal: Leméac 1991.

Marcotte, Gilles. *Une Littérature qui se fait*. Montreal: HMH 1962.

– Papineau, de Gaulle et le vieil espion." Review of *Papineau ou l'épée à double tranchant*, by Claire de Lamirande (among others). *Actualité* 5.7 (July 1980): 58.

Marron, Kevin. *Witches, Pagans and Magic in the New Age*. Toronto: Seal Books 1990.

Martel, Réginald. "Trois sur trois, naturellement." Review of *Ville-Dieu*, by François Barcelo. *La Presse*, 5 March 1983, E3.

Martin, Biddy, and Chandra Mohanty. "Feminist Politics: What's Home Got to Do with It?" In *Feminist Studies/ Critical Studies*. Ed. Teresa de Lauretis. Bloomington, IN: Indiana University Press 1986, 191–212.

Martin, Sandra. "Ode to Joy." In Fischman et al., "Ode to Joy," 5.

Mauss, Marcel. "Essai sur le don: forme archaïque de l'échange." In *L'Année sociologique* (1923–24). Reprinted as *The Gift: The Form and Reason for*

Exchange in Archaic Societies. Trans. W.D. Halls. London and New York: Routledge 1990.

Maxwell, D.E.S. "Landscape and Theme." *Commonwealth Literature: Unity and Diversity in a Common Culture.* Ed. John Press. London: Heinemann Educational Books 1965, 82–9.

McDonald, Larry. "Post modernism, Canadian style." Review of *The Canadian Postmodern: A Study of Contemporary English Canadian Literature,* by Linda Hutcheon. *Canadian Forum* 68.782 (October 1989): 29–30.

McDougall, Russell, and Whitlock, Gillian, eds. and intro. *Australian/ Canadian Literatures in English: Comparative Perspectives.* North Ryde, NSW: Methuen Australia 1987.

McGregor, Gaile. *The Wacousta Syndrome: Explorations in the Canadian Landscape.* Toronto: University of Toronto Press 1985.

McHale, Brian. *Postmodernist Fiction.* New York and London: Methuen 1987.

McLuhan, Marshall, and Quentin Fiore. *The Medium is the Massage.* New York: Random House 1967.

Memmi, Albert. *Portrait du colonisé.* Includes "Les Canadiens français sont-ils des colonisés?" Montreal: L'Etincelle 1972.

Menton, Seymour. "Jorge Luis Borges, Magic Realist." *Hispanic Review* 50 (1982): 411–26.

Merivale, Patricia. "Framed Voices: The Polyphonic Elegies of Hébert and Kogawa." *Canadian Literature* 116 (spring 1988): 68–82.

Meyer, Bruce, and Brian O'Riordan. "Joy Kogawa: A Matter of Trust." *University of Toronto Review* 9 (spring 1985): 28–31.

Michaud, Ginette. "Récits postmodernes?" *Etudes françaises* 21.3 (winter 1985–86): 67–88.

Michon, Jacques. "Romans." Letters in Canada 1981. *University of Toronto Quarterly* 51.4 (summer 1982): 334–43.

Miller, Orlo. *Death to the Donnelleys.* Toronto: Macmillan 1975.

Minh-ha, Trinh T. *Women, Native, Other: Writing Postcoloniality and Feminism.* Bloomington and Indianapolis, IN: Indiana University Press 1989.

Mink, Louis O. "History and Fiction as Modes of Comprehension." *New Literary History* 1 (1970): 541–58.

– "Narrative Form as a Cognitive Instrument." In *The Writing of History: Literary Form and Historical Understanding.* Eds. Robert H. Canary and Henry Kozicki. Madison, WI: University of Wisconsin Press 1978, 129–49.

Mishra, Vijay, and Bob Hodge. "What is Post(-)colonialism?" In Williams and Chrisman, eds., *Colonial Discourse,* 276–90.

Moi, Toril. *Sexual/Textual Politics: Feminist Literary Theory.* London and New York: Methuen 1985.

Monière, Denis. *Le Développement des idéologies au Québec: des origines à nos jours.* Montreal: Editions Québec/Amérique 1977.

– *Ideologies in Quebec: The Historical Development.* Trans. Richard Howard. Toronto: University of Toronto Press 1981.

Monkman, Leslie. *A Native Heritage: Images of the Indian in English-Canadian Literature.* Toronto: University of Toronto Press 1981.

– "Visions and Revisions: Contemporary Writers and Exploration Accounts of Indigenous Peoples." In King, Calver, and Hoy, eds., *The Native in Literature*, 80–98.

Morazain, Jeanne. "Un antidote à notre amnésie collective: la grande paix de Montréal de 1701." *Le Devoir*, 30 July 1992, 11.

Morgan, Janice, and Colette T. Hall, eds. *Redefining Autobiography in Twentieth-Century Women's Fiction.* New York and London: Garland Publishing 1991.

Morissette, Brigitte. "Lointaine et proche Anne Hébert." *Châteleine* 24.2 (February 1983): 47–54.

Morris, Welsey A. "Beginnings." *The Georgia Review* 30.3 (fall 1976): 736–44.

Moss, John George. *Patterns of Isolation in English Canadian Fiction.* Toronto: McClelland and Stewart 1974.

– *Present Tense: The Canadian Novel.* Vol. 4. Toronto: NC Press 1985.

– ed. and intro. *Future Indicative: Literary Theory and Canadian Literature.* Ottawa: University of Ottawa Press 1987.

Mukherjee, Arun P. "Whose Post-Colonialism and Whose Postmodernism?" In Mukherjee, King, and Bayard, "Post-Colonialism," 1–9.

Mukherjee, Arun P., Thomas King, and Caroline Bayard. "Post-Colonialism and Postmodernism: A Panel." *World Literature Written in English* 30.2 (autumn 1990): 1–29.

Mulvey, Laura. "Magnificent Obsession." *Parachute* 42 (1986): 6–12.

Murray, Heather. "Reading for Contradiction in the Literature of Colonial Space." In Moss, ed., *Future Indicative*, 71–84.

Naves, Elaine Kalman. "The Magnificient Voyage of Jovette Marchessault." *Books in Canada* 22.6 (September 1993): 27–31.

Nelson, Joyce. "Speaking the Unspeakable." *Canadian Forum* 68.787 (March 1990): 15–16.

Nepveu, Pierre. *L'Ecologie du réel: mort et naissance de la littérature québécoise contemporaine.* Montreal: Boréal 1988.

– "A (Hi)story that Refuses the Telling: Poetry and the Novel in Contemporary Québécois Literature." *Yale French Studies* 65 (1983): 90–105.

Newman, Shirley. Introduction to *Figures Cut in Sacred Ground*, by Angela Bowering. Edmonton, AB: NeWest Press 1989.

Neuman, Shirley, and Smaro Kamboureli, eds. *A Mazing Space: Writing Canadian Women Writing.* Edmonton, AB: Longspoon Press/NeWest Press 1986.

New, William H. *Among Worlds: An Introduction to Modern Commonwealth and South African Fiction.* Erin, ON: Press Porcépic 1975.

– *A Political Act: Essays and Images in Honour of George Woodcock.* Vancouver: University of Vancouver Press 1978.

– ed. *Native Writers and Canadian Writing*. Special issue of *Canadian Literature*. Vancouver: UBC Press 1990.

Newton, Judith. "History as Usual?: Feminism and the 'New Historicism.'" *Cultural Critique* 9 (spring 1988): 87–121.

Nicholson, Colin, and Peter Easingwood, eds. *Canadian Story and History, 1885–1985: Papers Presented at the Tenth Annual Conference of The British Association for Canadian Studies*. Edinburgh: University of Edinburgh 1985.

O'Hagan, Howard. *Tay John*. 1939. Toronto: McClelland and Stewart 1974.

Ondaatje, Michael. *The Collected Works of Billy the Kid*. Toronto: Anansi 1970.

– *Coming through Slaughter*. Toronto: Anansi 1976.

O'Neill-Karch, Mariel, ed. "Humour Québec." *Thalia: Studies in Literary Humour* 8.1 (spring/summer 1985).

Ong, Walter J. *Interfaces of the Word: Studies in the Evolution of Consciousness and Culture*. Ithaca, NY: Cornell University Press 1977.

– *Orality and Literacy: The Technologizing of the Word*. London and New York: Methuen 1982.

Orenstein, Gloria F. "Les voyages visionnaires de trois créatrices féministes-matristiques: Emily Carr, Jovette Marchessault et Gloria Orenstein." *Voix et Images* 47 (winter 1991): 253–61.

– "Jovette Marchessault: The Ecstatic Vision-Quest of the New Feminist Shaman." In Godard, ed., *Gynocritics/La Gynocritique*, 179–97.

Osachoff, Margaret Gail. "Louis Riel in Canadian Literature: Myth and Reality." In Nicholson and Easingwood, eds., *Canadian Story*, 61–9.

Ouellette, Francine. *Au nom du père et du fils*. Montreal: La Presse 1984.

Ouellette-Michalska, Madeleine. *L'Echapée des discours de l'Œil*. N.p.: Nouvelle Optique 1981.

– "Jovette Marchessault: Après la chute." Review of *La Mère des herbes*, by Jovette Marchessault. *Le Devoir*, 9 February 1980, 27.

– *La Maison Trestler ou le 8e jour d'Amérique*. Montreal: Québec/Amérique 1984.

Owens, Craig. "The Discourse of Others: Feminists and Postmodernism." in *The Anti-Aesthetic: Essays on Postmodern Culture*. Ed. Hal Foster. Washington, DC: Bay Press 1983, 57–82.

Pache, Walter. "The Fiction Makes Us Real: Aspects of Postmodernism in Canada." In Kroetsch and Nischik, eds., *Gaining Ground*, 64–78.

Palencia-Roth, Michael. *Myth and the Modern Novel: García Márquez, Mann and Joyce*. New York and London: Garland 1987.

Patai, Daphne. *Myth and Ideology in Contemporary Brazilian Fiction*. London and Toronto: Associated University Presses 1983.

Paterson, Janet M. *Moments postmodernes dans le roman québécois*. Ottawa: Les Presses de l'Université d'Ottawa 1990.

Pavel, Thomas. Review of *Agénor, Agénor, Agénor et Agénor* and *La Tribu*, by François Barcelo. *Lettres québécoises* 26 (summer 1982): 34–6.

Payette, Lise. *Appelez-moi Lise*. Télévision de Radio-Canada, Montreal. September 1972 to October 1976.

Pearlman, Mickey, ed. *Canadian Women Writing Fiction*. Jackson, MS: University Press of Mississippi 1993.

Pellerin, Gilles. Review of *Papineau ou l'épée à double tranchant*, by Claire de Lamirande. In *Livres et auteurs québécois 1980*. Quebec: Les Presses de l'Université Laval 1981, 45–7.

Pelletier, Jacques. Review of *Les Têtes à Papineau*, by Jacques Godbout. In *Livres et auteurs québécois 1981*. Quebec: Les Presses de l'Université Laval 1982, 52–3.

Perry, Reginald. "A Deckchair of Words: Post-colonialism, Post-modernism, and the Novel of Self-Projection in Canada and New Zealand." *Landfall* 159 40.3 (September 1986): 310–23.

Peterson, Jacqueline, and Jennifer S.H. Brown. *The New Peoples: Being and Becoming in North America*. Winnipeg, MB: University of Manitoba Press 1985.

Petrone, Penny. *Native Literature in Canada from the Oral Tradition to the Present*. Toronto: Oxford University Press 1990.

Philpot, Robin. *Oka: dernier alibi du Canada anglais*. Montreal: VLB Editeur 1991.

Piette, Alain. "Les Langues à Papineau: comment le texte national se fait littérature." *Voix et images* 9.3 (spring 1984): 113–27.

Plumwood, Val. "Nature, Self, and Gender: Feminism, Environmental Philosophy, and the Critique of Rationalism." *Hypatia* 6.1 (spring 1991): 3–27.

Ponte, Cecilia. "Au Carrefour du réalisme merveilleux." In *Actes du colloque: tradition et modernité dans les littératures francophones d'Afrique et d'Amérique*. Sainte-Foy, QC: GRELCA 1988, 99–116.

– *Le Réalisme merveilleux dans Les Arbres musiciens de Jacques-Stéphen Alexis*. Sainte-Foy, QC: GRELCA 1987, 1.

Popol Vuh: The Definitive Edition of the Mayan Book of the Dawn of Life and the Glories of Gods and Kings. Trans. Dennis Tedlock. New York: Simon and Schuster 1986.

Potter, Robin. "Moral – In whose Sense? Joy Kogawa's *Obasan* and Julia Kristeva's *Powers of Horror*." *Studies in Canadian Literature* 15.1 (1990): 117–39.

Potvin, Claudine. "Jovette Marchessault, autodidacte: en marge de l'institution littéraire ou les limites de la marge." In *Women's Writing and the Literary Institution*. C. Potvin and J. Williamson, eds., *Women's Writing*, 151–9.

– "Présentation: Jovette Marchessault. A-ma-zone/Ecrire dans la marge." *Voix et Images* 47 (winter 1991): 214–15.

Potvin, C., and J. Williamson, eds., in collaboration with S. Tötösy de Zepetnek. *Women's Writing and the Literary Institution/Ecriture au féminin et l'institution littéraire*. Edmonton, AB: Research Institute for Comparative Literature 1992.

Poulet, Georges. *Etudes sur le temps humain*. Paris: Plon 1950. 4 vols. *La Distance intérieure*. Vol. 2. 1952. *Le Point de départ*. Vol. 3. 1964. *Mesures de l'instant*. Vol. 4. 1968.
– *Les Métamorphoses du cercle*. Paris: Plon 1961.
Poulin, Jacques. *Les Grandes Marées*. Montreal: Leméac 1978.
– *Volkswagen Blues*. Montreal: Québec/Amérique 1984.
Powe, Bruce Allen. *The Aberhart Summer*. Toronto: Lester and Orpen Dennys 1983.
Powe, B.W. "Fear of Fryeing: Northrop Frye and the Theory of Myth Criticism." In *A Climate Charged: Essays on Canadian Writers*. Oakville: Mosaic Press 1984, 34–54.
Prémont, Laurent. *Le Mythe de Prométhée dans la littérature française contemporaine*. Quebec: Les Presses de l'université Laval 1964.
Prentice, Susan. "Taking Sides: What's Wrong with Eco-feminism?" *Women and Environments* 10.3 (Spring 1988): 9–10.
Propp, Vladimir. *Morphologie du conte*. [1928]. Paris: Seuil 1970.
Proust, Marcel. *A la recherche du temps perdu*. [1913–27]. Paris: Gallimard 1954.
Rasporich, Beverly. "The Literary Humour of Roch Carrier." In O'Neill-Karch, ed., "Humour Québec," 37–49.
Reaney, James. "To the Avon River Above Stratford, Canada." In *Twelve Letters to a Small Town*. Toronto: Ryerson Press 1962, 1.
Recherches amérindiennes au Québec 17.3 (autumn 1987). Special number on "L'Indien imaginaire."
Redekop, Magdalene. "The Literary Politics of the Victim." Interview with Joy Kogawa. *Canadian Forum* 68.783 (November 1989): 14–17.
Répertoire bibliographique: auteurs amérindiens du Québec. Saint-Luc, QC: Centre de recherche sur la littérature et les arts autochtones du Québec 1993.
Ricci Della Grisa, Graciela N. *Realismo Mágico y Conciencia Mítica en América Latina: Textos y Contextos*. Buenos Aires: Fernando García Cambeiro 1985.
Richardson, John. "Ode to Joy." in Fischman et al., 5.
Richer, Stephen, and Lorna Weir, eds. *Beyond Political Correctness: Toward the Inclusive University*. Toronto: University of Toronto Press 1995.
Ricou, Laurie. "Phyllis Webb, Daphne Marlatt and Simultitude: Journal Entries from a Capitalist Bourgeois Patriarchal Anglo-Saxon Mainstream Critic." In Neuman and Kamboureli, eds., 205–15.
Riemenschneider, Dieter, ed. *The History and Historiography of Commonwealth Literature* . Tübingen: Narr 1983.
Ringuet [Philippe Panneton]. *Trente arpents*. Montreal and Paris: Fides 1967.
Risco, Antón. "Le Postmodernisme latino-américain." *Etudes littéraires* 27.1 (summer 1994): 63–76.
Roa Bastos, Augusto Antonio. *I, the Supreme*. Trans. Helen Lane. New York: Knopf 1986.

Robertson, Heather. *Willie: A Romance*. Toronto: James Lorimer 1983.

Robin, Régine. "Postface: de nouveaux jardins aux sentiers qui bifurquent." In her *La Québécoite*. 2d ed. Montreal: Typo 1993, 207–24.

Roh, Franz. *El realismo mágico*. Trans. Fernando Vela. Madrid, Revista de Occidente 1927.

– *Nach Expressionismus (Magischer Realismus)*. Leipzig: Klinkhardt und Bierman 1925.

Rose, Margaret A. *Parody: Ancient, Modern, and Post-Modern*. Cambridge: Cambridge University Press 1993.

– *Parody/Meta-Fiction: An Analysis of Parody as a Critical Mirror to the Writing and Reception of Fiction*. London: Croom Helm 1979.

Rose, Marilyn Russell. "Politics into Art: Kogawa's *Obasan* and the Rhetoric of Fiction." *Mosaic* 21.2–3 (spring 1988): 215–26.

Rosenfield, Martha. "The Development of a Lesbian Sensibility in the Work of Jovette Marchessault and Nicole Brossard." In Lewis, ed., *Traditionalism*, 227–39.

Ross, Sinclair. *As for Me and My House*. Toronto: McClelland and Stewart 1957.

Rostas, Susanna. "Mexican Mythology: Divine Androgyny but 'His' Story: The Female in Aztec Mythology." In Larrington, ed., *Feminist Companion*, 362–87.

Roy, Alain. "La Sagesse de Mireille." *Liberté 212* 35.6 (December 1993): 72–108.

Ruether, Rosemary Radford. "The *Faith and Fratricide* Discussion: Old Problems and New Dimensions." In Davies. ed., *Antisemitism*, 230–56.

Said, Edward W. *Beginnings: Intention and Method*. New York: Basic Books 1975.

– *Orientalism*. 1978. New York: Vintage Books 1979.

– "Representing the Colonized: Anthropology's Interlocutors." *Critical Inquiry* 15.2 (winter 1989): 205–25.

– *The World, the Text, and the Critic*. Cambridge, MA: Harvard University Press 1983.

Salutin, Rick. *Marginal Notes: Challenges to the Mainstream*. Toronto: Lester and Orpen Dennys 1984.

Sartre, Jean Paul. *L'Etre et le néant: essai d'ontologie phénoménologique*. Paris: Gallimard 1943.

St-Andrews, B.A. "Reclaiming a Canadian Heritage: Kogawa's *Obasan*." *International Fiction Review* 13.1 (winter 1986): 29–31.

Scarpetta, Guy. *L'Impureté*. Paris: Bernard Grasset 1985.

Scholes, Robert. *The Fabulators*. New York and Oxford: Oxford University Press 1967.

Scobie, Stephen. "Cohen, Webb, and the End(s) of Modernism." In Lecker, ed., *Canadian Canons*, 57–70.

Scott, Chris. *Antichthon*. Dunvegan, ON: Quadrant 1982.

– "A Bum Rap for Poor George Vancouver." Review of *Burning Water*, by George Bowering. *Books in Canada* 9 (November 1980): 9.

Segal, Robert A. "Frazer and Campbell on Myth: Nineteeth- and Twentieth-Century Approaches." *The Southern Review* 26 (spring 1990): 470–6.

Séjourné, Laurette. *Burning Water: Thought and Religion in Ancient Mexico*. Trans. Irene Nicholson. New York: The Vanguard Press n.d.

Semujanga, Josias. "Onomastique littéraire et compétences de lecture: l'exemple des *Têtes à Papineau* de J. Godbout." *Protée* 21.2 (spring 1993): 77–84.

Shakespeare, William. *A Midsummer Night's Dream*. Ed. F. C. Horwood. London: Oxford University Press 1956.

– *The Tempest*. London: Cornmarket Press 1969.

Simon, Paul. "Slip Slidin' Away." Words and music by Paul Simon. Columbia 10630, 1977.

Simon, Sherry. "The Language of Difference: Minority Writers in Quebec." Comments by Christl Verduyn, J.D. Rayfield, and Barbara Godard. *Canadian Literature*. Supplement 1 (May 1987): 119–37.

Simon, Sherry, Pierre L'Hérault, et al. *Fictions de l'identitaire au Québec*. Montreal: XYZ 1991.

Singleton, C.S., ed. *Interpretation: Theory and Practice*. Baltimore, MD: Johns Hopkins University Press 1969.

Sioui, Georges E. *Pour une Autohistoire amérindienne: essai sur les fondements d'une morale sociale*. Quebec: Presses de l'Université Laval 1989.

Sioui Durand, Yves. *Atiskenandahate ou Voyage au pays des morts*. Manuscript, 1988. Play presented in Montreal, November 1988, at the studio theatre Alfred-Laliberté.

Sirois, Antoine. "Bible, mythe et fous de bassan." *Canadian Literature* 104 (spring 1985): 178–82.

– *Mythes et symboles dans la littératures québécoise*. Montreal: Triptyque 1992.

Slemon, Stephen. "Magic Realism as Post-Colonial Discourse." *Canadian Literature* 116 (spring 1988): 9–24.

– "Post-Colonial Allegory and the Transformation of History." *Journal of Commonwealth Literature* 23 (1988): 157–68.

– "The Scramble for Post-colonialism." In Ashcroft, Griffiths, and Tiffin, eds., 45–52.

Smart, Ninian. "Buddhism." In *The Encyclopedia of Philosophy*. Vol 1. Paul Edwards, ed. London: Collier-Macmillan 1967, 416–20.

Smart, Patricia. "Culture, Revolution, and Politics in Quebec." *Canadian Forum* 62.718 (May 1982): 7–10.

– "L'Espace de nos fictions: quelques réflexions sur nos deux cultures." *Voix et images* 10.1 (autumn 1984): 23–36.

– "Filming the Myth." Review of Jacques Godbout's film "Deux épisodes dans la vie d'Hubert Aquin." *Canadian Forum* 60.702 (September 1980): 20–1.

- "My Father's House: Exploring a Patriarchal Culture." *Canadian Forum* 67.774 (December 1987): 28–35.
- "Postmodern Male Narratives." In "Symposium: Feminism and Postmodernism in Quebec: The Politics of the Alliance." *Québec Studies* 9 (fall/winter 1989–90): 146–50.
- "Women as Object, Women as Subjects, and the Consequences for Narrative: Hubert Aquin's *Neige noire* and the Impasse of Post-Modernism." *Canadian Literature* 113–14 (summer/fall 1987): 168–78.
Smith, André. *L'Univers romanesque de Jacques Godbout*. Montreal: Editions Aquila 1976.
Smith, Derek G. "Native People, Religion." *Canadian Encyclopedia*. 2d ed. Edmonton, AB: Hurtig Publishers 1988, 1458–9.
Smith, Donald. "Jacques Godbout et la transformation de la réalité, une entrevue de Donald Smith." *Lettres québécoises* 25 (spring 1982): 53–61.
- "Jovette Marchessault: de la femme tellurique à la démythification sociale." *Lettres québécoises* 27 (autumn 1982): 53–8.
Smith, Paul. "The Will to Allegory in Postmodernism." *Dalhousie Review* 62.1 (spring 1982): 105–22.
Socken, Paul. *The Myth of the Lost Paradise in the Novels of Jacques Poulin*. Cranbury, NJ: Associated University Presses 1993.
Söderlind, Sylvia. *Margin/Alias: Language and Colonization in Canadian and Québécois Fiction*. Toronto: University of Toronto Press 1991.
Solecki, Sam. "Giant Fictions and Large Meanings: The Novels of Rudy Wiebe." *Canadian Forum* 60.707 (March 1981): 5–8.
Spencer, Herbert. *The Principles of Psychology*. 2d ed. 2 vols. 1870–72. London: Williams and Norgate 1890.
Spicer, Keith. "Les Acadiens aux yeux bridés." Review of *Obasan*, by Joy Kogawa. *Actualité* 7.10 (October 1982): 28.
Spivak, Gayatri. "Allégorie et historie de la poésie: hypothèse de travail." *Poétique* 8 (1971): 427–41.
- *In Other Worlds: Essays in Cultural Politics*. New York: Methuen 1987.
- "Thoughts on the Principle of Allegory." *Genre* 5 (October 1972): 327–52.
Stanton, Julie. "Pour Jovette Marchessault, ç'a été: 'tu crées ou tu crèves.'" *Châtelaine* 22 (June 1981): 110–14, 116, 118, 120.
Stead, C.K. *All Visitors Ashore*. London: Harvill Press 1984.
Steele, Lisa. "Committed to Memory: Women's Video Art Production in Canada and Quebec." In Tregebov, ed., *Work in Progress*, 39–63.
Stevens, Peter, "Kogawa, Joy." In *Oxford Companion to Canadian Literature*, ed. Toye.
Stevenson, W. Taylor. "Myth and the Crisis of Historical Consciousness." in Gibbs and Stevenson, eds., *Myth*, 1–17.
Stocking, George W., Jr. *Victorian Anthropology*. New York: The Free Press 1987.

– ed. *Observers Observed: Essays on Ethnographic Fieldwork*. Madison, WI: The University of Wisconsin Press 1983.

Stratford, Philip. *All the Polarities: Comparative Studies in Contemporary Canadian Novels in English and French*. Toronto: ECW Press 1986.

Strunk, Volker. "Canadian Literary Criticism and the Problem of 'National Literature.'" In Riemenschneider, ed., *History*, 66–77.

Stuewe, Paul. *Clearing the Ground: English-Canadian Literature after Survival*. Toronto: Proper Tales Press 1984.

Sullivan, Rosemary. "The Fascinating Place Between: The Fiction of Robert Kroetsch." *Mosaic* 11.3 (spring 1978): 165–76.

– "Northrop Frye: Canadian Mythographer." *Journal of Commonwealth Literature* 18.1 (1983): 1–13.

Sunahara, Ann Gomer. *The Politics of Racism: The Uprooting of Japanese-Canadians during the Second World War*. Toronto: James Lorimer 1981.

Sutherland, Roland. *The New Hero: Essays in Comparative Quebec/Canadian Literature*. Toronto: Macmillan 1977.

– *Second Image: Comparative Studies in Quebec/Canadian Literature*. Toronto: New Press 1971.

Swift, Graham. *Waterland*. 1983. London: Pan Books and William Heinemann 1984.

Thérien, Gilles. "L'Indien du discours." In Thérien, ed., *Figures*, 355–67.

– "L'Indien imaginaire: une hypothèse." *Recherches amérindiennes au Québec* 17.3 (autumn 1987): 3–21.

– "La Littérature québécoise: une littérature du tiers-monde?" *Voix et Images* 34 (autumn 1986): 12–20.

– ed. *Les Figures de l'Indien*. Les Cahiers du département d'études littéraires, no. 9. Montreal: Université du Québec à Montréal 1988.

Thiher, Allen. *Words in Reflection: Modern Language Theory and Postmodern Fiction*. Chicago: University of Chicago Press 1984.

Thomas, Clara. "The Chariot of Ossian: Myth and Manitoba in *The Diviners*." *Journal of Canadian Studies* 13.3 (fall 1978): 55–63.

– "A Conversation About Literature: An Interview with Margaret Laurence and Irving Layton." *Journal of Canadian Fiction* 1.1 (winter 1972): 65–9.

Thomas, Hilda L. "A Time to Remember." Review of *The Politics of Racism*, by Ann Gomer Sunahara, and of *Obasan*, by Joy Kogawa. *Canadian Literature* 96 (spring 1983): 103–5.

Thomas, Peter. "Trickster at the Wake of History: *The Studhorse Man*." In *Robert Kroetsch*. Studies in Canadian Literature Series. Vancouver: Douglas and McIntyre 1980, 51–67.

Tiffin, Helen. "Post-Colonialism, Post-Modernism, and the Rehabilitation of Post-Colonial History." *Journal of Commonwealth Literature* 23.1 (1988): 169–81.

– "Post-Colonial Literatures and Counter-Discourse." *Kunapipi* 9.3 (1987): 17–34.

Tournier, Michel. *Gilles et Jeanne*. Paris: Gallimard 1983.

– *Vendredi ou les limbes du Pacifique*. Paris: Gallimard 1972.

Toye, William, ed. *The Oxford Companion to Canadian Literature*. Toronto: Oxford University Press 1983.

Tregebov, Rhea, ed. *Work in Progress: Building Feminist Culture*. Toronto: Women's Press 1987.

.Trehearne, Brian. *Aestheticism and the Canadian Modernists: Aspects of a Poetic Influence*. Montreal and Kingston: McGill-Queen's University Press 1989.

Tremblay, Victor-Laurent. *Au commencement était le mythe*. Ottawa: Les Presses de l'Université d'Ottawa 1991.

Turgeon, Pierre. "Présentation." *Liberté 196–97* 33.4–5 (August–October 1991): 3–5.

Tuttle, Lisa. *Encyclopedia of Feminism*. Essex and London: Longman Group 1986.

Twigg, Alan. *For Openers: Conversations with Twenty-Four Canadian Writers*. Madeira Park, BC: Harbour Publishing 1981.

Ueki, Teruyo. "*Obasan*: Revelations in a Paradoxical Scheme." *Melus* 18 (winter 1993–94): 5–20.

Ursell, Geoffrey. *Perdue: Or How the West Was Lost*. Toronto: Macmillan 1984.

Vachon, André. "Qui serions-nous?" *Liberté 212* 36.2 (April 1994): 113–26.

Vallières, Pierre. *Nègres blancs d'Amérique: autobiographie précoce d'un terroriste*. Quebec: Editions Parti Pris 1968.

Van Gelder, Lindsy. "It's Not Nice to Mess with Mother Nature." *Ms.* 17.7–8 (January–February 1989): 60–3.

van Herk, Aritha. "Mapping as Metaphor." *Zeitschrift der Gesellschaft für Kanada Studien* 2, no. 1 (1982): 75–86.

van Toorn, Penny. *Rudy Wiebe and the Historicity of the Word*. Edmonton, AB: University of Alberta Press 1995.

Vancouver, George. *Voyage of Discovery to the North Pacific Ocean and Round the World*. 3 vols. New York: Da Capo Press 1967.

Vardey, Lucinda. *Belonging: A Book for the Questioning Catholic Today*. Toronto: Lester and Orpen Dennys 1988.

Varga, A Kibédi. "Le Récit postmoderne." *Littérature* 77 (February 1990): 3–22.

Vargos Llosa, Mario. *The War of the End of the World*. Trans. Helen R. Lane. New York: Farrar, Straus, Giroux 1984.

Varsava, Jerry. "History and/or His Story?" In D'haen and Berten, eds., *History and Post-War Writing*, 205–25.

Vautier, Marie. "Fiction, Historiography, and Myth: Jacques Godbout's *Les têtes à Papineau* and Rudy Wiebe's *The Scorched-Wood People*." *Canadian Literature* 110 (fall 1986): 61–78.

– "Les Métarécits, le postmodernisme, et le mythe postcolonial au Québec: un point de vue de la marge." *Etudes littéraires* 27.1 (summer 1994): 43–61.

- "Le Mythe postmoderne dans quelques romans historiographiques québécois." *Québec Studies* 12 (spring-summer 1991): 49–57.
Veyne, Paul. *Comment on écrit l'histoire: essai d'épistémologie*. Paris: Seuil 1971.
Viau, Robert. *Les Fous de papier*. Montreal: Editions du Méridien 1989.
Vickery, John B. *The Literary Impact of The Golden Bough*. Princeton, NJ: Princeton University Press 1973.
- *Myths and Texts: Strategies of Incorporation and Displacement*. Baton Rouge, LA: Louisiana State University Press 1983.
- ed. *Myth and Literature: Contemporary Theory and Practice*. Lincoln, NE: University of Nebraska Press 1966.
Vico, Giambattista. *The New Science*. 1725. Ithaca, NY: Cornell University Press 1948.
Visser, Carla. "Historicity in Historical Fiction: *Burning Water* and *The Temptations of Big Bear*." *Studies in Canadian Literature* 12.1 (1987): 90–111.
Vizenor, Gerald. Review of *The Fencepost Chronicles*, by W. P. Kinsella. *American Indian Quarterly* 1.13 (Winter 1989): 111–12.
Walcott, Derek. "The Muse of History." *Carifesta Forum* 76 (1976): 111–28.
Wall, Kathleen. *The Callisto Myth from Ovid to Atwood: Initiation and Rape in Literature*. Montreal: McGill-Queen's University Press 1988.
Waring, Wendy. "Strategies for Subversion: Canadian Women's Writing." In Tregebov, ed., *Work in Progress*, 13–37.
Warwick, Jack. *The Long Journey: Literary Themes of French Canada*. Toronto: University of Toronto Press 1968.
Waterston, Elizabeth. "Disunity Remembered." in Nicholson and Easingwood, eds., *Canadian Story*, 102–8.
Watson, Sheila. *The Double Hook*. Toronto: McClelland and Stewart 1959.
Waugh, Patricia. *Feminine Fictions: Revisiting the Postmodern*. New York: Routledge 1989.
- *Metafiction: The Theory and Practice of Self-Conscious Fiction*. London and New York: Methuen 1984.
Webb, Barbara J. *Myth and History in Caribbean Fiction: Alejo Carpentier, Wilson Harris, and Edouard Glissant*. Amherst, MA: University of Massachusetts Press 1992.
Weinstein, Mark A. "The Creative Imagination in Fiction and History." *Genre* 9.3 (1976): 263–77.
Weisgerber, Jean. "Le Réalisme magique: la locution et le concept." *Rivista di litterature moderne e comparate* 35.1 (1982): 27–53.
West, Benjamin. *The Death of Wolfe*. [1770]. Reproduction in *European and American Painting, Sculpture, and Decorative Arts*. Vol. 1. Ed. Myron Laskin, Jr and Michael Pantazzi. Ottawa: National Gallery of Canada/National Museum of Canada 1987, 299.
Whalley, George. "The Mariner and the Albatross." *University of Toronto Quarterly* 16 (1946–47): 381–98.

– *Studies in Literature and the Humanities: Innocence of Intent*. Eds. Brian Crick and John Ferns. Montreal and Kingston: McGill-Queen's University Press 1985.

Wheeler, Anne. Director. *The War between Us*. CBC-TV. Produced by Atlantis Films and Troika Films. 10 December 1995.

Wheeler, Kathleen M. *Sources, Processes, and Methods in Coleridge's Biographia Literaria*. Cambridge: Cambridge University Press 1980.

White, Hayden. "Frye's Place in Contemporary Cultural Studies." In Lee and Denham, eds., *Northrop Frye*, 28–39.

– "Getting Out of History." *Diacritics* 12.3 (fall 1982): 2–13.

– *Metahistory: The Historical Imagination in Nineteenth-Century Europe*. Baltimore, MD: Johns Hopkins University Press 1973.

– *Tropics of Discourse: Essays in Cultural Criticism*. Baltimore, MD: Johns Hopkins University Press 1978.

White, John J. *Mythology in the Modern Novel: A Study of Prefigurative Techniques*. Princeton, NJ: Princeton University Press 1971.

White, Richard. *The Middle Ground: Indians, Empires, and Republics in the Great Lakes Region, 1650–1815*. Cambridge: Cambridge University Press 1991.

Whorf, Benjamin Lee. "Languages and Logic." In *Languages, Thought, and Reality: Selected Writings by Benjamin Lee Whorf*. Ed. John B. Carroll. Cambridge, MA: MIT Press 1956, 233–45.

– "Science and Linguistics." In Whorf, *Language, Thought and Reality* 207–19.

Wiebe, Rudy. *A Discovery of Strangers*. Toronto: Alfred A. Knopf 1994.

– "On the Trail of Big Bear." In Keith, ed., *Voice*, 132–41.

– *The Scorched-Wood People*. New Canadian Library Series 156. Toronto: McClelland and Stewart 1977.

– *The Temptations of Big Bear*. Toronto: McClelland and Stuart 1973.

Wiebe, Rudy, and Eli Mandel. "Where the Voice Comes From." in Keith, ed., *Voice*, 150–5.

Williams, Patrick, and Laura Chrisman, eds. *Colonial Discourse and Post-Colonial Theory: A Reader*. New York: Columbia University Press 1994.

Williams, Raymond L. *Gabriel García Márquez*. Boston: Twayne 1984.

Willis, Gary. "Speaking the Silence: Joy Kogawa's *Obasan*." *Studies in Canadian Literature* 12.2 (1987): 239–49.

Wilson, Robert R. "On the Boundary of the Magic and the Real: Notes on Inter-American Fiction." *The Compass* 6 (1979): 37–53.

– "Playpens for Leviathan: Canadian Uses of 'Postmodern.'" *Australian-Canadian Studies: A Journal for the Humanities and the Social Sciences* 8.1 (1990): 35–45.

– Review of *Magic Realism*, by Geoff Hancock. *Quarry* 32.2 (spring 1983): 84–91.

Wimsatt, W. K. "Nothrop Frye: Criticism and Myth." in Krieger, ed., *Northrop Frye*, 74–107.

Woodcock, George. "Prairie Writers and the Métis: Rudy Wiebe and Margaret Laurence." *Canadian Ethnic Studies* 14.1 (1982): 9–22.

– *Odysseus Ever Returning: Essays on Canadian Writers and Writing*. Toronto: McClelland and Stewart 1970.

Yardley, M. Jeanne. "The Maple Leaf as Maple Leaf: Facing the Failure of the Search for Emblems in Canadian Literature." *Studies in Canadian Literature* 12.2 (1987): 251–63.

Young, Robert. *White Mythologies: Writing History and the West*. London and New York: Routledge 1990.

Zabus, Chantal. "A Calabanic Tempest in Anglophone and Francophone New World Writing." *Canadian Literature* 104 (spring 1985): 35–50.

Zwicker, Heather. "Canadian Women of Color in the New World Order: Marlene Nourbese Philip, Joy Kogawa, and Beatrice Culleton Fight Their Way Home." In Pearlman, ed., *Canadian Women*, 142–53.

Index